Continua of Biliteracy

BILINGUAL EDUCATION AND BILINGUALISM
Series Editors: Professor Colin Baker, *University of Wales, Bangor, Wales, Great Britain* and Professor Nancy H. Hornberger, *University of Pennsylvania, Philadelphia, USA*

Other Books in the Series

At War With Diversity: US Language Policy in an Age of Anxiety
James Crawford
Bilingual Education and Social Change
Rebecca Freeman
Cross-linguistic Influence in Third Language Acquisition
J. Cenoz, B. Hufeisen and U. Jessner (eds)
Dual Language Education
Kathryn J. Lindholm-Leary
English in Europe: The Acquisition of a Third Language
Jasone Cenoz and Ulrike Jessner (eds)
Identity and the English Language Learner
Elaine Mellen Day
An Introductory Reader to the Writings of Jim Cummins
Colin Baker and Nancy Hornberger (eds)
Language and Literacy Teaching for Indigenous Education: A Bilingual Approach
Norbert Francis and Jon Reyhner
Language Minority Students in the Mainstream Classroom (2nd Edition)
Angela L. Carrasquillo and Vivian Rodriguez
Languages in America: A Pluralist View
Susan J. Dicker
Language, Power and Pedagogy: Bilingual Children in the Crossfire
Jim Cummins
Language Rights and the Law in the United States: Finding our Voices
Sandra Del Valle
Language Revitalization Processes and Prospects
Kendall A. King
Language Socialization in Bilingual and Multilingual Societies
Robert Bayley and Sandra R. Schecter (eds)
Learning English at School: Identity, Social Relations and Classroom Practice
Kelleen Toohey
Learners' Experiences of Immersion Education: Case Studies of French and Chinese
Michèle de Courcy
The Native Speaker: Myth and Reality
Alan Davies
Power, Prestige and Bilingualism: International Perspectives on Elite Bilingual Education
Anne-Marie de Mejía
The Sociopolitics of English Language Teaching
Joan Kelly Hall and William G. Eggington (eds)
World English: A Study of its Development
Janina Brutt-Griffler

Please contact us for the latest book information:
Multilingual Matters, Frankfurt Lodge, Clevedon Hall,
Victoria Road, Clevedon, BS21 7HH, England
http://www.multilingual-matters.com

BILINGUAL EDUCATION AND BILINGUALISM 41
Series Editors: Colin Baker and Nancy H. Hornberger

Continua of Biliteracy

An Ecological Framework for Educational Policy, Research, and Practice in Multilingual Settings

Edited by
Nancy H. Hornberger

MULTILINGUAL MATTERS LTD
Clevedon • Buffalo • Toronto • Sydney

Library of Congress Cataloging in Publication Data
Continua of Biliteracy: An Ecological Framework for Educational Policy, Research, and Practice in Multilingual Settings/Edited by Nancy H. Hornberger.
Bilingual Education and Bilingualism: 41
Includes bibliographical references and index.
1. Education, Bilingual. 2. Literacy. 3. Multiculturalism.
I. Hornberger, Nancy H. II. Series.
LC3719 .C67 2003
370.117–dc21 2002015984

British Library Cataloguing in Publication Data
A catalogue entry for this book is available from the British Library.

ISBN 1-85359-655-8 (hbk)
ISBN 1-85359-654-X (pbk)

Multilingual Matters Ltd
UK: Frankfurt Lodge, Clevedon Hall, Victoria Road, Clevedon BS21 7HH.
USA: UTP, 2250 Military Road, Tonawanda, NY 14150, USA.
Canada: UTP, 5201 Dufferin Street, North York, Ontario M3H 5T8, Canada.
Australia: Footprint Books, PO Box 418, Church Point, NSW 2103, Australia.

Typeset by Florence Production Ltd.
Printed and bound in Great Britain by the Cromwell Press Ltd.

Contents

Foreword

I remember clearly my excitement when I first read Nancy Hornberger's article *Continua of Biliteracy*. It seemed to provide a unified framework for considering the rapidly expanding range of issues encompassed by the terms *bilingualism* and *literacy*. Disciplines that had previously kept a safe and sometimes disdainful distance from each other were suddenly in contact. In political contexts where issues related to both literacy and bilingualism had become intensely confrontational, the *Continua* framework defined and illuminated the landscape such that complex relationships were suddenly visible and could potentially be debated more rationally than had hitherto been the case. Any literacy event or practice could be located within the multidimensional space provided by the framework and analyzed from a variety of disciplinary perspectives in relation to a matrix of intersecting continua.

As this volume so eloquently testifies, the *Continua* framework has served as a powerful heuristic in stimulating a variety of investigations of literacy theory, policy, and practice in multilingual situations. As any useful framework should, it has expanded and refined itself to accommodate new findings and perspectives. It has built on its own foundation while at the same time forging linkages to other frameworks that are attempting to address similar phenomena. Most prominent among these is the *Multiliteracies* framework (Cope & Kalantzis, 2000) whose relation to the *Continua* framework is discussed by Hornberger and Skilton-Sylvester (this volume).

These developments together with the empirical and theoretical work reported in this volume appear to me to be extremely fruitful. The *Continua* framework has evolved from a comprehensive but perhaps somewhat static taxonomy into a potent tool to conceptualize and effect change in the education of bilingual children. It occurs to me that one way of furthering these directions might be to add an ancillary dimension to the *Continua* framework, namely *actors of biliteracy*. How should the various participants (e.g. policy-makers, educators, parents) whose actions shape the conditions under which children acquire (multi)literacies define their roles? What identities do they envisage for children as they choose to promote and implement certain options rather than others in relation to the contexts, development, media, and content of biliteracy children will experience? To what extent do the choices these actors make challenge coercive relations of power in the broader society or, alternatively, reinforce these relations of power? These points are elaborated below.

The initial *Continua* framework created an intellectual space for considering the phenomenon of biliteracy (and multiliteracy) in an integrated, comprehensive, and interdisciplinary way. It implied but did not explicitly chart directions for change in contexts such as the United States where the development of biliteracy among bilingual children was under constant assault. On a daily basis in the early 1990s (and subsequently), media soundbites served to undermine the rich linguistic and intellectual resources of individual children, communities, and the nation itself. The target has been bilingual education. The collateral damage has encompassed the lives of individual children who lose their first language (L1), the relationships between children and parents (and grandparents) who no longer share a language, and the 'intelligence' that any nation requires to exist and thrive in a global environment characterized by cultural, linguistic, and religious diversity.

However, despite my initial excitement, I didn't know how to use the original *Continua of Biliteracy* framework in talking with bilingual and ESL teachers committed to challenging these coercive power relations and promoting biliteracy among linguistically and culturally diverse students. I didn't know where to start. The complexity of the relationships embodied in the framework clearly reflected the complexity of the phenomenon of biliteracy itself. But this complexity represented (at least for me) a barrier in discussing directions for change with educators dedicated to helping students from marginalized communities succeed in school. A framework oriented towards changing restrictive conditions for biliteracy development would have to identify clearly the kinds of actions that policy-makers and educators should take to bring about change. It would have to specify how these actors position themselves in relation to historical and current power relations that construct (and frequently constrict) the contexts, media, and content of biliteracy development. In a context of increasing hierarchical control of education focused on attainment of rigid curriculum standards policed by English-only standardized tests, what options are available to individual teachers, principals, and administrators to create interpersonal spaces for powerful biliteracy development?

My attempt to articulate a conceptual framework focused on the power of educators to make choices that directly affect the conditions and prospects for children's biliteracy development assigns a central role to the process of *negotiating identities* in the interactions between educators and students (Cummins, 2001). The interactions orchestrated by educators are always located along a continuum ranging from challenging coercive relations of power in the wider society on the one hand, to reinforcing coercive relations of power on the other. For example, teachers who encourage children to write and publish dual-language books within the classroom are challenging the societal discourse that proclaims children's L1 an impediment to the learning of English. Through the choices they have made and the interactions they orchestrate in the classroom, these teachers are reinforcing biliteracy as a positive facet of children's identities. By contrast, teachers who simply follow the curriculum (or read the script) will likely focus only on English literacy, thereby constricting the interpersonal space for literacy development and inadvertently reinforcing the coercive societal discourse that views children's L1 as an impediment rather than a resource.

The recent evolution of the *Continua* framework opens up the possibility of aligning in a powerful way its detailed mapping of biliteracy contexts, development, media, and content with the explicit change orientation of the *Negotiating Identities* framework. The revised *Continua* framework elaborated in this volume has added a critical dimension, with contested power relations infused throughout the continua. Although the original framework made clear that literacy and biliteracy were not neutral phenomena, the more recent version has elaborated the fact that each of the continua is embedded in a historical and contemporary matrix of intergroup power relations. Pedagogical implications are also more explicitly elaborated, with linkages made to the *Multiliteracies* four-stage pedagogical framework that specifies *situated practice, overt instruction, critical framing*, and *transformed practice* as a way of conceptualizing how multiliteracies might be promoted both in school and in out-of-school contexts.

The recent evolution of the framework towards more overtly critical perspectives and towards explicit consideration of pedagogical issues highlights the question of how various actors concerned with children's education will emphasize the less powerful ends of the continua necessary to promote bi- and multiliteracy. The *Negotiating Identities* framework addresses this issue by highlighting the ways in which educators, individually and collectively, define their roles and identities in relation to societal power relations. Individual educators are never powerless, although they frequently work in conditions that are oppressive for both them and their students. While they rarely have complete freedom, educators do have choices in the way they structure the patterns of interactions in the classroom. They determine for themselves the social and educational goals they want to achieve with their students. They are responsible for the role definitions they adopt in relation to culturally diverse students and communities. Even in the context of English-only instruction, educators have options in their orientation to students' language and culture, in the forms of parent and community participation they encourage, and in the way they implement pedagogy and assessment.

In short, educators define their own identities through their practice and their interactions with students. Students, likewise, go through a continual process of defining their identities in interaction with their teachers, peers, and parents. This process of negotiating identities can never be fully controlled from the outside, although it is certainly influenced by many forces. Thus, educators, individually and collectively, have the potential to work towards the creation of contexts of empowerment, defined as the collaborative creation of power. Within these interactional spaces where identities are negotiated, students and educators together can generate power that challenges structures of injustice in small but significant ways. The collaborative generation of power in educator–student interactions is 'small' insofar as the lives of individual students rather than the futures of entire societies are at stake; it is significant, however, for precisely the same reason. The future of societies depends on the intelligence and identities generated in teacher–student interactions in school.

The *Continua* framework permits the various actors who influence the conditions of students' biliteracy development to examine in detail the choices available to them in relation to contexts, development, media, and content of biliteracy. They can examine the educational structures within which they currently operate and envisage options for changing or, in some cases, undermining these structures. These actors can examine explicitly how their own identities reflect and are formed by the choices they make in relation to their students' biliteracy development. Most significantly, they can come to realize that the classroom interactions they orchestrate with culturally and linguistically diverse students are never innocent. Regardless of how precisely the curriculum is followed, classroom instruction and educator identity choices are always implicated in a matrix of societal power relations. Frequently, a commitment to fully educating bilingual and biliterate students requires that educators challenge the coercive relations of power that are infused in the official curriculum (e.g. in post-Proposition 227 California).

This sketch of ways in which the *Continua* framework might be related to the *Negotiating Identities* framework by means of the construct *actors of biliteracy* illustrates, I believe, the potential of the *Continua* framework to exert a dramatic influence on policy, research, and practice in countries around the world in the coming years. It has become a dynamic tool for mapping the literacy landscape and for highlighting the extremely limited conceptions of literacy embedded in many educational policies. Furthermore, it enables us to analyze with precision and detail the social injustices perpetuated by policies that intentionally eradicate the multilingual literacies that children bring to school.

This volume will undoubtedly stimulate further discussion and application of the *Continua* framework in a variety of contexts around the world where literacy policies and issues are hotly debated. Of equal importance, it will stimulate exploration of how the framework can be integrated fruitfully and forcefully with other conceptualizations of literacy and biliteracy development that are oriented towards the promotion of social justice. As such the contributions of Nancy Hornberger and her colleagues represent not only an impressive intellectual accomplishment but also a powerful tool for social action in a global context characterized simultaneously and paradoxically by increasing inequity and xenophobia and by a serious international commitment to promote universal literacy and education.

Jim Cummins
Toronto, August 2002

References

Cope, B. and Kalantzis, M. (2000) *Multiliteracies*. London: Routledge.

Cummins, J. (2001) *Negotiating Identities: Education for Empowerment in a Diverse Society* (2nd edn). Los Angeles: California Association for Bilingual Education.

Introduction

NANCY H. HORNBERGER

Continua of Biliteracy: An Ecological Framework

What should you do when large (or small) numbers of children arrive at your school speaking a language other than the language of instruction? What is the best way to design bilingual education in a community where oral traditions in the local language are highly valued and, at the same time, the language of power (language of wider communication) is highly sought after? Is codeswitching in the bilingual classroom something to be avoided at all costs? How can we incorporate the perspectives and identities of language minority learners in the school curriculum when there are few written materials available in their language?

These and many other questions address instances of *biliteracy* – the use of two or more languages in and around writing – an increasingly inescapable feature of our lives and schools worldwide, yet one which most educational policy and practice continues blithely to ignore. The *continua of biliteracy*, featured in the present volume, offers a comprehensive yet flexible model to guide educators, researchers, and policy-makers in designing, carrying out, and evaluating educational programs for the development of multilingual learners, each program adapted to its own specific context, media, and contents.

The continua framework represents a synthesis of key findings on multilingualism and literacy, as gleaned from research of the past several decades and ongoing. It is a concise yet inclusive model which invites and enables both application and analysis of those findings, in every aspect of educational programming including policy, curriculum, teacher and staff professional development, classroom interaction, student assessment, and program evaluation. In the years since it was first proposed in 1989, the model has come to inform multilingual educational practice, policy, and research in a range of settings around the world. The present volume presents a collection of some of that work in 16 chapters, three of them reprints of my original publications on the continua (one co-authored with my former student), and 13 original chapters prepared for this volume: seven by my former or current students and six by colleagues from the US and abroad.

Biliteracy can be defined as 'any and all instances in which communication occurs in two (or more) languages in or around writing' (Hornberger, 1990: 213), a definition which follows from Heath's definition of literacy events as 'occasions in which written language is integral to the nature of participants' interactions and their interpretive processes and strategies' (Heath, 1982: 50, 1983: 386). Unlike Heath's definition which focuses on the literacy event, my definition of biliteracy refers to instances, a term encompassing events, but also biliterate actors, interactions, practices, activities, programs, situations, societies, sites, worlds, etc. (Hornberger & Skilton-Sylvester, 2000: 98; Hornberger, 2000: 362). Also unlike Heath's, the above definition of biliteracy refers explicitly to the use of two or more language varieties. In common with Heath's definition, however, the centrality of communication in and around writing, via processes and strategies of interaction and interpretation, is understood here as key to defining and understanding biliteracy.

Among early references to biliteracy are Goodman, Goodman and Flores' (1979) use of the term in a report on issues of reading in bilingual education; and Lado, Hanson and D'Emilio (1980), who argued for and demonstrated the value of preschool biliteracy in their Spanish Education Development Center Preschool Reading Project involving 50 children aged three to five from low-income families in Washington DC. In a number of early papers, the meaning of the term 'biliteracy' was left implicit or assumed to be, roughly, reading (and writing) in two languages (or in a second language) (e.g. Genesee, 1980; Cummins, 1981; Valdés, 1983; see Hornberger, forthcoming, for more on this).

Niyekawa, on the other hand, explicitly defines biliteracy as 'an advanced state of bilingualism where the person can not only speak two languages fluently but also read and write these two languages' (Niyekawa, 1983: 98), excluding from her definition not only those who are less than fluent but also those who are biliterate but not bilingual; her definition is thus considerably more strict than mine in disallowing 'lopsided' bilingual or biliterate instances. Fishman's definition of biliteracy as 'the mastery of reading in particular, and also of writing, in two (or more) languages' (Fishman *et al.*, 1985: 377, perhaps a reprinting of Fishman, 1980, cited by Spolsky, 1981) is, like Niyekawa's, more specific than mine, in that it focuses on mastery; yet it shares with mine a perspective encompassing not just the use of two languages, but of two (or more) languages (or language varieties).

Beyond these few early references, there was in the 1980s very little scholarly work attending explicitly to biliteracy (the conjunction of bilingualism and literacy), so I looked instead to its component parts, i.e. the literatures on bilingualism and the teaching of second/foreign languages and the literatures on literacy and the teaching of reading/writing. A common ground in these literatures was that, although we often characterize dimensions of bilingualism and literacy in terms of polar opposites, such as first versus second languages (L1 vs L2), monolingual versus bilingual individuals, or oral versus literate societies, in each case those opposites represent only theoretical endpoints on what is in reality a continuum of features (see Kelly, 1969: 5). Further, when we consider biliteracy as the conjunction of literacy and bilingualism, it becomes clear that these continua are interrelated dimensions of one highly complex whole; and that in fact it is in the dynamic, rapidly changing, and sometimes contested spaces along and across the intersecting continua that most biliteracy use and learning occur. These insights became the basis for the continua of biliteracy framework, proposed in Hornberger (1989) and revised in Hornberger and Skilton-Sylvester (2000).

The framework uses the notion of intersecting and nested continua to demonstrate the multiple and complex interrelationships between bilingualism and literacy and the importance of the contexts, media, and content through which biliteracy develops. The notion of continuum is intended to convey that, although one can identify (and name) points on the continuum, those points are not finite, static, or discrete. There are infinitely many points on the continuum; any single point is inevitably and inextricably related to all other points; and all the points have more in common than not with each other.

Specifically, the continua model depicts the development of biliteracy along intersecting first language – second language, receptive–productive, and oral–written language skills continua; through the medium of two (or more) languages and literacies whose linguistic structures vary from similar to dissimilar, whose scripts range from convergent to divergent, and to which the developing biliterate individual's exposure varies from simultaneous to successive; in contexts that encompass micro to macro levels and are characterized by varying mixes along the monolingual–bilingual and oral–literate continua; and with content that ranges from majority to minority perspectives and experiences, literary to vernacular styles and genres, and decontextualized to contextualized language texts.

Figures 2.1 and 2.2 schematically represent the framework by depicting both the nested and intersecting nature of the continua, while Figure 2.3 summarizes all 12 continua (four nested sets of three intersecting continua each). It is worth noting that Figures 2.1 and 2.2 are not intended to represent the continua model per se, but are meant rather as aids to visualization of the relationships among the continua. Figure 2.1 depicts the continua as a series of nested boxes representing contexts, media, content, and development of biliteracy respectively, while Figure 2.2 shows that each box is a cluster of its three intersecting continua. Not only is the three-dimensionality of any one set of three intersecting continua representative of the interrelatedness of those three constituent continua, but it should be emphasized that the interrelationships extend across the four sets of continua as well.[1]

The notion of continuum conveys that all points on a particular continuum are interrelated, and the intersecting and nested relationships among the continua convey that all points across the continua are also interrelated. The model suggests that the more their learning contexts and contexts of use allow learners and users to draw from across the whole of each and every continuum, the greater are the chances for their full biliterate development and expression (Hornberger, 1989: 289). Implicit in that suggestion is a recognition that there has usually *not* been attention to all points and that movement along the continua and across the intersections may well be contested (Hornberger & Skilton-Sylvester, 2000: 99).

The continua model of biliteracy offers a framework in which to situate research, teaching, and language planning in linguistically diverse settings. In order to understand any particular instance of biliteracy, we as educators, researchers, community members, or policy makers need to take account of all dimensions represented by the continua. At the same time, the advantage of the model is that it allows us to focus for pedagogical, analytical, activist, or policy purposes on one or selected continua and their dimensions without ignoring the importance of the others.

Finally, the continua model of biliteracy is premised on a view of multilingualism as a resource (see Ruiz, 1984) and on the metaphor of ecology of language. Specifically, it incorporates the language evolution, language environment, and language endangerment themes of the ecology of language metaphor (see Hornberger, Chapter 14, this volume). The very notion of bi- (or multi-)literacy assumes that one language and literacy is developing in relation to one or more other languages and literacies (*language evolution*); the model situates biliteracy development (whether in the individual, classroom, community, or society) in relation to the contexts, media, and content in and through which it develops (i.e. *language environment*); and it provides a heuristic for addressing the unequal balance of power across languages and literacies (i.e. for both studying and counteracting *language endangerment*).

The sections which follow take up the continua of biliteracy model in considerable detail. My own chapters, including the chapter co-authored with Ellen Skilton-Sylvester, which appear in the introductory and concluding sections of the book, are reprints of previously published papers on the continua model, setting forth the literature from which it is drawn, the dimensions that make it up, and the ideological underpinnings upholding it. The four sections in the body of the volume explore particular dimensions of the continua model, in relation to specific cases the authors are especially familiar with. The whole is framed by a foreword by Jim Cummins and an afterword by Brian Street, leading scholars in bilingualism and literacy, respectively.

Overview of the Book

The first section, Continua of Biliteracy, offers reprinted versions of the original papers laying out the framework as a heuristic in which to situate research, teaching, and language planning in linguistically diverse settings. Hornberger (1989) draws from the literatures on literacy, bilingualism, and the teaching of reading, writing, and second and foreign languages to propose that the complex array of possible biliteracy configurations can be accounted for by understanding biliteracy in terms of interrelated continua defining the contexts, media, and development of biliteracy. An understanding of the intersecting and nested nature of the continua has implications for teaching and research in biliteracy; specifically, the review concludes with the suggestion that the more their learning contexts allow learners to draw on all points of the continua, the greater are the chances for their full biliterate development.

Hornberger and Skilton-Sylvester (2000) revisit the continua model a decade later in the light of work undertaken in the intervening years. Based on Skilton-Sylvester's research in the Cambodian community of Philadelphia in the 1990s, the authors propose an expanded continua model which takes into account not only biliterate contexts, media, and development, but also, crucially, the content of biliteracy. Further, based on continuing work in both the Philadelphia context and internationally, and taking a critical perspective, they argue that, in educational policy and practice regarding biliteracy, there tends to be an implicit privileging of one end of the continua over the other such that one end of each continuum is associated with more power than the other (e.g. written development over oral development) and that there is a need to contest that traditional power weighting by paying attention to and granting agency and voice to actors and practices at what have traditionally been the less powerful ends of the continua.

The second section of the book, Language Planning, initiates the presentation of US and international cases illustrating and probing dimensions of the continua. These first three cases highlight policy contexts in which biliteracy is practiced and promoted. Colin Baker analyzes literacy traditions within Wales, showing that the continua model (1) enables a deeper explanation and interpretation of the long history of Welsh literacy; (2) is valuable for understanding the current drive for language monitoring and performance indicators for Welsh-language revitalization; (3) provides a framework for analyzing Welsh and English literacy in the Welsh National Curriculum; (4) anticipates the concept of 'transliteracy' where two languages are combined in a strategic way to teach Welsh and English literacy in schools; and (5) provides the conceptual tool to examine the crucial language planning issue of the role of diglossia in Welsh language revitalization.

Carole Bloch and Neville Alexander outline South Africa's recent language planning and policy initiatives promoting multilingualism and the African languages, initiatives which offer an ideal situation for the empowerment of those who, in effect, constitute a social minority even though demographically (linguistically) they are the majority. The authors then describe a programme being carried out by the Project for the Study of Alternative Education in South Africa (PRAESA), which uses the continua as heuristic in exploring ways of putting the new language in education policy into practice. This has involved developing multilingualism and mother tongue education through additive bilingualism. In a social climate where English is still believed to equal good education and future prosperity, the programme is developing Xhosa and English biliteracy, and generally seeking to raise the status of Xhosa in the classroom amongst teachers and young children.

Likewise, in the United States, favorable contexts for the practice and promotion of biliteracy and multilingualism are highly dependent on policy. Mihyon Jeon depicts a comprehensive rationale for Two-Way Immersion (TWI), one of few educational program types in the United States with an explicit goal of biliteracy. After profiling TWI programs in the United States, she provides an account of Korean–English TWI program policy, analyzing it within theories of language-policy ideology and the continua of biliteracy framework. She argues that the predictive and explanatory powers of the continua of biliteracy provide a rationale for Korean–English TWI program policy and for TWI program policies everywhere.

The third section of the book turns to cases of Learners' Identities as expressed and constructed through the resources, voices, and 'errors' they bring to their biliteracy development and practices. Felicia Lincoln presents a case analysis of two language minority and two language majority public high school students in rural Arkansas. The continua of biliteracy model is used in two ways: first, to understand language minority students' academic struggles and sometime academic failure, even in situations where there is evidence of adequate dual language facility; and second, to predict ways to enhance these students' agency and allow their voices to inform and impact their educational experiences.

Carmen Mercado examines instances of spontaneous biliteracy resulting from the diversification and growth of the Latino community among first and second generation Latino youth who have lived in the United States most of their lives. Although students' bilingual and biliterate potential grows from the need to participate in the society that surrounds them, this potential is misunderstood or devalued by the wider society and remains an untapped resource for learning in mainstream school settings. Three comparative cases are presented to understand the dynamics among contexts of biliteracy, development and variation, and communication media in shaping social practices in and around the symbolic representation of meaning and the presentation of self.

Melisa Cahnmann uses the core aspects of the continua of biliteracy – monolingual–bilingual norms, oralcy–literacy, and micro–macro – to understand the struggle and contradiction involved in teachers' assessment and correction of students' oral and written productions. She presents an expanded definition of biliteracy and uses this definition to explore the development, media, context, and content of biliteracy errors and correction. She concludes that the answer to whether a teacher should or should not correct a student's work is better understood as a continuum of complex and multifaceted considerations.

Three US cases in the fourth section focus on Empowering Teachers to take control of the content, media, and contexts through which they and their learners develop biliteracy. Bertha Pérez, Belinda Bustos Flores, and Susan Strecker apply the continua to two groups of bilingual teacher education candidates in the US southwest: US resident 'normalistas' (graduates of a Mexican normal school) and home-grown 'paraprofessionals.' Participants exhibited varying degrees of contextual situatedness and multiple social roles and identities in their texts and discourses, as revealed through both the media and content of their biliterate expression. The situatedness along the cultural content continua was most obvious during the tutoring sessions. Findings suggest that field experiences allow bilingual teacher candidates to realize the language and power issues within bilingual education and promote the use of the native language as a conduit for the acquisition of equity and power.

In rural midwestern US, Joel Hardman focuses on the differing roles of English language learners, ESL/bilingual teachers, mainstream classroom teachers, and other school personnel in the control of content in an ESL/bilingual program. A point of tension is described at the intersection of the continua of media and content – between 'content of the school's (or mainstream classroom teachers') choosing' and 'no content at all' (language-only). Another tension is outlined at the intersection of the continua of content and context (e.g. the language policies of the school system) – between content which ESL/bilingual teachers perceive to be in the students' best interests aside from mainstream classroom needs, and content they think will support the students' mainstream classroom success. He argues that both learners and teachers are disempowered in a system where these tensions are left unaddressed.

In yet another US context, this time urban Philadelphia, Diana Schwinge uses the model of the continua of biliteracy, and especially the content and development continua, to analyze the curricular modifications made by two elementary school teachers working with Latino biliterate learners. She shows that, while there is a growing trend in American education for schools (such as the school studied here) to adopt standardized curricula like the Success for All reading program, some bilingual education teachers act as bottom-up language and literacy planners by adapting and elaborating on the suggested activities and the content of the mandated programs to better enable their students to become bilingual, biliterate, and bicultural.

The last two cases demonstrate how the Sites and Worlds (see Hornberger, 2000: 362–4) in which biliteracy is practiced, promoted, and developed define biliterate media and content in ways unique to each context. Holly R. Pak describes one particular US Korean church and its heritage language school as a context that foregrounds being Korean and speaking Korean. In the context of this church and school, the Korean adults attempt to cultivate in their children a sense of who they are as Koreans in America. The context is perceived differently by the adults and children, however, and she discusses how in each of the four Continua – context, media, development, and content – the power relations between English and Korean are reversed from outside the Korean church context; and how the tension from this reversal is revealed through the children's expression of cultural identity.

A similar L1–L2 reversal is depicted by Viniti Basu, in her exploration of literacy practices regarding L2 acquisition in two government-run schools in New Delhi, India – Sarvodaya Kanya Vidyalaya (SKV), and Nagar Nigam Bal Vidyalaya (NNBV). In this case, the reversal is that the Hindi language is first language (L1) in one school and second language (L2) in the other. In the SKV, the second language of the children is English, which is also the medium of instruction, and their first language is Hindi. In the NNBV, the L2 is Hindi, which is the medium of instruction and the L1 is a dialect of Hindi. Also, starting from 1 July 2000 the children of the NNBV are being taught basic English skills. Thus both schools have some sort of a bilingual education policy, constituting a great step forward in empowering the masses. The author uses the continua model of biliteracy to seek to understand why it is that, despite the far reaching and progressive goal of the bilingual education policies, the bilingual education program of the SKV is not able to make its students as proficient in the L2 as does the NNBV.

The final, Conclusion, section of the book offers my paper exploring the ideologies underlying multilingual language policies and suggesting the continua of biliteracy framework as ecological heuristic for situating the challenges faced in implementing them. The paper applies the continua to analyzing community and classroom challenges facing the implementation of post-apartheid South Africa's new Constitution of 1993 and of Bolivia's National Education Reform of 1994.

There follows Brian Street's afterword, offering his comments, a few critical questions, and his personal 'take' on the individual contributions. He concludes that the continua of biliteracy framework, harnessed to other powerful conceptual tools, makes a demonstrable contribution to a sense of optimism, shared by the contributors here, that linguists and language educators can and must work hard alongside language planners and language users to fill the ecological spaces opened up by multilingual language policies wherever and whenever they occur, in order to promote the development and practice of biliteracy in and through as many contexts, contents, and media as possible.

Continua-ing On

I borrow Cahnmann's coinage, continua-ing, to serve as a reminder that the continua model is an ongoing project. As demonstrated here, it has been applied in a range of contexts and to a variety of issues in the US and internationally, including interpretation of language minority student voices in Arkansas, analysis of biliteracy development among Latino youth in New York City, bilingual teacher preparation in the US southwest, bilingual and ESL classroom practice in urban and rural US schools, Korean language education in immersion and heritage language programs, bilingual education in India, multilingual classroom teaching in South Africa, and language planning and the National Curriculum in Wales. Its usefulness in a variety of contexts and for a range of purposes is testimony to a certain versatility, enabled perhaps by its complexity. That same complexity has been one of the drawbacks of the model as well; it is a difficult framework to grasp intuitively and has proven resistant to easy representation. Similarly, existing representations of the continua model (e.g. Figures 2.1, 2.2, 2.3) are sometimes misinterpreted as conveying a static, bounded, dichotomized view rather than the fluid, flexible, and infinitely expanding model intended. Those who struggle with the framework long enough to grasp the dynamic nature of the intersecting and nested continua, however, eventually conclude that its complexity is also perhaps its greatest virtue, in that the phenomena it intends to represent are complex and too easily reified by over-simplification.

There remain unanswered questions about the continua model. It has proven useful in ethnographic research, but has yet to be tested as a basis for experimental or survey research. Likewise, it originated as a descriptive framework, but has evolved toward predictive and explanatory uses (Jeon, Chapter 5, this volume). Such extensions need further exploration through continuing research in a wide range of settings and circumstances.

More importantly, basic questions about biliteracy remain unanswered or partially answered. Questions like: Who becomes biliterate and where, when, how, and why do they do so? How can biliteracy best be acquired, nurtured, maintained, and promoted? What is the role of the family, the home, the school, the community, and the wider society in biliteracy acquisition and use? It is my hope that the continua model can contribute to answering some of these questions more fully than they have been answered up to now.

Note

1. Nevertheless, the box metaphor is unsatisfactory in that it implies a bounded space, which is clearly not consistent with the infinity of the continua. Other possible visualizations of the model that I have considered or that have been suggested to me include: a twelve-edged box with the four clusters of continua intersecting at each of the four corners; a bucket of paint with multiple colors

mixed in different proportions; a set of refracting lenses lined up one behind the other; a sphere with all the continua intersecting in the middle, or an anchor attached to a rope of twelve intertwining strands. The point is not to try to pin down the model with one visual representation, but to use a variety of visual representations as ways of thinking about the complex relationships among the continua.

References

Cummins, J. (1981) Biliteracy, language proficiency, and educational programs. In J. Edwards (ed.) *The Social Psychology of Reading* (Vol. Language and Literacy, pp. 131–46). Silver Spring, MD: Institute of Modern Languages.

Fishman, J.A. (1980) Ethnocultural dimensions in the acquisition and retention of biliteracy. Paper presented at the Mina Shaughnessy Memorial Conference.

Fishman, J.A., Gertner, M.H., Lowy, E.G. and Milán, W.G. (1985) *The Rise and Fall of the Ethnic Revival: Perspectives on Language and Ethnicity*. Berlin: Mouton.

Genesee, F. (1980) Bilingualism and biliteracy: A study of cross-cultural contact in a bilingual community. In J.R. Edwards (ed.) *The Social Psychology of Reading*. Silver Spring, MD: Institute of Modern Languages.

Goodman, K., Goodman, Y. and Flores, B. (1979) *Reading in the Bilingual Classroom: Literacy and Biliteracy* (ERIC Doc No. ED 181 725 ed.). Arlington, VA: NCBE.

Heath, S.B. (1982) What no bedtime story means: Narrative skills at home and school. *Language in Society* 11 (1), 49–76.

Heath, S.B. (1983) *Ways with Words: Language, Life and Work in Communities and Classrooms*. New York: Cambridge University Press.

Hornberger, N.H. (1989) Continua of biliteracy. *Review of Educational Research 59* (3), 271–96.

Hornberger, N.H. (1990) Creating successful learning contexts for bilingual literacy. *Teachers College Record 92* (2), 212–29.

Hornberger, N.H. (2000) Afterword: Multilingual literacies, literacy practices, and the continua of biliteracy. In M. Martin-Jones and K. Jones (eds) *Multilingual Literacies: Reading and Writing Different Worlds* (pp. 353–67). Philadelphia: John Benjamins.

Hornberger, N.H. (2002) Multilingual language policies and the continua of biliteracy: An ecological approach. *Language Policy 1* (1), 27–51.

Hornberger, Nancy H. (forthcoming) Biliteracy. In R. Beach, J. Green, M. Kamil and T. Shanahan (eds) *Multidisciplinary Perspectives on Literacy Research* (2nd edn). New York: Hampton Press.

Hornberger, N.H. and Skilton-Sylvester, E. (2000) Revisiting the continua of biliteracy: International and critical perspectives. *Language and Education: An International Journal 14* (2), 96–122.

Kelly, L.G. (ed.) (1969) *The Description and Measurement of Bilingualism: An International Seminar*. Toronto, Canada: University of Toronto Press.

Lado, R., Hanson, I. and D'Emilio, T. (1980) Biliteracy for bilingual children by Grade 1: The SED Center Preschool Reading Project, Phase 1. In J. Alatis (ed.) *Current Issues in Bilingual Education* (pp. 162–7). Washington, DC: Georgetown University Press.

Niyekawa, A.M. (1983) Biliteracy acquisition and its sociocultural effects. In M.C. Chang (ed.) *Asian- and Pacific-American Perspectives in Bilingual Education* (pp. 97–119). New York: Teachers College Press.

Ruiz, R. (1984) Orientations in language planning. *NABE Journal 8* (2), 15–34.

Spolsky, B. (1981) Bilingualism and biliteracy. *Canadian Modern Language Review 37* (3), 475–85.

Valdés, G. (1983) Planning for biliteracy. In L. Elías-Olivares (ed.) *Spanish in the US Setting: Beyond the Southwest* (pp. 259–62). Arlington, VA: National Clearinghouse for Bilingual Education.

Acknowledgments

The continua of biliteracy framework featured here was originally proposed in a literature review I undertook in connection with my Literacy in Two Languages project, an ethnographic research project begun in Philadelphia in 1987. Little did I guess at the time that the continua would go on to inform not only my own and my students' research in Philadelphia over the next decade-plus, but also my own and others' research in multilingual sites across the US and, indeed, the globe.

While *Continua of Biliteracy* is an unfinished work, with many chapters (and perhaps volumes) yet to be written, I want to thank those who encouraged and assisted me in putting this first volume together at this time. First and foremost, I thank my colleagues and students whose work is included here for their remarkable work and for the confidence they inspired in me to continue with the continua. I am especially grateful to Colin Baker, with whom I co-edit the book series in which this volume appears, for planting and nurturing the idea of my contributing a book on biliteracy for our series. His unfailing wisdom, graciousness, and humility are a model for all scholars. Likewise, I am indebted to Francis Hult, Ph.D. student in Educational Linguistics at the University of Pennsylvania, who ably assisted me in assembling the final manuscript for publication. His ability to dive into the project midstream and his careful and consistent attention to both detail and overall scope have been invaluable in bringing the book into final form. I thank, always, my husband Steve and our children Ch'uyasonqo and Kusisami, the pride and joy of my life and my unfailing support team. Finally, I thank the many bilingual and multilingual individuals, both those who appear in these pages and the many, many more who do not, for the living examples they provide of the inevitability, uniqueness, and unquenchability of biliteracy in our world.

Nancy H. Hornberger
Philadelphia, June 2002

About the Authors

Editor and Author

Nancy H. Hornberger is professor of Education and Director of Educational Linguistics at the University of Pennsylvania Graduate School of Education, where she also convenes the annual Ethnography in Education Research Forum. She specializes in sociolinguistics, language planning, bilingualism, biliteracy, and educational policy and practice for indigenous and immigrant language minorities in the United States, Latin America, and internationally. Professor Hornberger writes, teaches, lectures, and consults extensively on these topics throughout the world. Her published books include *Indigenous Literacies in the Americas: Language Planning from the Bottom Up* (Mouton, 1996), *Sociolinguistics and Language Teaching* (Cambridge, 1996, co-edited with S. McKay) and *Bilingual Education and Language Maintenance: A Southern Peruvian Quechua Case* (Mouton, 1988).

Contributing Authors

Neville Alexander is director of the Project for the Study of Alternative Education in South Africa (PRAESA). He has played a key role as advisor on language policy to various government departments in South Africa, including drawing up the outline for a national language plan. This plan has served as guideline for legislation pertaining to language issues. Until March 1998, he was also Vice-Chairperson of the Pan South African Language Board. He is currently a special advisor on language policy and planning to the Minister of Arts, Culture, Science and Technology and a member of the Western Cape Language Committee. Alexander is known especially as an educator in South Africa but he has a high political profile as a left-wing critic and community activist. He has written many books and articles and writes regularly on issues of ethnic and racial prejudice and on the politics of identity.

Colin Baker obtained a First Class Honours degree in Educational Studies and a subsequent Ph.D. in Social Psychology from the University of Wales. He holds a Personal Chair of the University of Wales and is currently a Professor of Education at the University of Wales, Bangor, and Director of Research Centre Wales. He is a member of the Welsh Language Board, one of Europe's foremost language planning organisations. His published books include: *Aspects of Bilingualism in Wales* (1985), *Attitudes and Language* (1992), the *Encyclopedia of Bilingualism and Bilingual Education* (1998, with Sylvia Prys Jones), *Foundations of Bilingual Education and Bilingualism* (1993, 1996, 2001) and *The Care and Education of Young Bilinguals* (2000).

Viniti Basu is a lecturer at the National Institute of Education in Singapore. She is a Ph.D. candidate at the University of Pennsylvania Graduate School of Education. Her interests include multilingualism and its implications for empowerment and identity.

Carole Bloch is an early literacy specialist at the Project for the Study of Alternative Education in South Africa (PRAESA), University of Cape Town. She works in the domain of early childhood development, focusing on young children's mother tongue literacy and biliteracy learning and development in South African and other African multilingual situations. She is currently involved in developmental and ethnographic research, teacher training, and materials development.

Melisa Cahnmann is an assistant professor in the Department of Language Education at the University of Georgia. Her research interests include biliteracy, bilingualism, multicultural education, and enhancing qualitative approaches to inquiry through poetic and arts-based approaches. She has been published in scholarly journals such as the *Urban Review* (in press), *Bilingual Research Journal*, *Educators for Urban Minorities*, *Symposium About Language and Society – Austin (SALSA)*, *Working Papers in Educational Linguistics*, and in several literary publications.

Jim Cummins teaches in the Department of Curriculum, Teaching and Learning at the University of Toronto. His research focuses on the challenges educators face in adjusting to classrooms where cultural and linguistic diversity is the norm. He has published widely in the areas of language learning, bilingual education, educational reform, and the implications of technological innovation for education. Among his publications are *Brave New Schools: Challenging Cultural Illiteracy through Global Learning*

Networks (with Dennis Sayers, St. Martin's Press, 1995) and *Negotiating Identities: Education for Empowerment in a Diverse Society* (California Association for Bilingual Education, 1996).

Belinda Bustos Flores is an assistant professor in the College of Education and Human Development, the University of Texas at San Antonio. She completed her Ph.D. at the University of Texas at Austin in Curriculum and Instruction with a specialization in Multilingual Studies and Educational Psychology. Dr Flores' research interests include bilingual teacher preparation, teacher belief systems, and ethnic identity, self-concept, and teaching efficacy in relation to teachers.

Joel Hardman is an assistant professor in the Department of English Language and Literature at Southern Illinois University Edwardsville. He works mostly in their MA specialization in Teaching English as a Second Language. He obtained a Ph.D. in Educational Linguistics at the University of Pennsylvania in 1994, when his research focused on family biliteracy development in a Cambodian community in Philadelphia. More recently he has become interested in language teacher education and teacher development. He is working now on how research, theory, beliefs, knowledge, experience, and practices all relate to each other in the work and thinking of practicing teachers.

Mihyon Jeon is a Ph.D. candidate in Educational Linguistics in the Graduate School of Education at the University of Pennsylvania. She was formerly a teacher in Seoul, Korea, and currently teaches Korean to secondary and university students in Philadelphia. Her research interests include minority language maintenance through heritage language education, language ideologies, and bilingual education.

Felicia Lincoln received her Ph.D. in Educational Linguistics from the University of Pennsylvania. While in Philadelphia, she taught English as a second language to international students at Penn, and also taught college English courses at several area universities. Prior to that she taught high school English in her home state of Arkansas. At present, she is on faculty in the Curriculum and Instruction Department at the University of Arkansas in Fayetteville, Arkansas. Her research interests concern language and education planning for language minority populations in Middle America. Other interests are ESL pedagogy and attitudes towards educating language minorities.

Carmen Mercado is the product of public schooling in New York City, where she has been a student, a teacher in a dual language program and, since 1988, a faculty member in the Department of Curriculum and Teaching at Hunter College of CUNY. She completed doctoral studies on language and literacy at Fordham University and her areas of expertise include participatory action research, multiliteracies, nontraditional assessments, and curriculum design in multidialectal, multilingual urban settings. One of her major research interests is language as a pedagogical and intellectual resource and as a tool for social change. She consults nationally and locally on matters pertaining to the formulation and implementation of policies affecting language and literacy instruction and is an active member of the National Latino Education Research Agenda Project of *El Centro de Estudios Puertorriquenos* at Hunter College.

Holly R. Pak is a Ph.D. candidate in Educational Linguistics in the Graduate School of Education at the University of Pennsylvania. She was formerly an instructor at the English Language Programs at the University of Pennsylvania. Currently, she teaches English at a high school near Philadelphia. Her research interests include language planning for heritage language maintenance, language and identity, and bilingual education.

Bertha Pérez is a professor in the College of Education and Human Development, the University of Texas at San Antonio. She completed her Ed.D. in Teacher Education at the University of Massachusetts at Amherst. Dr. Pérez's research interests are in biliteracy and language and literacy development in bilingual settings.

Diana Schwinge is currently a doctoral student in the Educational Linguistics program at the University of Pennsylvania. She has taught English as a second or foreign language in Puerto Rico, Thailand, and New York City. Her dissertation research is an ethnographic discourse analytic study of a second-grade bilingual classroom that examines how students use linguistic, cultural, and textual resources to make intertextual connections. Her research interests include biliteracy, language and literacy policy, second language pedagogy, and the impact of comprehensive school reform on English language learners.

Ellen Skilton-Sylvester is an assistant professor in Temple University's department of Curriculum, Instruction and Technology in Education. Her research interests include US language policies concerning immigrant and refugee education, bilingualism and biliteracy, particularly among Cambodians in the United States, the use of anthropological methods to address language education questions, and service-learning in teacher education. She received her doctorate from the University of

Pennsylvania in educational linguistics and received the Phi Delta Kappa and Council on Anthropology in Education Outstanding Dissertation awards.

Susan Strecker is an assistant professor in the College of Education and Human Development, the University of Texas at San Antonio. She completed her Ph.D. at the University of Texas at Austin in Curriculum and Instruction with a specialization in Language and Literacy. Dr. Strecker's research interests include early literacy, fluency and literacy in diverse cultural settings.

Brian Street is professor of Language in Education at King's College, London University and visiting professor of Education in the Graduate School of Education, University of Pennsylvania. He undertook anthropological fieldwork on literacy in Iran during the 1970s and taught social and cultural anthropology for over 20 years at the University of Sussex, before taking up the Chair of Language in Education at King's College, London. He has written and lectured extensively on literacy practices from both a theoretical and an applied perspective. Professor Street has a long-standing commitment to linking ethnographic-style research on the cultural dimension of language and literacy with contemporary practice in education and in development. Books include his authored *Literacy in Theory and Practice* (Cambridge University Press, 1985), and edited *Cross-Cultural Approaches to Literacy* (CUP, 1993), *Social Literacies* (CUP, 1995), and *Literacy and Development: Ethnographic Perspectives* (Routledge, 2000).

Part 1: Continua of Biliteracy

Chapter 1

Continua of Biliteracy*

NANCY H. HORNBERGER

As public schools in the United States increasingly serve speakers of languages other than English in a predominantly English-speaking society, the need for an understanding of biliteracy becomes more pressing. Among the 18 research priorities recently established by the US Department of Education, the first listed is 'the teaching and learning of reading, writing, or language skills particularly by non- or limited English speaking students' (Department of Education, 1988).

It is not that such teaching and learning does not occur. Consider the following three narrative vignettes. In an urban fourth-grade class composed of 11 Asian and 17 Black children, Sokhom,[1] age 10, has recently been promoted to the on-grade-level reading group and is doing well. She is no longer in the school's pull-out English for Speakers of Other Languages (ESOL) program and spends her whole day in the main-stream classroom. At home, she pulls out a well worn English–Khmer dictionary that she says her father bought at great expense in the refugee camp in the Philippines. She recounts that, when she first came to the United States and was in second grade, she used to look up English words there and ask her father or her brother to read the Cambodian word to her; then she would know what the English word was. Today, in addition to her intense motivation to know English ('I like to talk in English, I like to read in English, and I like to write in English'), Sokhom wants to learn to read and write in Khmer, and in fact has taught herself a little via English.

In another urban public school across the city, Maria, a fifth grader who has been in a two-way maintenance bilingual education program since prekindergarten, has both Spanish and English reading every morning for one and a quarter hours each, with Ms Torres and Mrs Dittmar, respectively. Today, Mrs Dittmar is reviewing the vocabulary for the story the students are reading about Charles Drew, a Black American doctor. She explains that 'influenza' is what Charles's little sister died of; Maria comments that 'you say it [influenza] in Spanish the same way you write it [in English].'

In the same Puerto Rican community, in a new bilingual middle school a few blocks away, Elizabeth, a graduate of the two-way maintenance bilingual program mentioned above, hears a Career Day speaker from the community tell her that, of two people applying for a job, one bilingual and one not, the bilingual has an advantage. Yet Elizabeth's daily program of classes provides little opportunity for her to continue to develop literacy in Spanish; the bilingual program at this school is primarily transitional.

All three of these girls are part of the biliterate population of the United States. The educational programs they are experiencing are vastly different with respect to attention to literacy in their first language, ranging from total absence to benign neglect to active development; and from mainstream with pull-out ESOL to transitional bilingual education to two-way maintenance bilingual education. Biliteracy exists, as do educational programs serving biliterate populations. Yet, provocative questions remain to be answered, primarily about the degree to which literacy knowledge and skills in one language aid or impede the learning of literacy knowledge and skills in the other.

A framework for understanding biliteracy is needed in which to situate research and teaching; this review attempts to address that need. Because biliteracy itself represents a conjunction of literacy and bilingualism, the logical place to begin to look is in those two fields. This seems particularly appropriate because the twin, and some suggest conflicting (Fillmore & Valadez, 1986: 653), goals of bilingual education and ESOL programs in elementary public schools in the United States are for students to (a) learn the second language (English) and (b) keep up with their monolingual peers in academic content areas.

The fields of literacy and bilingualism each represent vast amounts of literature. There is a relatively small but increasing proportion of explicit attention to (a) bilingualism within the literature on literacy and literacy within the literature on bilingualism and (b) second or foreign languages within the literatures on the teaching of reading and writing and reading and writing within the literatures on second or foreign language teaching. Perhaps the reason for the relative lack of attention is that, when one seeks to attend to both, already complex issues seem to become further muddled. For example, Alderson (1984: 24) explored one such muddled area: If a student is having difficulty reading a text in a foreign language, should this be construed as a reading problem or a language problem?

It turns out, however, as this review will show, that by focusing findings from the two fields on the common area of biliteracy, we elucidate not only biliteracy itself but also literacy and bilingualism. All the above literatures were considered for this review, with special focus on those studies and papers that explore the area of overlap, that is, biliteracy.

Neither a complete theory of literacy nor a complete theory of bilingualism yet exist. In both fields, the complexity of the subject; the multidisciplinary nature of the inquiry, including educators, linguists, psychologists, anthropologists, sociologists, and historians; and the interdependence between research, policy, and practice make unity and coherence elusive objectives (see Hakuta, 1986: x; Langer, 1988: 43; Scribner, 1987: 19).

This review proposes a framework for understanding biliteracy, using the notion of continuum to provide the overarching conceptual scheme for describing biliterate contexts, development, and media. Although we often characterize dimensions of bilingualism and literacy in terms of polar opposites, such as first versus second languages (L1 vs L2), monolingual versus bilingual individuals, or oral versus literate societies, it has become increasingly clear that in each case those opposites represent only theoretical endpoints on what is in reality a continuum of features (see Kelly, 1969: 5). Furthermore, when we consider biliteracy in its turn, it becomes clear that these continua are interrelated dimensions of one highly complex whole.

Figures 1.1–1.3 schematically represent the framework by depicting both the continua and their interrelatedness. The figures show the nine continua characterizing contexts for biliteracy, the development of individual biliteracy, and the media of biliteracy, respectively. Not only is the three-dimensionality of any one figure representative of the interrelatedness of its constituent continua, but it should be emphasized that the interrelationships extend across the contexts, development, and media of biliteracy as well (see Figures 1.1–1.3).

The notion of continuum is intended to convey that, although one can identify (and name) points on the continuum, those points are not finite, static, or discrete. There are infinitely many points on the continuum; any single point is inevitably and inextricably related to all other points; and all the points have more in common than not with each other. The argument here is that, for an understanding of biliteracy, it is equally elucidating to focus on the common features and on the distinguishing features along any one continuum.

In an attempt to disentangle the complexities of biliteracy, the sections that follow introduce the nine continua one at a time, citing illustrative

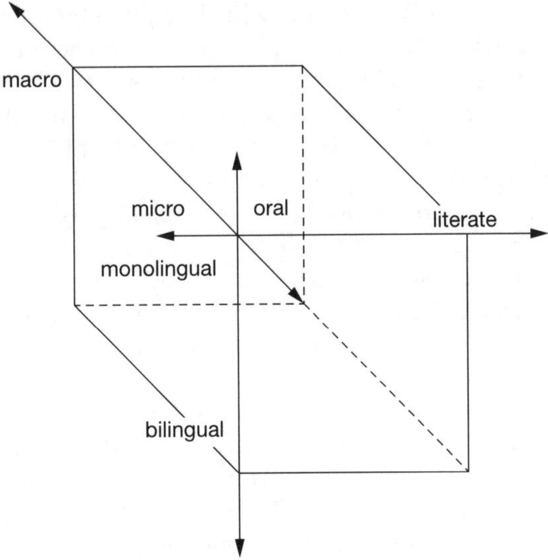

Figure 1.1 The continua of biliterate contexts

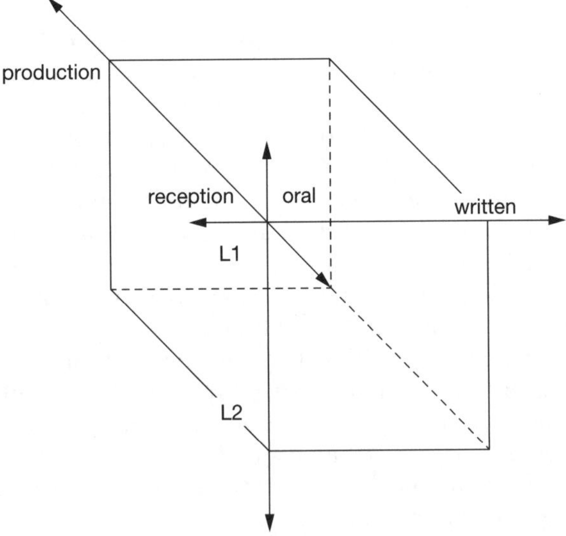

Figure 1.2 The continua of biliterate development in the individual

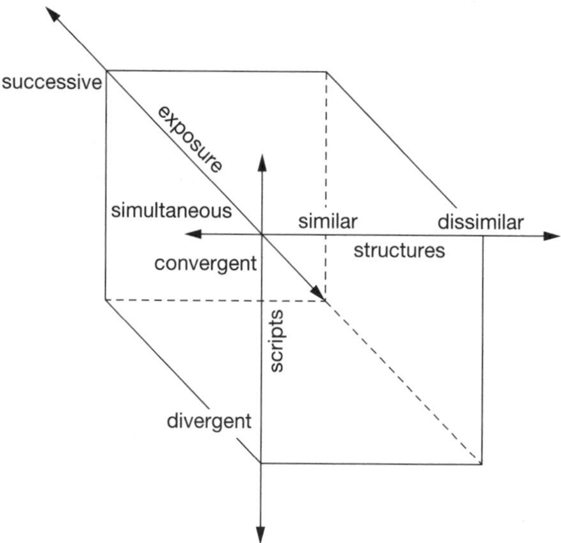

Figure 1.3 The continua of biliterate media

works from the literatures mentioned above in support of each one. In the first section, represented in Figure 1.1, contexts for biliteracy are defined in terms of three continua: micro–macro, oral–literate, and monolingual–bilingual. The second section, represented in Figure 1.2, introduces the continua that characterize the development of the biliterate individual's communicative repertoire: reception–production, oral language–written language, and L1–L2 transfer. The third section, represented in Figure 1.3, describes three continua characterizing the relationships among the media through which the biliterate individual communicates: simultaneous–successive exposure, similar–dissimilar structures, and convergent–divergent scripts. Throughout the discussion of the nine continua, the interrelationships among them are also brought out. The paper concludes with comments on the implications of the continua for research in and teaching of biliteracy.

Contexts of Biliteracy

An interest in context as an important factor in all aspects of language use dates back at least to the early 1960s and the beginnings of sociolinguistics and the ethnography of communication (Fishman, 1968; Hymes,

1964; Pride & Holmes, 1972). Building from communicative theory and work by Roman Jakobson published in 1953 and 1960, Hymes suggested an array of components that might serve as a heuristic for the ethnographic study of speech events, or more generally, communicative events, where such events refer to activities or aspects of activities that are directly governed by rules or norms for the use of language and that consist of one or more speech acts.[2] This array of components included participants, settings, topics, goals, norms, forms, genres, and so forth and was later formulated by Hymes (1974: 53–62) into the mnemonic SPEAKING (*S*etting, *P*articipants, *E*nds, *A*ct, *K*ey, *I*nstrumentalities, *N*orms, *G*enres).

From within the ethnography of communication have come occasional calls for the ethnography of writing (Basso, 1974) and the ethnography of literacy (Szwed, 1981). In a recent paper Dubin (1989) assured those attending the Communicative Competence Revisited Seminar that the ethnography of communication is alive and well in the literacy field, and she went on to describe her own current study of what she termed the 'mini-literacies' of three biliterate immigrants.

Indeed, in the last decade the literacy field has seen a series of persuasive arguments for the significance of context for understanding literacy. Heath is one who has explicitly undertaken the study of literacy in context, within an ethnography of communication framework. She noted that reading varies in its functions and uses across history, cultures, and 'contexts of use as defined by particular communities' (1980: 126) and went on to document this in her 1983 study. Scribner and Cole (1981) drew from their study of literacy in Liberia to argue that 'literacy is not simply learning how to read and write a particular script but applying this knowledge for specific purposes in specific contexts of use' (236). Gee (1986) contended that literacy has no meaning 'apart from particular cultural contexts in which it is used' (734). Also, Langer (1988) found one of three new emphases of books and articles on literacy in the 1980s to be 'the effects of context and culture on literacy,' and went on to suggest that all three literacy volumes she reviewed (Bloome, 1987; de Castell *et al.*, 1986; Olson *et al.*, 1985) share a concern with literacy in context (or what Olson *et al.* called literacy as situational).

Street (1984) rejected what he labeled the autonomous model of literacy and argued for the ideological model, which assumes that the 'meaning of literacy depends upon the social institutions in which it is embedded' (8). Therefore, he continued, it makes more sense to refer to multiple literacies than to any single literacy; he described such a case from his own fieldwork in Iran (see also Gee, 1986: 719). Thus, he opted for a contextualized rather than a decontextualized view of literacy.

Biliteracy, like all literacies, can be taken to be 'radically constituted by [its] context of use' (Erickson, 1984: 529). What do the literatures on bilingualism, literacy, and biliteracy tell us about the contexts of biliteracy? This review suggests that there is an implicit, and at times explicit, understanding in the literatures that any particular context of biliteracy is defined by the intersection of at least three continua – the micro–macro continuum, the oral–literate continuum, and the monolingual–bilingual continuum – and that any attempt to understand an instance of biliteracy by attending to only one of these contextual continua produces at best an incomplete result.

The micro–macro continuum

Sociolinguists have recognized a distinction between micro and macro levels of analysis from the beginning. Indeed, one can characterize areas of sociolinguistic inquiry in a quadrant model that distinguishes between micro and macro levels of analysis of social interaction and micro and macro levels of linguistic analysis (see Figure 1.4). Such a model makes

		LEVELS OF SOCIAL INTERACTION	
		MICRO	MACRO
LEVELS OF LINGUISTIC ANALYSIS	MICRO	*Micro–Micro* Ethnomethodology Discourse analysis Interactionist sociolinguistics	*Macro–Micro* Variationist sociolinguistics
	MACRO	*Micro–Macro* Ethnography of communication	*Macro–Macro* Sociology of language

Figure 1.4 Micro and macro sociolinguistics

clear the range of contexts for the analysis of language use. Thus, generalizing broadly, at the micro–micro level of context a particular feature of language (e.g. cohesion, rhythm, or a phoneme) is examined in a particular piece of text or discourse; at the micro–macro level, patterns of language use are examined in the context of a situation or a speech event; at the macro–micro level, a particular feature of language is examined in the context of a society or a large social unit; and at the macro–macro level of context, patterns of language use are examined within or across societies or nations.

Insights from a consideration of bilingualism in context include, for example, at the micro–macro level, the recognition that the bilingual individual keys language choice to characteristics of the situation (e.g. Grosjean, 1982: 127–145). At the macro-macro level are the insights that there may exist domains[3] associated with one or another language in bilingual societies (e.g. Fishman, 1986 [1972]; Grosjean, 1982: 130–2), or that a language may fulfill one of a range of functions in the society. These functional roles include the high or low variety in a diglossic situation,[4] such as classical and colloquial Arabic in Arabic-speaking societies (Ferguson, 1959); a second language of widespread use, such as English in Singapore (Williams, 1987); a foreign language (e.g. Alderson & Urquhart, 1984); or a language of wider communication (LWC), such as Swahili in East Africa.

On the other hand, insights from a consideration of literacy in context include, for example, Bloome and Green's (1984) differentiation within the micro–micro context between the intrapersonal and interpersonal contexts of reading, where the former encompasses 'the individual's background knowledge, skills, and general approach to reading' and the latter refers to 'the organization of reading events, the interaction of participants involved in reading events, the influences that the interaction of participants had on the reading process, as well as how the reading process influenced the interaction of participants' (413). Lytle and Botel (1988: 12) represented micro and macro levels of context schematically with successively larger concentric circles consisting of student; classroom; school as a community; home, neighborhood, town/city, state, and region; and national, cultural, and multicultural environment.

The point to be emphasized here is that micro and macro levels of context are perhaps best represented in neither a dichotomous nor a layered relationship, but as a continuum. Any particular instance of biliteracy is defined at one point along the continuum, whether it is a child using an L1–L2 dictionary to learn her L2 at the micro end or a language minority population making only minimal use of its L1 in written form at the macro end. This does not deny that other levels of context impinge on that instance; it was noted earlier, with respect to all the continua, that any one point is inevitably and inextricably related to all other points. Yet, if we are to begin to understand biliteracy we must be careful to define each instance by its particulars.

A number of studies of biliteracy make one or another end of the continuum salient while revealing the continuity between them. At the macro level, biliteracy often exists in a context of unequal power relations: one or another literacy becomes marginalized (Baynham, 1988); or literacies become specialized by functions – Amharic, Arabic, and English literacy in Ethiopia (Ferguson, 1985: 137) or English, Hindi, and Fijian literacy in Fiji (Mangubhai, 1987: 190–3, 201–4). Changing societal contexts lead to changing biliteracy configurations: whereas the literate minority among the Panjabi in Northern India used to learn literacy in either Hindi or Urdu, 'the expansion of education; expanded roles of regional languages in education and public life; and the reluctance of Sikhs to be identified with either Hindus or Muslims' led many Panjabis to adopt literacy in their mother tongue (Ferguson, 1985: 178).

At the micro level, situational factors such as the roles of public writers, the juxtaposition of traditional and modern uses of literacy in and outside of school, the use of the individual writing board, and memorization and oral recitation for learning lessons all bear on literacy in French, standard Arabic, and Moroccan Arabic in Morocco (Wagner *et al.*, 1986).

The oral–literate continuum

The above studies point to the relevance of the micro–macro continuum for an understanding of biliterate contexts. They also suggest, however, that a complete picture of biliteracy necessarily entails the other two: the oral–literate and monolingual–bilingual continua. Consider the following series of contextual barriers to literacy for the Northern Ute people in northeastern Utah. The barriers to literacy range from the macro to micro level, across Ute and English, and from oral to literate uses.

Barriers to literacy in Ute include the implicit new model of social organization literacy brings – literates versus nonliterates as opposed to kinship ties and sodalities; the reversal of traditional leadership patterns ensuing from literacy acquisition by the younger generation; the limited 'real world' usefulness of Ute literacy; the potential inappropriateness (in spiritual terms) of expressing Ute in writing; the relative drabness of print as compared to beadwork, basketry, ceremonial dress, and other visual communication already in use; and the relative lack of flexibility and potential for individual variation in response to different situations in written Ute as compared to oral Ute expression. On the other hand, contextual barriers to literacy in English include the pervasive influence of Ute patterns of discourse in students' written English, schooling as a painful experience for the Ute, and the limited usefulness of English literacy given high unemployment rates unaffected by literacy (Leap, 1987: 18–48).

The example of Ute oral discourse patterns in English written by Utes is an example of the oral–literate continuum, which is the second of the defining continua for contexts of biliteracy. Any particular instance of biliteracy is located at a point on the oral–literate continuum, but there is also a close relationship between oral and literate uses of language, as exemplified in the Ute case.

Heath (1982) demonstrated how a familiar literacy event in mainstream US culture, the bedtime story, is embedded in oral language use. In addition, her study (Heath, 1983) of the functions and uses of literacy in mainstream, black working-class, and white working-class homes in the southeastern United States clearly reveals not only that speech and literacy are interrelated in each group, but that differences among the groups are not so much along the lines of oral versus literate cultures as along the lines of which literacies most closely resemble those of the school.

There may be, in any one society, many varieties of literacy, including uses of literacy 'for storytelling and reading . . . for immediate functional purposes in the home and work; for leisure and pleasure purposes; and for personal exploration as in diaries and private notebooks' (Street, 1988b). Yet all these literacies are not equally 'powerful' in society. As Cook-Gumperz (1986) illustrated, there has been, in Western society, a shift from the eighteenth century onward from 'a *pluralistic* idea about literacy as a composite of different skills related to reading and writing for many different purposes and sections of a society's population, to a twentieth-century notion of a single, standardised *schooled literacy*' (22).

Street (1988a) argued that 'literacy practices are always embedded in oral uses, and the variations between cultures are generally variations in the *mix* of oral/literate channels' (5) and *not* due to a dichotomous difference between the oral and literate worlds, as Ong (1982), for example, proposed and many writers still accept (e.g. Parry, 1987: 63). Street refuted the idea of the 'great divide' between orality and literacy (see Scribner & Cole, 1981: 4), where the oral world is characterized with terms such as 'formulaic, conservative, [and] homeostatic' and the literate world with terms such as 'abstract, analytic, [and] objective (1988a: 1). He noted that the characteristics that Ong would attribute to literacy are, in fact, 'those of the social *context* and specific culture in which the literacy being described is located' (Street, 1988a: 5; see also Gee, 1986: 728).

Street further noted, as did Murray (1988: 351, 370), that even some of the recent papers discussing the relation between orality and literacy as a continuum continue to reinforce the concept of the great divide. Street (1988c: 64, 70) went on to examine and refute various 'literacy myths' that divide literacy from orality on grounds of cohesion, connectedness, lexical versus paralinguistic features to encode meaning, and degree of situational embeddedness. Earlier, Tannen (1985) suggested that what many have called features of spoken versus written language (specifically, degrees of contextualization and devices of cohesion) are, in fact, features reflecting relatively more or less focus on interpersonal involvement, which may characterize either spoken *or* written language.

Both Street and Murray have argued for less emphasis on the supposed differences between written and oral language use and more on the contexts in which speakers choose between written and oral media in the same way they make other linguistic choices (Murray, 1988: 352, 370). Murray (1988: 353, 368–9) drew from Hymes's and Halliday's models and proposed a taxonomy of those aspects of the context of situation (field, speaker/hearer, setting) that contribute to choice of medium (face to face, telephone, paper, or computer) and mode (specific subtypes within medium) within the speech community of an IBM research laboratory.

In sum, orality and literacy share many common features and the features that have been identified with one or the other have more to do with the context in which language is used than with oral versus literate use.

The monolingual–bilingual continuum

The same can be said for the third defining continuum for contexts of biliteracy, the monolingual–bilingual continuum. At the macro level, consider the specialization of functions for languages and varieties. In monolingual societies, different varieties of one language may be firmly identified with high and low functions (Ferguson, 1959; see also Duranti and Ochs, 1986: 219, on Samoa). So, too, in bilingual societies, different languages may experience specialization of function (Fishman, 1967). The important distinction appears to be less the difference in languages than the differences in contexts, functions, and use (see also Gee, 1986: 728).

Similarly, at the micro level, the difference between monolingual and bilingual individuals is not so much that bilinguals possess two complete sets of functions and uses of language, one for each language. Rather, bilinguals switch languages according to specific functions and uses, whereas monolinguals switch styles in the same contexts. 'Bilingualism . . . is a special, salient case of the general phenomenon of linguistic repertoire. No normal person, and no normal community, is limited to a single way of speaking' (Hymes, 1986 [1972]: 38). Grosjean (1985) argued for a bilingual ('wholistic') rather than a monolingual (fractional) view of bilingualism. In the bilingual view, bilinguals are perceived to have unique and specific linguistic configurations that are different from those of monolinguals in either language, in the same way that a hurdler is neither a sprinter nor a high jumper but something completely different (see also Gumperz, 1969: 244).

Zentella (1981) showed that code-switching,[5] stigmatized because it is believed to reflect the bilingual's lack of complete knowledge and control of the two languages, in fact reflects a highly sensitive response to contextual factors. In her study, she grouped contextual factors into three categories from the point of view of the observer: 'on the spot' (factors of setting and participants), 'in the head' (communicative factors such as style, functions, and conversational strategies), and 'out of the mouth' (linguistic factors such as language of the switch, loans, and grammaticality). That is, code-switching represents highly competent, context-specific language use.

The argument here is that monolingualism and bilingualism are more alike than different. The functions and uses to which different varieties and styles are put in a monolingual individual or society are the same ones to which different languages are put in a bilingual individual or society.

Contexts of biliteracy are defined, then, by these three continua. Any particular instance of biliteracy is located at a point of intersection among the three. To return to our opening vignettes, Sokhom's use of the English–Khmer dictionary to learn L2 words represents an instance toward the micro, oral, and monolingual ends of the continua; the bilingual middle school's predominant use of written L2 represents an instance toward the macro, literate, and bilingual ends of the continua. With the wide range of possible biliterate contexts as defined by these three continua for background, we will now turn to a consideration of the biliterate individual's development of communicative competence in biliterate contexts.

Biliterate Development in the Individual

Within the ethnography of communication framework, the term *communicative competence* designates the knowledge and ability of individuals for appropriate language use in the communicative events in which they find themselves in any particular speech community. This competence is, by definition, variable within individuals (from event to event), across individuals, and across speech communities. Individuals draw on their communicative repertoire to participate appropriately in any given context. This review suggests that, for the biliterate individual, that repertoire is crucially defined by at least three continua: reception–production, oral language–written language, and L1–L2 transfer (see Figure 1.2).

Further, the development of biliteracy in individuals occurs along the continua in direct response to the contextual demands placed on these individuals:

> The environmental press that requires the successful interactant to use distinct subsets of linguistic and sociolinguistic knowledge can change from moment to moment in face to face interaction, and from one discourse unit to another in a written text with which ego is confronted. Interaction with these verbal and written texts, and with the text producers, constitutes practice in language use. (Erickson, 1989: 5)

Finally, it should be clarified that the notion of continuum in development is not intended to suggest that development is necessarily continuous or gradual; it may, in fact, occur in spurts and with some backtracking. Rather, the argument is that development within any one continuum draws on features from the entire continuum (see Heath, 1986: 150 on the 'single developmental model').

The reception–production continuum

One of the longstanding theories of language development in both the reading and the foreign language teaching literatures has involved a dichotomy between oral and written language and one between receptive and productive skills. The assumption has been that oral language development (listening and speaking) precedes written language development (reading and writing) and that receptive skills (listening and reading) precede productive ones (speaking and writing). Thus, the 'logical sequence' of language development was believed to be listening, speaking, reading, and writing (e.g. Smith, 1967: 54–7). Along with the other dichotomies presented in this review, the reception–production dichotomy (and the oral–written dichotomy discussed next) have been superseded by a view that recognizes that receptive and productive development occurs along a continuum, beginning at any point, and proceeding, cumulatively or in spurts, in either direction.

In second-language acquisition research, a decade or more of attention to 'comprehensible input'[6] as crucial to the learner's acquisition of the second language has recently been extended to a recognition that learners must also have the opportunity to produce 'comprehensible output'[7] (Pica *et al.*, 1989; Swain, 1985). That is, speaking, as well as listening, contributes to the negotiation of meaning in interaction, which in turn is said to lead to language acquisition. In a review article exploring lessons from first-language acquisition for second-language acquisition, Gathercole (1988) argued that recent research shows that 'the relationship between comprehension and production is not unidirectional – that progress in either may lead to progress in the other' (426).

In the reading field, Goodman and Goodman (1983) have argued that 'people not only learn to read by reading and write by writing but they also learn to read by writing and write by reading' (592). Hudelson (1984: 229) added that this is true for second as well as first languages.

A number of studies in biliterate settings have confirmed the interrelationship of skills along the reception–production continuum. In a study among immigrant children in Israel, Feitelson (1987: 178–9) found that being read to in formal primary school settings prepared students for subsequent reading comprehension. In Fiji, Mangubhai (1987: 200) found that, as a result of the Book Flood Project, receptive skills in English (reading and listening comprehension) improved and apparently transferred to other related language skills. In highland Puno, Peru, Quechua-speaking children taught via their first language as medium of instruction showed not only improved oral participation but increased reading and writing performance in school (Hornberger, 1988: 190–8).

The oral language–written language continuum

As the research cited above already suggests, not only do listening–speaking and reading–writing development occur along a continuum, but so too does oral–written development. As noted above in the discussion of the oral–literate continuum, many literacy events occur embedded in oral language use (see Heath, 1982). The counterpart to this embeddedness in the development of literacy is that children learn to read and write through heavy reliance on spoken language. Goodman and Goodman have shown how oral miscues[8] provide clues as to the development of reading (Goodman, 1982: 89–168; Grove, 1981: 11–13). Similarly, Wilde (1988) argued that children's use of their own 'invented' spellings, based at the beginning on children's knowledge of the sounds of the language (and later on patterns and meaning relationships), helps them in language development.

Bi- and multilingual readers provide evidence that, like listening–speaking and reading–writing development, development along the oral–written language continuum is not necessarily unidirectional. In the rote learning and memorization of the Koran in Muslim societies, emphasis is placed on 'reading' a text that is of a 'conceptual and linguistic complexity far beyond the understanding of the young children who memorize it' (Baynham, 1988). The level of the reading outstrips the children's speaking knowledge of the language; yet they do read it.

Hudelson (1984: 224, 231) pointed out that children learning English as a second language can and do both read and write English before they have mastered the oral and written systems of the language. Hudelson concluded:

> The processes of writing, reading, speaking, and listening in a second language are interrelated and interdependent. It is both useless and, ultimately, impossible to separate out the language processes in our teaching ... or to try to present ESL [English as a second language] material in a linear sequence of listening, speaking, reading, and writing. (1984: 234)

The LI–L2 transfer continuum

Biliterate development is defined not only by continuities between spoken and written language, between listening and speaking, and between reading and writing, but also by those between the first language (L1) and the second language (L2). Recognizing the close connections between development in one and the other language, researchers have attempted to determine to what extent knowledge of one language transfers to the other (and aids learning) and to what extent knowledge of the one interferes with the other (and impedes learning).

Researchers have approached the question of transfer versus interference in two general ways, both focused on the search for evidence of positive transfer. They have asked what kinds of *positive* effects reading instruction in one language might have on reading achievement in the other and what kinds of *negative* effects the *absence* of reading instruction in one language might have on reading achievement in the other. These questions have usually been framed in terms of transfer from L1 to L2, and occasionally in terms of transfer from L2 to L3 (see Wagner *et al.*, 1989 and below) or L2 to L1 (Canadian immersion studies).

Research on the question of negative effects has generally revealed that the absence of L1 reading instruction does not necessarily have a negative effect; however, in almost every case, researchers have been careful to note that whether or not direct L2 instruction will have a negative effect depends substantially on the context in which it occurs.

For example, a series of studies investigated whether initial instruction in L1 or L2 is more conducive to successful acquisition of L2 literacy skills. Engle (1975) and Dutcher (1982) reviewed a number of these studies and arrived at conclusions that buttress the view that the context of language use, rather than the language per se, is the deciding factor. In a review of eight studies in seven multilingual countries on the use of first and second languages in primary education, including Modiano's (1973) Mexico study, the Canadian immersion programs (Lambert & Tucker, 1972; Lambert, 1985), and the Rock Point Navajo School (Rosier & Holm, 1980), Dutcher (1982) concluded that there is no one answer to the question of what is the best choice of language as the initial language of instruction for children in primary school. Rather, the answer varies from case to case depending on micro and macro contextual factors such as the child's cognitive and linguistic development in L1 (see also Niyekawa, 1983: 104–13), parental attitudes and support for the languages and the school, and the status of both languages in the wider community (Dutcher, 1982).

In an earlier review drawn on by Dutcher, Engle (1975) also found that neither what she called the 'direct approach' (i.e. instruction in L2) nor the 'native language approach' (i.e. instruction in L1) was clearly superior to the other for the teaching of initial reading and subject matter in multilingual contexts; rather, a series of contextual issues needed to be taken into account.

Tucker (1986: 362–3) reiterated this point with reference to the transferability of the Canadian immersion model to US settings. He listed the following as salient contextual attributes that contribute to the success of Canadian immersion programs: The children's L1 is a language of high social and economic status; the children come from families of middle socioeconomic status backgrounds; participation is voluntary; parents play a strong and catalytic role in the programs; formal L2 instruction occurs from the very beginning; teachers are native L2 speakers; an L1 language arts component is added to the curriculum by Grade 2; and L1 is used for content instruction beginning at Grade 3 or 4.

More recently, Wagner *et al.* (1989), who found that instruction in their second language did not necessarily put Berber monolingual children at a disadvantage with respect to their Arabic-speaking peers by the fifth year of primary school, offered a number of contextual explanations for this 'counter-example' to the UNESCO (1953) mother tongue literacy axiom: lack of competing literacy in Berber, Arabic as the language of Islam, the ascendancy of spoken Moroccan Arabic in the small-town context of the study, and the usefulness of the Koranic preschool experience for promoting reading skills. The same study found that both Berber- and Arabic-speaking children's acquisition of their second literacy (French) was substantially dependent on their first literacy (Arabic) acquisition.

This last finding directly addresses the other of the two transfer questions (i.e. what kinds of positive effects literacy in one language might have on literacy in the other). The two general lines of findings in the research in this area are that (a) what appears to be interference from L1 in L2 is better construed as evidence for learning in that it represents the *application* of L1 knowledge to L2, and (b) the stronger the foundation and continuing development in L1, the greater the potential for enhanced learning of L2.

Consider the example of errors in oral second-language acquisition. In the audiolingual method of second-language teaching, popular in the 1940s to 1960s, errors in the second language were seen as the result of first-language habits *interfering* with the acquisition of second-language habits. Today, in contrast, with the advent of transformational grammar and first-language acquisition research, a new view has emerged. In this view the learner is 'credited with having an interlanguage . . . [incorporating] characteristics of both the native and target language of the learner,'[9] and errors are seen as clues to the nature of the interlanguage and the process of second-language acquisition (Hakuta & Cancino, 1977: 297). That is, what was once seen as simply interference from the first language into the second is now recognized as evidence of the creative application of L1 knowledge to L2 learning. Just as miscues and invented spellings provide clues as to the development of reading and writing, interlanguage provides clues as to the development of the second language.

In studies of biliterate development, as well, the notion of interference has given way to that of transfer. Edelsky (1986) refuted the interference 'myth,' arguing that children in the bilingual program she studied *applied* what they knew about first-language writing to second-language writing:

> they were applying everything from specific hypotheses about segmentation, spelling, and endings to general strategies for literacy acquisition (e.g. use the input – Spanish print does not have k's; English print does not have tildes and accents), to high level knowledge (that texts are contextually constrained), to a crucial process (orchestration of cuing systems). (73, 117; see also Edelsky, 1982)

This accords with Thonis's (1981: 150–4) and Hakuta's (1987) suggestions that most transfer of skills from L1 to L2 occurs in a global way, rather than point by point; that is, transfer is not word for word, but rather involves processes and strategies. Wald, too, found that both 'English language skills (such as knowledge of syntactic devices for organizing information) and cross-language literacy skills (such as strategies for organizing information in writing) interact in the acquisition of English literacy [for East Los Angeles Hispanic bilingual advanced high school students]' (1987: 180). Research on Spanish and English reading lessons in a bilingual school in Philadelphia suggests that the strategy of 'attacking' new words by identifying roots and suffixes may transfer between the two languages (Hornberger & Micheau, 1988). Finally, two studies using the Sentence Verification Technique in Spanish and English with sixth- and seventh-grade students in transitional bilingual education programs showed that (a) listening and reading skills transferred from L1 to L2, and (b) subject matter knowledge acquired by means of L1 transferred to L2 (Carlo *et al.*, 1989).

Work in the field of contrastive rhetoric has shown that native language discourse patterns have an impact on writers' learning of a second language and its discourse patterns. Söter's (1988: 202) study comparing one writing task (a simple bedtime story) carried out by Vietnamese, Arabic-speaking Lebanese, and native English-speaking students in Sydney, Australia, demonstrated the influence of the students' prior knowledge of literacy and literary experiences on their current experiences and writing performance. Indrasuta's (1988: 222) comparison of writing by a group of Thai writers in Thai and English found that the writers brought L1 rhetorical style and appropriateness to their L2 writing.

Leap (1987) analyzed English compositions by Ute fourth graders and argued that Ute discourse strategies are at work in their English writing. Such strategies include 'non-exhaustive presentation of detail, . . . active engagement of the reader as well as the writer in the construction and presentation of meaning,' and choosing 'to write a "personal opinion" essay in . . . "corporate terms"' (Leap, 1987: 36, 38).

Influence of L1 on L2 along the L1–L2 writing development continuum can be seen as interference or transfer, depending on the writer's goals. The aim in contrastive rhetoric has generally been to make the biliterate's ESL writing more congruent with English rhetorical style (e.g. Kaplan, 1988: 278), that is, eradicating interference. Leap (1987: 44–6), on the other hand, noted that Ute students should be able to choose whether they will acquire the rhetorical patterns associated with written standard English or stay with Ute rhetorical patterns in writing English, and thus communicate Ute-centered perspectives more effectively (i.e. a choice between eradicating interference and making creative use of transfer).

As noted above, the second line of argument concerning L1–L2 transfer is that the potential and benefit for positive transfer of reading/writing skills to L2 increase with the greater development of L1 skills. Studies by Rosier and Holm (1980), Reyes (1987), and Roller (1988) point to cumulative effects of bilingual instruction with benefits for L2 literacy becoming more evident each year after the third grade (see also Genesee, 1987: 43, 129). Moll and Diaz (1985) found that strong reading skills in Spanish could be drawn on to improve reading in English by fourth-grade bilingual students. In a study of second-, third-, and fourth-grade Spanish-speaking students in a transitional bilingual program, Zutell and Allen (1988: 338–9) found that the more successful spellers differentiated between Spanish and English systems, whereas poorer spellers' English spellings were influenced by the effect of Spanish phonology on their pronunciation of English words.

Such results find theoretical support in Cummins's linguistic interdependence hypothesis[10] and in Lambert's notions of additive and subtractive bilingualism.[11] They also accord with Thonis's (1981) claims that 'hasty, premature introduction to the second writing system may result in two weak sets of [reading/writing] skills' (178) and Niyekawa's (1983) assumption that 'the higher the grade level at the time of transfer to an L2 school, the less time it should take the children to catch up because they have more knowledge to serve as context and more skills to transfer' (112).

Finally, a note about the question Alderson (1984: 24) posed as to whether a learner's difficulties with reading a foreign text stem from a reading problem or a language problem. It is relevant here to note that he concluded that both are probably involved, but for low levels of foreign language competence the problem is likely one of language. Clarke (1981: 78) had similar findings for adult ESL readers (see also Carrell, 1987: 3). Edelsky (1982) also found that 'the child's second language proficiency was the factor that most directly influenced the relative syntactic simplicity of the English texts [they wrote]' (226), even though the child's knowledge of more complex syntax in the first language might be high. Similarly, in a study that focused on the transfer of decoding skills from Spanish to English in beginning reading, Faltis (1986) found that, in addition to the extent of mastery of decoding in Spanish, the students' 'proficiency in English as a second language played a central role in affecting transfer' (156). In other words, highly efficient reading/writing ability in L1 does not make up altogether for lack of knowledge of L2.

That is, development along one continuum is crucially affected by development along the others. This is not to imply, however, that development occurs in one straight line along all three continua simultaneously from, say, oral receptive L1 competence to written productive L1–L2 competence. In fact, depending on the particular context, development is likely to zigzag across points within the three-dimensional space defined by the three continua. Thus, a more exact answer to Alderson's question might be: both, either, or neither, depending on the context. To return again to the initial vignettes, Sokhom's biliterate development could be characterized as beginning at a point near the L1 oral receptive ends of the continua, moving through a point near the L2 written receptive space and toward a point near the middle of all three continua. In contrast, Maria's biliterate development could be characterized as starting at a point near the L1 oral receptive ends of the continua, moving through a point near the middle of all three continua and toward a point midway along the reception–production and oral–written continua, near the L2 end.

In sum, the individual's biliterate development occurs along all three continua simultaneously and in relation with each other; this is why the notion of transfer has been such a tenacious and, at the same time, frustratingly elusive one. The potential for transfer along and across the continua is apparently infinite. Not only are the three continua of biliterate development related to each other, they are also related to the continua of biliterate contexts, as we have seen in the above discussion, and to the continua of biliterate media, as we will see below.

The Media of Biliteracy

It is, after all, through the media of the two languages that the biliterate individual communicates in any particular context. Indeed, the media are a part of that context. The continua that define the relationship between the media are simultaneous–successive exposure, similar–dissimilar structures, and convergent–divergent scripts. Each of these continua is argued to have a bearing on the individual development of biliteracy, and especially on the potential for transfer in that development; however, research has not yet clarified which, if either, end of the continuum is the more conducive to positive transfer.

The simultaneous–successive exposure continuum

In the bilingualism field, a distinction is often made between simultaneous and successive bilingual language acquisition (McLaughlin, 1985) or early and late bilingualism (Lambert, 1985: 120). Early bilinguals are those who become bilingual in infancy; late bilinguals do so in adolescence. Similarly, a child who acquires two languages before age three is doing so simultaneously; one who acquires one language before age three and the other after age three is doing so successively.

Differences are attributed to the kinds of bilinguals; for example, it was suggested that early bilinguals have more compounded language systems and late bilinguals more coordinated ones (Lambert, 1985: 120).[12] Nevertheless, there is increasing recognition that type and degree of bilingualism have more to do with systematic use of the two languages than with age of acquisition. Genesee (1989), for example, has recently refuted the hypothesis that children who learn two languages simultaneously have a unitary, undifferentiated language system, arguing instead that 'bilingual children develop differentiated language systems from the beginning and are able to use their developing languages in *contextually sensitive ways*' (161, italics added).

It should be emphasized that the findings that a stronger first language leads to a stronger second language do not necessarily imply that the first language must be fully developed before the second language is introduced. Rather, the first language must not be abandoned before it is fully developed, whether the second language is introduced simultaneously or successively, early or late, in that process. This too accords with Lambert's notion of additive bilingualism and is reiterated by Hakuta *et al.* (1986), who found that positive cognitive effects, including increased metalinguistic awareness and the use of language as a tool of thought, are found in additive bilingual situations (where the second language is acquired without loss of the mother tongue) that involve a somewhat systematic use of two languages.

It is worth noting that a number of configurations exist as to the simultaneous or successive development of biliteracy and that these involve varying degrees of development of L1. A few examples will suffice to illustrate this point. There are cases where L2 literacy follows on varying levels of L1 literacy: transitional bilingual education, as practiced in the United States, builds L2 literacy on minimal L1 literacy development; secondary schooling in a language of wider communication, such as English in many African nations, builds L2 literacy on moderate L1 literacy development; and foreign language studies at the college level build L2 literacy on highly developed L1 literacy.

Alternatively, there are cases where L1 literacy of varying levels of development follows on L2 literacy development: French immersion programs in Canada introduce English-speaking children to literacy through French, and later bring English literacy into the program, continuing to develop both throughout the years of schooling. On the other hand, immigrants who have been schooled in their second language may later apply their literacy skills to literacy in their first language, probably only for limited uses (Niyekawa, 1983: 114). Finally, there are cases where L1 and L2 literacy are simultaneously acquired, for example, a US Hispanic adult acquiring Spanish and English literacy in the same class (e.g. Lewis, 1988).

The similar–dissimilar language structures continuum

Niyekawa (1983: 98–9) suggested that learning to read in a second language that has no linguistic relation to the first language (e.g. Asian or Pacific language speakers learning European languages) will be 'quite different' from learning a second language that is linguistically related to the first language (e.g. French and English). This would, in turn, be different than the case of two dialects of one language, or a pidgin and a language. Thus, not only multilingual settings, but also multidialectal settings (Collins, 1986; Collins & Michaels, 1986; Ferguson, 1985: 140; Michaels, 1986; Simons & Murphy, 1986), and pidgin and creole settings (see Au *et al.*, 1986: 242; Durán, 1987: 48), provide contexts for the study of biliteracy.

The convergent–divergent scripts continuum

Ferguson (1985: 140) noted that cases around the world exemplify a range of possibilities as to writing systems: literacy in two languages with different writing systems (e.g. Bengali and English), in one language with two writing systems (e.g. Hindi and Urdu), or in two languages with one writing system (e.g. Marathi and Hindi). He invited research on consequences of this range of possibilities for literacy acquisition.

Thonis (1981: 150), Barnitz (1982: 565), Niyekawa (1983: 97–102), and Feitelson (1987: 180) suggested that the more characteristics two orthographic systems have in common, the greater or more immediate the potential for transfer of reading skills or strategies. On the other hand, Fillmore and Valadez (1986: 662) reported that, when students are learning to read in two languages at the same time, different writing systems (e.g. English and Chinese) appear to lead to less interference than do similar writing systems (e.g. English and French). Edelsky (1982: 223, 225) found that, although children in the bilingual program she studied generally used Spanish orthography when writing in English, they reserved the letter *k* for English and the tilde and accent for Spanish, thus reflecting knowledge of differences between the two writing systems from an early stage.

Fishman concluded from his study of four ethnolinguistic schools in New York City:

> With respect to mastering the various graphic systems employed in the ethnolinguistic schools we have studied [earlier he noted that the four graphic systems involved – Hebrew, Greek/Armenian, and French – may be said to be ordered on a continuum of decreasing divergence from English], it was our impression that divergence from or proximity to English made no noticeable difference in the rate or level of literacy acquisition by the time the second or third grade was reached (Fishman *et al.*, 1985: 385).

In this case, whether because of transfer or not, convergence or divergence between the biliterates' two writing systems seemed to have little influence on the reading and writing of either.

Conclusion

Biliteracy is a complex phenomenon. In the course of this review, numerous biliteracy and, indeed, multiliteracy configurations have been cited. The motivation here was to contribute to theory, research, and practice with respect to biliteracy by attempting to elucidate that complexity. I have presented a framework for understanding biliteracy that uses the notion of continuum as its basis. It suggests that the nine continua provide a way to identify both relevant questions and incipient answers in research on biliteracy.

The important question as to the degree to which literacy knowledge and skills in one language aid or impede the learning of literacy knowledge and skills in the other has been answered partially through an understanding of the interrelated and nested nature of the continua. That is, the interrelatedness of the continua allows us to see why there is potential for positive transfer across languages and literacies, whereas the nested nature of the continua allows us to see that there are a myriad of contextual factors that may abet or impede such transfer.

Many unresolved issues remain for research with respect to the nature and development of biliteracy. Nevertheless, what is already known does have implications for the teaching of biliterate populations in our schools (see Hornberger, 1989, for more discussion on implications for teaching). Somewhat ironically, the framework outlined here suggests that the hope for understanding biliteracy, as well as literacy and bilingualism, seems to lie in the complexity of biliteracy. Once it is recognized that every instance of biliteracy shares in being situated on the same series of continua, it no longer seems to matter which particular configuration is under consideration. The important point becomes recognizing and understanding what the continua are and how they are related to each other. To return one final time to Sokhom, Maria, and Elizabeth, the implications of the model of biliteracy outlined here are that the more the contexts of their learning allow Sokhom, Maria, and Elizabeth to draw on *all* points of the continua, the greater are the chances for their full biliterate development.

Notes

* This paper originally appeared in *Review of Educational Research* 59 (3): 271–96. It is reprinted here with permission from the American Educational Research Association (AERA).

1. Names in the vignettes are pseudonyms.
2. Speech act is the minimal unit of the following set: speech act, speech event, speech situation, and speech community. Hymes (1974) gave an example: 'a party (speech situation), a conversation during the party (speech event), a joke within the conversation (speech act)' (52). He also defined speech community as a 'community sharing knowledge of rules for the conduct and interpretation of speech' (Hymes, 1974: 51).
3. A *domain*, as defined by Fishman (e.g. 1972, 1986 [1972]) is a construct based on congruencies between patterns of language use and social situations, where social situations are made up by a particular conjunction of setting (place and time) and role relationships of the participants. The aggregates of situations in which place, time, role relationship, and patterns of language use correlate in the culturally appropriate way are termed *domains*.
4. Ferguson (1959) originally introduced the term *diglossia* to refer to the speech community where 'two varieties of a language exist side by side throughout the community, with each having a definite role to play' (325). The languages he selected to exemplify this concept were classical and colloquial Arabic in Arabic-speaking countries; katharevousa and demotiki in Greece; standard and Swiss German in Switzerland; and French and Haitian creole in Haiti. Fishman (1967: 29) later extended the concepts of diglossia and of functional specialization to include not only varieties of one language but different languages.
5. Code-switching refers to the switch from one code to another (i.e. one language to another) by a speaker within an 'unchanged' speech event or situation (see Blom & Gumperz, 1986 [1972]; Gumperz, 1972).
6. Krashen (1987) claimed that comprehensible input is the 'true and only causative variable in second language acquisition' (40; see also Krashen, 1985). His argument that the best form of input to the second-language learner is language that includes input that is a bit beyond the learner's current level

(i + 1) but still comprehensible has influenced a number of language-teaching approaches (e.g. the natural approach) (McLaughlin, 1985: 116; Krashen & Terrell, 1983).

7. According to Swain (1985: 252), learners must have the opportunity to produce comprehensible output in order to move from a purely semantic analysis to a syntactic analysis of the language (see also Pica, 1988; Pica *et al.*, 1989).
8. The beginnings of miscue analysis were in the 1960s, with a paper Goodman presented at the 1964 American Educational Research Association meetings, titled 'A Linguistic Study of Cues and Miscues in Reading' (reprinted in Goodman, 1982). Working from the premise that a reader actively reconstructs a message from written language by using language cues, miscue analysis examines 'errors' readers make in oral reading as a clue to understanding the reading process. In that first paper, Goodman divided the cues into sets: those within words (e.g. letter-sound relationships), those in the flow of language (e.g. structural markers), those external to language and the reader (e.g. pictures), and those within the reader (e.g. conceptual background).
9. Ellis (1986: 47–8) explained that the term *interlanguage* refers to (a) 'the structured system which the learner constructs at any given stage in his development' and (b) ' the series of interlocking systems which form . . . the interlanguage continuum.' The L2 learner is seen as progressing along the interlanguage continuum by means of hypothesizing about the nature of the language they are learning. The notion of L1 interference is not rejected entirely, but is seen as one of five principal processes operating in the interlanguage (others include overgeneralization of target language rules and transfer of training). L. Selinker's (1972) paper marked the first appearance of the term *interlanguage*.
10. Cummins's (1979b) linguistic interdependence hypothesis posits that 'the level of L2 competence which a bilingual child attains is partially a function of the type of competence the child has developed in L1 at the time when intensive exposure to L2 begins' (233). This hypothesis, along with the distinction between basic interpersonal communication skills (BICS) and cognitive/academic language proficiency (CALP) (Cummins, 1979a), later expanded into a four-quadrant model of language proficiency (Cummins, 1981), and the threshold hypothesis (which posits that there is a lower threshold of linguistic competence that a bilingual child must attain to avoid cognitive deficits and a higher threshold to gain positive cognitive effects), were offered as a way of explaining seemingly contradictory research results in bilingual education (Canadian immersion vs US transitional bilingual education) and bilingualism (positive vs negative cognitive effects). (See also Cummins, 1985)
11. For Lambert, an additive form of bilingualism is one in which a second, socially relevant language is added to one's repertory of skills without displacing or replacing the first or 'home' language, whereas a subtractive form of bilingualism is the one 'experienced by many ethnic minority groups who, because of national educational policies and social pressures of various sorts, are forced to put aside their ethnic language for a national language' (1985: 119–20).
12. The compound/coordinate distinction refers to whether or not the two languages of a bilingual are fused into one language system. The distinction originated with Uriel Weinreich's (1963: 9–11) discussion of possible

relationships between a sign and a semanteme (unit of meaning) in bilingualism. In his discussion (a) a coordinative relationship meant that a word in either language had its own distinct referent, (b) a compound relationship was one where words from both languages shared one and the same referent, and (c) a subordinative relationship meant that access to the referent of a word in language A was made only *through* language B. Although Weinreich suggested that a person's or a group's bilingualism need not be entirely of one or another of these three types, the compound/coordinate distinction has been widely interpreted (beginning with Ervin & Osgood, 1954: 141) to refer precisely to bilingual types, an interpretation not without its problems (see Hakuta, 1986: 95–101).

References

Alderson, J.C. (1984) Reading in a foreign language: A reading problem or a language problem? In J.C. Alderson and A.H. Urquhart (eds) *Reading in a Foreign Language* (pp. 1–27). London: Longman.

Alderson, J.C. and Urquhart, A.H. (eds) (1984) *Reading in a Foreign Language*. London: Longman.

Au, K.H., Crowell, D., Jordan, C., Sloat, K., Speidel, G., Klein, T. and Tharp, R. (1986) Development and implementation of the KEEP reading program. In J. Orasanu (ed.) *Reading Comprehension: From Research to Practice* (pp. 235–52). Hillsdale, NJ: Lawrence Erlbaum.

Barnitz, J.G. (1982) Orthographies, bilingualism and learning to read English as a second language. *Reading Teacher* 35 (5), 560–7.

Basso, K. (1974) The ethnography of writing. In R. Bauman and J. Sherzer (eds) *Explorations in the Ethnography of Speaking* (pp. 425–32). Cambridge: Cambridge University Press.

Baynham, M. (1988) Literate, biliterate, multiliterate? Some issues for literacy research. In B. Street and P. McCaffery (eds) *Literacy Research in the U.K.: Adult and School Perspectives* (pp. 51–63). Lancaster: RaPAL.

Blom, J.P. and Gumperz, J. (1986 [1972]) Social meaning in linguistic structure: Code-switching in Norway. In J.J. Gumperz and D. Hymes (eds) *Directions in Sociolinguistics* (pp. 407–34). New York: Holt, Rinehart, and Winston.

Bloome, D. (ed.) (1987) *Literacy and Schooling*. Norwood, NJ: Ablex.

Bloome, D. and Green, J. (1984) Directions in the sociolinguistic study of reading. In P.D. Pearson (ed.) *Handbook of Reading Research* (pp. 395–421). New York: Longman.

Carlo, M.S., Sinatra, G.M. and Royer, J.M. (1989, March) Using the sentence verification technique to measure transfer of comprehension skills from native to second language. Paper presented at the Annual Meeting of the American Educational Research Association, San Francisco, California.

Carrell, P. (1987) Introduction. In J. Devine, P.L. Carrell and D.E. Eskey (eds) *Research in Reading in English as a Second Language* (pp. 1–7). Washington, DC: TESOL.

Clarke, M.A. (1981) Reading in Spanish and English: Evidence from adult ESL students. In S. Hudelson (ed.) *Learning to Read in Different Languages* (pp. 69–92). Washington DC: Center for Applied Linguistics.

Collins, J. (1986) Differential instruction in reading groups. In J. Cook-Gumperz (ed.) *The Social Construction of Literacy* (pp. 117–37). New York: Cambridge University Press.

Collins, J. and Michaels, S. (1986) Speaking and writing: Discourse strategies and the acquisition of literacy. In J. Cook-Gumperz (ed.) *The Social Construction of Literacy* (pp. 207–22). New York: Cambridge University Press.

Cook-Gumperz, J. (ed.) (1986) *The Social Construction of Literacy*. New York: Cambridge University Press.

Cummins, J. (1979a) Cognitive/academic language proficiency, linguistic interdependence, the optimum age question and some other matters. *Working Papers on Bilingualism 19*, 197–205.

Cummins, J. (1979b) Linguistic interdependence and the educational development of bilingual children. *Educational Research* 49 (2), 222–51.

Cummins, J. (1981) The role of primary language development in promoting educational success for language minority students. In California State Department of Education, *Schooling and Language Minority Students: A Theoretical Framework* (pp. 3–49). Los Angeles: Evaluation, Dissemination and Assessment Center, California State University.

Cummins, J. (1985) The construct of language proficiency in bilingual education. In J. Alatis and J. Staczek (eds) *Perspectives on Bilingualism and Bilingual Education* (pp. 209–31). Washington, DC: Georgetown University Press.

de Castell, S., Luke, A. and Egan, K. (eds) (1986) *Literacy, Society and Schooling: A Reader*. New York: Cambridge University Press.

Department of Education (1988) Final research priorities; establishment. Federal Register, 20 June, pp. 23192–5.

Dubin, F. (1989) Situating literacy within traditions of communicative competence. *Applied Linguistics* 10 (2), 171–81.

Durán, R. (1987) Factors affecting development of second language literacy. In S. Goldman and H. Trueba (eds) *Becoming Literate in English as a Second Language* (pp. 33–55). Norwood, NJ: Ablex.

Duranti, A. and Ochs, E. (1986) Literacy instruction in a Samoan village. In B.B. Schieffelin and P. Gilmore (eds) *The Acquisition of Literacy: Ethnographic Perspectives* (pp. 213–32). Norwood, NJ: Ablex.

Dutcher, N. (1982) The use of first and second language in primary education: Selected case studies (World Bank Staff Working Paper 504). Washington, DC: World Bank.

Edelsky, C. (1982) Writing in a bilingual program: The relation of L1 and L2 texts. *TESOL Quarterly* 16 (2), 211–28.

Edelsky, C. (1986) *Writing in a Bilingual Program: Había una Vez*. Norwood, NJ: Ablex.

Ellis, R. (1986) *Understanding Second Language Acquisition*. Oxford: Oxford University Press.

Engle, P.L. (1975) *The Use of Vernacular Languages in Education: Language Medium in Early School Years for Minority Language Groups*. Washington, DC: Center for Applied Linguistics.

Erickson, F. (1984) School literacy, reasoning, and civility: An anthropologist's perspective. *Review of Educational Research* 54 (4), 525–46.

Erickson, F. (1989) Advantages and disadvantages of qualitative research design for foreign language research. Unpublished manuscript. Later published as Erickson, F. (1991) Advantages and disadvantages of qualitative research design on foreign language research. In B.F. Freed (ed.) *Foreign Language Acquisition Research and the Classroom* (pp. 338–53). Lexington, MA: D.C. Heath.

Ervin, S. and Osgood, C. (1954) Second language learning and bilingualism. *Journal of Abnormal and Social Psychology, Supplement* 49, 139–46.

Faltis, C. (1986) Initial cross-lingual reading transfer in bilingual second grade classrooms. In E. Garcia and B. Flores (eds) *Language and Literacy Research in Bilingual Education* (pp. 145–57). Arizona: Center for Bilingual Education, Arizona State University.

Feitelson, D. (1987) Reconsidering the effects of school and home for literacy in a multicultural cross-language context: The case of Israel. In D. Wagner (ed.) *The Future of Literacy in a Changing World* (pp. 174–85). Oxford: Pergamon Press.

Ferguson, C.A. (1959) Diglossia. *Word* 15, 325–40.

Ferguson, C.A. (1985) Patterns of literacy in multilingual situations. In J. Alatis and J. Staczek (eds) *Perspectives on Bilingualism and Bilingual Education* (pp. 135–43). Washington, DC: Georgetown University Press.

Fillmore, L.W. and Valadez, C. (1986) Teaching bilingual learners. In M.C. Wittrock (ed.) *Handbook of Research on Teaching* (pp. 648–85). New York: Macmillan.

Fishman, J.A. (1967) Bilingualism with and without diglossia: Diglossia with and without bilingualism. *Journal of Social Issues* 23 (2), 29–38.

Fishman, J.A. (ed.) (1968) *Readings in the Sociology of Language*. The Hague: Mouton.

Fishman, J.A. (1972) The relationship between micro- and macro-sociolinguistics in the study of who speaks what language to whom and when. In J.B. Pride and J. Holmes (eds) *Sociolinguistics: Selected Readings* (pp. 15–32). New York: Penguin Books.

Fishman, J.A., Gertner, M., Lowy, E.G. and Milán, W.G. (eds) (1985) *The Rise and Fall of the Ethnic Revival: Perspectives on Language and Ethnicity* (Vol. 37). Berlin: Mouton.

Fishman, J.A. (1986 [1972]) Domains and the relationship between micro- and macrosociolinguistics. In J.J. Gumperz and D. Hymes (eds) *Directions in Sociolinguistics* (pp. 435–53). New York: Holt, Rinehart, and Winston.

Gathercole, V.A. (1988) Some myths you may have heard about first language acquisition. *TESOL Quarterly* 22 (3), 407–35.

Gee, J.P. (1986) Orality and literacy: From the savage mind to ways with words. *TESOL Quarterly 20* (4), 719–46.

Genesee, F. (1987) *Learning through Two Languages: Studies of Immersion and Bilingual Education*. Cambridge, MA: Newbury House.

Genesee, F. (1989) Early bilingual development: One language or two? *Journal of Child Language* 16 (1), 161–79.

Goodman, K. (1982) *Language and Literacy: The Selected Writings of Kenneth S. Goodman* (Volumes I and II). Boston, MA: Routledge & Kegan Paul.

Goodman, K. and Goodman, Y. (1983) Reading and writing relationships: Pragmatic functions. *Language Arts* 60 (5), 590–9.

Grosjean, F. (1982) *Life with Two Languages: An Introduction to Bilingualism.* Cambridge, MA: Harvard University Press.

Grosjean, F. (1985) The bilingual as a competent but specific speaker-hearer. *Journal of Multilingual and Multicultural Development* 6 (6), 467–77.

Grove, M.P. (1981) Psycholinguistic theories and ESL reading. In C.W. Twyford, W. Diehl and K. Feathers (eds) *Reading English as a Second Language: Moving from Theory* (pp. 3–20). Bloomington, IN: Indiana University.

Gumperz, J.J. (1969) How can we describe and measure the behavior of bilingual groups? In L.G. Kelly (ed.) *Description and Measurement of Bilingualism: An International Seminar.* Toronto, Canada: University of Toronto Press.

Gumperz, J.J. (1972) Verbal strategies in multilingual communication. In R. Abrahams and R.C. Troike (eds) *Language and Cultural Diversity in American Education* (pp. 184–95). Englewood Cliffs, NJ: Prentice Hall.

Hakuta, K. (1986) *Mirror of Language: The Debate on Bilingualism.* New York: Basic Books.

Hakuta, K. (1987) Properties of the bilingual mind. Paper presented at the Harvard Institute on Bilingual Education: Research to Policy to Practice.

Hakuta, K. and Cancino, H. (1977) Trends in second language acquisition research. *Harvard Educational Review* 47 (3), 294–316.

Hakuta, K., Ferdman, B.M. and Diaz, R. (1986) *Bilingualism and Cognitive Development: Three Perspectives and Methodological Implications* (Technical Report Series). Los Angeles: CLEAR.

Heath, S.B. (1980) The functions and uses of literacy. *Journal of Communication* 30 (1), 123–33.

Heath, S.B. (1982) What no bedtime story means: Narrative skills at home and school. *Language in Society* 11 (1), 49–76.

Heath, S.B. (1983) *Ways with Words: Language, Life and Work in Communities and Classrooms.* New York: Cambridge University Press.

Heath, S.B. (1986) Sociocultural contexts of language development. In California State Department of Education, *Beyond Language: Social and Cultural Factors in Schooling Language Minority Students* (pp. 143–86). Los Angeles: Evaluation, Dissemination and Assessment Center, California State University.

Hornberger, N.H. (1988) *Bilingual Education and Language Maintenance: A Southern Peruvian Quechua Case.* Berlin: Mouton.

Hornberger, N.H. (1989) Teaching for biliteracy: What do TESOL and reading tell us about it? Unpublished manuscript.

Hornberger, N.H. and Micheau, C. (1988, October) Teaching reading bilingually. Paper presented at Ninth Conference on Spanish in the United States, Miami.

Hudelson, S. (1984) Kan Yu Ret an Rayt en Ingles: Children become literate in English as a second language. *TESOL Quarterly* 18 (2), 221–38.

Hymes, D.H. (1964) Introduction: Toward ethnographies of communication. *American Anthropologist* 66 (6), 1–34.

Hymes, D.H. (1974) *Foundations in Sociolinguistics: An Ethnographic Approach.* Philadelphia: University of Pennsylvania Press.

Hymes, D.H. (1986 [1972]) Models of the interaction of language and social life. In J. Gumperz and D. Hymes (eds) *Directions in Sociolinguistics: The Ethnography of Communication* (pp. 35–71). New York: Holt, Rinehart, and Winston.

Indrasuta, C. (1988) Narrative styles in the writing of Thai and American students. In A.C. Purves (ed.) *Writing Across Languages and Cultures: Issues in Contrastive Rhetoric* (pp. 206–26). Newbury Park, CA: Sage.

Kaplan, R.B. (1988) Contrastive rhetoric and second language learning: Notes toward a theory of contrastive rhetoric. In A.C. Purves (ed.) *Writing Across Languages and Cultures: Issues in Contrastive Rhetoric* (pp. 275–304). Newbury Park, CA: Sage.

Kelly, L.G. (ed.) (1969) *The Description and Measurement of Bilingualism: An International Seminar*. Toronto, Canada: University of Toronto Press.

Krashen, S.D. (1985) *The Input Hypothesis: Issues and Implications*. London: Longman.

Krashen, S.D. (1987) Applications of psycholinguistic research to the classroom. In M. Long and J. Richards (eds) *Methodology in TESOL: A Book of Readings* (pp. 33–44). Rowley, MA: Newbury House.

Krashen, S.D. and Terrell, T. (1983) *The Natural Approach*. Hayward, CA: Alemany Press.

Lambert, W. (1985) Some cognitive and sociocultural consequences of being bilingual. In J. Alatis and J. Staczek (eds) *Perspectives on Bilingualism and Bilingual Education* (pp. 116–31). Washington DC: Georgetown University Press.

Lambert, W.E. and Tucker, G.R. (1972) *The Bilingual Education of Children: The St Lambert Experiment*. Rowley, MA: Newbury House.

Langer, J.A. (1988) The state of research on literacy. *Educational Researcher* 17 (3), 42–6.

Leap, W.L. (1987) Pathways and barriers to literacy-building on the Northern Ute Reservation. Paper presented at the annual meeting of the American Anthropological association. Later published as Leap, W.L. (1991) Pathways and barriers to Indian language literacy-building on the Northern Ute reservation. *Anthropology and Education Quarterly* 22 (1), 21–41.

Lewis, M. (1988) Adult literacy students: Perceptions of reading held by English and Spanish speakers. Paper presented at the Modern Language Association Right to Literacy Conference, Columbus, Ohio.

Lytle, S. and Botel, M. (1988) *The Pennsylvania Comprehensive Reading and Communication Arts Plan II (PCRP II): Reading, Writing and Talking Across the Curriculum*. Harrisburg, PA: Pennsylvania Department of Education.

Mangubhai, F. (1987) Literacy in the South Pacific: Some multilingual and multiethnic issues. In D. Wagner (ed.) *The Future of Literacy in a Changing World* (pp. 186–206). Oxford: Pergamon Press.

McLaughlin, B. (1985) *Second-language Acquisition in Childhood: Volume 2: School-age Children*. Hillsdale, NJ: Lawrence Erlbaum.

Michaels, S. (1986) Narrative presentations: An oral preparation for literacy with first graders. In J. Cook-Gumperz (ed.) *The Social Construction of Literacy* (pp. 94–116). New York: Cambridge University Press.

Modiano, N. (1973) *Indian Education in the Chiapas Highlands*. New York: Holt, Rinehart & Winston.

Moll, L. and Díaz, S. (1985) Ethnographic pedagogy: Promoting effective bilingual instruction. In E.E. García and R.V. Padilla (eds) *Advances in Bilingual Education Research* (pp. 127–49). Tucson, AZ: University of Arizona Press.

Murray, D.E. (1988) The context of oral and written language: A framework for mode and medium switching. *Language in Society* 17 (3), 351–73.

Niyekawa, A.M. (1983) Biliteracy acquisition and its sociocultural effects. In M.C. Chang (ed.) *Asian- and Pacific-American Perspectives in Bilingual Education* (pp. 97–119). New York: Teachers College Press.

Olson, D., Torrance, N. and Hildyard, A. (eds) (1985) *Literacy, Language, and Learning: The Nature and Consequences of Reading and Writing*. London: Cambridge University Press.

Ong, W. (1982) *Orality and Literacy: The Technologizing of the World*. London: Methuen.

Parry, K.J. (1987) Reading in a second culture. In J. Devine, P. Carrell and D.E. Eskey (eds) *Research in Reading in English as a Second Language* (pp. 59–70). Washington, DC: TESOL.

Pica, T. (1988) Interlanguage adjustments as an outcome of NS-NNS negotiated interaction. *Language Learning* 38, 45–73.

Pica, T., Holliday, L., Lewis, N. and Morgenthaler, L. (1989) Comprehensible output as an outcome of linguistic demands on the learner. *Studies in Second Language Acquisition* 11, 63–90.

Pride, J.B. and Holmes, J. (1972) *Sociolinguistics: Selected Readings*. Harmondsworth: Penguin Books.

Reyes, M. de la Luz (1987) Comprehension of content area passages: A study of Spanish/English readers in third and fourth grade. In S.R. Goldman and H.T. Trueba (eds) *Becoming Literate in English as a Second Language* (pp. 107–26). Norwood, NJ: Ablex.

Roller, C.M. (1988) Transfer of cognitive academic competence and L2 reading in a rural Zimbabwean primary school. *TESOL Quarterly* 22 (2), 303–18.

Rosier, P. and Holm, W. (1980) *The Rock Point Experience: A Longitudinal Study of a Navajo School Program* (Bilingual Education Series 8). Washington, DC: Center for Applied Linguistics.

Scribner, S. (1984) Literacy in three metaphors. *American Journal of Education* 93 (1), 6–21.

Scribner, S. (1987) Introduction. In D. Wagner (ed.) *The Future of Literacy in a Changing World* (pp. 19–24). Oxford: Pergamon Press.

Scribner, S. and Cole, M. (1981) *The Psychology of Literacy*. Cambridge, MA: Harvard University Press.

Selinker, L. (1972) Interlanguage. *International Review of Applied Linguistics* 10, 209–30.

Simons, H.D. and Murphy, S. (1986) Spoken language strategies and reading acquisition. In J. Cook-Gumperz (ed.) *The Social Construction of Literacy* (pp. 185–206). New York: Cambridge University Press.

Smith, J. (1967) *Creative Teaching of the Language Arts in the Elementary School*. Boston: Allyn and Bacon.

Söter, A.O. (1988) The second language learner and cultural transfer in narration. In A.C. Purves (ed.) *Writing Across Languages and Cultures: Issues in Contrastive Rhetoric*. Newbury Park, CA: Sage.

Street, B. (1984) *Literacy in Theory and Practice*. New York: Cambridge University Press.

Street, B. (1988a) A critical look at Walter Ong and the 'Great Divide'. *Literacy Research Center* 4 (1), 1, 3, 5.

Street, B. (1988b) Literacy, pedagogy and nationalism. *Occasional Papers*. New York: Teachers College, Columbia University.

Street, B. (1988c) Literacy practices and literacy myths. In R. Saljo (ed.) *The Written World* (pp. 59–72). New York: Springer Press.
Swain, M. (1985) Communicative competence: Some roles of comprehensible input and comprehensible output in its development. In S. Gass and C. Madden (eds) *Input in Second Language Acquisition* (pp. 235–53). Rowley, MA: Newbury House.
Szwed, J.F. (1981) The ethnography of literacy. In M.F. Whiteman (ed.) *Writing: The Nature, Development, and Teaching of Written Communication* (Vol. 1: 13–23). Hillsdale, NJ: Lawrence Erlbaum.
Tannen, D. (1985) Relative focus on involvement in oral and written discourse. In D. Olson, N. Torrance and A. Hildyard (eds) *Literacy, Language, and Learning: The Nature and Consequences of Reading and Writing* (pp. 124–47). London: Cambridge University Press.
Thonis, E. (1981) Reading instruction for language minority students. *Schooling and Language Minority Students: A Theoretical Framework* (pp. 147–81). Los Angeles: Evaluation, Dissemination and Assessment Center, California State University.
Tucker, G.R. (1986) Implications of Canadian research for promoting a language competent American society. In J.A. Fishman (ed.) *The Fergusonian Impact* (Volume 2: Sociolinguistics and the Sociology of Language: 361–9). Berlin: Mouton de Gruyter.
UNESCO (1953) *The Use of Vernacular Languages in Education* (Monograph of Fundamental Education 8). Paris: UNESCO.
Wagner, D.A., Messick, B.M. and Spratt, J. (1986) Studying literacy in Morocco. In B.B. Schieffelin and P. Gilmore (eds) *The Acquisition of Literacy: Ethnographic Perspectives* (pp. 233–60). Norwood, NJ: Ablex.
Wagner, D., Spratt, J.E. and Ezzaki, A. (1989) Does learning to read in a second language always put the child at a disadvantage? Some counter-evidence from Morocco. *Applied Psycholinguistics* 10, 31–48.
Wald, B. (1987) The development of writing skills among Hispanic high school students. In S. Goldman and H.T. Trueba (eds) *Becoming Literate in English as a Second Language* (pp. 155–85). Norwood, NJ: Ablex.
Weinreich, U. (1963) *Languages in Contact: Findings and Problems*. The Hague: Mouton.
Wilde, S. (1988) Teaching skills or learning language? Spelling in the whole language classroom. Paper presented at the Modern Language Association Right to Literacy Conference, Columbus, Ohio.
Williams, J. (1987) Production principles in non-native institutionalized varieties of English. Ph.D. dissertation, University of Pennsylvania.
Zentella, A.C. (1981) 'Hablamos los dos. We Speak Both': Growing up Bilingual in El Barrio. Ph.D. dissertation, University of Pennsylvania.
Zutell, J. and Allen, V. (1988) The English spelling strategies of Spanish-speaking bilingual children. *TESOL Quarterly* 22 (2), 333–40.

Chapter 2

Revisiting the Continua of Biliteracy: International and Critical Perspectives*†

NANCY H. HORNBERGER AND ELLEN SKILTON-SYLVESTER

Introduction

The continua model of biliteracy offers a framework in which to situate research, teaching, and language planning in linguistically diverse settings. The model uses the notion of intersecting and nested continua to demonstrate the multiple and complex interrelationships between bilingualism and literacy and the importance of the contexts, media, and content through which biliteracy develops (see Figures 2.1 and 2.2).[1] Specifically, it depicts the development of biliteracy along intersecting first language–second language, receptive–productive, and oral–written language skills continua; through the medium of two (or more) languages and literacies whose linguistic structures vary from similar to dissimilar, whose scripts range from convergent to divergent, and to which the developing biliterate individual's exposure varies from simultaneous to successive; in contexts that encompass micro to macro levels and are characterized by varying mixes along the monolingual–bilingual and oral–literate continua; and (as revised here) with content that ranges from majority to minority perspectives and experiences, literary to vernacular styles and genres, and decontextualized to contextualized language texts (Hornberger, 1989; Skilton-Sylvester, 1997).

Biliteracy, in this model, refers to 'any and all instances in which communication occurs in two (or more) languages in or around writing' (Hornberger, 1990: 213), a definition which by no means originated the use of the term, but which attempted to clarify it. In order to understand any particular instance of biliteracy – be it an individual biliterate actor, interaction, practice, program, situation, or society – we as educators,

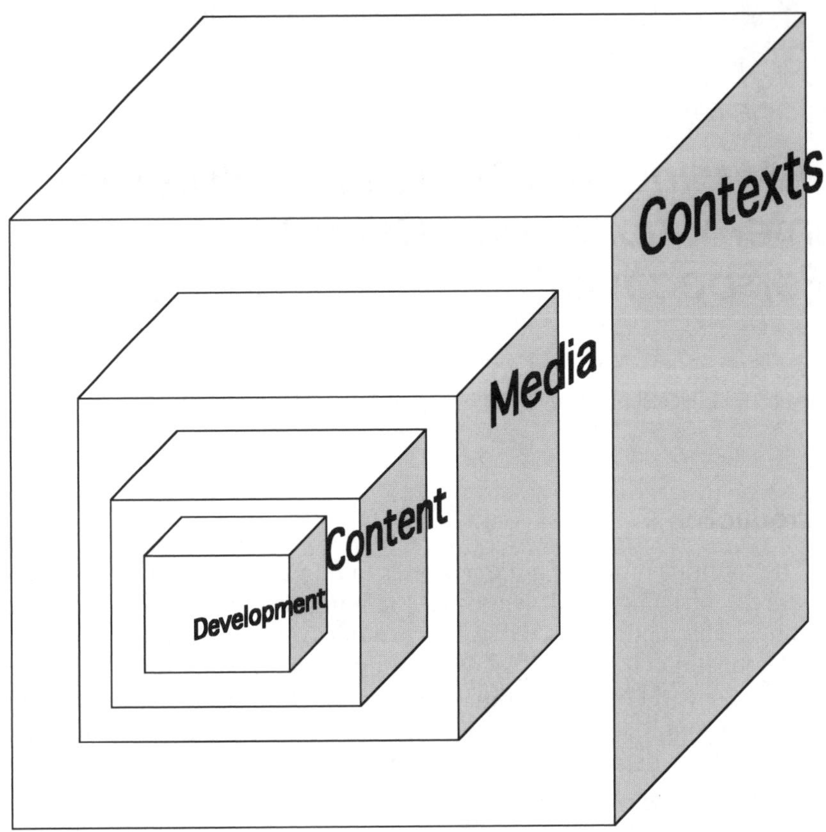

Figure 2.1 Nested relationships among the continua of biliteracy

researchers, community members, or policy makers need to take account of all dimensions represented by the continua. At the same time, the advantage of the model is that it allows us to focus for pedagogical, analytical, activist, or policy purposes on one or selected continua and their dimensions without ignoring the importance of the others.

In 1989, Hornberger emphasized a balanced attention to both ends of the continua and all points in between. The notion of continuum was 'intended to convey that although one can identify (and name) points on the continuum, those points are not finite, static, or discrete. There are infinitely many points on the continuum; any single point is inevitably and inextricably related to all other points; and all the points have more

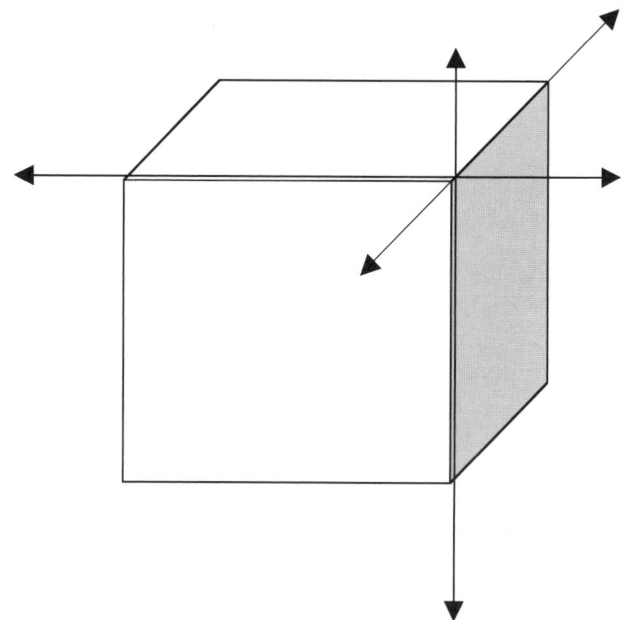

Figure 2.2 Intersecting relationships among the continua of biliteracy

in common than not with each other' (1989: 274–5). Arguing from the model, and citing examples of Cambodian and Puerto Rican students in Philadelphia's public schools as illustrative of the challenge facing American educators, Hornberger suggested that the more their learning contexts allow learners to draw on all points of the continua, the greater are the chances for their full biliterate development (1989: 289). Implicit in that argument was a recognition that there had in fact *not* been attention to all points.

In the intervening years since the model was proposed, Hornberger and her students and colleagues have continued to use the continua model in their work on biliteracy in Philadelphia and internationally. Given a decade of accumulated work, the moment seems propitious for revisiting the continua model to see how it has held up through the new perspectives we have acquired. One revision which has already been alluded to above and to which we will return is the addition of the continua of biliterate content (Skilton-Sylvester, 1997).

In what follows, we will be drawing primarily on two kinds of new perspectives we are bringing to the continua of biliteracy, perspectives which are distinguishable but also complementary and overlapping: (1) international perspectives deriving from Hornberger's work in South America and from the growing international literature on multiple literacies, multilingual literacies, and multiliteracies; and (2) critical perspectives deriving from Skilton-Sylvester's and Hornberger's ongoing work in Philadelphia and from the growing international literature on critical pedagogy, critical realism, critical literacy, critical discourse analysis, and related fields.

Throughout, what we will be emphasizing is an emerging explicit emphasis on power relations in the continua model (see Figure 2.3). We are arguing that, in educational policy and practice regarding biliteracy, there tends to be an implicit privileging of one end of the continua over the other such that one end of each continuum is associated with more power than the other (e.g. written development over oral development). In investigating biliterate contexts, development, media, and content, one can see the ways in which power is negotiated through language by individuals and institutions and that some language practices seem to garner more power than others. Corson describes the ways in which power and language are inextricably linked:

> For most everyday human purposes, power is exerted through verbal channels: Language is the vehicle for identifying, manipulating, and changing power relations between people . . . In short, the struggle for power in any setting is really a struggle for the control of discourses. (1999: 14–15)

In investigating the complexity of biliteracy using the continua as a theoretical framework, one sees the ways in which certain practices, varieties, contextual features, and instructional strategies have been tools for gaining and/or sustaining power, while others have not. What Hornberger was arguing for in 1989 when she first proposed the continua of biliteracy, though not as explicitly as we will do here, is the need to contest the traditional power weighting of the continua by paying attention to and granting agency and voice to actors and practices at what have traditionally been the less powerful ends of the continua.

We are not suggesting that particular biliterate actors and practices at the traditionally powerful ends of the continua (e.g. policies which promote written, monolingual, decontextualized, standardized texts) are immutably fixed points of power to be accessed or resisted, but rather that, though those actors and practices may currently be privileged, they need not be. Indeed, we are suggesting that the very nature and definition of what is powerful biliteracy is open to transformation through what

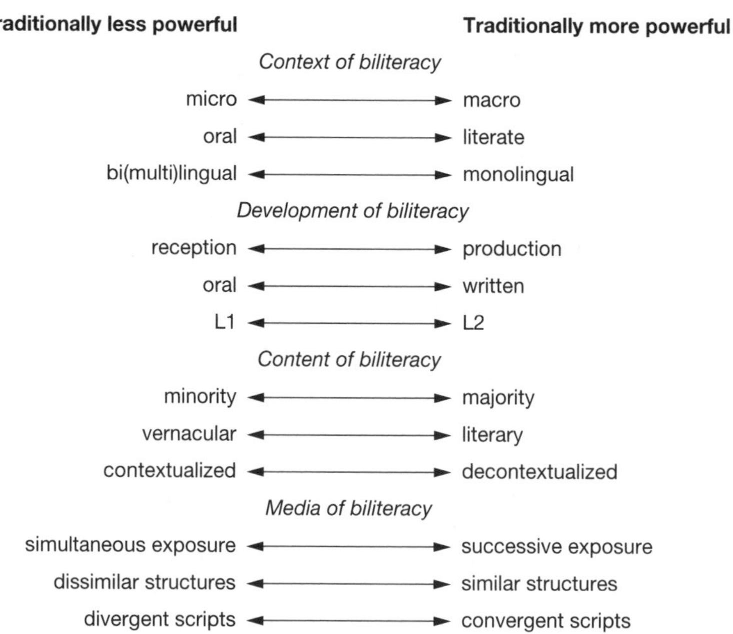

Figure 2.3 Power relations in the continua model

actors – educators, researchers, community members, and policy makers – do in their everyday practices. In this we concur with Street, who suggests that 'for educationalists concerned with . . . power, the question is not "how can a few gain access to existing power", nor "how can existing power structures be resisted", but rather how can power be transformed' (1996). Street follows Foucault and Bourdieu in putting forward a 'process' (as opposed to 'quantity') model of power, arguing that power varies between sites and contexts and is exercised through force, through discourse, and through acquisition of cultural and symbolic capital. One route to transforming existing power, he argues, is through a critical reflexivity that

> focuses attention on the daily lived reality of power relations and helps us recognize how we are all involved in both control and resistance; rather than assuming that power always lies somewhere else, this view assumes that *power lies in each of us* and our immediate personal and social relations, as well as in institutional formations. (Street, 1996; emphasis added)

Similarly, our purpose in pointing to the privileged, powerful ends of the continua is not to reify that power but rather to emphasize that the privileging can be transformed through critical reflection by the various actors involved – educators, researchers, community members, and policy makers – on how their own everyday biliteracy practices do or do not exercise and maintain power. This is particularly important for language teachers to consider as they teach linguistically diverse students. Critical reflection about language and power in and out of the classroom can allow new speakers, readers, and writers of a language to see that the values placed on particular languages and varieties are not fixed, but socially and culturally constructed. This can make classrooms places where a diversity of linguistic practices can be valued and given voice. Peirce's (1995) discussion of helping students claim the 'right to speak' is a useful construct in understanding how agency and voice are connected to power relationships. She suggests that those who are learning a new language need to believe that they have the 'right to speak,' that what they say will be heard and responded to with interest, respect, and action. Drawing on Bourdieu's (1977) work, she suggests that we cannot assume that listeners always grant those who are speaking (or writing) English as a second language the 'right to speak' and that, as teachers, we need to help students claim the right to speak in and out of the classroom context. Peirce goes on to describe the powerless and powerful positions learners are 'allowed' to take in particular situations. For example, one adult learner initially saw all of the communication problems she had when talking to native speakers as related to her own limitations as an immigrant; as time went on and she began to see herself as a multicultural citizen of the United States, she began to be able to speak more freely and command the attention of her listeners.

Critical reflection is important not only for those who are speaking a new language, but also for those who are listening – educators, researchers, community members, and policy makers. In looking at the ways in which power is constructed through language and in interaction, actors can begin to see themselves as agents who have the power to transform practices and not merely as recipients of already decided upon norms. In discussing the relationship between action and power, Giddens (1984: 14) offers a helpful description of agency. He explains, 'Action depends upon the capability of the individual to "make a difference" to a pre-existing state of affairs or course of events. An agent ceases to be such if he or she loses the capability to "make a difference," that is, to exercise some sort of power.' This paper takes the position that all of us have the capability to transform the traditional power weighting of the continua of biliteracy, to 'make a difference' to this 'pre-existing state of affairs.'

In what follows, then, we revisit the continua, paying explicit attention to dimensions of power, drawing on recent international and critical perspectives to do so, and making a plea for research, teaching, and language planning which grant agency and voice to those who have traditionally been powerless. Corson has recently suggested that neutrality is in any case a problematic stance in applied fields, since it often means condoning an unsatisfactory status quo (1997: 166). Instead, he suggests that applied practitioners, and in particular in this case applied linguists, might take inspiration from the critical realism of Roy Bhaskar, a British philosopher of science, whose theory of being includes as real entities the 'reasons and accounts that people use or offer, to direct or effect social or individual behavior or change' (Corson, 1997: 169). Such an approach, Corson suggests, might lead to reform in several areas of applied linguistics, including not only dictionary-making and linguistic nomenclature, but also language planning, treatment of standard and nonstandard varieties, and second language program delivery; in most cases such reform would involve the devolution of 'research and decision-making processes down as much as possible to the least of the stakeholders' (1997: 177).

Similarly, Ruiz has recently argued that 'voice and agency are central to critical pedagogy' and that 'without them, there is no such thing as "empowerment"' (Ruiz, 1997: 327). Indeed, he takes issue with the way the term empowerment has been used in the literature, as if it were a gift bestowed on the powerless, rather than the result of their own initiative in taking control and taking power. Agency and voice are, then, central to empowerment; and they will be central to the argument we present below.

Contexts and Development of Biliteracy: International Perspectives

Contexts of biliteracy

Implicit in consideration of the contexts for biliteracy is society's tendency to weight power toward the macro, literate and monolingual ends of the continua. Hornberger (1992) showed how biliteracy contexts for Puerto Rican and Cambodian students in Philadelphia in the 1980s were framed and constrained by national policies which emphasized English acquisition at the expense of minority language maintenance (e.g. the proposed English Language Amendment to the Constitution, the 1984 and 1988 renewals of the Bilingual Education Act of 1968, and the Immigration Reform and Control Act of 1986), by an educational system which used minority languages only to embed the more powerful English literacy, and by the assimilative 'charm' of English which pulled students' biliterate development toward English. For the United States to achieve its goals of education for all, she argued, policy, curriculum, and community language and literacy use would have to change in ways that would encourage, rather than inhibit, biliterate individuals' drawing on all points of the continua for their full biliterate development. What was not stated explicitly there, but is worth stating now, is that one of the ways to make those changes happen is to pay attention to and grant agency and voice to oral, bilingual interaction at the micro level.

Such is precisely the emphasis in recent developments in language policy and educational reform in Peru, Ecuador, and Bolivia, where bilingual intercultural education is gaining ground as a vehicle for moving societal discourse away from the openly racist ideology of the past and toward a more inclusive, intercultural one. Due to a confluence and evolution of such factors as Peru's Revolutionary Government of the 1970s, the gathering momentum of Ecuador's indigenous grassroots movement in the 1980s, and the leadership of Bolivia's first indigenous Vice-President in the 1990s, new worlds of possibility for the historically oppressed indigenous languages and their speakers have been opened up, beginning with the 1975 Officialization of Quechua in Peru, and followed by the creation of the National Directorate of Bilingual Intercultural Education in Ecuador in 1988 and the launching in 1994 of the National Education Reform of Bolivia which sets out to make all of Bolivian education bilingual and intercultural.

In a recent paper, Hornberger (2000) has explored the degree to which the shift in these three Andean countries toward a more inclusive, intercultural ideology can be seen as truly substantive and not merely rhetorical, examining the use and meanings of the term 'intercultural' in official policy documents and in short narratives about intercultural practice by indigenous and non-indigenous educational professionals. The narratives reveal first of all that the cultural (social) identities (groups) involved are more complex than essentialized designations by language name (e.g. Quechua speakers or Spanish speakers) would suggest, and that there is an incipient recognition that interculturality must be based on dialogic interaction among different cultural groups, self-consciously defined. What is most revealing, however, is that the narratives also provide evidence that local actors are actively engaged in making use of oral, bilingual resources at the micro level to change the longstanding macro level discourse of racism and discrimination to one of intercultural understanding and collaboration.

Two practitioner narratives illustrate this point.[2] Early in her career, Bolivian teacher of English and Quechua Julia Pino Quispe was assigned to a school in a mining center. Upon her arrival on the first of May, the Director told her that one of her responsibilities was to organize the annual celebration of Mother's Day later that month. She worked hard and organized 'dances, funny toys, presents for the mothers, and other activities'; but what stands out most in her memory of that event is:

> a girl who was frequently marginalized in her class because she was of peasant origin and this was still noticeable in her speech; and she offered to participate with a poem in Quechua which told of someone who had lost her mother and could not be consoled in her grief. The poem, of course, made the greatest impression and all were astonished because the form in which she interpreted the poem in Quechua could not have provided more originality nor more sense of life to all those who had the good fortune to be present. After this event, the girl was no longer excluded from any group; on the contrary it served to enable her to value her capacity to be included and it also served as a good example to her classmates.

In a second narrative, Concepción Anta tells of her work in an urban secondary school in Cajamarca (northern Peru), where she finds that using local materials and natural resources enables her to work successfully with her students, who come from the outskirts of the city and are of very limited economic means. For example:

> in a language class, where I am working with stories, I prefer to choose a peasant story, from a district or province of Cajamarca, worthy material from the locality, rather than choose a foreign story. First, I tell them the story and then with them we proceed to dramatize the story, using local materials from their own area; and finally with them we select some music to make a song from the story; this is something which they find very entertaining . . . what I seek is for all aspects of the student or the person to continue functioning always as an integrated whole, . . . where man's lived experience is in conjunction with the life of the animals, the plants, the hills, the cliffs, the rivers, the stars, the fields, etc.

Teacher Julia and the little girl who performs a poem in Quechua, and teacher Concepción and her class performing a local peasant story with local materials and local music, are engaged in micro-level contestation of dominant discourse practices by making use, in school contexts, of language and content which have historically been excluded from the school. As we will address more fully in discussing the content continua, they are infusing vernacular and minority content (as opposed to literary and majority content) into a formal schooling context that often excludes the histories and voices of those who speak minority languages. They have used their discourse to serve a purpose different from that dictated by macro-level, hegemonic, Spanish, Western, urban, formal education practice; and have taken control of oral, bilingual, micro-level interactional contexts to do so.

Another example of the need and potential for actors at the oral, bilingual micro-level of context to take control away from macro-level, monolingual literacies comes from Watson-Gegeo and Gegeo's work on language socialization in Kwara'ae (Solomon Islands). Watson-Gegeo (1992) argues for the value of thick explanation, which integrates both macro and micro-levels of contextual data in seeking to explain a particular problem, in this case Kwara'ae children's problems with succeeding in school. Having first sought an explanation through micro-level study of language socialization patterns in the home and classroom discourse patterns in the school, she and co-researcher Gegeo found that, contrary to expectation, Kwara'ae language socialization practices (in particular the discourses known as 'shaping the mind') emphasize precisely the kind of direct, verbally mediated teaching of intellectual and cultural skills that should be successful preparation for school discourse. On the other hand, study of actual discourse in the classroom revealed use of a restricted version of English in the context of inadequate, irrelevant materials and poorly trained teachers. A 'thin' explanation would have attributed the children's problems to differences between home and school in terms of language use, sociocultural meaning, interactional rules, and behavioral expectations.

Not satisfied with this explanation, however, Watson-Gegeo and Gegeo looked to the macro-level context, carrying out an institutional analysis based on document review; interviews with parents, teachers, Ministry of Education officials; and the recoding of their data. They uncovered a larger social context in the Solomons in which rapid school expansion resulting in outdated and incomplete materials and poorly trained teachers using oral recitation and rote memorization, along with a national development plan which privileged urban over rural schools, and an emerging class system assisted by the schools as gatekeepers, had all contributed to a deep ambivalence among Kwara'ae adults toward the schools, an ambivalence which they consciously or unconsciously communicated to their children (for example, in 'shaping the mind' discourses) and which served to undercut children's motivation to succeed. Watson-Gegeo concludes that 'children's problems with succeeding in school have less to do with home socialization than with larger societal processes that shape the nature of schooling in the Solomons' (1992: 63). While Watson-Gegeo uses the case to argue for the value of understanding the macro context in explaining a micro-level phenomenon, the example also serves to make the opposite point; namely the role of the oral, Kwara'ae shaping-the-mind discourses in the home in resisting dominant English literacy schooling imposed from the macro-level.

Internationally, it is perhaps the New Literacy Studies which have done the most to draw our attention to just these kinds of contestations of macro-level, dominant, monolingual literacy practices, with their documentation of 'multiple literacies' – the multiple social and cultural constructions of literacy in practice. Street criticizes what he calls the autonomous model of literacy, a model which conceives of literacy as a uniform set of techniques and ascribes direct cognitive and social benefits to the acquisition of these skills; he suggests instead an ideological model, wherein literacies are seen as multiple and socially constructed (Street, 1993: 1–21). Using key concepts like literacy event (Heath, 1982: 50) and literacy practice (Street, 1995: 2), researchers have produced a growing body of work on reading and writing as social practices embedded in particular historical and cultural contexts; and their work has encompassed multilingual literacies as well. This work has explicitly drawn attention to the fact that literacies may be implicated in operations of social power, as well as in the formation of identities and subjectivities (Collins, 1995: 81).

A recent study by Martin-Jones and Bhatt (1998) shows how the everyday multilingual literacy practices of young Gujerati speakers in urban Leicester (UK) contribute to the construction of their social identities, identities which for these young people are multiple and changing over time. In contradistinction to the usual concern expressed 'in contemporary debates about the language education of young people in multilingual urban contexts in Britain ... about how best to support literacy development in English beyond the initial stages' (1998: 37), these authors explore 'the different literacies that bilingual learners have access to and the ways in which they draw on these literacies as they explore and affirm different identities' (1998: 37). Specifically, they present evidence for a variety of literacies: including the literacies associated with particular cultural inheritances (e.g. reading Gujerati in Sunday prayers, letter-writing in Gujerati as a shared family activity, learning and performing songs in Gujerati, Arabic literacy and Islamic studies), individual and shared literacy activities in English (sharing books and magazines, exchanging notes and letters with friends, collecting memorabilia), and the school literacies in which the young people participate. Although we will discuss the content continua more fully in a later section, here again we can see the overlapping of context and content. The situation Martin-Jones and Bhatt (1998) discuss in relation to Gujerati speakers in the UK is a typical one in which vernacular and minority content is relegated to personal rather than school contexts. In limiting the discourse in official school contexts to monolingual, written, literary texts from the majority culture, the richness of multilingual, oral discourse, vernacular writing, and literary texts from minority cultures is left outside of the school walls.

More generally, looking at the role of context in schooling is important to illustrate the ways in which linguistic and intellectual development have typically been discussed in decontextualized terms. Looking closely at biliterate contexts, and specifically at multilingual, oral interaction at the micro-level, allows us to see how measures of intelligence and school achievement have ignored those ways of speaking and knowing that have not been valued inside of school contexts. As Kincheloe and Steinberg have suggested, 'Intelligence is not an innate quality of a particular individual, but rather something related to the interrelationship among ideas, behaviors, contexts and outcomes . . .' (1993: 229). Paying attention to the traditionally less powerful ends of the continua of biliterate contexts illuminates ways in which a contextualized view of learning and cognition can have important consequences for defining and measuring school success.

Development of biliteracy

The last two examples above – of Kwara'ae children and of multilingual urban youth in Britain – are as much about the development of biliteracy in the individual as about biliterate contexts. Both demonstrate a societal tendency to weight power toward the L2 (second language), written, production ends of the continua of biliterate development. In both cases, national policy and school curricula are focused primarily on English (L2) literacy development as evidenced in school performance (usually standardized tests), even in the face of other language and literacy resources in the community.

All too often, the focus on productive L2 literacy development is accompanied by a skills-based view of literacy. Hornberger and Hardman (1994) reported on their study of adult biliteracy programs for Puerto Ricans and

Cambodians in Philadelphia, making an argument for the inadequacy of an autonomous, cognitive skills-based view of literacy with its emphasis on a single, standardized schooled literacy in the L2 and arguing for a complementary ideological, cultural practice view (1994: 168). What was not stated explicitly there, but is worth stating here, is that one of the features of the ideological, cultural practice view, with respect to the continua of biliterate development, is that, when put in practice in literacy teaching, it can assist learners in claiming the 'right to speak' through use of their L1 (first language), oral, and receptive skills as well as the L2, written, productive ones.

This becomes clear when we take a closer look at the findings presented by Hornberger and Hardman. In an ESL literacy class for Cambodian adults, Hardman found evidence of a cultural practice approach in student-directed social learning strategies including prompting, collaboration and using Khmer (the L1) to answer questions, talk with other students, and take notes; he further noted that students were most comfortable with repeating, copying, and reading aloud, activities which as he pointed out use both receptive and productive skills (and oral–written ones too, in the case of reading aloud) (Hornberger & Hardman, 1994: 151–6). These findings give direct evidence of the space for learners to use their L1, oral, and receptive skills in a cultural practice approach.

Hornberger too found that in the bilingual GED program run by ASPIRA (a non-profit Puerto Rican education-advocacy organization established in 1961 in New York City), while the focus was on mastering the discrete skills needed to pass the GED exam, at the same time the program embedded this literacy as cultural practice at every level in ways which sought to give voice and agency to the learners' Spanish language and Puerto Rican cultural identity. For example, the program explicitly taught Puerto Rican culture and cultural awareness to both the Spanish-dominant and English-dominant groups, offered opportunities for students to act in solidarity with other Latin Americans, connected the students to a network of ASPIRA-sponsored organizations and programs that support the Puerto Rican community, drew on the Puerto Rican community to support students' development, allowed the students to accommodate the highly individualized competency-based program to the more collaborative learning approach they seemed to prefer, and acknowledged and addressed tensions between the Spanish-dominant Puerto Rican-born and English-dominant Philadelphia-born groups. One evidence of the success of this approach in creating a context where students' expressions are voiced and heard came in the very lively election campaign for class officers and ASPIRA Club Board representatives, including a several-verse rap song in Spanish spontaneously composed by a group of students (Hornberger & Hardman, 1994: 163–7).

Similar counter-power weighting of the continua of biliterate development, toward the oral, L1, receptive end is evident in an indigenous teacher education program in the Amazonian rainforest which Hornberger visited in 1997 (Hornberger, 1998):

> Every year since 1983, this course sponsored by the Comissão Pró-Indio do Acre (CPI) has been held during the summer months (January–March) in or just outside Rio Branco, Brazil. For the past several years, it has been held at an outdoor site whose spaces and buildings are consistent with the indigenous teachers' own community spaces. The 1997 session was attended by some 25 *professores indios* 'indigenous teachers', representing eight different ethnic groups whose languages are in varying stages of vitality, from those with about 150 speakers to those with several thousand.[2]
>
> One of the striking features of the course is that the *professores indios* are simultaneously learners and teachers-in-formation; that is, they are simultaneously learning the school curriculum themselves for the first time, while also preparing themselves to return to their *aldeias*, or communities, to teach it. Another feature of the course is the emphasis on reflexive practice, epitomized in the keeping of class diaries during the school year, a practice which some of the *professores indios* have employed since 1983.[4] The third striking feature is the clear language-as-resource orientation, used here in Ruiz' (1984) sense. The language-as-resource orientation in the CPI course means that the indigenous languages are not only encouraged and used as medium and subject of instruction in both the course and the schools, but that the *professores indios* encourage and exchange among each other across their different languages.
>
> One activity of the course in which all three of these features converge is the *professores indios'* authorship of teaching materials in the indigenous languages which are reflective of indigenous culture, history, and artistic expression; these materials serve as documentation of the *professores'* own learning while also serving as a teaching resource for their own classrooms. Interestingly, this activity in which they are all engaged means that they listen to and read each other's languages even when they do not actually speak (or write) those languages themselves.

That is, the course creates a context in which the multiple oral (and written), L1 expressions of the indigenous teachers are voiced and heard.

The documents produced also make it possible for minority-authored texts to become part of the content of the curriculum, for both teachers-in-training and the students they will teach.

This 'multiple literacies' approach is further enabled by the pedagogy of 'multiliteracies' employed in the course. Multiliteracies, as defined by the New London Group (New London Group, 1996: 63), refers to the multiplicity of communications channels and media in our changing world (and secondarily to the increasing saliency of cultural and linguistic diversity); the concept extends literacy beyond reading and writing to other domains, such as the visual, audio, spatial, and behavioral. In the case of the indigenous teacher education course, these other literacies reinforce the reading/writing literacies, since the teachers live and study in a traditional space familiar to all of them, follow their traditional behaviors (e.g. sleeping in hammocks in communal houses, bathing frequently during the day, etc.), and make extensive use of drawing in addition to reading and writing in producing their materials.

Furthermore, the indigenous teacher education course embodies all four components of the 'how' of a pedagogy of multiliteracies, as defined by the New London Group: situated practice, overt instruction, critical framing, and transformed practice. In their dual role as learners and teachers-in-formation, the indigenous teachers in the CPI course have opportunity for situated practice through immersion in meaningful practices among their peers, and subsequently for transformed practice as they enact their learnings as teachers in their own village schools. As noted above, a central feature of the course has always been reflexive practice, which means that the teachers of the course take seriously the need for scaffolded instruction and critical framing, and the indigenous teacher-learners have long since been socialized to a critical pedagogical approach.

In addition to defining multiliteracies and the 'how' of a pedagogy of multiliteracies, the New London Group also addresses the question of 'what' a pedagogy of multiliteracies is about (1996: 73–6), namely that it is about designing in the sense of making/taking meaning from available designs to create new transformed designs (which are never purely created nor purely reproduced). Available designs include grammars (of languages and other semiotic systems) and orders of discourse, and we redesign these in the same way that we make/take meaning from texts/discourses to create new texts/discourses (see Fairclough, 1992 on intertextuality). In the case of the CPI indigenous teacher education course, we already noted that the *professores indios* are engaged in producing teaching materials in the indigenous languages which are reflective of indigenous culture, history, and artistic expression and which serve as documentation of the *professores'* own learning while also serving as a teaching resource for their own classrooms, an example par excellence of 'designing.' The 'what' of a pedagogy of multiliteracies brings us to the content of biliteracy, with which we introduce the next section.

Content and Media of Biliteracy: Critical Perspectives

Content of biliteracy

Implicit in consideration of the content of biliteracy is society's traditional power weighting of the continua toward the majority and literary ends (as opposed to the minority and vernacular ends). Indeed, the clear power weighting here was what first drew Hornberger's attention to the power dimension of the continua. There are also significant power-related weightings in the decontextualized–contextualized continuum, but the relationship is not as immediately visible.

In her study of literacy, identity and educational policy among Cambodian women and girls in Philadelphia, Skilton-Sylvester found it necessary to supplement the continua model with these content dimensions that would allow for looking not only at how language was used and learned, where it was used and learned, and what aspects of it were used and learned, but also the kinds of meanings expressed in particular biliterate contexts, during particular aspects of biliterate development, and through specific biliterate media. Whereas the media continua focus on the forms literacy takes, the content continua focus on the meaning those forms express. She argued for the importance of including minority, vernacular, and contextualized whole language texts in these learners' literacy experiences.

If voice and agency are indeed central to critical pedagogy, the importance of making whole texts that include the experiences of language minority students a part of that pedagogy becomes immediately evident. In this way, knowing two languages is inextricably linked to knowing two cultures. Through the content continua, biliteracy becomes linked to bicultural literacy. In their construction of a post-Piagetian cognitive theory that is informed by and extends critical, feminist, and postmodern thought, Kincheloe and Steinberg (1993) suggest something called 'post-formal thinking.' This theory of cognition holds that:

> the frontier where the information of the disciplines intersects with the understandings and experience that individuals carry with them to school is the point where knowledge is created (constructed). The

> post-formal teacher facilitates this interaction, helping students to reinterpret their own lives and uncover new talents as a result of their encounter with school knowledge .... unless students are moved to incorporate school information into their own lives, schooling will remain merely an unengaging rite of passage into adulthood. (1993: 301)

It is in this intersection of school knowledge and personal knowledge that the importance of paying attention to the minority end of the content continua (rather than the majority end) is most important. Examples from Skilton-Sylvester's research include one eleventh-grade high school student named Ty, who, when encountering Maxine Hong Kingston's *Woman Warrior* for the first time, asked 'Is she the only Asian writer?' This young Cambodian woman had been able to go through 11 years of school without realizing there were Asian writers who wrote in English. This realization provided a springboard for her to reflect on her own experiences, to see that her process of being a second-language learner in a US school was not just a local/personal phenomenon. She went on to say:

> She seems like me ... in the story, she goes to school and then she's silent. You know, she doesn't usually, like raise her hand and like participate and answer the questions her teacher asks.... When I read the story, it kind of like reminded me of myself when I used to be in elementary school. ... She's Asian and of course, I'm Asian too. It made me kind of look back, you know. (Skilton-Sylvester, 1997: 244)

The reading of this text fell at the minority end of the content continua and at the same time at the literary end usually encountered in the classroom. Although this was a literary text, it addressed some of Ty's own experiences with school. As such, it opened a door for her to be a part of literary discourse in a new way.

An even less powerful aspect of literacy is the vernacular. The vernacular end of the literary–vernacular content continuum is often completely absent from school discourse. This was certainly the case for Cambodian students in Philadelphia and mirrors some of the findings of Martin-Jones and Bhatt (1998), mentioned earlier, in their study of Gujerati speakers in the UK. Skilton-Sylvester found that students who were proficient vernacular writers (writing letters, plays for friends and family members to perform, etc.) were often framed as 'non-writers' in schooling contexts. At home with her siblings and cousins, one young woman named Nan was in a constant state of performance of the plays and stories she had written. In her ESOL class, she was sometimes able to use her performance skills to augment texts that she had written. For example, she was able to read her journal aloud. This was one of the very few ways that her vernacular ways of reading and writing were valued in the classroom. This particular example is especially interesting because performance is so inextricably linked to literacy in Cambodia. As Thierry has said:

> Whether they are written or oral, there is no question for them of the second aspect, since writing does not imply a silent reading in their view. The story is told. If it is read, it is read in a loud voice, and not only for oneself, but for an audience. (1978: 86)

More than any of the other girls in Skilton-Sylvester's study, Nan wrote and performed stories she had written spontaneously, of her own volition. However, she struggled painfully with school writing assignments. The role of performance in vernacular writing was rarely evident in school contexts for Nan. Where it was, she was seen as a writer; where it wasn't, she was seen as a non-writer.

The decontextualized–contextualized continuum has a particularly complicated relationship to power, a relationship also inherent in Street's (1984) distinction between autonomous and ideological perspectives on literacy. Within the scientific tradition and much academic writing, decontextualized meanings are the meanings that count. This tradition has certainly maintained a powerful place in academic discourse generally (Kennedy, 1997), such that being able to state truths that hold, regardless of context, has been a part of speaking the language of power. At the most decontextualized end of this continuum are decontextualized parts of language followed by decontextualized wholes.

Some researchers (Anyon, 1980; Skilton-Sylvester, 1998) have discussed the ways in which those in poverty are often not given exposure to whole tasks that require problem solving but instead are exposed primarily to tasks that require rote memorization of the parts or what Anyon (1980: 427) has called unexplained fragmented procedures.[5] For the purposes of this paper, we are highlighting the fact that an exclusive emphasis on decontextualized parts of language makes it so that students do not learn how to construct wholes with academically appropriate parts. For example, in discussing an ESL class in which the parts of language were stressed at the expense of rather than in conjunction with wholes, Warschauer (1998) describes a student named Jon, who:

> was not challenged to develop the skills of abstraction, system thinking, experimental inquiry, or collaboration that are crucial in today's economy (Reich, 1991) . . . [nor] to 'talk and write about language as such, to explain and sequence implicit knowledge and

rules of planning, and to speak and write for multiple functions in appropriate forms' (Heath, 1992). (Warschauer, 1998: 76)

In the late twentieth century, an ability to construct wholes with appropriate parts is quite important if one wants to speak the language of power.

A particularly interesting illustration of the ways in which language parts divorced from the wholes leave learners powerless comes in looking at Chamran's experiences (Skilton-Sylvester, 1997). As Chamran entered first grade, and during the first three years of schooling, she struggled to decode and to spell. Most of her assignments were ones in which she was asked to copy something from the board or from a homework sheet. Regularly, Skilton-Sylvester would ask Chamran if she wanted to write a story, but she typically said 'no.' After three years, she finally answered 'yes,' and proceeded to write 'Spelling Test' at the top of the page and number down the left hand side from 1 to 15. Skilton-Sylvester was struck by the fact that Chamran had chosen a spelling test, but then realized that her knowledge of literacy had remained at the letter and sight word level. It was with these parts of language that she felt most comfortable. She knew the spelling test genre inside and out. She had learned the spelling test format, but had not learned other formats for expressing her thoughts in writing (1997: 255).

This moment was particularly poignant because in all of the spelling lists Chamran and the other young women (from the ages of 6–17) had studied, never did they understand the meaning of the words they were being asked to spell. So, not only was Chamran's 'story' a set of parts rather than a whole, it was also a practice that was devoid of meaning for her and for many others. It is then no surprise that writing whole texts is quite difficult for these students when they reach other levels of schooling and are asked to summarize, synthesize, and evaluate in their writing.

If we now turn to the contextualized end of the continuum, it is important to first stress the value of contextualized parts, parts of language that are analyzed and understood in the context of a whole text or texts. Although an exclusive emphasis on decontextualized parts can keep language minority students from learning the language of power, being able to use parts of language correctly is one key element of being able to speak the language of power. As Delpit (1995) suggests, students of color are often not given access to the intricacies of the parts of academic discourse. That is, they are often not taught how to use pieces of language to construct meaningful, articulate, whole texts. In the service of allowing students to create whole texts, turning one's back on the parts of language can keep students from learning powerful discourse. The key to making it so that students can use the parts of language to construct articulate wholes comes in contextualizing those parts so that students see how they fit into the creation of a whole text.

At the most contextualized end of this continuum, we see that contextualized whole texts, that is texts that acknowledge the position of the reader or writer, are, like vernacular texts, usually absent from school contexts. However, in current debates about what kinds of content count, there is an increased emphasis on paying more attention to the contextualized end of this continuum. In the applied linguistics field alone, there has been an ever-increasing emphasis on contextualized, particular knowledge (Davis, 1995). An example of this kind of emphasis was seen in Skilton-Sylvester's (1997) research in an adult education class that a Cambodian woman attended. In Soka's process of writing a letter to her former teacher (contextualized content that had meaning to her as a person), her teacher found out that she had a very complex understanding of the structure of personal letters (even though her English skills were relatively limited). Soka was able to explain how the structure of writing letters in Khmer is different than in English and how this is connected to language and culture (Skilton-Sylvester, 1997: 227). Starting with contextualized content in an academic context allowed her to analyze language and even rhetorical structure in a more decontextualized, powerful way.

If students' whole contextualized texts, with all of their imperfections, could be used as a starting point, meaning would be insured and students could intrinsically see the links between decontextualized and contextualized language, and between the literary and the vernacular. If minority texts could be chosen as a part of the literary content of the classroom, links could also be made between the content students bring with them to school and the content they encounter at the school door.

Skilton-Sylvester's contribution of the content continua to the continua model of biliteracy parallels other developments in the study of language and literacy. It is true that 'there is a longstanding tradition in linguistics which is concerned with the form rather than the content of language' (Malcolm, 1997), which perhaps explains the missing content dimension in the original continua model. It is also true that, in recent years, there has been greater attention to content. Malcolm mentions Gary Palmer's (1996) work on cultural linguistics and its origins in Boasian linguistics, ethnosemantics, and the ethnography of communication. There are also the various critical perspectives on language and literacy, as expressed for example in critical discourse analysis (Fairclough 1995; Norton 1997), critical language awareness (Clark *et al.*, 1990, 1991), and critical literacy (Lankshear, 1997), as well as critical ethnography (May, 1997) and critical pedagogy (Goldstein, 1997), all of which demand attention to content.

Lankshear suggests that 'two essential elements of any and all critical practice ... [are] the element of evaluation or judgement ... and the requirement of knowing closely ... that which is being evaluated' (1997: 43). To think critically about language, discourse, or literacy, one must first know it closely; that is, one must pay attention to what it is – its content. In terms of literacy, Lankshear specifies three possible contents, or 'potential objects of critique: ... literacies per se, ... particular texts, [and] ... wider social practices, arrangements, relations, allocations, procedures, etc.' (1997: 44). These he in turn relates to discourse and Discourse, in Gee's sense (1990), where discourse with a small 'd' refers to the language components of Discourse with a capital 'D', which refers to social practices or 'ways of being in the world.' Indeed, Gee suggests in his introduction to Lankshear's volume that critical literacy is in fact 'the ability to juxtapose Discourses, to watch how competing Discourses frame and re-frame various elements' (Gee in Lankshear, 1997: xviii).

Gee's discourse/Discourse distinction is akin to Fairclough's discussion of discourse types which make up the 'orders of discourse associated with particular institutions or domains of social life' (1992: 284). Fairclough goes on to specify discourse types as genre, activity type, style, and discourse itself: where *genre* is the overarching type that corresponds closely to social practice types (e.g. informal chat, counseling session, newspaper article); *activity type* refers to a structured sequence of actions and the participants involved; *style* varies according to tenor (e.g. formal, casual, etc.), mode (e.g. written or spoken), and rhetorical mode (e.g. argumentative, descriptive, etc.); and '*discourses* correspond roughly to dimensions of texts which have traditionally been discussed in terms of content' (1992: 286; emphasis added). By drawing attention to the majority–minority perspectives and experiences (*discourses and activity types*), as well as the literary and vernacular *genres and styles*, of texts available to Cambodian women and girls, Skilton-Sylvester attends precisely to the ways in which discourses make up the Discourses, or possible ways of being in the world, that are made available (or unavailable) to these language minority readers.

Available Discourses are multiple, indeed innumerable: 'e.g. gangs, academic disciplines, bar gatherings, ethnic groups, friendship networks, types of men, women, gays, children, students, classrooms, workers, workplaces, etc. and etc.' (Gee in Lankshear, 1997: xv). Yet, they are not equally available to all; rather they are ordered hierarchically within the politics of daily life (Lankshear, 1997: 39). By calling attention to the importance of whole contextualized texts/discourses that give voice and agency to minority discourses and activities and vernacular genres and styles, we are arguing for attention to the traditionally powerless ends of the continua of biliteracy content.

Media of biliteracy

One of the reasons for revisiting the continua was as a vehicle for analyzing ongoing data collection on two-way bilingual programs in Philadelphia's Puerto Rican community, as well as to revisit data which had been collected earlier, some of which had never been analyzed and written up.[6] Focusing on the media of biliteracy as they are put in practice in these two-way bilingual programs, we wondered: Would the argument we had been developing, about the need to pay attention to the powerless as well as powerful ends of the continua, hold up?

We concur with Valdés' (1997) cautionary note about underlying societal power relationships and their possible negative effects on two-way bilingual programs (dual-language immersion programs), especially in light of the appeal of these programs to both bilingual educators concerned about the education of language minority children and foreign-language educators interested in developing second-language proficiencies in mainstream American children. Specifically, she suggests three issues that deserve closer attention: (1) the degree to which modifications that may be made in the use of the minority language (to accommodate language majority children) may in fact be detrimental to the primary language development of minority children; (2) the ways in which intergroup relations among children in school are shaped by societal attitudes and structures outside the school despite the best intentions of those within the school; and (3) the question of who will in fact be the main beneficiaries of the language resources developed in the program; i.e. will the two-way program serve to simply give the majority yet another way (bilingualism) to displace the minority in the larger societal power structure? (412–20).[7]

Similarly, we found, once we focused on the media of biliteracy in the two-way programs we are familiar with, that faculty and staff continually face challenging decisions touching implicitly on larger questions of power. Specifically, decisions constantly arise with regard to: (1) placement of students in English-dominant and Spanish-dominant streams in the two-way program; (2) distribution of English and Spanish in the program structure and the classroom; and (3) the co-existence of various standard and nonstandard varieties of English and Spanish and the implications of this for instruction and assessment. The first two issues relate to the question of simultaneous versus successive exposure to (or acquisition) of the languages/literacies; while the last touches on the matter of language varieties' structures and scripts. We argue that the implicit weighting in most educational approaches to biliteracy (whether bilingual or monolingual) is toward successive acquisition and similar, convergent, standard language varieties. To contest that weighting requires attention to simultaneous acquisition and to dissimilar, divergent, nonstandard language varieties.

Hornberger's earlier work had noted the issues of student placement and language distribution in the programs to some degree, and the issues of standard and nonstandard varieties only in passing. With regard to the placement of students in English-dominant and Spanish-dominant streams:

> When students first arrive at Potter Thomas, they are assigned to the Anglo or Latino stream according to their home language, that is, the dominant language in the home, as reported by the parents. Parental preference also plays a role in children's placement; parents may choose, for linguistic or cultural reasons, to place their child in the Anglo stream, even if the child is Spanish-dominant; or vice versa. Thus Anglo and Latino are neither clear cultural nor monolingual language categories, but reflect two clusters along a continuum of language use, as well as a range of attitudes toward Spanish language maintenance and assimilation to US culture. (Hornberger, 1991: 230)

What was not explicitly stated then, but is worth stating here, is that English-dominant and Spanish-dominant *could not* be self-evident categories, given the myriad constellations of language use, ability, and exposure present in a community where ongoing circular migration from Puerto Rico to Philadelphia and back is a fact of life for nearly everyone to one degree or another. The fact is that most Puerto Rican children do not grow up with just one (dominant or only) mother tongue and then acquire the second language in school, but rather that they are constantly crossing back and forth between both languages and the meanings and identities they convey.

Similarly, Rampton, in his work on language crossing among Anglo, Afro-Caribbean, and Panjabi adolescents in the UK, has suggested that 'native speaker' and 'mother tongue' are problematic terms, given that the assumptions underlying them are now widely contested; it can no longer be assumed, for example, that a particular language is inherited (genetically or socially); that people either are or are not native/mother tongue speakers; or that people are native speakers of one mother tongue. He proposes instead that we think in terms of expertise, affiliation, and inheritance, where expertise has to do with a speaker's skill, proficiency, and ability to operate with a language; and affiliation and inheritance are two different, socially negotiated routes to a sense of allegiance to a language, i.e. identification with the values, meanings, and identities the language stands for (Rampton, 1995: 336–44). Although Rampton focused in his work on oral language use, Martin-Jones and Bhatt (1998) use these same concepts in showing how the range of multilingual literacy expertise developed by multilingual youth in Leicester is affected by the opportunities available to them as well as by the kinds of allegiances they feel at different points in time; in some cases, for example, young people reclaim in later adolescence an inheritance that they had earlier left behind.

Students arriving (and re-arriving) at school with widely different constellations of biliterate expertise, affiliations and inheritances pose a complex challenge to schools seeking to develop a two-way bilingual program that builds on both languages for all students. One such challenge occurred when Julia de Burgos Middle School sought to implement a targeted two-way program for an initial cohort of 60 gifted students assigned to Spanish-dominant and English-dominant sections:

> A problem has arisen, however, in that the Spanish language proficiencies of the English-dominant section encompass a great range, from [non-Puerto Rican] African-American students who have never had any Spanish instruction at all to Latino students who are fluently bilingual and in some cases biliterate in Spanish and English. The English language proficiencies of the Spanish-dominant section likewise span a range from the recent arrivals from Puerto Rico who are beginners in English to fluently bilingual and, in some cases, biliterate students. (Hornberger and Micheau, 1993: 44–5)

Hornberger (1991: 230–3) described how Potter Thomas School sought to address a similar challenge through a complex stream and cycle structure, where students regularly cycled through heterogeneously grouped homeroom classes in the Anglo and Latino streams where bilingual language use was the norm, and homogeneously grouped reading classes where language separation was expected, and back again. A study of how one fourth/fifth-grade homeroom teacher at Potter Thomas created successful learning contexts for her students' biliterate development, specifically how she built students' interaction with text, highlighted how she 'allows small-group peer interaction to occur spontaneously and a-systematically as a natural outgrowth of shared cultural values, emphasizes her students' community-based prior knowledge, and seeks to help her students to "connect and transfer" strategies across languages' (Hornberger, 1990: 227). Retrospectively, it appears that this teacher had in fact found ways to build on the biliterate affiliations, inheritances, and expertise that her students brought with them to school. What was not stated explicitly then, but is worth stating now, is that such an approach made a strength rather than a weakness out of students' criss-crossed, simultaneous (rather than successive) acquisition of two languages and literacies.

A third issue which poses challenges for these two-way programs is the co-existence of standard and non-standard varieties of English and Spanish in the school community's repertoire, and the implications of these for instruction and assessment. While earlier fieldwork (by Hornberger and her students) had taken note in passing of the existence of Puerto Rican, Cuban, and other Latin American varieties of Spanish, and of school standard and African-American varieties of English, all in use within one school (see Zentella, 1997: 41 on the repertoire of Spanish and English varieties on New York City's *el bloque*), the focus in terms of the continua of biliterate media had been more on the relative similarities and convergences *between* the two languages (Spanish and English) and their writing systems as potential resources for transfer of literacy from one to the other, rather than on dissimilarities and divergences across varieties *within* the two languages which might impede literacy development even in one.

To pose a (partially hypothetical) example: a school with a two-way program serving Puerto Rican children in Philadelphia decides, after many years of English language standardized testing, to inaugurate Spanish language standardized testing as well, in an effort to obtain a more representative picture of their students' biliterate accomplishments; the only trouble is that the only standardized testing materials available reflect Mexican, not Puerto Rican language varieties and identities and, thus, hardly promise to render a truer picture of the Puerto Rican students' expertise. Similarly, another school elects to develop portfolio assessment in Spanish and calls in an English-language expert on the subject, who is in turn stymied by the discovery that the teachers in the school, who speak varieties of Puerto Rican, Cuban, and other Latin American Spanishes, cannot agree on the 'correct' form of Spanish to use.

The problem of multiple varieties of Spanish has been around for some time, but has received relatively little attention. Among the first to draw attention to it were Gary Keller and Guadalupe Valdés. In a 1983 article, Keller posed the question: Which variety of Spanish to use in the classroom? He pointed out that the answer has often been made in the form of one of two extremes: either the local vernacular or world standard Spanish; but that sociolinguists chart instead a middle course that fosters bidialectalism. In the meanwhile, he said, the debate was being worked out in classrooms and programs across the country. A 1974 National Institute of Education project evaluating approximately 1000 titles in Spanish bilingual education found that eight types of Spanish were in use, as follows: (1) world standard Spanish, (2) regional or social varieties from outside the US (e.g. Bolivian), (3) all US regional and ethnic varieties, (4) eastern US ethnic varieties, (5) western US ethnic varieties, (6) nonstandard non-Spanish (i.e. bad translations), (7) regional and ethnic varieties *and* world Spanish, and (8) controlled world Spanish (i.e. only those forms for which there are not alternate regionalisms or ethnic varieties). Noting his dissatisfaction with the fact that there were too many Spanishes being promoted in the classroom, he suggested that some of the above alternatives are certainly more appropriate than others (e.g. types 1, 4, 5, and 8); and he concluded that resolution of this corpus planning issue would be extremely difficult to achieve without the conferral of power and authority (that is, voice and agency) on a group of corpus planners (Keller, 1983: 257–64).

Valdés too made an early plea for language planning on this issue. Her 1983 article, entitled 'Planning for biliteracy,' called for *lingüistas comprometidos* 'committed linguists' to be involved in training bilingual teachers, developing community activities for out-of-school bilingual adults, and, most relevant for our topic here, teaching Spanish as a subject in high school and college to Hispanic bilinguals, with a 'focus on the written language and not on eradicating the students' home dialect' (1983: 259). In her 1981 co-edited book, she had reported on a series of studies on Spanish language classes designed for Hispanic students in which the disturbing picture which emerged was one of language classes 'designed to show speakers of that language that theirs is not really that language – perhaps is not really *any* language' (Ruiz, 1997: 320, commenting on Valdés, 1981). Ruiz cites this as an example of instances of 'language planning in which the 'inclusion' of the language of a group has coincided with the exclusion of their voice' (Ruiz, 1997: 320).

For those voices to be included requires attention to divergence and dissimilarity across varieties of the language, and not an unreflexive legitimizing of only the standard variety. We have already noted above Corson's suggestion that applied linguists' adoption of a critical realist stance could lead to reform in the treatment of standard and nonstandard varieties; specifically, he suggests that it is the participants in any given context of situation who should determine the variety(ies) of a language that will be accorded status in that situation. As Ruiz suggests, though, this goes beyond matters of language or dialect, to those of voice and agency.

'Efforts on behalf of subordinate groups to "denaturalise" standard dialects and dominant Discourses are increasingly evident,' says Lankshear (1997: 34), going on to name three such sorts of initiative: bilingualism as an educational demand/ideal, 'bidialectism' in education, and 'multidiscoursal' education. To illustrate the last two, he cites the case of West Indian Creole dialects and standard English involving students at the University of the Virgin Islands, as described by Anderson and Irvine (1993). 'These students channeled their anger at being assigned to a non-credit remedial English class into a critical investigation of language and dialects', which, ultimately, had an impact on their language practices in and out of class. They began to write 'consciously in a variety of genres: using standard English for research papers, letters to editors, etc.; Creole for fictional stories addressed to other West Indians on themes of shared interest; and Creole for letters of thanks to guest speakers from the community, etc.' (Lankshear, 1997: 36–8). What is interesting about this example is that it is not just about the use of different dialects, but also of the orders of discourse and ways of being that those dialects entail; hence, the idea of not just bidialectal, but also multidiscoursal, education.[8]

A two-way bidialectal approach to the education of Aboriginal students in Western Australia provides another example (Malcolm, 1997). This work began in 1994 out of Edith Cowan University, as part of a teacher development project called 'Language and Communication Enhancement for Two-Way Education.' In partnership with the state Education Department of Western Australia, the project involves a 'team of Aboriginal and non-Aboriginal linguists and educators at the University . . . working with Aboriginal education workers from schools across the state and the teacher-partners they have nominated.' One bicultural team is carrying out research on the varieties of Aboriginal English spoken (and in particular the cultural imagery, or discourses, it represents); while another makes use of material from the accumulating semantic and pragmatic data base, as they prepare curriculum that both meets the state curricular requirements and reflects the underlying discourses (dialects, genres, styles, and voices) of Aboriginal English. The material is then trialed by the teams in the schools. The project operates under the basic premise that most Aboriginal people today are functioning in complex bicultural contexts, employing different varieties of English which represent different and sometimes competing discourses, identities, and cultural schemas for behaving and interpreting behavior, and that it is the job of education to recognize and allow learners to build on those resources.

One final note about this project, one which takes us back to the continua of biliterate contexts. The project aims intentionally at both macro (systemic) and micro (school) levels:

> The idea of giving recognition to Aboriginal English, rather than simply condemning it, is still not fully accepted at the staffroom level although the Education Department . . . has accepted the principle of bidialectal education. The work at the school level is fundamental, in that our experience has shown that a school can be transformed by a teacher who has his or her eyes opened to the reality of Aboriginal English by being engaged in action research on it. (Malcolm, 1997)

Conclusion

As our 're-visit' to the continua of biliteracy draws to a close, the recurrent theme which has emerged is the need for schools to become bi(multi)literate instances where student voices are heard and where students are able to 'make a difference' with the language(s) they speak. For voice and agency to be available, teachers, administrators, researchers, policy makers, community members, and students themselves must contest the traditional power weighting of the continua. With regard to the *contexts* of biliteracy, we have seen some evidence of such contestation occurring at the oral, bilingual, micro level in, for example, school language practices in the Peruvian highlands, language socialization practices in Kwara'ae, and literacy practices among urban multilingual youth in Britain. With regard to the *development* of biliteracy, we have seen that a cultural practice model of literacy allows for learners' voice and agency through use of their L1, oral, and receptive skills as well as the L2, written, productive ones. With regard to the *content* of biliteracy, we have argued for the importance of contextualized whole texts/discourses that give voice and agency to minority discourses and activities and vernacular genres and styles. With regard to the *media* of biliteracy, we have suggested the value of program structures and instructional approaches which make a strength rather than a weakness out of learners' criss-crossed, simultaneous acquisition of (exposure to) two languages and literacies, and the need for language planning that devolves agency and voice to those whose varieties and discourses are at stake.

As Cummins (1994) has suggested, exploring and exposing the invisible screen that obscures power relationships in schools is a key element in providing equitable education for all:

> In culturally diverse societies, a central goal of education should be to create interactional contexts where educators and students can critically examine issues of identity and experience and collaboratively deconstruct the myths that are inherited from one generation to the next. . . . For educators to create an educational context with their students where the assumptions and lies underlying dominant group identity become the focus of scrutiny rather than the invisible screen that determines perception is to challenge the societal power structure. Educational equity requires no less. (1994: 153)

This paper has been an attempt to make visible the ways in which school practices surrounding literacy and bilingualism have acted as a powerful invisible screen both nationally and internationally, and the ways in which this screen can lose and is losing some of its power by paying attention, at both micro and macro levels, to the traditionally less powerful ends of the continua of biliteracy. We agree with Corson that only an inclusive epistemology meets the three basic ethical principles of equal treatment, respect for persons, and benefit maximization (Corson, 1997: 183), and we argue from that epistemology that inclusion of learners' voice and agency is the only ethically acceptable solution when it comes to educating a linguistically and culturally diverse learner population. In today's world, that means every learner in every classroom.

Notes

* Reprinted from *Language and Education: An International Journal* 14 (2), 96–122 (2000), also published by Multilingual Matters.

† This is a revised version of a paper originally presented at the Symposium on Sociolinguistic and Ethnographic Studies on Linguistic Diversity: Looking Back and Looking Forward, as part of the annual meetings of the American Educational Research Association in San Diego, April 1998. We are grateful for comments from those present at the session. We also thank *Language and Education* editor David Corson and the two referees for very helpful comments as we prepared the paper for publication. Any errors of concept or interpretation are of course our own.

1. Figures 2.1 and 2.2 are not intended to represent the continua model per se, but are meant rather as aids to visualization of the relationships among the continua. Figure 2.1 depicts the continua as a series of nested boxes representing contexts, media, content, and development of biliteracy respectively, while Figure 2.2 shows that each box is a cluster of its three intersecting

continua. Other possible visualizations of the model that we have considered or that have been suggested to us include: a twelve-edged box with the four clusters of continua intersecting at each of the four corners; a bucket of paint with multiple colors mixed in different proportions; a set of refracting lenses lined up one behind the other; a sphere with all the continua intersecting in the middle, or an anchor attached to a rope of twelve intertwining strands. The point, we believe, is not to try to pin down the model with one visual representation, but to use a variety of visual representations as ways of thinking about the complex relationships among the continua.

2. Translations from the Spanish are by Hornberger; names are pseudonyms.
3. The ethnic groups represented in the 1997 course were, in order of total estimated number of speakers from greatest to smallest: Asheninca or Kampa – of which there are only 560 in Brazil, but 55,000 in Peru; Kaxinawá – with 2700 in Brazil and another 1200 in Peru; Apurinã – 2800; Jaminawá – 370 in Brazil and 600 in Peru; Katukina – 650; Arara or Shawandawa – 300; Yawanawá – 230; and Manchineri – 152 (Brasil, 1994).
4. See Monte (1996) for a description and analysis of the diaries; and Cavalcanti (1996) for insight into the reflexive nature of the cross-cultural interaction between the *professores indios* and one of the *professores broncos*, 'white teachers', who provide instruction in the course.
5. This analysis of fragmented, decontextualized school work builds on Bowles and Gintis's (1976) discussion of the fragmentation of tasks in the workplace for workers of lower socioeconomic classes.
6. We are grateful to students and staff of the Potter Thomas Elementary School and the Julia de Burgos Middle School, as well as to the School District of Philadelphia, for ongoing research and collaboration relationships since 1987. Warm appreciation also goes to Melisa Cahnmann (University of Pennsylvania Ph.D. student) for current collaboration at Potter Thomas School and in the revisiting of earlier data.
7. As a case in point, David Corson reports that work with francophone minority students in Ontario suggests that programs of the two-way type can gradually reduce the children's use of and proficiency in their French first language (personal communication, 19 July 1999).
8. In this regard, it is perhaps worth noting that, in a more recent formulation of the discourse types making up orders of discourse, Fairclough (in New London Group, 1996) has given greater salience to both dialect and voice, including them among the discourse types, where in 1992 they were not included.

References

Anderson, G. and Irvine, P. (1993) Informing critical literacy with ethnography. In C. Lankshear and P. McLaren (eds) *Critical Literacy: Politics, Praxis and the Postmodern* (pp. 81–104). Albany, New York: SUNY Press.

Anyon, J. (1980) Social class and the hidden curriculum of work. *Journal of Education* 162, 67–92.

Bourdieu, P. (1977) The economics of linguistic exchanges. *Social Science Information* 16, 645–68.

Bowles, S. and Gintis, H. (1976) *Schooling in Capitalist America*. New York: Basic Books.

Brasil (1994) *Banco de Dados do Programa Povos Indígenas no Brasil*. São Paulo, Brasil: CEDI/Instituto Socioambiental, November.

Cavalcanti, M. (1996) An indigenous teacher education course in Brazil: Cross-cultural interaction, voices and social representation. Paper presented at University of Pennsylvania Graduate School of Education: Language in Education Division Colloquium, November.

Clark, R., Fairclough, N., Ivanic, R. and Martin-Jones, M. (1990) Critical language awareness, Part I: A critical review of three current approaches to language awareness. *Language and Education* 4 (4), 249–60.

Clark, R., Fairclough, N., Ivanic, R. and Martin-Jones, M. (1991) Critical language awareness, Part II: Towards critical alternatives. *Language and Education* 5 (1), 41–54.

Collins, J. (1995) Literacy and literacies. *Annual Review of Anthropology* 24, 75–93.

Corson, D. (1997) Critical realism: An emancipatory philosophy for applied linguistics? *Applied Linguistics* 18 (2), 166–88.

Corson, D. (1999) *Language Policy in Schools*. Mahwah, NJ: Lawrence Erlbaum.

Cummins, J. (1994) Lies we live by: National identity and social justice. *International Journal of the Sociology of Language* 110, 145–54.

Davis, K. (1995) Qualitative theory and methods in applied linguistics research. *TESOL Quarterly* 29 (3), 427–55.

Delpit, L. (1995) *Other People's Children: Cultural Conflict in the Classroom*. New York: The New Press.

Fairclough, N. (1992) Intertextuality in critical discourse analysis. *Linguistics and Education* 4, 269–93.

Fairclough, N. (1995) *Critical Discourse Analysis: The Critical Study of Language*. London: Longman.

Gee, J.P. (1990) *Social Linguistics and Literacies: Ideology in Discourses*. London: Taylor and Francis.

Gee, J.P. (1997) Foreword: A discourse approach to language and literacy. In C. Lankshear *Changing Literacies* (pp. xiii–xix). Buckingham: Open University Press.

Giddens, A. (1984) *The Constitution of Society: Outline of the Theory of Structuration*. Berkeley: University of California Press.

Goldstein, T. (1997) Language research methods and critical pedagogy. In N.H. Hornberger and D. Corson (eds) *Research Methods in Language and Education* (pp. 67–77). Dordrecht: Kluwer Academic Publishers.

Heath, S.B. (1982) What no bedtime story means: Narrative skills at home and school. *Language in Society* 11 (1), 49–76.

Heath, S.B. (1992) Literacy skills or literate skills? Considerations for ESL/EFL learners. In D. Nunan (ed.) *Collaborative Language Learning and Teaching* (pp. 40–55). Cambridge: Cambridge University Press.

Hornberger, N.H. (1989) Continua of biliteracy. *Review of Educational Research* 59 (3), 271–96.

Hornberger, N.H. (1990) Creating successful learning contexts for bilingual literacy. *Teachers College Record* 92 (2), 212–29.

Hornberger, N.H. (1991) Extending enrichment bilingual education: Revisiting typologies and redirecting policy. In O. García (ed.) *Bilingual Education: Focusschrift in Honor of Joshua A. Fishman on the Occasion of his 65th Birthday* (pp. 215–34). Philadelphia: John Benjamins Publishers.

Hornberger, N.H. (1992) Biliteracy contexts, continua, and contrasts: Policy and curriculum for Cambodian and Puerto Rican students in Philadelphia. *Education and Urban Society* 24 (2), 196–211.

Hornberger, N.H. (1998) Language policy, language education, and language rights: Indigenous, immigrant, and international perspectives. *Language in Society* 27 (4).

Hornberger, N.H. (2000) Bilingual education policy and practice in the Andes: Ideological paradox and intercultural possibility. *Anthropology and Education Quarterly* 31 (2), 173–201.

Hornberger, N.H. and Hardman, J. (1994) Literacy as cultural practice and cognitive skill: Biliteracy in a Cambodian adult ESL class and a Puerto Rican GED program. In D. Spener (ed.) *Adult Biliteracy in the United States* (pp. 147–69). Washington DC: Center for Applied Linguistics.

Hornberger, N.H. and Micheau, C. (1993) 'Getting far enough to like it': Biliteracy in the middle school. *Peabody Journal of Education* 69 (1), 30–53.

Keller, G.D. (1983) What can language planners learn from the Hispanic experience with corpus planning in the United States? In J. Cobarrubias and J.A. Fishman (eds) *Progress in Language Planning: International Perspectives* (pp. 253–65). Berlin: Mouton.

Kennedy, M.M. (1997) The connection between research and practice. *Educational Researcher* 26 (7), 4–12.

Kincheloe, J. and Steinberg, S. (1993) A tentative description of post-formal thinking: The critical confrontation with cognitive theory. *Harvard Educational Review* 63 (3), 296–320.

Lankshear, C. (1997) *Changing Literacies*. Philadelphia: Open University Press.

Malcolm, I. (1997) Two-way bidialectal education. Paper presented at the annual conference of the American Association for Applied Linguistics, Orlando, Florida.

Martin-Jones, M. and Bhatt, A. (1998) Literacies in the lives of young Gujarati speakers in Leicester. In A. Durgunoglu and L. Verhoeven (eds.) *Literacy Development in a Multilingual Context: Cross-cultural Perspectives* (pp. 37–50). Mahwah, NJ: Lawrence Erlbaum.

May, S.A. (1997) Critical ethnography. In N.H. Hornberger and D. Corson (eds) *Research Methods in Language and Education* (pp. 197–206). Dordrecht: Kluwer Academic Publishers.

Monte, N.L. (1996) *Escolas da Floresta: Entre o Passado Oral e o Presente Letrado*. Rio de Janeiro, Brasil: Multiletra.

New London Group (1996) A pedagogy of multiliteracies: Designing social futures. *Harvard Educational Review* 66 (1), 60–92.

Norton, B. (1997) Critical discourse research. In N.H. Hornberger and D. Corson (eds) *Research Methods in Language and Education* (pp. 207–16). Dordrecht: Kluwer Academic Publishers.

Palmer, G.B. (1996) *Toward a Theory of Cultural Linguistics*. Austin: University of Texas Press.

Peirce, B.N. (1995) Social identity, investment and language learning. *TESOL Quarterly* 29 (1), 9–31.

Rampton, B. (1995) *Crossing: Language and Ethnicity among Adolescents.* London: Longman.

Reich, R. (1991) *The Work of Nations: Preparing Ourselves for 21st Century Capitalism.* New York: Knopf.

Ruiz, R. (1984) Orientations in language planning. *NABE Journal* 8 (2), 15–34.

Ruiz, R. (1997) The empowerment of language-minority students. In A. Darder, R. Torres and H. Gutierrez (eds) *Latinos and Education: A Critical Reader* (pp. 319–28). New York: Routledge.

Skilton-Sylvester, E. (1997) Inside, outside, and in-between: Identities, literacies, and educational policies in the lives of Cambodian women and girls in Philadelphia. Ph.D. dissertation, University of Pennsylvania.

Skilton-Sylvester, P. (1998) Putting school/work back together?: A comparison of organizational change in an inner city school and a Fortune 500 company. Ph.D. dissertation, University of Pennsylvania.

Street, B.V. (1984) *Literacy in Theory and Practice.* New York: Cambridge University Press.

Street, B.V. (ed.) (1993) *Cross-Cultural Approaches to Literacy.* Cambridge: Cambridge University Press.

Street, B.V. (1995) *Social Literacies: Critical Approaches to Literacy in Development, Ethnography, and Education.* London: Longman.

Street, B.V. (1996) Literacy and power? *Open Letter* 6 (2), 7–16. (Sydney, Australia: UTS).

Thierry, S. (1978) Etude d'un corpus de contes Cambodgiens traditionnels. Unpublished Thesis, University of Paris.

Valdés, G. (1981) Pedagogical implications of teaching Spanish to the Spanish-speaking in the United States. In G. Valdés, A.G. Lozano and R. Garcia-Moya (eds) *Teaching Spanish to the Hispanic Bilingual: Issues, Aims, and Methods.* New York: Teachers College Press.

Valdés, G. (1983) Planning for biliteracy. In L. Elías-Olivares (ed.) *Spanish in the US Setting: Beyond the Southwest* (pp. 259–62). National Clearinghouse for Bilingual Education.

Valdés, G. (1997) Dual-language immersion programs: A cautionary note concerning the education of language-minority students. *Harvard Educational Review* 67 (3), 391–429.

Warschauer, M. (1998) Online learning in sociocultural context. *Anthropology and Education Quarterly* 29 (1), 68–88.

Watson-Gegeo, K.A. (1992) Thick explanation in the ethnographic study of child socialization: A longitudinal study of the problem of schooling for Kwara'ae (Solomon Islands) children. *New Directions for Child Development* 58, 51–66.

Zentella, A.C. (1997) *Growing Up Bilingual: Puerto Rican Children in New York.* Oxford: Blackwell.

Part 2: Language Planning

Chapter 3
Biliteracy and Transliteracy in Wales: Language Planning and the Welsh National Curriculum

COLIN BAKER

Introduction

This chapter demonstrates that the Continua of Biliteracy model enables a fresh understanding of both Welsh literacy traditions and emerging perspectives in Wales about biliteracy. It will be shown that the comprehensive and holistic nature of the Continua framework (Hornberger, 1989; Hornberger & Skilton-Sylvester, 2000) creates an analytical tool for elucidating historical, contemporary political, and recent innovative perspectives on biliteracy in Wales.

The first section provides a brief standard historical perspective of biliteracy in Wales, and then asks whether the Continua enable a deeper explanation and understanding of Welsh literacy history than is typically provided. The second section addresses a belief in Wales that literacy in the minority language is a key performance indicator of Welsh language vitality and revitalization (or decline). This section asks whether the Continua aid the interpretation and understanding of biliteracy in language monitoring.

In the third section, the limited view of literacy practice embedded in the new Welsh National Curriculum is presented. It is argued that the Continua provide a thorough analytical framework for a critique of that literacy approach. In the fourth section, in contrast to the National Curriculum biliteracy approach, academics in Wales have begun to advocate 'translanguaging' and 'transliteracy' as a learning strategy both to increase competence in Welsh and English and to raise achievement levels in students across the curriculum. This idea is explained along with remarks about how the Continua anticipate and accommodate an innovative idea about biliteracy strategies in the classroom.

In the fifth section, the relationship between biliteracy and language planning in Wales is discussed. In particular, this final section examines the Welsh view that there should be no functional separation between English and Welsh, including in biliteracy, if the minority language is to be maintained and revitalized. Welsh language planning currently tends to reject a diglossic view of the separate uses for the two languages. This section reveals how the Continua of Biliteracy framework provides a conceptual tool to examine the issues.

Historical Perspectives on Welsh Literacy

This section begins by indicating that Welsh language literacy in Wales has a long tradition with a remarkably high status. A very brief résumé of the 'standard history' is provided (for details see Baker, 1985, 1993; J. Davies, 1993, 1994, 2000; R.R. Davies, 1990; Jenkins, 1993; Morgan, 1990; Williams, 1999). This is followed by exemplification of how the Continua (Hornberger, 1989; Hornberger & Skilton-Sylvester, 2000) enable a wider historical analysis and can generate new perspectives. The argument is that an historical analysis of biliteracy (in any country) is valuably assisted by use of the Continua framework. It enables the asking of key pertinent questions about historical developments in literacy practices ensuring an extended and deeper historical perspective.

By the end of the eleventh century, Welsh was the language spoken by almost everyone throughout Wales. It also had developed one of the longest and strongest literary traditions in Europe. For example, the Welsh Law Books and the collection of stories known as the 'Mabinogi' (which were written down some time between 1050 and 1170) are regarded as a major and distinctive contribution to European medieval literature. The first printed book in Welsh appeared in 1547.

From those early days until the present, Welsh language poetry has always had a high status throughout the Welsh-speaking nation, almost unparalleled throughout the world. One third of all books in Welsh purchased by adults contain Welsh poetry (Davies, 2000). Not just among the literary minded or cultural elites, the prestige of the poet among the populace continues to be almost internationally unique. For example, there is a high-status national competition on an annual basis for the best poets in the land. At the National Eisteddfod, one of the best poets is given a costly crown to wear and is treated like royalty (for the remainder of their life). Their fame and status for years to come, throughout the

Welsh-speaking nation, is guaranteed. The Welsh poet is more of a hero for Welsh speakers than the novelist, singer or actor. Such is the strength and status of the Welsh literacy tradition.

A major part of the standard history of Welsh literacy is also the strong religious context that encouraged and supported Welsh literacy. Indeed, all school students are taught that it was biblical literacy that saved the Welsh language from virtual extinction (such language death having occurred with our Welsh language Celtic cousins, the Manx and Cornish languages).

To elucidate, the translation of the Bible into Welsh in 1567 has long been popularly regarded as the savior of the Welsh language. Particularly in the 'Welsh language decline' decades of the nineteenth and twentieth centuries, it was compulsory for almost all people in a Welsh-speaking community not only to attend a Welsh chapel or church but to develop the ability to read the Bible in Welsh with speed and diligence. Given the strongly religious nature of the Welsh (particularly but not exclusively non-conformist Christianity), all children were taught to read the Bible as part of salvation. From the 1730s onwards, Sunday schools were established with a solid focus of teaching children to read the Bible. In the eighteenth century, it is estimated that over a quarter of a million children in over 3000 Sunday schools across more than 1500 villages and towns in Wales became functionally literate in Welsh through the Bible (Davis, 1993). Such literacy in turn gave the Welsh language prestige and status, stimulating other religious publications in the indigenous language.

The standard history of Welsh literacy includes the idea that the Welsh language Bible provided standardization of the Welsh language from the sixteenth century onwards. The Bible in Wales has historically been a main tool of corpus planning, ensuring that dialects of Welsh had a common denominator in high status biblical language. Welsh religious literacy over the last two centuries has been regarded as an essential (but insufficient by itself) element in Welsh language maintenance and revitalization.

While Welsh literacy traditions have high status and much credit in language maintenance and vitality, the contemporary engagement in Welsh literacy practices by the populace is markedly lower. Two 'performance indictors' provide the evidence for less frequent Welsh literacy use among Welsh speakers compared with Welsh oracy and historical use of Welsh literacy:

(1) The size of the Welsh-speaking population has decreased rapidly, particularly in the last century. Following immigration, particularly of English language speakers, emigration, colonization, mass communication, transport, tourism, industrialization, urbanization/

suburbanization, the decline of religion and the growing dominance of English in most domains of language life (from the eighteenth century to the present), the Welsh language has declined. Here decline refers to raw numbers of speakers, geographical saturation in communities, and status and use of Welsh in different domains. For example, those counted by a decennial Census as Welsh speaking has declined from around 50% in the early 1900s to 20% at the end of the twentieth century (National Assembly for Wales, 2000b; OPCS, 1994).

Of those declaring themselves in the Census as Welsh speaking, around 70% are literate in Welsh (although this includes those with developing literacy competences). In the 1991 Census, 18.7% reported themselves as Welsh speaking (no differentiation is made in the Census question between ability and use). In contrast, 16.3% declared that they 'read in Welsh', 14.1% that they 'write in Welsh' and 13.6% as 'reading and writing in Welsh' (National Assembly for Wales, 2000b; OPCS, 1994). Again, no difference is made between ability and actual involvement in literacy practices. Since Welsh is compulsory as L1 or L2 in the National Curriculum of Wales (see later), most students have literacy skills – but relatively few seemingly engage in Welsh literacy events outside school and homework.

(2) In a review of the Welsh Books Council by the Welsh Language Board (1999), it was found that: (a) only one in five Welsh speakers (18.2%) buy Welsh language books (although only 50.3% of the sample bought a book in any language) – in a Welsh-speaking population of close to half a million, only 90,000 will buy a Welsh book; and (b) with an annual subsidy equivalent to close to one million US dollars, and with the production of around 600 new titles each year, only 50% to 60% of (relatively small) print runs are sold. Following the establishment of the Welsh Books Council in 1961, almost all Welsh language books have received financial support. Support funding is also provided for children's leisure and school books in Welsh, such books amounting to a third of all books published in Welsh.

Having provided a very brief standard 'potted history' of Welsh language literacy, use of the Continua opens up new perspectives and raises new questions that can both challenge and enhance the 'standard' perspective. This section can do no more than briefly illustrate this: a full historical analysis would take a book in itself. This section makes the point that the Continua provide a valuable tool for historical analysis of literacy within and across countries. The standard history can be refined and elaborated through use of Continua dimensions.

The Continua remind us that historical analysis and explanations should encompass *contexts* that show the interrelationship of oracy and literacy (e.g. in religious meetings where Bible reading, sermons as expositions and praying, for example, are integrated). Also Wales has developed from monolingual literacy in Welsh among much of the populace to bilingualism and biliteracy as the norm in Welsh-speaking communities. In Wales, there is little analytical history of the contextual shift from monoliteracy in Welsh to biliteracy among around 70% of the Welsh-speaking population (and in all children who take their education bilingually – see Baker and Jones, 2000). The Continua serve to prompt that important line of historical enquiry of movement from minority language monoliteracy to biliteracy and the power dimensions in that movement.

While the Continua framework does not provide an explanation, its dimensions provide the spectacles through which to seek causes and catalysts of historical change in literacy practices. In the development of biliteracy in Wales, the change from receptive to productive uses of literacy in Welsh schools from the eighteenth to the twenty-first century requires treatment. Simple explanations (e.g. changes in religious practices) need to be joined by analyzing power relations (e.g. a decline in the power of the pulpit), and a movement to similar infrastructures (e.g. mass media) supporting literacy in English and Welsh. Biliteracy in Wales has also been aided by convergent scripts in the media of biliteracy. Whereas the standard history typically seeks to maintain differences and boundaries between Welsh and English literacies, the move to biliteracy has surely been helped by similar language scripts.

The content of biliteracy reminds us that, for example, power struggles lie beneath changing historical patterns of literacy practice (e.g. in mass communications, the rise of UK newspapers and international WWW links). The changing politics of power and economic advancement (societal and individual) enrich religious explanations of literacy as Welsh language salvation. The power of conformity in local chapels, the resistance to the English invader, the political marginalization of Welsh-speaking miners and farmers in remote rural areas are examples of how the political content of biliteracy in the new Continua is an essential element to a literacy history.

The argument is thus that the Continua aid historical explanation of the fortunes of minority language literacy and biliteracy by providing a wider set of conceptual dimensions for analysis. The Continua prompt us to ask an extensive and expansive set of questions about literacy evolution, seeking re-framing and re-analysis and avoiding a standard description or a simplistic conclusion.

Literacy as Performance Indicator in Language Planning

For Welsh scholars of geolinguistics, language planning and language demography, and not least for the many prophets of the future of the Welsh language, literacy in the minority language (and hence biliteracy) has been regarded as a key performance indicator of Welsh language decline or vitality. That is, the percentage of people at a national, regional and community level who report themselves on a Census as literate in Welsh (and by implication biliterate) provides a barometer of the present and future language climate. Simple and inexact, nevertheless the Census data is an almost irreplaceable gauge of language decline, maintenance or reversal due to its sampling of the complete population in Wales.

There are two Census literacy measures used to detect the health and prospects of the indigenous language (OPCS, 1994). First, the percentage within a geographical area (as large as a District (County) or as small as the smallest community) who are literate in Welsh can be compared with a previous Census (a Census is held in Wales every 10 years). Where there is decline in that percentage over time, the indigenous language would appear to be weakening.

Second, analyses of Census data spotlight geographical areas where there are relatively higher percentages of Welsh speakers who are not literate in Welsh (Baker, 1985). Where there is oracy without literacy, the language is predicted to decline in the coming decades in those areas. When someone can speak a minority language and not write in that language, the number of functions and prestige of that language is diminished. This is the case in Wales where employment and promotion in employment increasingly requires biliteracy and bilingualism. This is the intended reversal of the colonialization of Wales where indigenous Welsh speakers were required to acquire majority language literacy if they were to stand a good chance of employment in the bureaucracy and infrastructure of the ruling elites. Currently, language planning in Wales (see later) aims to make Welsh functional literacy important for employment (e.g. in the customer interface).

Analysis of Welsh language Census data shows that, where bilingualism exists without biliteracy, there is an increased likelihood of language decay (Baker, 1985). Welsh Census analysis of oracy without literacy is a way of locating places where language literacy planning is needed (e.g. by the injection of central government funds into community initiatives – called *Mentrau Iaith*).

Thus literacy (or illiteracy) in Welsh is regarded as a key monitoring device to evaluate if government Welsh language planning measures are seemingly effective (e.g. the government in Wales gives the equivalent of a 1.25 million US dollar subsidy per annum to the Welsh Books industry via the Welsh Books Council). However, much caution is needed in using this performance indicator, and the Continua framework is a valuable tool for ensuring a cautious approach to such language monitoring. This section therefore proceeds to suggest that the Continua (Hornberger, 1989; Hornberger & Skilton-Sylvester, 2000) valuably help examine the 'biliteracy as a performance indicator view' and suggests that a simple statistical analysis and 'monitoring' approach can become more profound when viewed through the multidimensional spectacles of the Continua. Three examples will be given to illustrate this.

First, the Continua urge a multidimensional approach to viewing biliteracy, ensuring sensitivity to a wide variety of literacy practices. A Census takes a black and white snapshot (each person is either literate in Welsh or not) whereas the multidimensioning reminds us that there are degrees of biliteracy (e.g. oral to literate dimension in Contexts and oral to written in Development of Biliteracy).

Second, the micro to macro dimension reminds us that societal analyses do not reflect the individuality of local community or personal profiles of biliteracy. The Census simplicity of 'reading and writing in Welsh' masks the complexity of contextualized and decontextualized content with frequent moving 'to and fro' on the minority–majority dimension. A Census simplifies unsympathetically. The Continua justifiably complexifies so that literacy life at local and personal level can be expressed in its variety, individuality and intricacy.

Third, Hornberger and Skilton-Sylvester's (2000) revisiting of the Continua emphasizes that power relations become an essential part of any biliteracy analysis. When there are government statistics that are used for language planning purposes, such power relations are always close at hand. Welsh language literacy must not be viewed in political or analytical isolation from majority language literacy. Welsh literacy is in a competitive market (e.g. books, local newspapers, advertising) with unequal revenues, lower political power and less status in the populace.

This third point is particularly important in Wales. Statistics are often presented as objective measures, exact and definitive. When, as in Wales, they show language decline, they can then be used to cast doubts on the money spent on supporting the indigenous language (the equivalent of over 150 million US dollars a year is spent, for example, on Welsh language TV and radio, Welsh language curriculum support and a Welsh language government planning agency).

The new Continua remind us that power relationships are crucial to explaining and understanding the status and health of indigenous literacy practice. Such status difference is not merely symbolic. Literacy in the minority language means that a person is also subject to majority language print media. Majority language media will contain dominant and powerful viewpoints, the attitudes of the center, and the values and the beliefs of the majority language. Minority language literacies allow the possibility of minority language culture, political and ideological viewpoints to be presented, but they do not work in isolation of central power structures nor majority language status pressures.

Statistics showing the decline of the Welsh literacy across Census from the early 1900s to the present imply that dominant political and ideological viewpoints from the conquering language (English) have risen in power. With a decrease in Welsh literacy goes a movement away from values, beliefs, ideas, attitudes and perspectives that have been transmitted by Welsh literacy practices. Welsh cultural forms conveyed through such practices, with their embedded ways of constructing and experiencing the world, will have declined in favor of a hegemonic English literacy experience. This theme is continued and exemplified in the next section that examines biliteracy in the National Curriculum in Wales.

Literacy in the National Curriculum in Wales

In this section, the view of literacy practice embedded in the new Welsh National Curriculum is presented. It is argued that the Continua (Hornberger & Skilton-Sylvester, 2000) provide an analytical framework for a critique of that literacy approach.

Literacy is variously said to cultivate values, norms of behavior and codes of conduct, to create benign citizens, develop powers of thinking and reasoning, enculturate, emancipate and empower, provide enjoyment and emotional development, develop critical awareness, foster religious devotion, community development, and not least to be central to academic success across the curriculum. Literacy can also empower and liberate low-status, marginalized communities, emancipating those politically subjugated and despised. In contrast, the National Curriculum in Wales takes a much more narrow view of literacy and biliteracy (National Assembly for Wales, 2000a).

Wales has a National Curriculum with the core subjects defined as English, Mathematics, Science and Welsh (when taught as a first language). Its view of literacy is contained in a definitive National Curriculum document: 'Key Stages 1 and 2 of the National Curriculum in Wales' (National Assembly for Wales, 2000a). A few key quotes reveal its stance on literacy in English and Welsh.

On language development:

> Pupils should be given opportunities to: understand the importance of standard English, with appropriate sensitivity to their patterns of speech, and recognize some of the features that distinguish standard English, including subject–verb agreement and the use of the verb 'to be' in past and present tenses. (National Assembly for Wales, 2000a: 35)

> Pupils should be taught to: write each letter of the alphabet, use their knowledge of sound–symbol relationships and phonological patterns, recognize and use simple spelling patterns, write common letter strings within familiar and common words, spell commonly occurring simple words, spell words with common prefixes and suffixes, check the accuracy of their spelling and use word books and dictionaries, identifying initial letters as the means of locating words, experiment with the spelling of complex words and discuss misapplied generalizations and other reasons for misspellings; close attention should be paid to word families. (National Assembly for Wales, 2000a: 38)

> Pupils should be taught that writing communicates meaning, and they should be given opportunities to express themselves in writing so that they begin to develop as independent writers, both creatively and factually, using conventional spelling, punctuation, grammatical organization, and handwriting which is legible. Pupils' knowledge, understanding and skills should be developed within an integrated programme of speaking and listening, reading and writing. (National Assembly for Wales, 2000a: 33)

On language development in Welsh:

> Pupils should be taught to: write correctly and robustly, with attention to aspects of grammar, in order to promote accuracy so that they: use Welsh syntax, use verb forms (tense and person) correctly, form negative sentences correctly, conjugate prepositions correctly, use the correct prepositions after a verb/noun, mutate appropriately, are aware of the gender of nouns, are able to differentiate between similar words. (National Assembly for Wales, 2000a: 65)

The National Curriculum view of literacy (Welsh and English) in Wales is thus highly functional, about technical skills, decoding symbols, correctness and accuracy. It concerns linguistics rather than communication, legitimacy rather than diversity. Its assimilative and superordinate view of citizenship is implicit in the frequent reference to the importance of 'standard English'. Despite the presence of dialects of English in Wales and a strong literacy tradition of English from Welsh writers (e.g. Dylan Thomas), it is standard 'England's English' that is sought. Despite the National Curriculum of Wales originating from Cardiff and not London, the 'doffing of the cap' to the English educational power in London is still omnipresent. Despite having its own parliament (National Assembly), the Welsh education system continues to regard England as its source of educational ideas. This is no more evident than Wales' National Curriculum's conception of literacy.

The Continua framework (Hornberger, 1989; Hornberger & Skilton-Sylvester, 2000) provides the analytical apparatus for a powerful critique of the Welsh National Curriculum approach to literacy in English and Welsh. The Continua indicate the very limited contexts in which Welsh National Curriculum literacy practice is situated. Indeed, there is a highly decontextualized view of literacy.

While some credence is given to the oral–literate continuum, no credence is given to the monolingual–bilingual continuum. There are separate 'Orders' (requirements) for Welsh and English literacy. Welsh literacy and English literacy are treated totally separately in the National Curriculum document as autonomous and unconnected. Thus, a fractionalist view of languages is presented with no linkage or interaction between the Welsh and English literacy curriculum. Any connections or L1–L2 transfer on the biliterate development dimension of the Continua have to be made inside the student's head, not inside the curriculum. A holistic biliterate development is ignored by the Welsh National Curriculum.

As the new Continua (Hornberger & Skilton-Sylvester, 2000) remind us, this is not purely a curriculum issue. There are power and status dimensions. When such a fractional view of biliteracy is presented, there may well be an increase in the status distance between the two languages and literacies. The majority–minority divide is maintained and reinforced by a fractionalist approach. English literacy is promoted; Welsh literacy is marginalized and demoted to inferior and subordinate status. This is illustrated by some statistics.

All students in Wales have English literacy lessons; around 12% will have Welsh language literacy throughout their schooling (Baker & Jones, 2000). Almost all Welsh children become literate in English. Despite Welsh being a compulsory subject in the National Curriculum from 5 to 16 years of age (as an L1 or an L2), only a minority of children gain full

Welsh language literacy and hence biliteracy. An even smaller percentage (e.g. 5%) engage in Welsh literacy practices outside school.

Thus a fractionalist approach to biliteracy in the National Curriculum maintains a separation and differentiation in the status of Welsh and English literacy. It reinforces a system that gives English literacy power and status, dominance and superiority, while Welsh literacy is relegated to minority margins, with inferiority in educational use. The skills-based view of literacy serves to promote a view of literacy that maintains a low power base for Welsh literacy. It emphasizes the functional value of standard English while failing to engage a critical literacy for those with minority language and minority status.

The political climate in Wales is one of raising standards, monitoring progress, quality enhancement, increasing effectiveness, better value, value addedness and proven efficiency. One result is a 'back-to-basics' emphasis in literacy in school and an emphasis on functional literacy. The Continua are valuable for showing that beneath simple policies are multiple dimensions and hidden politics. Political spins and pious simplicity in Wales' curriculum prescriptions are challenged by the Continua's multiple lenses. Such multiple lenses allow microscopic deconstruction, binoculars to envisage holistically, and not least a periscope to uncover power and prestige realities resting beneath the political rhetoric.

Transliteracy

In contrast to the National Curriculum, some academics and teachers in Wales have begun to advocate 'transliteracy'. This idea is explained in this section along with an analysis as to whether the Continua of Biliteracy framework (Hornberger, 1989; Hornberger & Skilton-Sylvester, 2000) accommodates a new idea about biliteracy strategies in the classroom.

Cen Williams (1994) developed a theory and conducted research on the 'translanguaging' development of language skills across the high school curriculum. Williams (1994) maintains that it is not the amount of time allotted to each language in a lesson or in the curriculum that is most significant. Rather, the use made and the activities allocated to each language are paramount. Building on the framework of Jacobson (1990), Williams particularly examines how the strategic concurrent use of two languages in a classroom can contribute to a deeper understanding of curriculum content and to the development of both languages. The use of translanguaging (a translation of Cen Williams' (1994) Welsh term *trawysieithu*) is claimed to contribute to a deeper understanding of the subject matter being studied.

This section initially introduces the notion of translanguaging (and transliteracy), and then examines whether the Continua accommodate this innovative idea from Wales. However, it must initially be stated that translanguaging is only relevant when a student has a sufficiently developed L1 and L2 to use those languages for curriculum content learning.

Imagine the following routine. The teacher briefly introduces a topic in English, making a few side comments in Welsh. Stimulus reading and worksheets are in English. Class activities (e.g. teamwork) are carried out in the students' preferred language. The teacher interacts with small groups and individual students in a mixture of Welsh and English, but with English dominant. The students complete the worksheet in English. This pattern of interaction is unlikely to result in biliteracy. The languages have an unequal status. Literacy is being developed in English and not Welsh. To allow students to make progress in both languages and to maximize academic achievement, Williams (1994) urges that bilingual classrooms should engage in strategic classroom language planning by translanguaging and transliteracy.

Cen Williams' (1994) high school and tertiary level research suggests that there are curriculum strategies that develop both languages successfully and also result in highly effective content learning. In particular, he found translanguaging and transliteracy to be highly successful. These terms describe the hearing or reading of a lesson, a passage in a book or a section of work in one language and the development of the work (e.g. by discussion, writing a passage, completing a work sheet, conducting an experiment) in the other language. That is, input and output are deliberately in a different language, and this is systematically varied. Thus translanguaging is a more specific term than the general umbrella term 'concurrent use of two languages'. In translanguaging, the input (reading or listening) will be in one language, and the output (speaking or writing) in the other language. Across different lessons this is varied to ensure progress in both languages across the curriculum.

For instance, a science worksheet in English is read by students. The teacher then initiates a discussion on the subject matter in Welsh, switching to English to highlight particular science terms. The students then do their written work in Welsh. Next lesson, the roles of the languages are reversed. In this example, the literacy input is in one language, the literacy output in a different language. Therefore transliteracy may be an apt descriptor.

Translanguaging and transliteracy have four potential advantages. First, they may promote a deeper and fuller understanding of the subject matter. As one teacher remarked in Williams' (1994) research, 'If the students have understood it in two languages, they've really understood it'. To read and discuss a topic in one language, and then to write about it in another language, means that the subject matter has to be processed, reprocessed and 'mentally digested'. While full conceptual reprocessing need not occur, linguistic reprocessing is likely to help in deeper conceptualization and assimilation.

Second, translanguaging and transliteracy may help students develop competence in their weaker language. Students might otherwise attempt the main part of the work in their stronger language and then undertake less challenging, related tasks in their weaker language. Translanguaging and transliteracy are attempts to develop academic language skills in both languages and fuller bilingualism and biliteracy.

Third, the joint use of languages can facilitate home–school cooperation. If a child can communicate curriculum content to a minority language parent in their home language, the parent can support the child in their school work. Thus, a policy of translanguaging and transliteracy may encourage parents to become more involved in literacy support in the home. At its best, this includes using literacy practices that are part of the language minority culture.

Fourth, the integration of fluent English speakers and English learners of various levels of attainment is helped by translanguaging. If English learners are integrated with first language English speakers, and if sensitive and strategic use is made of both languages in class, then learners can develop their second language ability concurrently with content learning.

There are potential problems in the complexity of managing, allocating and organizing such a use of two languages. However, the value of the idea is that the teacher plans the strategic use of two languages, thinks consciously about use of two languages in the classroom, reflects on and reviews what is happening linguistically, and attempts to cognitively stimulate students by 'language provocative' and 'language diversified' lessons.

Having presented the idea of translanguaging and transliteracy, the focus switches to how the Continua of Biliteracy framework allows for this classroom strategy, and how it helps refine and extend, and possibly challenge the notion of transliteracy.

The Continua anticipate and valuably extend the notion of translanguaging and transliteracy. First, transliteracy in classrooms can be placed on the Continua at the bilingual end of the bilingual–monolingual dimension in micro classroom contexts. The notion of translanguaging and transliteracy is anticipated by the oral–literate continuum. In terms of biliterate development, the notion of translanguaging and transliteracy involves strategic movement along the production and reception continuum, between the L1 and L2 transfer, and between the oral and written continuum. That is, the three dimensional continua of biliterate development in the individual (see Hornberger, 1989: 274) provide the schema for strategic variation by moving between these three continua. In terms of media of biliteracy, the simultaneous end of the exposure continuum is regarded by translanguaging and transliteracy as important, rather than successive exposure.

The new Continua (Hornberger & Skilton-Sylvester, 2000) also provide a reminder of the tensions that will typically be present in translanguaging and transliteracy. Production, the written form, and the L2 as a majority language all contain more prestigious forms of literacy. Thus, when there is a strategic choice of which language to use for input, throughput (process) and output, the power and prestige balance needs careful consideration. For example, a strategy of the equal use of the two languages may be simplistic as the languages will already have unequal value and status in the eyes of the students. A balance that is tilted towards the minority language may be needed to try to adjust the balance that favors the majority language in many in-school (e.g. playground) and out-of-school domains.

Translanguaging is essentially about developing full biliteracy with no curriculum separation in literacy learning outcomes (other than in Welsh as a subject where Welsh literature, and particularly poetic forms, will be taught). Translanguaging thus partly assumes equality in literacy usage and smooth transitions between two literacies, with usage and practice available in either. The new Continua warn that such equality will be difficult to achieve. The politics of languages and power dimensions may leave equality a difficult goal to attain.

The Continua of Biliteracy framework also extends the idea of transliteracy and how it may be achieved. Hornberger and Skilton-Sylvester (2000) suggest that 'the more their learning contexts allow learners to draw on all points of the Continua, the greater are the chances for their full biliterate development' (96). That is, translanguaging and transliteracy needs strategically to consider all the dimensions of the Continua to create full biliteracy in students. In particular, the consideration of micro and macro contexts, transfer between L1 and L2, the relationship between the majority and minority language, and contextualized and decontextualized content are each needed added dimensions to pedagogic thinking about transliteracy. Not least, the new Continua's dimension of power relations is vital to situating transliteracy in its political reality of the majority–minority relationship in Wales. That is, when translanguaging and transliteracy engage all the dimensions of the Continua, the aim of full biliteracy in students may be more maximally achieved.

By bringing the new Continua's (Hornberger & Skilton-Sylvester, 2000) dimensions of power into translanguaging, the functional allocation of languages in a diglossic arrangement is also challenged, and this is now considered in the final section.

Functional Allocation of Literacy in Wales

The notion of translanguaging latently contains the dominant language planning (e.g. Welsh Language Board) perspective in Wales that is critical of diglossic arrangements. Translanguaging is an attempt to raise Welsh literacy to similar status levels to English literacy. While this is nigh impossible, the Welsh language planning view is that it has to be attempted.

To explain, the Welsh language situation is moving to Fishman's (1972, 1980) 'bilingualism without diglossia'. In this situation, most people will be bilingual and will not restrict one language to a specific set of purposes. Either language may be used for almost any function. Fishman (1972, 1980) regards such communities as unstable and in a state of change. Where bilingualism exists without diglossia, the prediction is that the majority language will become even more powerful and extend its use. The other language may decrease in its functions and decay in both status and usage.

However, this is not the only outcome. In Wales, for example, the attempt is for the minority language (Welsh) to be increasingly available in hitherto English language domains (e.g. in education, television, pop music), giving bilinguals a choice. A 'High' use of Welsh means, for example, encouraging its use in local and national government where there is higher status and prestige.

It is believed in Wales that allocating separate functions for Welsh and English will relegate the Welsh language to low status and subordinate uses. Welsh would have sentimental and not instrumental (e.g. economic) value. Thus the Welsh view is that a functional separation of languages in Wales will inevitably lead to language decline (except where the minority language has prestigious uses such as for religious purposes). The Basques have created a similar argument against a diglossic functional separation and are working for the normalization of bilingualism. This is related to (but not the same as) Sridhar (1996) who suggests that, rather than compartmentalization of languages in a diglossic situation, the reality is often of an overlapping and intermeshing use of languages.

Fishman (2001a, 2001b) disagrees, arguing that keeping up with the prestige and power of a worldwide language such as English is impractical and impossible. 'All functions for the minority language' sets the wrong goal for that language. Instead, the minority language must be safeguarded in the home and community. For Fishman, a minority language is safeguarded when it is preserved and dominant in intimate language functions in the home and local community.

Nevertheless, Welsh language planners believe that Welsh should be used in all domains (Welsh Language Board, 2000). The argument has been, first, that a diglossic relationship between Welsh and English will relegate Welsh to domains where there is less power, prestige and status. If Welsh is consigned only to intimate family and community domains (with religious usage increasingly infrequent among the populace), the language will die. Welsh language and Welsh literacy practices must achieve a modern usage that has status and power.

Second, in order to support intergenerational transmission and the learning of Welsh as an L2 in school, language functions with status must all be promoted. Only when Welsh is used in higher status areas (e.g. government, mass media, education, employment) will families and communities be interested in intergenerational transmission. That is, relegating a language to affective, integrative domains is too romantic a notion of the function and value of language in a new century. For twenty-first century families to raise their children in the minority language, and for schools to have a secure *raison d'être* for using the minority language to transmit curriculum content requires instrumental, economic and employment value for a language and literacy (as well as integrative value).

Thus Welsh language planning maintains that there is a higher probability of revitalizing the Welsh language by attempting to ensure Welsh can be used in as many status domains as possible: Welsh curriculum materials (for all ages, all curriculum areas, all ability levels and all special needs (e.g. blind children)), subsidization for Welsh literature, separate Welsh language TV and radio channels, Microsoft Windows in Welsh, Welsh signage and packaging and WWW sites in Welsh. In terms of literacy, the equivalent of some three million dollars per annum is spent on producing Welsh curriculum materials, and the equivalent of one million dollars is spent on subsidizing and promoting Welsh books. Strong attempts are thus made to provide all bilinguals in Wales with the opportunity to engage in Welsh literacy practices. While it is acknowledged that, against the all-pervading power and status of international English, such attempts can only imperfectly be achieved, nevertheless it raises probabilities of language survival beyond the pessimistic scenario of the compartmentalization of Welsh to low power dimensions.

There are undoubted risks in this approach to language planning. There is no equal choice of Welsh and English. As the new Continua (Hornberger & Skilton-Sylvester, 2000) remind us, power is unequally distributed between minority and majority languages. English will seemingly have, for many people most of the time, the status usage. The Continua are valuable here in analyzing this argument. Hornberger and Skilton-Sylvester (2000) show how each of their listed 12 dimensions (in a $3 \times 3 \times 3 \times 3$ framework) has traditionally more powerful ends to each dimension. Within the content of biliteracy continua there are particularly the more powerful majority language, decontextualized and literary endpoints.

Within the conceptualization of the Continua, minority language literacy has to find locations on all relevant dimensions that remain its preserve (functional allocation) and to defend those locations. This is the diglossic approach of Fishman. Alternatively, as in the Wales and Basque positioning, the aim becomes to move along all relevant dimensions as far as possible to the 'traditionally more power' ends of the 12 dimensions (Hornberger & Skilton-Sylvester, 2000: 99).

That is, within the Welsh and Basque viewpoint, the Continua set the challenge and define the agenda. This is to move successively along the 12 literacy dimensions towards increasing power for Welsh language literacy. For example, this involves continuing to celebrate Welsh literacy in its written production forms, but also 'contesting the traditional power weighting of the continua by paying attention to and granting agency and voice to actors and practices that have traditionally been the less powerful ends of the continua' (Hornberger & Skilton-Sylvester, 2000: 99).

Between the 1920s and the 1990s, the Welsh protested about power structures and resisted English dominance. This has now changed to beginning to believe that power lies within, that Welsh language and its attendant literacy should have political voice, taking the initiative in gaining power and control (e.g. the recent establishment of Wales' own parliament – the National Assembly). Where there is still 'doffing the cap to England' as in the literacy formulations of Wales' National Curriculum, voice and agency are beginning to be seized by Welsh language and Welsh literacy interests (e.g. transliteracy classrooms).

Concluding Remarks about the Continua

Not for the geometrically faint hearted, the Continua of Biliteracy (Hornberger, 1989; Hornberger & Skilton-Sylvester, 2000) provide a comprehensive and highly developed conceptual framework for sociolinguists and educationalists and a conceptually clarifying tool that ensures a deep analytical approach to biliteracy. This chapter demonstrates that the Continua are productive in interpreting and especially reinterpreting Welsh minority language literacy and biliteracy. In this chapter, the Welsh situation is utilized to demonstrate that the Continua are valuable in analysis beyond education, enriching historical, contemporary and predictive perspectives on the Welsh language.

The Continua framework successfully outlines crucial parameters and processes, attempts to explain the biliteracy phenomena, helps integrate a diversity of findings, locates key parameters and interactions, helps predict outcomes and patterns of biliterate behavior, and lucidly expresses the various conditions that allow the framework to be appropriate in a variety of contexts.

The Continua tend to escape the typical limitations of many frameworks and typologies: (1) frameworks often inadvertently suggest static systems whereas the interactive and integrative multidimensioning of the Continua ensures that personal and societal evolution and change is not only possible but expected; (2) frameworks may stereotype and restrict difference and variety in, for example, educational practice – to its credit, the Continua framework, partly by its complexity, expects wide and many variations within and across different environments; (3) frameworks often address 'inputs' and 'outputs' of, for example, the education system, but less frequently address the more complex classroom process. The Continua relate directly and explicitly to micro contexts and thereby to processes along a variety of dimensions (Hornberger, 1990). As the discussion of 'transliteracy' revealed, it anticipates debates about process strategies and classroom actions; and (4) frameworks typically do not, by themselves, explain success or failure and the relative effectiveness of practices, or predict outcomes. The Continua framework successfully provides a comprehensive starting point for the analysis of success and effectiveness. It is also a conceptual tool for policy makers who have to predict the consequences of their actions.

The Continua educate us to include an expansive range of issues and depth of treatment in such policy analyses and, as this chapter has exemplified, provide a robust tool for critiquing systems (e.g. for biases, absences, unequal power relations). Indeed, it is the new Continua of

Hornberger and Skilton-Sylvester (2000) with their power and status dimensioning that serves to politically enlighten, engaging key issues of politics and policy, not least in Wales.

References

Baker, C. (1985) *Aspects of Bilingualism in Wales*. Clevedon: Multilingual Matters.

Baker, C. (1993) Bilingual education in Wales. In H.B. Beardsmore (ed.) *European Models of Bilingual Education* (pp. 7–29). Clevedon: Multilingual Matters.

Baker, C. and Jones, M.P. (2000) Welsh language education: A strategy for revitalisation. In C.H. Williams (ed.) *Language Revitalisation: Policy and Planning* (pp. 116–37). Cardiff: University of Wales Press.

Davies, J. (1993) *The Welsh Language*. Cardiff: University of Wales Press.

Davies, J. (1994) *A History of Wales*. London, New York: Penguin Books.

Davies, J. (2000) Welsh. In G. Price (ed.) *Languages in Britain and Ireland*. (pp. 78–108). Oxford: Blackwell.

Davies, R.R. (1990) *Conquest, Coexistence and Change, 1063–1415*. Oxford: Clarendon Press.

Fishman, J.A. (1972) *The Sociology of Language*. Rowley, MA: Newbury House.

Fishman, J.A. (1980) Bilingualism and biculturalism as individual and as societal phenomena. *Journal of Multilingual and Multicultural Development* 1 (1), 3–15.

Fishman, J.A. (2001a) Conclusions: From theory to practice (and vice versa). In J.A. Fishman (ed.) *Can Threatened Languages be Saved?* (pp. 451–83). Clevedon: Multilingual Matters.

Fishman, J.A. (2001b) Why is it so hard to save a threatened language? In J.A. Fishman (ed.) *Can Threatened Languages be Saved?* (pp. 1–22). Clevedon: Multilingual Matters.

Hornberger, N.H. (1989) Continua of biliteracy. *Review of Educational Research* 59 (3), 271–96.

Hornberger, N.H. (1990) Creating successful learning contexts for bilingual literacy. *Teachers College Record* 92 (2), 212–29.

Hornberger, N.H. and Skilton-Sylvester, E. (2000) Revisiting the continua of biliteracy: International and critical perspectives. *Language and Education* 14 (2), 96–122.

Jacobson, R. (1990) Allocating two languages as a key feature of a bilingual methodology. In R. Jacobson and C. Faltis (eds) *Language Distribution Issues in Bilingual Schooling* (pp. 3–17). Clevedon: Multilingual Matters.

Jenkins, G.H. (1993) *Foundations of Modern Wales: 1642–1780*. Oxford: Oxford University Press.

Morgan, K.O. (1990) *Rebirth of a Nation, 1880–1980*. Oxford: Oxford University Press.

National Assembly for Wales (2000a) *Key Stages 1 and 2 of the National Curriculum in Wales*. Cardiff: National Assembly for Wales.

National Assembly for Wales (2000b) *Digest of Welsh Local Area Statistics 2000*. Cardiff: National Assembly for Wales.

OPCS (Office of Population, Censuses and Surveys) (1994) *Cyfrifiad 1991, Cymraeg/1991 Census, Welsh Language*. HMSO: London.

Sridhar, K.K. (1996) Societal multilingualism. In S.L. McKay and N.H. Hornberger (eds) *Sociolinguistics and Language Teaching* (pp. 47–70). Cambridge: Cambridge University Press.

Welsh Language Board (1999) *Review of the Publishing Grant Administered by the Welsh Books Council*. Cardiff: Welsh Language Board.

Welsh Language Board (2000) *The Welsh Language: A Vision and Mission for 2000–2005*. Cardiff: Welsh Language Board.

Williams, C. (1994) Arfarniad o ddulliau dysgu ac addysgu yng nghyd-destun addysg uwchradd ddwyieithog. Unpublished Ph.D. thesis. Bangor: University of Wales.

Williams, G. (1999) *Wales and the Reformation*. Cardiff: University of Wales Press.

WWW site for further information:

Welsh Language Board, available at http://www.bwrdd-yr-iaith.org.uk/.

Chapter 4

A Luta Continua![1]: *The Relevance of the Continua of Biliteracy to South African Multilingual Schools*

CAROLE BLOCH AND NEVILLE ALEXANDER

Language Policy and Planning in South Africa

For reasons connected with the recent history of South Africa, one of the most interesting developments in national language policy and planning has been taking place during the past five years. In order to understand the significance of this development in terms of the continua of biliteracy model, we give a brief sketch of the language situation in the country.

There are 11 official languages. Of these, English is the dominant and hegemonic language because of its global status as the language of business, the internet, etc., but also because it has served in the course of many decades of struggle as the, to some extent mythical, language of national unity and language of liberation. There is no doubt at all that it has been, and continues to be, the language of wider communication for all middle-class South Africans, including the current political class.

Situated along the micro–macro context continuum, between English and the indigenous African languages, is Afrikaans. This language has a very special South African history, which cannot be discussed in any detail in the present context. It came to be associated with the struggle of the Afrikaner people against British imperialism for the domination of the wealth and of the black people of South Africa and specifically with the racist policies and practices of the Afrikaner nationalist movement, which was the author of apartheid. As a result black South Africans came to regard it as 'the language of the oppressor'. This negative language attitude is only now beginning to abate somewhat. However, the real power of Afrikaans as the lingua franca of the commercial farming zone and of the formerly white-dominated rural towns makes it a language that it is still necessary to learn for purely economic reasons. The actual, as opposed to the reputed, policy of the present government tends to scale down the importance and status of the language in the public domain and this is giving rise to passionate resistance on the part of the majority of native Afrikaans-speaking people, including those who are not labelled 'white' (some 50%).

Close to the micro end of the continuum lie clustered together the nine indigenous African languages which were accorded official status in 1993–4. The hierarchy even among these languages is of major significance in the South African context since the allocation of the meagre resources that are available for the development and modernisation of these languages (called 'marginalised languages' in new-South African speak) depends on where in terms of power/status along the continua they are officially deemed to be located. Roughly, we could say that Zulu, Xhosa, Tswana, Pedi, Sotho, Tsonga, Swati, Ndebele and Venda in that order constitute a segment of the steep gradient of South Africa's official languages. They all have very few high-status functions and the attitude of most of their native speakers could be described by the term 'static maintenance syndrome' (*pace* Baker, 1996), i.e. they are prepared to keep their languages alive for community and family uses but see no point in trying to develop and modernise them for higher economic, political and cultural functions.[2]

At the very weakest end are found the other indigenous (mainly Khoisan) languages, which do not have official status and can be described without melodrama as endangered languages. Spread across this particular continuum at various points is a large number of so-called heritage, or ancestral, languages of mostly European and Asian provenance. None of these obtains official financial support from government (unlike the Khoisan languages) but they are constitutionally recognised as languages to be respected and permitted freedom of usage.

Constitutionally, the government of South Africa is obliged to 'develop' the African languages and to afford all official languages 'parity of esteem and equitable usage' in the public domain. This noble injunction has, however, hitherto been honoured in the breach because of the hegemonic status of English and the apparently irresistible drift towards official unilingualism in the public service. The dynamic of the situation is best described in the following manner. Like every South African, the members of the government know that with very few exceptions every native South African grows up knowing at least two South African languages to one or other degree of proficiency. They know, therefore, that the foundations for a policy of bilingual education exist and that, with appropriate retraining of the teaching corps, such a policy could be translated into practice without much cost within a period of five to 10 years. Such a commitment would have major positive implications for economic development as well as for the promotion of national unity and national identity. One of the provisos for the success of such a policy (which exists on paper already) is that all Afrikaans and English speakers should be encouraged to learn one of the official African languages as a first or second additional language. For reasons connected with recent reviews of educational policy, the government is inching its way towards realisation of such a language policy in education (see note 4). Moreover, every single independent committee and board which the government has appointed in order to plan and to help formulate language policy consistent with the principles of the constitution has reported in ways that unambiguously point to the realisation of a multilingual dispensation in which all the official languages will share high-status and other functions.[3]

It would be wrong to say that members of the present government are opposed to the modernisation and development of the African languages. Indeed, there are a few stalwarts among them who are fully committed to this goal. However, the majority of government functionaries seem not to understand the connection between economic growth, democracy and social stability on the one hand and an optimal language policy on the other. Since the relevant provisions of the constitution, if truth be told, are the consequence of the Afrikaners' passion for Afrikaans and the insistence, therefore, of the Afrikaner nationalist negotiators during the Codesa talks in 1990–3 on the continued equality of Afrikaans and English in the public domain, there is very little real drive and commitment on the part of the black political elite. Most of them would be perfectly happy to let the situation develop as it did in most postcolonial African countries, where the former colonial language (English, French or Portuguese) became the only official language. This is what has happened most recently once again in Namibia. In their culpable short-sightedness, they justify this policy by means of spurious arguments about the 'costs of multilingualism'. The fact that this policy slide, which, by default, amounts to the implementation of a neo-apartheid language policy, implies that mediocrity and failure are necessarily programmed into most national undertakings is beyond the horizon of the leadership at present.

In effect, therefore, most of the rulers of the country find themselves in contradiction with their constitutional mandate. As in all such cases, short of tyrannical action, the bureaucratic class simply defers the evil moment, they filibuster and use amphibolous language in order to hide their discomfort. On the other hand, the same constitution affords many opportunities to those who, for whatever reasons, want to use the democratic space provided in the language provisions to promote the rights of their own and of other languages and to ensure the development, modernisation and empowerment of languages other than English. It is in this context that both the larger strategic moves made at the level of language planning and policy evolution, as well as grassroots and local initiatives at the level of pilot projects for the promotion of, for instance, bilingual education and biliteracy, should be evaluated. In some ways, these are attempts to pre-empt possible language conflict in the future and to anticipate the problems that must arise once this, or some successor, government eventually is compelled to implement the language clauses of the constitution and of the very progressive-sounding language legislation we are now crafting.

To put the situation in terms of contexts for biliteracy, it ought to be clear that what is at stake at the powerful ends of the continua is the gradual shift of power towards the languages of the majority of the people, who continue in linguistic terms to be treated as a social minority. At this level, many different political and social scenarios are possible. At present, the white Afrikaans-speaking population is mobilising for the retention of the status and powerful functions of Afrikaans, for example as a language of tuition at universities and other tertiary educational institutions. Strategically, the problem they have to overcome is to do this without slipping in the racist agenda of protecting the privileges of a segment of the white 'minority'. Some of the more insightful people, therefore, are trying to get them to accept that they can only attain their sociolinguistic (and other socio-political) goals if they create a coalition, not necessarily a formal one, with individuals and groups who represent the other African languages in order to fight for the equality of rights, resources and functions of all South African languages within a clearly understood framework of functional multilingualism, which does not depend on unnecessary duplication of documentation. In the process of forming such networks, inevitably the other language communities are beginning to make demands which hitherto have been latent but the articulation of which would have been seen by most of the leadership elements as demanding too much too soon or as upsetting the applecart. Such is the dialectic of South African history. As the consequence of Mephistophelean logic, we have the situation today where the gains made for Afrikaans to a large extent as a result of the privileging of the white Afrikaans-speaking community are being placed at the disposal of the languages of the black people. For example, dictionary units are being established for the African languages and the expertise of the Afrikaans lexicographers is being used to train others. Similarly, interpreting and translation techniques are being transferred gradually from Afrikaans practitioners to others.

It is clear, therefore, that the power shift and the struggle around discourses will characterise the language domain for a long time to come. At a micro level, the kind of projects described in what follows is demonstrating as well as reclaiming the power of the powerless. It is to be expected that the cumulative effect of these processes, multiplied in their thousands throughout the country as a matter of necessity, will eventually become manifest as a real change in the balance of power. Of course, this cannot be considered in isolation of other developments at the global level.

The Continua of Biliteracy and South African Multilingual Primary Schooling

The continua of biliteracy model provides a framework for reflection and action on multilingual education work in South Africa. We will provide an illustration of this through a description of some of the salient features of one of the few biliteracy programmes in the country, in one Cape Town school, Battswood Primary. In relation to the programme at Battswood, the model assists us by offering a kind of aerial view of the linguistic terrain, where the more and less fertile areas lie in stark contrast to each other. Because African languages in South Africa have low status as resources in South African economic life, the languages of the majority of the people of the country are treated like minority languages elsewhere, particularly in the realm of print. In terms of the struggle with power relations in the continua, this implies a different emphasis from that which applies to numerical minorities (such as immigrants) in countries of the north. While in no way diminishing the struggle for expression and development of the less powerful ends, it also includes asserting strongly the need for movement of African languages to the powerful ends of the continua. The programme we describe here is one aspect of a larger multilingual education project of PRAESA (Project for the Study of Alternative Education in South Africa). Among other things, PRAESA is trying to give body to the letter and the spirit of the official language policy in education, which was promulgated on 14 July 1997. This is a full-fledged policy of bilingual (or multilingual) education, which relies on additive bilingualism as the policy framework. Accordingly, it places the emphasis on home-language maintenance throughout the school career of the students and implicitly promotes the attainment of biliteracy as a policy goal.

But policy does not automatically change the myths in the minds of people or the practices that have come to make sense to them in their daily activities for many years. The belief that 'English is equal to education' prevails widely and is deeply carved into the psyche of people who have bitter memories of an inferior early education being forced on them through the medium of the mother tongue under apartheid. This has led people to view their own languages as impediments to progress. Some infer from this attitude of the speakers of the African languages that (in the interest of democracy) the language policy should be changed to a straight for English one (Taylor & Vingevold, 1999) and many teachers across the country feel that as parents want English, 'the sooner the better', this is what must be delivered. This syndrome has fatal influence in the schools too – from urban townships to rural situations, teachers express the view that they must teach in English like the 'multiracial' schools or else they will lose pupils (Gamede *et al.*, 2000; Pluddemann *et al.* 1998). Even at preschool level, where provision exists, the demand is for English (Bloch, 1999a). Many people see the situation as an 'either–or' one, rather than as mother tongue-plus (another one or two languages, one of which will usually be English).

About Battswood

Battswood Primary School is a formerly 'coloured' school, which has existed since 1891 in Wynberg, Cape Town, an area designated 'coloured' during the apartheid years. The school had Dutch Reformed Church ties from its earliest days – even today, the building belongs to the Church while the school falls under the control of the Western Cape Education Department. The school is well known in the area as a school that has produced community leaders. Initially Afrikaans medium, the school has, over the years, come to represent a dual language (Afrikaans/English) situation and in the early 1990s the school 'opened itself' to African language-speaking children as well. As the numbers of Xhosa-speaking children have increased, the medium rapidly shifted to become in effect English only.

Battswood is one of the many city schools where taxis full of children from the townships can be seen arriving and departing in 'transport' at beginning and end of each school day. African language-speaking families make tough financial and other sacrifices to send their children to the formerly 'coloured' and 'white' schools in the hope of getting them a good education. Wynberg is a very busy commercial area and a transport nodal point for Cape Town, with its large railway station and a route along which many taxis and buses travel regularly. Some parents work near the school as domestic, factory or railway workers, clerks and cleaners. Others, including a few who are teachers or social workers, work further afield.

While the majority of the Battswood children are now Xhosa speakers (see Table 4.1), the sensitive issue of how to support this reality by ensuring the presence of Xhosa-speaking teachers at school so that there can be communication between children and teachers has not yet been addressed effectively by government[4] and the teacher profile remains as it was before. This creates a structural communication problem between teachers and children. Of the 15 teachers at Battswood, the only staff who are not English- or Afrikaans-speaking have come through the programme we describe below, or by other ad hoc attempts by the school staff themselves. As at so many other schools, there is some openness towards improving the situation, and this positive intent leads the principal to write that 'we are multi-cultural and a multi-ethnic school in which there is a healthy respect for the different languages, cultures and traditions' (Battswood Primary School, 1998). It is, however, not possible for schools to make the kind of fundamental changes that are needed without substantial and committed support from the education department. Consequently, the school's cultural and linguistic climate tends 'naturally' to be an assimilative one for the relative newcomers, i.e. the Xhosa speaking children. Frustration levels have increased in schools where communication is impeded, and teachers complain that children increasingly lack discipline. Battswood is one of many schools open to some extent to suggestions for dealing with the 'language problem'. Often, schools with such a 'language problem' need assistance with much more than languages in classrooms since the 'language problem' is one aspect of a complex set of identity- and value-related intercultural issues which in fact need to be addressed urgently in the majority of South African schools.[5]

Table 4.1 Breakdown of children in Battswood Primary School in 2000 according to language

Afrikaans	*English*	*Xhosa*	*Other*	*Total*
89	51	404	10	554

Our Approach

Our intention is to develop, try out and demonstrate workable strategies for teaching and learning, using additive bilingualism approaches that can be adapted and used elsewhere in the country in comparable classroom situations. In doing so, our contexts are the less powerful micro, oral and multilingual ends of the continua as we develop ways to challenge the power relations that exist at macro, literate and monolingual English levels of the continua in the school[6] and the wider society.

While we engage with all aspects of the curriculum through the daily schedule, the children's mother tongue literacy and biliteracy development form the core of this work. Our focus is on a multilingual stream of children who are at the time of writing in their fourth year of primary school. A team consisting of Carole Bloch, a PRAESA early literacy specialist, and Ntombizanele Nkence, a Xhosa-speaking teacher employed by PRAESA, as well as Erica Fellies, a 'resident' Battswood teacher, worked closely with 30 Xhosa and 19 English/Afrikaans bilingual children from their first days in Grade 1 until the end of Grade 3.[7] Past apartheid language planning ensured English–Afrikaans bilingualism for most 'white' and 'coloured' people, but very few had the opportunity to learn an African language. Moreover, although most African language speakers are multilingual and know some English, enforced 'Bantu education' left many not knowing it well enough to be good role models for children to learn it competently from them. These facts, as well as the fact that the inferior nature of Bantu education, generally speaking, provided the poorest quality of teacher training for African language speakers, mean that one medium-term strategy is to combine and share pedagogical and linguistic resources through team teaching, an aspect of the programme we do not discuss any further in the present context.

The classroom community

The classroom situation that we have been developing provides all of the children with expanded linguistic opportunities and consequently with related opportunities for deepening mutual intercultural communication and acceptance that the other children in the school[8] as well as most other children in comparable former 'white' and 'coloured' schools do not have.[9]

We engage with aspects of all of the continua through our programme structure and teaching strategies. Regarding the media of biliteracy, we encourage simultaneous exposure for the Xhosa (XL1) and English speaking (EL1) children to both languages with an emphasis on the children's first language (L1). As we have indicated, most of the Afrikaans- and English-speaking children are actually already bilingual to varying extents – at home and in their community settings they are exposed to, and use, both languages for different purposes. Because Afrikaans is a relatively high-status language and because all of the children have in common their parents' wish for them to learn English, we are concentrating mainly on Xhosa and English, while at the same time not excluding Afrikaans.[10] Our ongoing challenge, in terms of Xhosa language learning for the English/Afrikaans speakers is to try and inspire them enough, and teach the language in ways that motivate them to learn 'against the odds' of any real incentives which promote Xhosa as either necessary or even desirable in the wider society. This is different for the Xhosa speakers; weighty incentives to tap into English with unrelenting focus seem to permeate the air we breathe. These range from homes, via the sacrifices parents make in order to send their children to an 'English medium' school, to the seduction of the English language print and other media they experience, as well as the English language that influential adult role models speak around them.

First principles

The pedagogical principles that guide our endeavour at Battswood are ones we understand to underpin sound educational practice in early childhood education (Bruce, 1987), early literacy (Goodman, 1986; Holdaway, 1979), and bilingual education (Cummins, 1996; Gregory, 1996) in overlapping and mutually reinforcing ways. For our purposes, we have summarised the main ones thus:

- Appropriate teaching begins with and builds on what children know. This principle applied in multilingual contexts supports prioritising and developing the language/s which the children already know and use.
- Language is viewed as a resource rather than as a problem.
- All aspects of language are interrelated and understandings in one aspect help to develop and support other aspects. Reading, writing, speaking, listening and, in a multilingual society, also translating and interpreting should all be developed and supported.
- The ways that children learn to write are similar to how they learn to speak – in a social environment children actively construct their own hypotheses about the nature of language, test these out and

reshape them in terms of real encounters in their daily lives (Ferreiro & Teberosky, 1993).
- Each of us is a learner and a teacher, and teachers and children learn from each other.
- Mistakes are critical – they offer insights about the learner's understandings.
- Children learning literacy benefit from teaching approaches that see literacy as social and cultural practices (Street, 1995), with concentration on involving children in using written language for real and personally meaningful reasons. Emphasis as children learn to read and write is on use, with mechanical skills being learned in context as teachers assist children to read and write for a range of purposeful reasons.

All of this means that children's linguistic strengths need to be encouraged, supported and maintained rather than inhibited or negated. For most of our children as they begin primary school this is their oral proficiency in their mother tongue.[11] At the same time we need to help them to build on these oral strengths by expanding these to include and explore the literacies of the languages of their homes and the classroom. We do this by establishing daily space for stories, for talk and writing about their concerns, ideas and feelings. This implies a concentration of energies diametrically opposed to that generally widespread in similar schools, i.e. remediating children's perceived deficits in English as well as other related deficiencies (Bloch, 1999b).

Parents, teachers and children have all had to invest in the endeavour by being prepared to take risks. All of the parents have had to set aside their fear that time spent using two languages in the classroom means their children get less English, take longer to learn it, and do not learn it well.

Apart from accepting the challenge of team teaching in two languages, the teachers have had to move from the safety of the decontextualised content of a rigid phonics-based part-to-whole skills programme to face the real evidence of what their pupils actually know and can do, thereby drawing on contextualised, vernacular, 'minority' (i.e. majority) knowledge.[12] This implies a real shift of pedagogical paradigm to a simple yet profound understanding of children as being capable of constructing knowledge and meaning. The children, already well in tune with the societally pervasive belief in early literacy learning as being 'copy and colour-in', have had to struggle to find or reclaim their own writing (and reading) process.

Considering Strategies for Teaching and Learning Biliteracy – Accessing Resources

Developing strategies for classroom literacy teaching, which view literacy as socio-cultural practice (Gee, 1990; Heath, 1983; Street, 1995), must begin from the premise that few South Africans have a well-developed culture of reading and writing in any language. These are usually the progeny of middle-class, overwhelmingly 'white', families. What environmental print there is to be seen in greater Cape Town and in the school (as in most similar South African schools) is usually in English. Unlike the situation in the countries of the economic North, we cannot assume that most young children will have come across written language in personally and socially meaningful ways as they enter primary school for the first time (Taylor & Dorsey-Gaines, 1988). Literature barely exists in the African languages for adults and even less so for young children.[13] In the vast majority of homes and schools, books are a rare luxury, and teachers certainly do not associate teaching reading and writing in the early years with engagement with stories in books[14] – talk about books in most school situations implies textbooks. It is normal in vast numbers of homes throughout the country to conduct daily business in oral rather than written mode; many young children encounter few or no regular social uses of literacy in the languages of their homes and communities, and thus have few if any opportunities to develop a propensity towards literacy (Holdaway, 1979). This is exacerbated by the first weeks and months of school being characterised by large doses of decontextualised phonics-laden reading and writing 'skills' that tend to crush creativity, initiative and interest in reading and writing at the outset. This is the situation for most children in most South African schools (Bloch, 1997; Gamede *et al.*, 2000), and certainly it is so at Battswood.

For these reasons, using the continua framework in multilingual 'third world' conditions exposes another dimension thereof. This can be thought of as a struggle for *access* to resources, both human and material in various languages for education generally and specifically for embedding literacy into the social and cultural practices of communities. It relates to paucity at one pole and abundance at the other, with sufficiency lying somewhere in the middle.

A task for teachers wanting to create conditions for biliteracy to flourish is to work towards providing sufficient access by creating a multilingual print-rich classroom environment that simultaneously takes substance from and feeds back into the children's daily home and community practices as they develop opportunities for stimulating them towards a variety of meaningful and real engagements with print. In this way, we carry out work similar to that discussed by Luis Moll, the approach which he explains is:

> influenced in great part by Vygotsky's (1978) and Luria's (1981) formulation of how social practices and the use of cultural artefacts mediate thinking, [and it] highlights how classrooms (or households) are always socially and culturally organised settings, artificial creations, whose specific practices mediate the intellectual work children accomplish. (Moll, 1992: 21)

In doing so, we engage continuously with the status of English (and to a lesser extent, Afrikaans) as the perceived 'legitimate' language for writing, as well as the related issue concerning the current scarcity of uses and materials for literacy in Xhosa. All of our strategies involve trying to improve the status of Xhosa as an oral and written language in the classroom, and where possible in the school.

We hold the view that there are various 'roots' of literacy (Goodman, 1984: 103) and that the 'funds of knowledge' in the children's homes and communities provide a crucial resource for learning (Moll, 1992). We are cautious not to focus myopically on what is a largely middle-class practice of storybook reading as the pinnacle of possible literacy practices as we are aware that there is a danger that we could neglect to recognise and support other real routes. However, under apartheid, the almost total disregard for real stories in teacher education and school curricula has contributed to the desert-like conditions for stimulating children's imaginations and creativity in early childhood classrooms. So we place equal importance on writing and reading, and within this we structure our programme around story reading and engagement with books as well as building ongoing opportunities for purposeful and authentic writing.

Language is talk and print

Many of the activities we engage in at a classroom curricular and pedagogical level challenge the more powerful ends of the media, development and content continua. Our working definition of biliteracy concurs with Hornberger's definition of biliteracy as referring to 'any and all instances in which communication occurs in two (or more) languages in or around writing' (Hornberger, 1990: 213). The children all receive simultaneous exposure to both Xhosa and English texts and to reading and writing in both languages illustrated by the following extract from Erica Fellies' (1998) diary:

> Monday 11th May 1998
>
> The day started off with the Xhosa speakers with Ntombi and the non-Xhosa speakers with me. We both told them a story about the sisters. I elaborated by asking the children to dramatise the events in the story. This was then followed by showing them the paper plates of different faces. . . . What I found very interesting was that Ntombi and myself work together after telling the story to the 2 groups. We put the faces up on the board and asked them to label the feelings. Here the children were exposed to both English and Xhosa terminology. The Xhosa speakers gave us the Xhosa terms and vice versa with the English speakers.

We encourage oral, mother tongue and bilingual interaction. When Teacher Ntombi speaks with the Xhosa speakers in Xhosa, and they to her, there is of course an easy communication, a lightness and quickness of voice. She is alert to the fact that one of her tasks is to counter 'the assimilative "charm" of English which pulls students' biliterate development towards English' (Hornberger & Skilton-Sylvester, 2000: 101) and will initiate conversations in Xhosa, or answer in Xhosa when she notices the swing to English. The impact of such smooth and effective communication on the attitudes of young English/Afrikaans speakers cannot be underrated as a means of combating the development of racist attitudes in a society like South Africa where innumerable African language role models tend to appear incompetent as a result of being 'forced' to communicate through a medium of which they have a limited grasp.

In Grade 1, to develop the children's linguistic repertoire, to enable play with language, language awareness and value for the classroom languages, the teachers sang many songs and did rhymes with the whole class, providing substance and support for the oral, receptive and L1 ends of the development continua. At first, the teachers were anxious that these young children might get confused if they made 'an issue' about which language they were using, and tended to use them spontaneously, but without being explicit. They came to realise that the children were already consciously and actively 'tuned into' the bilingualism of the situation. They began to build on these insights, by discussing the languages we use as positive achievements and useful resources. An initial strategy offering a direct route to developing mutual respect for each other's languages was to write up the words of the song or rhyme and display these on the walls. This, too, provided the teachers with further evidence that the children were more capable than they had thought. At first they were sceptical about displaying the songs or rhymes in printed form, as the children couldn't read yet. But the children did begin to help each other read the displays and both English and Xhosa speakers began to develop concepts about print that related to both languages.

In the absence of appropriate Xhosa material to use at school and to take home to read, we typed up the rhymes and songs, put them in plastic sleeves, an English one on one side, and a Xhosa one on the other.[15] The teachers suggested that the children 'read these to a friend who speaks a different language from you'. This strategy has been useful for enabling a balance of power among the English- and Xhosa-speaking children, each having something positive to offer on their mother tongue side of the sheet. It also reached out in a small way to challenge home life, and we received feedback from some parents that they were proud that their children were beginning to read another language and that they were learning from it too.[16]

We sometimes bump directly into situations where English print literally forces the children out of using Xhosa. In an early project about the food we eat, the children wrote about the kinds of food they eat at home and their favourite meals. The children loved the task – and they had the choice of using either Xhosa or English. They then moved into looking at real food items by using the 'junkmail' newspaper advertisements of foodstuffs available at the shops. While in the initial stages of this project many of the children had been working in Xhosa, with the introduction of junkmail products they noticed that everything printed was in English. When the teachers invited them to make an advertisement for their favourite product, these 'naturally' appeared in English. This incident was one of many which keep us alert to the fact that completely free choice about which language to use does not work, and that we need to exert ongoing emphasis on Xhosa writing.

Interactive writing

We give a lot of attention to vernacular, contextualised 'minority' (i.e. majority) (see note 12) content through interactive writing in order to change existing school-based notions of early writing as consisting of sets of decontextualised skills which have to be taught one after the other and in one print language after the other in bilingual contexts. Like Robinson *et al.* we felt that:

> It was not appropriate to think of authorship as something which happened after children had learned to write neatly and spell correctly. We knew that young children were able to function as

authors from the beginning and that it was experience of authorship which led to the refinement of writing. (1990: 11)

Interactive writing provides a means of igniting children's initiative to take the lead in developing writing for themselves and it counters the dearth of reading material in Xhosa. It also provides authentic samples of and reasons for writing and reading in Xhosa (and English) and offers children various ways to express themselves through print.

Robinson *et al.* explain how dialogue journals and letter writing makes writing easier for children because: 'although unfamiliar to many children, they allow children to write with their own voices. Writers are not made to look inadequate by a failure to understand literary genre conventions'(1990: 11). One of us wrote letters to the children in English, and another in Xhosa. Although at the time we were regular visitors to the classroom, there were often quite long spaces between our visits, and the children took to the idea of writing letters like ducks to water. The excitement and energy for self-expression and communication with others in the classroom is often palpable.

All the letters, except Letter 7, were responses to letters initiated by Carole Bloch and Babazile Mahlasela. They were about real 'happenings' (and sometimes their feeling around these) in their lives and their invitations to the children to respond. Letter 7 was a letter which the children wanted to write to President Mbeki because of their concern over the rising crime in the country, which affects many of their lives directly. They wrote to Neville, because their teachers suggested that this might be a reliable way of ensuring that the letters reached President Mbeki.

We have chosen Zindi's letters as typifying what we see to varying extents in most of the children: a developing fluency and willingness to engage in written communication in both languages over a period of time.

Letter 1 **15 February 99**: response to short introductory letters giving information about the things we do with our days and a question asked about what they were doing at school.

Letter 2 **15 June 99**: response to Carole's letter about getting cross and frustrated when the printer didn't work, and a question about what makes the children cross.

Letter 3 **15 June 99**: response to Babazile who had travelled to Swaziland, and she asked them where they have travelled.

Letter 4 **18 June 99**: response to Carole's inquiry about an outing to the local station.

Battswood Primary
Gosport Road
Wynberg
15 February 1999
Dear Miss Carole
Molo Miss Babazile
We bibi sums
From Zindi

Dear Miss Carole, Molo Miss Babazile,

We did sums, From Zindi.

Letter 1

Letter 5 **28 July 99**: response to a letter from Babazile asking the children to help her with a problem. She needed to go away to England for a year and was being asked to go without her little boy. What should she do?

Letter 6 **14 October 99**: response to Babazile, who did in the end have to go without her child, Simphiwe, and wrote from England, asking what present she should bring back to him.

Letter 7 **June 99**: letter to President Mbeki via Neville Alexander.

15 June 1999

Dear Miss carole

I go to My sister and I ask for a banana and she said No

wan I go to my Mothers bad She said get of my bad

wan I ask my Mother for a seet She said No

from zindi

Dear Miss Carole,

(What makes me cross is when) I go to my sister and I ask for a banana and she said no. When I go to my mothers bed (and) she said 'get off my bed'. when I ask my mother for a sweet she said 'no'.

From Zindi.

Letter 2

15 June 1999
Molo Miss Babazile from Zindi

1.badiya a Cradock
2.Kwa Zulunatali
3.badiyaa a monty   I went to Monti
4.badiya a bayi   " " eBhayi
5.badiya a Somasety   " " " Somerset

Molo Miss Babazile, from Zindi.
Bendiye eCradock, Kwa-Zulu Natal.
Bendiye eMonti.
Bendiye eBhayi.
Bendiye eSomerset.

We went to Cradock, Kwa-Zulu Natal. We went to East London. We went to Port Elizabeth. We went to Somerset.

Letter 3

18 June 1999 Molo Miss Carole
si Pumepaphe samaelinin Sahobasayaa
Stesheen sai fik sa nawkaizitepsi sa
gen Pasikeapbeyi sa Jykor gas koph sama
ky Plet form Samonteta se Phaizitepsy
from zindi

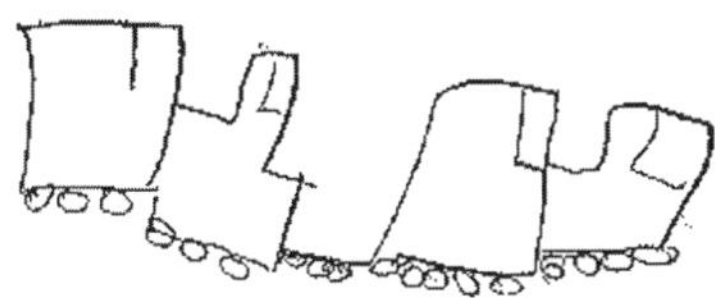

Molo Miss Carole,

Siphume apha sama elayini. Sahamba saya estishini. Sakafika sanyuka izitepsi sangena ? . Sanyuka ? sama kwi platform, sama satheta ezitepsini.

We got out (of the classroom) and lined up. We went to the station. We got there, we went up the steps and we got in ? . We went up ? and stood by the platform and we talked by the stairs.

Letter 4

28.07.99

Molo Miss Babazile Zindi

You can not live your BaBy

'Be cose He is to smol

Be cose He is going to Be Cross

You can go with hyim

Molo Miss Babazile,

You cannot leave your baby because he is too small [and] because he is going to be cross. You can go with him.

Zindi.

Letter 5

14 October 1999 Molo Miss Babazile
Kumandi kumu akuomand kuwe
mnadishushe gnakubagnu 25 dikuxelele
sihlobsam kufuneka umthengele
iroper koper uphinde umthengele iteki
Kumandi kwelilizwe lam kumandi esikolweni
kodwa kuyabethwa eskolweni kobwaggabt
weskoleni from Zindi

Molo Miss Babazile,

Kumnandi kum akhukho mnandi kuwe. Mna ndishushu ngokuba ngu 25. Ndikuxelele sihlobo sam kufuneka umthengele I 'Roper Koper'. Kufuneka umthengele iteki. Kumnandi kwelilizwe lam. Kumnandi esikolweni kodwa kuyabethwa esikolweni kodwa ? wesikolweni.

From Zindi.

I am fine. You are not fine [*without your child*].
I am warm, 25 degrees. I'm telling you my friend, you must buy him a 'Roper Koper'. Also buy him tackies [*canvas shoes*]. *It's very nice in my country. School is very nice. But at the school we are beaten. But ? to school.*

Letter 6

Dear Mr Nevile

I want you to stop the crime, Beacouse lots of peaple die of crime and this crime must. How did you become a presedent but you must write me back please. Beacouse when I am big I am going to be one. Write to me in xosa please. from Zindi mankayi

Letter 7

Writing journals

Journal writing gives another reason for writing that allows for 'minority', vernacular and contextualised content. It has also provided another way for the teachers to deepen their understanding of the children – to get to know them better, and to weave the hard work of literacy learning and teaching into the substance of their real lives, through their own voices. Even more so than with letter writing, the children are being given the space to write what they want to. The teachers write back, usually Erica uses English and Ntombi, Xhosa. It is also a significant (literacy) learning process for them. The texture and breadth of their own written responses are evolving gradually over time.[17] They are realising the value of such written dialogue and developing a heightened sense of responsibility and empathy, becoming people whom children can trust enough to confide in. Erica describes how:

> Ntombi and I absolutely love reading the journals because we get to know our children better. I find that the topics they choose . . . are so interesting because many of the children would write about their home life. . . . The children are so enthusiastic about their journals, and they don't see it as schoolwork. They get frantic when we leave their journals at home or if they can't find their journals. I remember one time when Ntombi was late and she had some journals with her, they basically attacked her when she came in because they had some things to write in their journals. They would also nag in the mornings to write in their journals. I absolutely love this idea. (Fellies, 2000)

Journal writing also offers direct routes to essential and relevant curriculum material. A child confided in her journal to Ntombi that she was afraid that her sister had caught Aids, because she had 'slept with' her cousin who has Aids. Ntombi inquired further and discovered that the child understood 'slept with' in the literal sense of sharing a sleeping space to be a way of transmitting the virus. Once they realised the need, the teachers could plan essential life skills lessons.

One journal extract from Zindi (using her original formulations and spellings), writing with Ntombi, shows vividly how home life experiences (vernacular, contextualised content), in this case 'the rural areas', can both connect with, and have a place in the classroom as well as help a child to discover more about her world. It seems as if Zindi was comparing cows with cars as a guide for checking on just how rural Mdantsane actually is:

> February 2000
>
> **Z**: *Bendiye emaxhoseni ndaleqwa hinkom ndiyigezele. Ndacol iswazi ndaybetha ndangena endlini.*
> (I was in the rural areas and a cow that I was teasing chased me. I picked up a stick and I hit the cow, chasing it away and I went in the house.)
>
> **T**: *Ubusithini xa ubuyigezela? Yhu unesibindi. Mna bendizakubaleka qha.*
> (How were you teasing it? Yhu, you are so brave. I would have just run away.)
>
> **Z**: *Bendiyinyonyzele ndayisuzela ndayi jula nga maanzi ndabetha ithole.*
> (I made funny faces and I farted at it and I threw water at it and I beat the cow's calf.)

T: *Uzoya nini ngoku emaxhoseni?*
(When are you going again?)

Z: *Ndizakuya ngeholidayi ezayo. Wena uzoyanini na wena?*
(I'm going in the next holidays. When are you going?)

T: *EMdantsane? Ngeholide kaDisemba.*
(To Mdantsane? During December holidays.)

Z: *Zikhona imoto apho. Zikhona inkomo apho. Zingapi.*
(Are there cars there? Are there cows there? How many are they?)

T: *Azikho iinkomo, kodwa zikhona iimoto. Zininzi andinokwazi ukuzibala.*
(There are no cows but there are cars. They are so many I wouldn't be able to count them.)

Z: *Baandi phazami utsho eziphi imoto. Zingaphi imoto zakho wenu. Zezo uzixelayo ezininzi zakowenu.*
(If I am not mistaken which cars are you talking about? How many cars [are there] at your house? Are these the many cars you are talking about at your house?

T: *Akukho moto ekhaya. Kodwa iitshomi zam zinee moto. Ipolo, Toyota neGolf. Zintle. Xa ndinemali ndokuyithenga nam. Unayo umama wakho imoto?*
(There are no cars at home. But my friends have got cars. They have Polo, Toyota and Golf. They are beautiful. When I have money I'll also buy one. Does your mother have a car?)

Z: *Hayi akanayo imoto kodwa utata wam unayo imoto. Yitoyota. Iblue.*
(No she doesn't have a car but my father does have a car. It is a Toyota. It's blue.)

T: *Unethamsanqa.*
(You are lucky.)

As this collaborative and interactive writing process develops over time, we have become increasingly aware of the potential of such direct, consistent and committed one-to-one relationships through writing for the development of meaningful education, not only for children, but for their teachers as well. We also see that progress takes time, for some children more so than for others. In giving priority to using this time, teachers and children together create models for nurturing authentic and purposeful writing and reading that is taking place at the pace and level of each child. It may be that this is the shortest cut that can be taken for rooting autonomous writing and reading habits into our classroom communities in one or more languages (and potentially at any level of schooling) in print-scarce environments.

Wallowing in stories

Sharing storybooks nurtures contextualised content, the reception and L1 ends of the development continua and provides simultaneous exposure to print in two languages. We have gathered an adequate selection of Xhosa picture storybooks translated from English and available in both languages.[18] The teachers read daily stories in both Xhosa and English (and sometimes Afrikaans). When possible, each language group has the story first in their own language, and subsequently hears it in the other language as well. When the children make comments or respond to teacher questions about the story, we can see that the Xhosa speakers' receptive and productive knowledge of Xhosa and English is more advanced than that of the English/Afrikaans speakers. The XL1 speakers respond generally in the language they have been addressed in or the language of the story. The E/AL1 children's responses indicate that they are developing understanding, but they answer in English. When browsing, the children choose books from either language, and often collaborate around the story in bilingual pairs or groups. There is also more formal reading instruction where the children are separated into home language groups, for both English and Xhosa reading. There are regular times for the children to wallow in storybooks. Like all of us, they need unpressurised time to explore the wholeness and richness of the language of books.

Developing and assessing multilingual strengths

The children have a lot to deal with as they move through their third year of schooling, beginning to read and write in two languages with an emphasis on communication and self-expression. It is easy to become insecure when we notice how much some of the children still have to learn, particularly with their spelling and in terms of neat handwriting. We remind ourselves how important it is to take into consideration the dimension of access, which affects most of our children. Time and nurturing are required for intellectual growth and more so with meagre access to essential resources which are so taken for granted in 'literate environments'. Several of the children in the class write with growing confidence in both languages, using invented spellings (Bissex, 1980; Kress, 2000) that are still far removed from conventional forms. On this matter of spelling we echo the words of Gunther Kress as he discusses examples of emergent writing, in the knowledge that our emerging biliterate children are walking sure-footedly, albeit along a dry dirt road:

> although the sense here is clear, the knowledge of words and their component elements is shaky. These spellings are based on having heard these words, not on having seen them: they are informed guesses in terms of the framings of the words and in terms of their grammatical function. Again, if we take this insight seriously, we see that spelling rests on a prior knowledge of language as a visual phenomenon, knowledge of the look of words. What is clear from these, is that spelling from sound alone is not enough. Spelling is deeply embedded in the shape, the *look* of words and their grammar. And all of these depend on a prior sense about their meaning. (Kress, 2000: 219)

Multilingual classroom community life along the lines that we outline here also involves the children in developing other valuable concepts as they slowly learn to spell in conventional ways, such as reciprocity. As a strategy to help with spelling, their teachers have given them little blank books in which they write new words for their journals and other writing each day. They are then encouraged to look up to see if they have the spelling of the Xhosa/English version of the word before getting help with spelling again. Erica asked them if they would assist her as well:

> I asked the children to help me to learn to speak Xhosa. I put up a sheet and asked them to write the Xhosa and English word for me ... at the present moment there's not a single space on that page because every minute they have they go and write some words. And I even found children that aren't that fluent in English – most of the time they're at that page. When they don't know the English equivalent they go and ask Ntombi or some other child in the class. (Fellies, 2000)

There is a related growing metalinguistic interest in and familiarity with both languages among English and Xhosa speakers. Teacher Ntombi explains in her diary how, with spelling:

> They love spelling words to me when I ask them to spell some words for me, whether it's English or Xhosa. With Xhosa, in words like bhala (count) or bala (write) that they tend to confuse, when you say bala or bhala, they will say does it have an 'h' and I will say yes. I don't have to tell them where the 'h' goes they know its after 'b'. . . . All of them love that, the English and the Xhosa children. They ask for a spelling exercise in both languages. We discuss the Xhosa words. I tell them in English what they mean, and I ask the Xhosa children to give me a sentence using that word in Xhosa and doing the same thing in English. (Nkence, 2000)

So we have to think about what it means to assess emergent biliteracy in children and to question whether the kinds of testing that are generally done can do justice to what the children are actually learning. The willingness to engage, the confidence to try and the ability to express and communicate profoundly are palpable. Skills, values and qualities are revealing themselves as ones that are not normally assessed in our schools. An extract from Carole Bloch's notes illustrates how one day, towards the end of the first term in 2000, the class held a performance session, where the children could read, tell a story, sing or recite a rhyme. They were using the languages of their choice, and many of their contributions were in Xhosa:

> I entered as a child began to tell a story in Xhosa. As usual, I cocked my head and began straining my mainly English senses to try and grasp the gist of what she was saying. All at once I felt an arm slip round my shoulder, as one of the girls quietly sat down next to me. Our eyes met, she smiled, leant towards me, and in a whisper she began to interpret the story for me.

There are currently neither assessment tools nor marks for this invaluable skill. On another recent occasion an English-speaking child came up to Carole waving her journal. 'Look,' she said proudly, 'Look what I've done.' The entry was a page of writing in Xhosa. She then explained how she had decided to write in Xhosa that day, and had got a friend to translate her words into Xhosa. Both of the children appeared deeply satisfied, both had executed appropriate strategies skilfully and smoothly – and yet translation is not valued and, therefore, not assessed, by our education system.

Conclusion

The Battswood project demonstrates clearly that, at the less powerful ends of all of the continua, much can be done to initiate changes in people's perceptions about making use of the possibilities for their languages and literacies as well as in their capabilities to take control of such changes. We have reason to believe that the window of opportunity will remain open for another few years and that the multiplication of such projects in different areas of South Africa involving all the different languages, even some which have not been officialised, notably South African sign languages, will shift the balance of power in favour of those for whom ostensibly the democratic transition was initiated. It remains a challenging and exhilarating task to ensure that the opportunity is used to the full and that the specificity of the South African transition is underlined by the contribution of the country's language workers and practitioners.

Notes

1. The term *'a luta continua'* means 'the struggle continues'. It was made popular during the freedom struggles in the Portuguese-speaking African countries in the seventies and was taken over by other liberation movements as well.
2. However, a recent survey has brought to light some unexpected findings about prevalent attitudes. By way of example, we cite the following:

   Almost 90% of people feel very strongly that the mother tongue should have a significant place in the education system. This finding contradicts impressions created in the media and held by many South Africans that English is the language of choice for schooling. Fewer than 10% of respondents argue for an English dominant Education system.

   The survey revealed that 45% of South Africans are unable to understand (or understand very little of) the information that prominent leaders are trying to convey, when this is done in English only. (PANSALB, 2000)
3. See especially LANGTAG (1996) and RSA Government Notice No. 383 of 9 May 1997 on Language In Education Policy (DOE, 1997). Also see DOE (2000).
4. Political will to implement the Language in Education Policy (LIEP) implies overcoming complex value-laden and economically sensitive challenges to find ways of appointing teachers who are speakers of the African languages of the pupils in multilingual schools, as well as ensuring ways of getting fluent additional language- (usually English-)speaking teachers to teach the additional language in schools where African languages are spoken by the majority of the children.
5. The government has recently begun addressing this through the commissioning of an investigation into Values in Education. This report names the value of multilingualism as one of six such values which should be promoted via the school system (see DOE, 2000).
6. Our long-term goal is to 'make micro more macro' by establishing a demonstration school, where everyone will be completely involved in developing models for multilingual education. For this we need the Education Department to support us by giving us a school to work in and paying the teachers salaries. Recent discussions with the member of the executive council of the government of the Western Cape Province responsible for education has rekindled the hope that this will happen soon. Even more significant is the suggestion that Battswood, given a few essential changes, might well become the demonstration school for multilingual education.
7. In their fourth year, the situation has changed to one where, due to internal staffing issues at the school, Erica did not 'move up' with the class, and they have a new class teacher. Ntombi now spends two full days a week with the children.
8. Our initial intention was to work with both Grade 1 classes, with the Xhosa-speaking teacher dividing her time between the two classes, but one of the class teachers found the experience of having 'that language' (i.e. Xhosa) an

imposition on the daily curriculum. She could not overcome her fear that the time spent on Xhosa would impact negatively on the children's developing fluency in English. As we wanted involvement to be positive, we ended the programme with her after the first term.

9. At the time of writing, most of these schools remain English (or Afrikaans) medium, and Xhosa-speaking children have few if any opportunities to use their home language/s for anything but playground talk at school.
10. During the first three years, Erica Fellies used Afrikaans when it seemed appropriate, the children have all learned greetings and songs and counting in Afrikaans, there are some storybooks available in Afrikaans, and if children wanted to speak or write in Afrikaans sometimes, they were encouraged to do so. From Grade 4, Afrikaans is phased in as a subject at Battswood.
11. For the vast majority of young South African children, most initial experiences with print are school ones. Preschool provision has only ever been available for a minority of mainly 'white' children. Most African language-speaking families' daily life practices involve predominantly oral transactions.
12. The African languages are 'minority' languages in terms of power relationship, but they are in fact the languages of the majority of the people in the country.
13. As yet, no storybooks for very young children of preschool age have been written in African languages, although an initiative called 'First Words in Print' is presently under way to address this. What does exist to some extent are translations from English and Afrikaans books.
14. The oral tradition, with its wealth of stories for young and old, is alive more in the memories of adults than in their practices with children (Bloch,1999a).
15. This enables XL1 children to join English/Afrikaans speakers in having the songs, rhymes and wordplay they love and know so well as early printed material.
16. In South Africa, for many historical reasons, it is notoriously difficult to enlist the active participation of parents in their children's education, among them overwork and underpay coupled with long distances to travel and poor transport. We thus tread lightly in that domain, while at the same time trying to make the most of whatever opportunities reveal themselves to provide information and get family members involved in unimposing ways.
17. See Bloch (2002) for a more detailed account of this journal-writing process.
18. We have done this with the help of the South African branch of Biblionef, an International Book Donation Agency which has as its mission to supply mother tongue literature to children.

References

Baker, C. (1996) *Foundations of Bilingual Education and Bilingualism*. Clevedon: Multilingual Matters.

Battswood Primary School (1998) *School Business Proposal 1998*. Unpublished manuscript.

Bissex, G. (1980) *Gnys at Wrk: A Child Learns to Write and Read*. Cambridge, MA: Harvard University Press.

Bloch, C. (1997) *Chloe's Story: First Steps into Literacy*. Cape Town: Juta and Co.

Bloch, C. (1999a) The potential of early childhood for developing and sustaining literacy in Africa. *Social Dynamics* 25 (1), 101–129.
Bloch, C. (1999b) Literacy in the early years: Teaching and learning in multilingual early childhood classrooms. *International Journal of Early Years Education* 7 (1), 39–59.
Bloch, C. (2002) Nurturing biliteracy through interactive writing. In Beckett, T. (compiler) *Reports on Mother-Tongue Education*. Cape Town: PRAESA, University of Cape Town.
Bruce, T. (1987) *Early Childhood Education*. London, Sydney: Hodder and Stoughton.
Cummins, J. (1996) *Negotiating Identities: Education for Empowerment in a Diverse Society*. Ontario, CA: California Association for Bilingual Education; and Stoke-on-Trent: Trentham Books.
DOE (Department of Education) Republic of South Africa (1997) *Government Notice No. 383: Language in Education Policy*. Pretoria: Department of Education.
DOE (Department of Education) Republic of South Africa (2000) *Values, Education and Democracy: Report of the Working Group on Values in Education*. Pretoria: Department of Education.
Fellies, E. (1998) Project diary. Unpublished manuscript.
Fellies, E. (2000) Project diary. Unpublished manuscript.
Ferreiro, E. and Teberosky, A. (1993) *Literacy Before Schooling*. London: Heinemann Educational Books.
Gamede, T., Mnisi, P. and Leibowitz, B. (2000) *Language in the Classroom: Towards a Framework for Intervention*. Pretoria: National Centre for Curriculum Research and Development (NCCRD).
Gee, J.P. (1990) *Social Linguistics and Literacies: Ideology in Discourses*. London: Taylor and Francis.
Goodman, Y. (1984) The development of initial literacy. In H. Goelman, A. Olberg and F. Smith (eds) *Awakening to Literacy* (pp. 102–9). Exeter, NH: Heinemann Educational.
Goodman, Y. (1986) Children coming to know literacy. In W.H. Teale and E. Sulzby (eds) *Emergent Literacy: Writing and Reading* (pp. 1–14). Norwood NJ: Ablex Publishing Corporation.
Gregory, E. (1996) *Making Sense of a New World: Learning to Read in a Second Language*. London: Paul Chapman.
Heath, S.B. (1983) *Ways with Words: Language and Life in Communities and Classrooms*. Cambridge: Cambridge University Press.
Holdaway, D. (1979) *The Foundations of Literacy*. Sydney: Ashton Scholastic.
Hornberger, N. (1990) Creating successful learning contexts for bilingual literacy. *Teachers College Record* 92 (2), 212–29.
Hornberger, N. and Skilton-Sylvester, E. (2000) Revisiting the continua of biliteracy: International and critical perspectives. *Language in Education: An International Journal* 14 (2), 96–22.
Kress, G. (2000) *Early Spelling Between Convention and Creativity*. London and New York: Routledge.
LANGTAG (Language Plan Task Group) (1996) *Towards a National Language Plan for South Africa: Final Report of the Language Plan Task Group*. Pretoria: State Language Services.

Moll, L. (1992) Bilingual classroom studies and community analysis: Some recent trends. *Educational Researcher* 21 (2), 20–4.

Nkence, N. (2000) Diary. Unpublished manuscript.

PANSALB (Pan South African Language Board) (2000) *Media Release: Pansalb Announces Major Findings – A Sociolinguistic Survey*. Pretoria: PANSALB. 7 September.

Pluddemann, P., Mati, X. and Mahlalela, B. (1998) *Problems and Possibilities in Multilingual Classrooms in the Western Cape*. Final Research Report for the Joint Education Trust (JET) – Presidents Educational Initiative (PEI) Research Initiative. Department of Education. University of Cape Town, South Africa: PRAESA (Project for the Study of Alternative Education in South Africa).

Robinson, A., Crawford, L. and Hall, N. (1990) *some day you will no all about me*. Suffolk: Mary Glasgow Publications.

Street, B. (1995) *Social Literacies: Critical Perspectives on Literacy in Development Ethnography and Education*. London: Longman.

Taylor, D. and Dorsey-Gaines, C. (1988) *Growing Up Literate: Learning From Inner-City Families*. Portsmouth, NH: Heinemann.

Taylor, N. and Vingevold, P. (eds) (1999) *Getting Learning Right*. Johannesburg: The Joint Education Trust.

Chapter 5

Searching for a Comprehensive Rationale for Two-way Immersion

MIHYON JEON

Introduction

As one of various language policies in the United States, two-way immersion (TWI) programs have been increasingly implemented and also researched. Two-way immersion programs are also referred to as two-way bilingual or dual language programs. TWI programs are defined as a program type that integrates language minority and language majority students[1] for all or most of the day, with the goals of promoting high academic achievement, bilingual development, and multicultural understanding for all students (see Christian, 1994; Christian *et al.*, 1996; Freeman, 1998; Howard & Christian, 1997; Lindholm-Leary, 2001; Montone & Loeb, 2000). More detailed description of the third goal of TWI programs is found in the following quote: 'An additional goal of many [TWI] programs is to create an environment that promotes linguistic and ethnic equality and fosters a positive cross-cultural attitude' (Christian *et al.*, 1996: 1).

Much research proposes a rationale for two-way immersion programs based on language-acquisition theories. A very commonly used rationale for TWI programs is as follows. First, content knowledge learned through the first language helps learners to acquire high levels of academic achievement in the second language. Second, minority students with strong oral language and literacy skills in their first language tend to acquire a higher level of second-language development. Third, a language is best learned when it is the medium of instruction (Christian *et al.*, 1996; Howard & Christian, 1997). Finally, a language is best learned through social interaction (Christian *et al.*, 1996; Genesee, 1999).

The need for a more comprehensive rationale for TWI programs arises from a gap between the three main goals of TWI programs and the current rationale for TWI programs. The first and second goals of TWI programs – namely, promoting academic achievement and bilingual development – are supported by the current rationale. However, it does not provide a theoretical reason why TWI programs should be implemented in order to promote multicultural understanding, the third goal of TWI programs, nor does it support the claim that TWI programs can achieve this third goal.

This chapter attempts to depict a more comprehensive rationale for TWI program policies by locating them in the context of language-policy theory and by analyzing them through a framework – the continua of biliteracy (Hornberger, 1989; Hornberger & Skilton-Sylvester, 2000). The purpose of this chapter is not to analyze and evaluate implementations of TWI programs and their outcomes in the United States. Rather, it aims to achieve a more comprehensive understanding of TWI programs as a language policy, and to describe language ideologies reflected in the policy. In so doing, it seeks to set up a more complete rationale for TWI programs which can then support all three goals of the programs.

The first section of this chapter provides a profile of TWI programs in the United States and explains why in this chapter the case of Korean–English TWI programs is used as an example of TWI programs. The second section recognizes Korean–English TWI program policy as a type of language policy. The third section is devoted to formulating a framework drawn from theories of language-policy ideology and the continua of biliteracy model. The fourth section analyzes the Korean–English TWI program policy using the framework introduced in the preceding section. The analysis provides a rationale for TWI program policy both for the specific case of Korean–English TWI and more generally.

Profile of TWI Programs

The first TWI program was implemented in 1963 at the Coral Way School in Dade County, Florida, in order to provide quality education for both native English-speaking majority students and native Spanish-speaking minority students (Pedraza-Bailey & Sullivan, 1979). Recognized as an effective means of educating not only language-minority students but also language-majority students, TWI programs have been receiving increased attention and funding in the United States since the early 1990s (Freeman, 1998). According to the *2001 Directory of Two-Way Immersion Programs in the United States,* which the Center for Applied Linguistics (2001) posts on the World Wide Web, currently 260 two-way immersion programs exist in 135 districts in 24 states in the United States

(September of 2001). Figure 5.1 indicates the dramatic increase in the number of TWI programs in the United States since the early 1990s.

There has also been considerable expansion within existing programs – many have added new grade levels each year, and 40 programs have been extended into middle- or high-school levels (Howard & Sugarman, 2000). Howard and Sugarman (2000) report that the majority of TWI programs are implemented in public schools, with the exception of four programs; and a few TWI programs, only 32, are whole-school programs. In terms of languages of instruction, most TWI programs are Spanish–English (244 out of 261). The CAL *2001 Directory* identifies TWI programs that use Korean and English (4), Chinese and English (5), French and English (6), and Navajo and English (2). One program uses both Spanish– and Chinese–English. As far as Korean–English TWI programs are concerned, according to *the Korean/English Dual Language Program brochure*,[2] five programs exist (for more information see the next section). Howard and Sugarman (2000) report that the large majority of students enrolled in TWI programs are native speakers of one or both languages of instruction, but in 37 programs there are more than 1% of the students whose native language is not used in the program. These students are referred to as third-language speakers.

The ratio of instructional time in each language varies. Christian (1994) identifies two major patterns in the allocation of the two languages – 90/10 or 80/20 and 50/50 approaches. In the former approach, the target

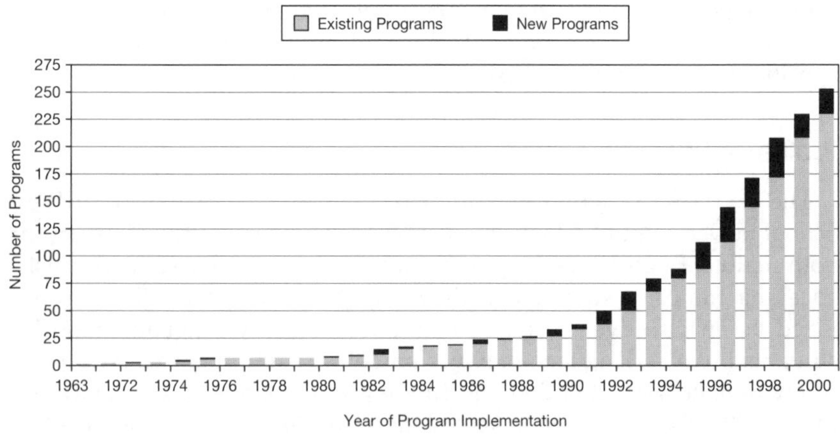

Figure 5.1 Growth of TWI programs in the United States

Source: Center for Applied Linguistics (2001)

non-English language is used for nearly all of the instruction time, up to 80–90%, in the lower elementary grades. English is introduced gradually up to 50% in the upper elementary grades in this approach. The latter approach allocates 50% of the time to each language in all grades. According to their survey (Howard & Sugarman, 2000), of 248 TWI programs in the United States, 42% of the programs use the 90/10 or 80/20 approach and 34% use the 50/50 approach. In addition to the 90/10 or 80/20 and the 50/50 approaches, Howard and Sugarman report that 13% of the TWI programs are middle- or high-school programs with neither of the two approaches; 9% of the programs provided no response; and 2% separate students by native language for part of the day in the primary grades. In both the 90/10 or 80/20 and the 50/50 approaches, the distribution of the two languages is achieved by designation of teacher, content areas, time allotment, or any combination of these (Freeman, 1998).

This chapter focuses on Korean–English TWI programs as an example of TWI program policy. While Spanish–English TWI programs have been intensively researched because of the large number of the programs and their relatively long history, the Korean–English TWI programs have not yet received much attention. This is because they have a short history and because of the relatively small number of Korean immigrants. One of the two elementary-level Korean–English TWI programs was implemented in 1992 and the other in 1993. The two secondary-level Korean–English TWI programs started in 1998 and 1999 respectively. Paying more attention to Korean–English TWI programs can contribute to the establishment of a comprehensive rationale for TWI programs, because the existence of these programs reflects an ideology that – regardless of the number of speakers of a minority language – a minority group has a right to enjoy their language and to have their language respected as a resource. Even though the focus is on the Korean–English TWI programs, the aim is to formulate a comprehensive rationale for all TWI programs in the United States.

Situating Korean–English TWI Program Policy in a Language-policy Context

In searching for an integrative definition of language policy, Cooper (1989: 97–8) introduces an accounting scheme for the study of language policy and planning – *what actors* attempt to influence *what behaviors of which people, for what ends, by what means, with what results, under what conditions*, and *how*? Haarmann (1990: 123) also raises a similar question

– *who* is engaged in planning *what language for whom* and *why*? Here, a combination of both questions is used to discuss Korean–English TWI program policy, by focusing on *who plans what for whom, for what ends, under what conditions, how,* and *why*? The element of *with what results* (from Cooper's scheme) is not included because the aim here is not to evaluate the implementation and outcomes of TWI programs. In addition, the element of *by what means* in Cooper's scheme is also incorporated into the element of *how,* which accounts for what decision-making process is involved in TWI programs. Depicting a more comprehensive rationale for TWI programs addresses the last element of the question, *why.*

All four Korean–English TWI programs (appearing in the *2001 Directory of Two-Way Immersion Programs in the United States*) are implemented in public schools in the Los Angeles United School District (LAUSD) in California. A brief profile of these four programs is shown Table 5.1 based on the information posted in the same directory above.

In both elementary-level Korean–English TWI programs, Korean is used up to 70% of the instruction time in the lower grades and English is gradually introduced up to 50% by the fourth grade. The two middle-school programs started in 1998 and 1999 respectively, in order to meet a need for providing a continuing program for the students finishing their elementary-level programs. These two middle-school level TWI programs plan to expand the programs to upper grades as the current students age; in the fall of 2001, a high-school program started. In each school, one class of each grade operates the TWI program.

In addition to these four Korean–English TWI programs, there is one more program, which is implemented in Wilton Place School in the same school district, according to the *Korean/English Dual Language Program* brochure (APOL, 2000). In this program, which started in 1994, two or three classes in K-1 grade levels participate in the Korean–English TWI program, and one class of each grade from second through fifth participates in the same program. Currently, there are about 600 students in these five Korean–English TWI programs (Merrill, personal communication, 22 April 2001). All five programs have a special funding source, namely Title VII, from the United States Government.

Who plans and how?

The following sections discuss the Korean–English TWI program policy based on the accounting scheme introduced above – *who plans what for whom, for what ends, under what conditions, how,* and *why*? The discussion about *who plans, under what conditions,* and *how* is based upon a personal

Table 5.1 Profile of Korean–English TWI programs in LAUSD

	Cahuenga Elementary School	*Denker Avenue School*	*John Burroughs Middle School*	*Robert E. Peary Middle School*
Grade level	K–5	K–5	6–7	6
Starting year	1992	1993	1998	1999
Program scope	Program-within-a-school	Program-within-a-school	Program-within-a school	Program-within-a-school
Program approach	70/30 (a variation of 90/10 approach)	70/30 (a variation of 90/10 approach)	50/50	50/50
Allocation of language	By teacher	By block of time By subject	By block of time By subject	By teacher By subject
% of students receiving a free or reduced-price lunch	Native Eng students: More than 76% Minority lang students: More than 76%	Native Eng students: 61–75% Minority lang students: 26–50%	Native Eng students: More than 76% Minority lang students: 51–75%	Native Eng students: 26–50% Minority lang students: Less than 5%
Average class size	K–3: 20 4–5: 32	K–3: 20 4–5: 15	6: 30 7: 30	6: 15
% of third-language students and languages spoken	15% Spanish, Tagalog, Burmese	N/A	0%	27% Spanish, Tagalog

Source: APOL, 2001

conversation with Mr Craig C. Merrill (15 April 2001) who has been involved in initiating and implementing the Korean–English TWI programs since their beginnings. The first actors of the Korean TWI program policy were a few individuals who wrote a grant in 1991, Dr Russ Campbell of UCLA and his students, including Chin Kim and others. The LAUSD was not involved at this stage. The proposal written in 1991 won a Title VII grant from the United States Government, and the first Korean–English TWI program was implemented in 1992. In this implementation stage, Merrill started working to implement the first program in Cahuenga Elementary School, as a full-time employee of the LAUSD. Over the ten-year period since its first implementation, Merrill has played a critical role in the program's expansion by writing several more Title VII grants, which have provided the necessary financial support. As the Korean–English TWI programs expanded, the LAUSD created an Asian Pacific and Other Language Office (APOL) with support for the implementation of the Korean–English TWI programs. Since then, Merrill has been working for that office with the Title VII programs coordinator, Schelly Kwock.

Based upon the history of the Korean–English TWI programs, the range of Korean–English TWI program policy makers seems to be multi-level, from individuals and the school district to the federal government. The most direct actors of the Korean–English TWI program policy are a few individuals such as Campbell, Kim, and Merrill. Personnel in the APOL who are involved in the Korean–English TWI programs are also direct actors in Korean–English TWI program policy making. The school district is an indirect policy maker through the creation of its APOL, which is currently involved in the programs' implementation and expansion through training teachers and writing new grants. The federal government is an indirect policy maker because of its role in establishing criteria, granting, and funding for Title VII grants. In terms of the element of *how* in the accounting scheme, the process of planning the Korean English TWI programs is a collaboration among the different levels of agents, such as the individual promoters, the APOL, the LAUSD, and the federal government.

Under what conditions?

The situational and informational conditions which influenced the initiation of the Korean–English TWI program policy follow. First, the demographic characteristics of the area where the Korean–English TWI programs are implemented are worthy of mention. The programs are located in Koreatown, within LAUSD. The Koreatown area consists of approximately 30% Korean immigrants, with 62% Latino and 3% other Asian and Pacific Islander (mostly Filipino) immigrants (Campbell, 1994, as cited in Rolstad, 1998). In this area, the majority of students are from low-income families, many of them receiving free or reduced lunch (Rolstad, 1998; see also Table 5.1). Second, information drawn from much research about successful TWI programs encouraged the initiation of the Korean–English TWI program policy. Third, low academic achievement and ethnic/racial separation among the students in the school district caused a need for an innovative program, such as the Korean–English TWI programs, in order to help the students achieve higher academic success and in order to increase cross-cultural understanding (Merrill, personal communication, 15 April 2001).

What?

What is planned in the Korean–English TWI program policy? Of the three foci of language policy – corpus, status, and acquisition (Cooper, 1989) – the Korean–English TWI program policy is mainly a language-acquisition policy. Kaplan and Baldauf use 'language-in-education policy' (1997: 125) in order to refer to language-acquisition policy. They suggest a number of areas of 'policy development for language-policy implementation,' such as curriculum, personnel, materials, community, and evaluation policies (Kaplan & Baldauf, 1997).

In terms of curriculum policy, the Korean–English TWI program policy determines the usage ratios of the medium of instruction, in this case both Korean and English. As mentioned earlier, all five Korean–English TWI programs adopt a 70/30 approach, a variation of the 90/10 approach. This mean that 70% of the day in kindergarten is taught in Korean, 30% in English, and the proportion of English increases each year until the fourth grade, when each language is used 50% of the day. Each lesson is taught using only one language and translation is not used. Except for the language of delivery, the academic curriculum in the Korean–English TWI program is the same as that of other LAUSD programs.

In terms of personnel policy[3], teachers in the programs should have a California BCLAD (Bilingual Cross-cultural Language Academic Development) certificate in Korean. To achieve this certificate, a candidate must have a certain level of spoken and written Korean proficiency. The individual principal in each school where the Korean–English TWI program is implemented has the right to choose all teachers, including those for the program.

In terms of material policy, the APOL supports teachers in the Korean–English TWI programs through Korean teaching materials, including textbooks in Korean. Some of the Korean textbooks are from Korea through the Korean Consulate in Los Angeles.

The community policy of the Korean–English TWI program policy emphasizes home/school collaboration. The *Korean/English Dual Language Program* brochure (APOL, 2000: 1) elucidates this emphasis by stating that 'parents are encouraged to participate and opportunities are created for parents to volunteer in the school in various capacities.'

Evaluation of the academic and bilingual development of students employs the Stanford 9 test administered in English for academic achievement in content areas, including English language arts, and in Korean for a Korean-language proficiency test developed by UCLA and LAUSD.

Although the Korean–English TWI program policy is primarily a language-acquisition policy, it is also a status policy which plans functional allocation of a language. Cooper (1989), citing Stewart (1968), introduces functions as targets of status planning,[4] functions such as official, provincial, wider communication, international, capital, group, educational, school subject, literacy, and religious. This Korean–English TWI program policy allocates to the Korean language the functions of education, school subject, and literacy.

For whom and for what ends?

The Korean–English TWI program policy is planned for students in the LAUSD, both native Korean-speaking students and native English-speaking students. The goals of the policy, as shown in the *Korean/English Dual Language Program* brochure (APOL, 2000), are to develop Korean and English biliteracy, high academic achievement, and multicultural understanding for all students. This third goal is also referred to as acquiring 'an appreciation for diversity.' These goals are in common with other TWI programs.

Why?

Why did the Korean–English TWI program policy-makers want to achieve these three goals? Why did they choose the Korean–English TWI program as a particular means of achieving these goals? What is the theoretical framework upon which this choice was made? These questions lead to a discussion about rationale for TWI programs, because goals are about what to achieve through a policy, whereas rationale is about why a particular policy is chosen in order to achieve them.[5] As introduced above, the current rationale provides a logic for arguing that, if they are successfully implemented, TWI programs will achieve the first and second goals – developing Korean and English biliteracy and high academic achievement. However, it does not provide any theoretical framework to justify the choice of TWI programs for achieving the third goal – enhancing multicultural understanding and/or appreciation for diversity. In searching for a more comprehensive rationale for TWI programs, my focus is to pay attention to this question – what kind of theoretical framework supports the claim that TWI programs contribute to achieving the third goal?

A Framework

In order to answer the question above, this section sets up a framework through which TWI program policy can be analyzed and which, as a result, provides a more comprehensive rationale for TWI programs. The framework is drawn from language-policy theories and the continua of biliteracy model.

Language-policy ideologies

Cobarrubias (1983) suggests a taxonomy of typical language ideologies which influence language policy, such as linguistic assimilation, linguistic pluralism, vernacularization, and internationalism. Here only the first two ideologies are taken up for further discussion, because they seem to be more directly related to language-acquisition policy with regard to minority languages in the United States than are the other two ideologies. Ruiz (1994) also identifies these two ideologies as the main ideologies surrounding the education of language minorities in the United States. The linguistic-assimilation ideology presupposes that 'all speakers of languages other than the dominant languages should be able to speak and function in the dominant language, regardless of their origin' (Cobarrubias, 1983). Hornberger (2002) discusses one kind of linguistic-assimilation ideology, the one language–one nation ideology. This ideology does not grant equal rights to language minorities (Cobarrubias, 1983); under it monolingualism is an ideal, natural state, while multilingualism is seen as an abnormal condition. Wiley (1996) points out that, in societies where the majority of the population is monolingual, especially in many Anglophone countries, there exists an underlying assumption that monolingualism is the normal condition (Wiley, 1996).

This means that linguistic assimilation is a predominant ideology in many societies.

On the contrary, the linguistic-pluralism ideology grants 'coexistence of different language groups and their rights to maintain and cultivate their languages on an equitable basis' (Cobarrubias, 1983: 65). Under this ideology, multilingualism is seen as a normal condition within a society. Cobarrubias (1983) distinguishes two main types of multilingualism. The first type is where linguistic coexistence is merely tolerated, whereas the second type is where languages other than the dominant language have some important but restricted functions such as religious rituals or education, or where official support is extended to those languages. Cobarrubias (1983) asserts that the latter is the strongest and most significant use of the term multilingualism, whereas the former is a weak form of multilingualism.

These two main ideologies coexist within a society. However, one can be dominant, and the tendency of dominance between these two ideologies is under constant change. According to Hornberger, 'ideological tensions between assimilationist and pluralist discourses about linguistic and cultural diversity are long-standing and persistent' (2000: 173). Writing about multilingual language policies with respect to their ideology and implementation, Hornberger (2002) emphasizes that the one language–one nation ideology (the linguistic assimilation ideology) is no longer the only available one, as multilingual language policies based on the linguistic-pluralism ideology are increasing.

These ideologies reflect not only the current situation in a society but also the vision of the future society. What kind of society and what kind of members does each ideology reflect and/or envision? In terms of power relationships existing within a society, the linguistic-assimilation ideology reflects coercive relationships of power (Cummins, 1986, 2000). Under this type of power relationship, minority-language speakers are forced to assimilate to the dominant language. On the other hand, the linguistic-pluralism ideology envisions a society where collaborative power relationships (Cummins, 1986, 2000) between minority and majority members operate.

These different power relationships and their underlying ideologies also influence the social-psychological state of members of a society. Liebkind (1999) identifies two main types of psychological states of members in a society – psychologically insecure and secure. Psychologically insecure majorities feel threatened in their majority position and thus discriminate against out-group members; and, at the same time, psychologically insecure minorities are not convinced of the values of their own language and culture (Liebkind, 1999). On the other hand, psychologically secure majorities are tolerant of minorities, and minorities tend to assert their own distinctiveness (Liebkind, 1999). I believe that coercive power relationships based on the linguistic-assimilation ideology exert an influence on the psychological insecurity of members of a society, whereas collaborative power relationships based on the linguistic-pluralism ideology promote psychologically secure majorities and minorities. However, Liebkind's description about secure majorities and minorities seems to be limited to a weak form of the multilingualism ideology. When a strong form of multilingualism ideology is predominant in a society, secure majorities not only tolerate minority languages, but also respect language rights of minority language speakers and support minority-language development. At the same time secure minorities enjoy their language rights and experience their language and culture as being valued by majorities.

Ruiz's three orientations in language planning – language-as-problem, language-as-right, and language-as-resource – are worthy of mention at this point. Ruiz uses the concept of orientations as 'a heuristic approach to the study of basic issues in language planning' (1984: 16). In my interpretation, the three orientations in language planning are based on different ideologies. The language-as-problem orientation reflects the language-assimilation ideology in that this orientation assumes that minority-language speakers have a handicap to overcome and they need to assimilate to the majority language in order to overcome this problem. The language-as-right orientation echoes a weak form of the linguistic-pluralism ideology, and the language-as-resource orientation echoes a strong form of the linguistic-pluralism ideology. The former assumes that language is a basic human right (Ruiz, 1984) – 'the right to freedom from discrimination on the basis of language' and 'the right to use your language(s) in the activities of communal life' (Macías, 1979, as cited in Ruiz, 1984: 22). The latter considers all languages, not only the language of majorities but also minority languages, as resources.

Ruiz (1984) suggests that the language-as-resource orientation can enhance the language status of minority languages and can relieve tensions between majority and minority communities. Ruiz, citing Feinberg (1970) that 'the nature of a full-fledged right is that it is not a mere "claim-to" something but also a "claim-against" someone' (Ruiz, 1984: 24), considers that the language-as-right orientation causes an automatic resistance and thus a tension between majority and minority communities. He also considers the language-as-right orientation to be quite different from the language-as-resource orientation. However, I believe that the former is a prerequisite for the latter. The language-as-resource orientation can be valid only when it is based on the language-as-right orientation. This is because, without acknowledging, accepting, and respecting others' language rights, perceiving their language(s) as resource does not have a significant meaning. My view is that the language-as-right orientation does not cause any problems. Whether minorities' claim to their language rights constitutes a claim against language majorities depends on what kind of power relationships operate in a society. Under coercive power relationships in a society, minorities' claim to their language rights is inevitably a claim against majorities and other minorities. And yet in a society where collaborative power relationships operate, the same claim does not mean a claim against someone else.

Language-policy ideologies and language policies

How do these ideologies – linguistic assimilation and linguistic pluralism – influence language policy? The former leads to the imposition of 'one-language-only policies' (Wiley, 1996). In the case of the United States, the dominant language is English; thus, this type of language policy is included under 'the diffusion-of-English paradigm' as one language-policy option (Phillipson & Skutnabb-Kangas, 1996: 436; Tsuda, 1994). In this language-policy paradigm, a language policy allocates resources to the dominant language and thus glorifies this language while it stigmatizes minority languages (Phillipson & Skutnabb-Kangas, 1996). Phillipson and Skutnabb-Kangas (1996: 437) argue that the underlying ideology of this paradigm, named *linguicism*, falsely claims that the learning of the majority language at the cost of minority languages is beneficial to and for the minorities; but in fact this falsification is always for the advantage of the majorities.

In terms of the perspective of language-planning goals (Wiley, 1996), the goal of the one-language-only policies under the diffusion-of-English paradigm is language shift. Language shift refers to 'the gradual or sudden move from the use of one language to another, either by individuals or a group' (Bright, 1992, as cited in Wiley, 1996: 122). When language shift occurs from the use of a minority language to a dominant majority, it entails minority language death. Wiley (1996) suggests that, when language diversity is seen as a problem, language shift is a goal for language-acquisition planning.

In contrast to the linguistic-assimilation ideology, the linguistic-pluralism ideology leads to both 'language maintenance' and 'language enrichment policies' (Wiley, 1996) with the goals of minority-language maintenance and enrichment, through the prevention and/or reversal of language shift. Fishman (1981, 1991) suggests language enrichment policies as ways to reverse language shift. Hornberger (2002) asserts that multilingual language policies based on the linguistic-pluralism ideology recognize ethnic and linguistic diversity as resources for nation-building. She further argues that

> these [multilingual language] policies, many of which envision implementation through bilingual intercultural education, open up new worlds of possibilities for oppressed indigenous and immigrant languages and their speakers, transforming former homogenizing and assimilationist policy discourse into discourse about diversity and emancipation. (Hornberger, 2002)

These multilingual language policies, based on the linguistic-pluralism ideology, fall within 'the ecology-of-language paradigm' (Tsuda, 1994; Phillipson & Skutnabb-Kangas, 1996: 436) as a language-policy option which offers an alternative to the diffusion-of-English paradigm. *Language ecology* refers to 'the study of interactions between any given language and its environment' (Haugen, 1972, as cited in Phillipson & Skutnabb-Kangas, 1996: 441; Hornberger, 2002). Phillipson and Skutnabb-Kangas assert that 'just as ecology is a "movement for environmental sanitation" (Haugen, 1972: 392), the ecology of language should be concerned with the cultivation and preservation of languages' (1996: 441). Hornberger (2002) elaborates the concept of ecology of language in the language-planning field, emphasizing that the 'ecology of language' metaphor underpins a multilingual approach to language planning and policy (Hornberger, 2002). Under the ecology-of-language paradigm, language policies aim to maintain and cultivate languages and cultures, based on the perspective of linguistic human rights, in order to promote 'a healthy and just ecology of language' (Phillipson & Skutnabb-Kangas, 1996: 447).

Incorporation of the continua of biliteracy

In this section, in order to set up a framework in which TWI program policy is situated, the continua of biliteracy model is incorporated into the discussion about language ideologies and language policies reflecting different ideologies. The continua of biliteracy model (Hornberger, 1989; Hornberger & Skilton-Sylvester, 2000) offers a comprehensive framework in which to situate not only research and teaching but also language planning in linguistically diverse settings (Hornberger, 2002). The model consists of four sets of continua defining the context, development, content, and media of biliteracy.

Hornberger and Skilton-Sylvester (2000) point out that 'in educational policy and practice regarding biliteracy, there tends to be an implicit privileging of one end of the continua over the other such that one end of each continuum is associated with more power than the other.' This point is shown in Figure 5.2. Hornberger and Skilton-Sylvester (2000) suggest that transforming the traditional power weighting of the continua of biliteracy through weighting equal power toward both ends of the continua is necessary in order to facilitate full biliterate development of learners.

The tendency of a society to weight power toward the macro, literate, and monolingual ends of the context continua indicates that the linguistic-assimilation ideology is predominant in the society. This ideology, as discussed earlier, is reflected in one-language-only policies. In contrast to the linguistic-assimilation ideology, the linguistic-pluralism ideology envisions a biliteracy context which weights equal power to both ends of

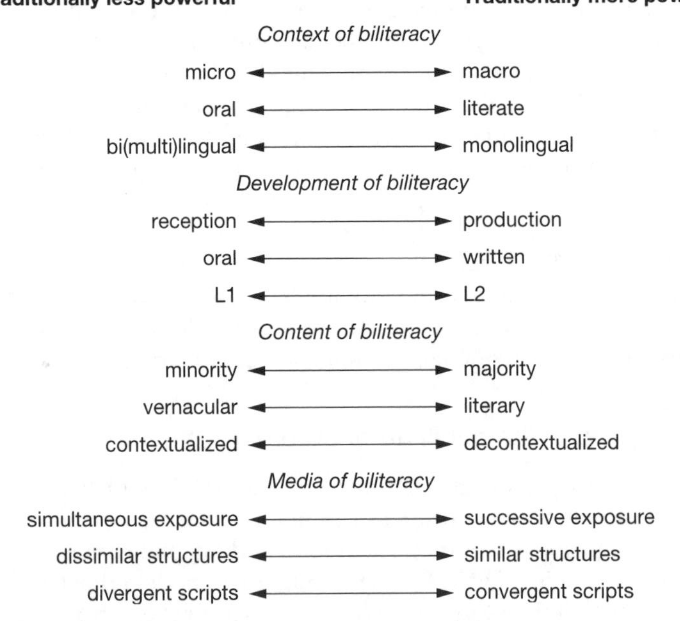

Figure 5.2 Power relations in the continua model

Source: Hornberger and Skilton-Sylvester (2000: 99)

the continua of biliterate context – micro–macro, oral–literate, and bi(multi)lingual–monolingual. This ideology is reflected in language maintenance and language enrichment policies.

Here specifically I use the continua of context to examine language-policy ideologies in relation to language policies. Furthermore, I use the continua of biliteracy model as a framework to analyze TWI program policy, and, in the next section, as a premise to provide a comprehensive rationale for that policy. The continua of development serve to analyze the goals of language-acquisition policy. In fact, these continua can also be used as a framework in which a learner's biliterate development is described and evaluated; but that is not the aim of this chapter. The content and media continua are used in examining curriculum policy and/or material policy – derivative categories of language-acquisition policy. Again, these two sets of continua are useful in examining the actual implementation process of language-acquisition policy, but our discussion is intentionally restricted to the policy-setting level.

In terms of the goals of language-acquisition policy, the one-language-only policy has the goal of developing only the majority language, emphasizing written language and production skills. The power weighting of the one-language-only policy is toward the right-hand ends of the continua of development of biliteracy. In contrast, multilingual language policy premised on a linguistic-pluralism ideology weights equal power toward both ends of the development of biliteracy continua, aiming for learners' full biliterate development in receptive–productive and oral–written language skills.

Accordingly, the tendency of weighting power in curriculum and materials policies, as derivative policies of language-acquisition policy, depends on what kind of ideologies the main language-acquisition policy reflects. The curriculum and materials policies based on the one-language-only policy, reflecting a linguistic-assimilation ideology, weight power only toward the right-hand ends of the continua of content and media of biliteracy – the majority, literary, and decontextualized ends (in the continua of content of biliteracy) and successive exposure, similar structures, and convergent scripts (in the continua of media of biliteracy). In contrast, curriculum and materials policies premised on language-maintenance and language-enrichment policies, reflecting a linguistic pluralism ideology, weight equal power toward both ends of the continua of content and media of biliteracy.

The continua model was based on and supported by extensive research about language use and development in multilingual educational settings. The model posits that counter-power weighting of each continuum, that is, weighting equal power toward both ends of each continuum – facilitates learners' biliterate development in their L1 (first language) oral and receptive skills, as well as their L2 (second language) written and productive skills. For example, in her rich and comprehensive ethnographic research on Cambodian women in Philadelphia, Skilton-Sylvester (1997) demonstrates that the continua of biliteracy constituted a useful descriptive framework for her observation and analysis of the biliterate development of Cambodian women. Her research also supports the premise that equally weighting power toward both ends of the continua facilitates biliterate development of Cambodian women.

I argue that, in addition to promising learners' full biliterate development, weighting equal power toward both ends of the continua of biliteracy facilitates minority-language maintenance and enrichment, since these are the main goals of language policies based on the linguistic-pluralism ideology. Transforming the traditional power weighting of the continua of biliteracy makes a difference not only in learners' biliterate development, but also in types of power relationships between majorities and minorities within a school and broadly within a society. By transforming the way of weighting power along the continua of biliteracy, the coercive power relationships will be transformed into collaborative power relationships. In terms of the social-psychological state of members of a society, weighting equal power toward both ends of the continua, based on the linguistic-pluralism ideology, promotes secure majorities and minorities who not only tolerate each other but are also able to respect each other's language rights and value the languages and cultures of each other as resources.

Based on both the discussion above and the research supporting the claims of the continua of biliteracy, we can conclude that the continua of biliteracy model, incorporated with the notion of language-policy ideology, provides descriptive power to describe the details of the policies, predictive power to anticipate language-acquisition policy outcomes, and explanatory power to elucidate why certain outcomes are anticipated. The concept of descriptive power is based on 'descriptive adequacy' of a framework or a theory, referring to 'our success in representing what happened in a given instance' (Cooper, 1989: 46–7). The concept of predictive power is based on 'predictive adequacy' referring to 'our ability to forecast events' (Cooper, 1989: 48–9). The concept of explanatory power is based on 'explanatory adequacy' referring to 'our ability to "account for" a particular outcome' (Cooper, 1989: 49–56).[6]

The descriptive power of the continua of biliteracy model is useful in examining a language-acquisition policy by looking at the power weighting of the policy. The predictive power of the continua of biliteracy model anticipates that, if a language-acquisition policy provides learning contexts which allow learners to draw on all points of the continua of biliteracy through weighting equal power toward both ends of the continua, the policy will promote secure majorities/minorities and a collaborative power relationship between these groups as well as full development of learners' biliteracy. The explanatory power of the continua model offers a rationale for a language-acquisition policy because the explanatory power of the continua of biliteracy model gives an adequate explanation of why particular policy outcomes can be anticipated. Based on the explanatory power, if a language-acquisition policy is anticipated to have the possible outcomes mentioned above, the policy is considered as having a rationale supporting a choice of the policy in order to achieve these outcomes.

Rationale for TWI Program Policy

What does the continua of biliteracy model tell us about TWI program policy and its rationale? Based on the continua of contexts of biliteracy, the Korean–English TWI program policy attempts to promote learning contexts which allow learners to draw on all points of the continua – oral, bilingual, and micro interactional contexts as well as macro, literate, and monolingual contexts. The Korean–English TWI program policy aims to provide students with a bilingual context where both majority and minority languages are used as media of instruction. This demonstrates that the Korean–English TWI is based on the linguistic-pluralism ideology.

An analysis of the curriculum and material policies of the Korean–English TWI program policy, using the content and media of biliteracy continua as descriptive framework, also reveals that the Korean–English TWI program policy weights power equally to both ends of each continuum. For example, the curriculum and material policies of the Korean–English TWI program policy allow students to have access to learning materials and contents in both the minority and majority language through providing textbooks and materials in both languages. The textbooks and materials in Korean allow the minority students in the program to develop their native-language literacy based on their Korean language skills, which they have already developed before entering the programs. The same textbooks and materials in Korean also allow the majority students to develop second-language proficiency in Korean. In terms of the development continua, one of the goals of the

Korean–English program policy, developing biliteracy proficiency in both Korean and English, shows that the program policy weights power towards both ends of the L1–L2, oral–written, and receptive–productive continua.

The Korean–English TWI policy reflects an ideology of linguistic-pluralism. Based on the predictive power of the continua of biliteracy, full biliteracy development of students is anticipated as an outcome of the full implementation of the policy. In addition, the Korean–English TWI policy is also anticipated to promote secure majority and minority students and a collaborative power relationship between them. Secure majority and minority students respect each other's language rights and experience their languages and cultures as being valued by each other. Thus the Korean–English TWI policy has a rationale to support not only its first and second goals but also the third goal of the policy – developing multicultural understanding/appreciation for diversity.

Conclusion

This chapter has depicted a more comprehensive rationale for TWI programs by locating them in the context of language-policy theory and by analyzing them through the continua framework. We have especially focused on a theoretical argument of why TWI programs should be implemented in order to promote multicultural understanding, which is the third goal of TWI programs, since the other two goals of TWI programs – promoting academic achievement and bilingual development – are supported by the commonly used rationale for TWI programs.

In developing a framework, I discussed two main language-policy ideologies. The linguistic-assimilation ideology leads to one-language-only policies and envisions insecure majorities and minorities under coercive power relationships, while the linguistic-pluralism ideology leads to language maintenance and enrichment policies and envisions secure majorities and minorities under collaborative power relationships.

The incorporation of the continua of biliteracy model with the notion of language-policy ideologies provided a framework to analyze a language-acquisition policy in bilingual education. Equal weighting of power toward both ends of the continua of biliteracy – the context, development, content, and media of biliteracy continua – facilitates students' full biliterate development, and reflects an ideology of language-pluralism. Thus, equal weighting of power toward both ends of the continua of biliteracy is also anticipated to promote secure majority and minority students.

An analysis of the Korean–English TWI program policy, based on the descriptive power of the continua of biliteracy, demonstrates that the policy weights equal power toward both ends of the continua of biliteracy and is based on the linguistic-pluralism ideology. In terms of the predictive power of the continua of biliteracy, the Korean–English program policy may be expected not only to facilitate students' full biliterate development, but also to promote secure majority and minority students who respect languages, cultures, and each other's language rights. The explanatory power of the model gives a rationale of why the outcome, the achievement of the third goal of TWI programs – promoting multicultural understanding/appreciation of diversity – is also to be expected. In sum, the analysis of the Korean–English TWI program policy by means of the continua of biliteracy model, incorporated with the notion of linguistic-pluralism ideology, provides a comprehensive rationale for TWI program policy.

Even though Korean–English TWI program policy is the example used, the rationale developed here is also valid for other TWI programs. This is based not only on the fact that the Korean–English TWI program policy shares its three main goals with other TWI programs, but also on what I take to be the 'theoretical adequacy' (Cooper, 1989: 46) of the continua of biliteracy model. Cooper tells us that

> Generalizations can be built up from individual cases by observing consistencies in the relationships among descriptive classifications. Such generalizations can be organized into theories designed to explain not simply a given individual case but *all* individual cases represented by the phenomenon of interest. The validity of the theory can then be tested against new data, gathered in terms of the descriptive classifications on which theory is built. (Cooper, 1989: 57)

He notes that the theoretical adequacy of a framework refers precisely to the ability to derive generalizations explaining a wide range of human behavior from a small number of propositions. It is then the theoretical adequacy of the continua of biliteracy model that enables us to derive legitimate generalizations for TWI programs generally from consideration of the rationale for Korean–English TWI program policy.

Notes

1. Following Tollefson (1999), in this chapter 'minority' refers to groups with relatively less power and fewer rights and privileges than one or more dominant groups. Thus, 'language minority' means groups of people whose first

language is neither an official language nor a dominant national language. In the US context, 'language minority' refers to groups of people whose first language is not English, and 'language majority' refers to groups of people whose first language is English.

2. This brochure is made by the Asian Pacific and Other Language Office in Los Angeles (see next section for detailed introduction to this office).
3. Information about the personnel, material, and evaluation policies of the Korean–English TWI program policy is from my personal conversation with Mr Merrill (22 April 2001), although the categorization of his comments according to Kaplan and Baldauf's scheme is my own.
4. In this paper, I make no distinction between policy and planning, even though there have been efforts to make this distinction.
5. I owe this distinction between goals and rationale to Dr Nancy H. Hornberger through e-mail correspondence (12 April 2001)
6. I prefer the term 'power' over 'adequacy' because power as used here means the ability of the model not only to fulfill the requirements but also to move current understanding beyond its present insights.

References

APOL (Asian Pacific and Other Language Office) (2000) *Korean/English Dual Language Program.* Los Angeles, CA: APOL.

Campbell, R.N. (1994) *Korean/English Bilingual Immersion Project: Title VII Developmental Bilingual Education Evaluation Report Year Two, 1993–1994.* Federal Grant #T003c20062–93. Los Angeles, CA.

Center for Applied Linguistics (2001) *2001 Directory of Two-Way Immersion Programs in the United States.* Washington, DC: CAL. On www at http://www.cal.org/twi/

Christian, D. (1994) *Two-way Bilingual Education: Students Learning Through Two Languages* (Educational Practice Rep. No. 12). Santa Cruz, CA/Washington DC: National Center for Research on Cultural Diversity and Second Language Learning.

Christian, D., Montone, C. and Carranza, I. (1996) *Two-Way Bilingual Education: Students Learning through Two Languages.* Washington, DC: Center for Applied Linguistics.

Cobarrubias, J. (1983) Ethical issues in status planning. In J. Cobarrubias (ed.) *Progress in Language Planning* (pp. 41–86). Berlin: Mouton.

Cooper, R.L. (1989) *Language Planning and Social Change.* New York: Cambridge University Press.

Cummins, J. (1986) Empowering minority students: A framework for intervention. *Harvard Educational Review 15,* 18–36.

Cummins, J. (2000) *Language, Power and Pedagogy: Bilingual Children in the Crossfire.* Clevedon, Buffalo, Toronto, Sydney: Multilingual Matters.

Fishman, J.A. (1981) Language policy: Past, present, and future. In C.A. Ferguson and S.B. Heath (eds) *Language in the U.S.A.* (pp. 516–26). Cambridge: Cambridge University Press.

Fishman, J.A. (1991) *Reversing Language Shift: Theoretical and Empirical Foundations of Assistance to Threatened Languages.* Clevedon, UK: Multilingual Matters.

Freeman, R.D. (1998) *Bilingual Education and Social Change*. Clevedon, Buffalo, Toronto, Sydney: Multilingual Matters.
Genesee, F.E. (1999) *Program Alternatives for Linguistically Diverse Students* (Education Practice Rep. No. 1). Santa Cruz, CA/Washington, DC: National Center for Research on Education, Diversity and Excellence.
Haarmann, H. (1990) Language planning in the light of a general theory of language: A methodological framework. *International Journal of the Sociology of Language* 86, 103–26.
Hornberger, N.H. (1989) Continua of biliteracy. *Review of Educational Research* 92 (2), 212–29.
Hornberger, N.H. (2000) Bilingual education policy and practice in the Andes: Ideological paradox and intercultural possibility. *Anthropology and Education Quarterly* 32 (2), 173–201.
Hornberger, N.H. (2002) Multilingual language policies and the continua of biliteracy: An ecological approach. *Language Policy* 1(1), 27–51.
Hornberger, N.H. and Skilton-Sylvester, E. (2000) Revisiting the continua of biliteracy. *Language and Education: An International Journal* 14 (2), 96–122.
Howard, E.R. and Christian, D. (1997) The development of bilingualism and biliteracy in two-way immersion students. Paper presented at the Annual Meeting of the American Educational Research Association, Chicago, IL.
Howard, E.R. and Sugarman, J. (2000) *Two-Way Immersion Programs: Features and Statistics*. Washington DC: Center for Applied Linguistics: Available at http://www.cal.org/twi/.
Kaplan, R.B. and Baldauf, R.B. (1997) *Language Planning from Practice to Theory*. Clevedon: Multilingual Matters.
Liebkind, K. (1999) Social psychology. In J.A. Fishman (ed.) *Handbook of Language and Ethnic Identity* (pp. 140–51). New York, Oxford: Oxford University Press, Inc.
Lindholm-Leary, K.J. (2001) *Dual Language Education*. Clevedon, UK: Multilingual Matters.
Merrill, C.C. (2001) Personal communication, 15 April, 2001.
Merrill, C.C. (2001) Personal communication, 22 April, 2001.
Montone, C.L. and Loeb, M.I. (2000) *Implementing Two-Way Immersion Programs in Secondary Schools*. Santa Cruz: Center for Research on Education, Diversity and Excellence.
Pedraza-Bailey, S. and Sullivan, T.A. (1979) Bilingual education in the reception of political immigrants: The case of Cubans in Miami, Florida. In R.V. Padilla (ed.) *Bilingual Education and Public Policy in the United States* (pp. 376–94). Eastern Michigan University: Bilingual Bicultural Education Programs.
Phillipson, R. and Skutnabb-Kangas, T. (1996) English only worldwide or language ecology. *TESOL Quarterly* 30 (3), 429–52.
Rolstad, K. (1998) Language minority children in a third language immersion context: Evidence for educational enrichment. Unpublished doctoral dissertation, University of California in Los Angeles, CA.
Ruiz, R. (1984) Orientations in language planning. *NABE Journal* 8 (2), 15–34.
Ruiz, R. (1994) Language policy and planning in the US. *Annual Review of Applied Linguistics* 14, 111–25.

Skilton-Sylvester, E. (1997) Inside, outside and in-between: Identities, literacies and educational policies in the lives of Cambodian women and girls in Philadelphia, Ph.D. dissertation, University of Pennsylvania.

Tollefson, J.W. (1999) *Planning Language, Planning Inequality: Language Policy in the Community*. London, New York: Addison Wesley Longman, Inc.

Tsuda, Y. (1994) The dominance of English and linguistic discrimination. *Media Development* 16, 32–34.

Wiley, T.G. (1996) Language planning and policy. In S. Mckay and N.H. Hornberger (eds) *Sociolinguistics and Language Teaching* (pp. 103–47). New York: Cambridge University Press.

Part 3: Learners' Identities

Chapter 6

Language Education Planning and Policy in Middle America: Students' Voices

FELICIA LINCOLN

> Rose seemed to have settled the identity question. It was a solution that she seemed to find satisfying. When I asked her, 'Which are you? Hispanic or American?' she made it a declaration. She was ambiguous, but not ambivalent, 'I am both.'

Recent research and writing in the field of language minority education have tended to support minority language maintenance as being the approach of most benefit to language minority students (Fishman, 1979; Thomas & Collier, 1997; Fillmore & Valadez, 1986). The issue that originally motivated my research was interest in the educational experience of language minority children in rural communities that have had little linguistic diversity in their history and with limited resources and support in terms of finances, legislation, or human resources. Specifically, then, this chapter considers the questions:

- What is the public school educational experience of language minority children in a non-urban community with no previous experience with language minorities?
- What are the implications of the above for language maintenance?
- How can these findings and implications inform language education planning and policy?

Language Minority Education in Middle America

Most studies of language minority education in the US have involved urban settings and regions of the US with a history and tradition of educating language minorities. These previous studies have done much to frame the issues and to establish the parameters of language planning and policy (LPP) discourse. They beg the question, however, of how those involved in school districts less commonly studied might describe the experience of educating language minority children, especially in areas of the US that do not have a history of language minority education. It is possible that rural education settings affect language minority students differently than do urban educational settings. If education research in the US has neglected rural settings (Jensen & Eggebeen, 1994; Sherman, 1992; Theobald, 1991), and the resources for language minority students in many rural education settings are limited, then this (language minority student) population is twice neglected. DeYoung (1991: xvii) is hopeful that research in non-urban America might spark increased interest in work that looks at the 'rural school not as an "anomaly" to be modernized, but as a *neglected source of useful information of scholarly interest*' (emphasis mine). He is hopeful that educators will look for ways to incorporate rural 'ways of knowing' and understanding educational issues into the canon.

Scholarship and writing in the area of LPP have tended to set forth theories, frameworks, and models that imply a preference for native language instruction and the valuing of culture as ways of successfully attending to the education of language minority students. Some of the most respected voices in the field hold the same opinion: language maintenance is important and native language instruction in bilingual education is the most effective, humane way to teach language minority students (Fishman, 1979; Holm & Holm, 1990; Morison, 1990; Thomas & Collier, 1997; Fillmore & Valadez, 1986). In the last few decades, LPP scholars have seemed to take this as given and have turned to issues of pedagogy, such as how to allocate the two languages in school (length of instructional time in each language) and what content material should be taught in what language (Fillmore & Valadez, 1986).

Thomas and Collier's report some thirty years after the passage of the Bilingual Education Act (BEA) does, in fact, provide evidence that bilingual education and native language (NL) instruction make a difference to language minority children in their educational success. Their research findings are that native language instruction is not only better than ESL pull-out programs, but also that the longer the NL is used as a medium of instruction, the better are the results cognitively and socially for language minority children. While this study and others with similar findings are encouraging for those educators and planners who advocate the use of native language in schools, the question still remains: what are the best practices for language minority student education in the decidedly different rural and isolated regions considered in this study, in what one of the participants calls 'Middle America' or those parts of the US that historically did not receive large numbers of immigrants?

Corson (1999) asserts that little attention has been paid to schools as a setting for language planning. If that is true, and if, as Faltis (1998) asserts, attention to schools as sites of language planning is much needed, then it is vital to begin to understand language minority education in this non-traditional setting. According to Corson (1999), policy can be deduced from interactions with students. The goal of K-12 education in a classic sense is to help young people gain the skills and understanding they need to become active, responsible citizens of the world. As Corson states, 'Language is the vehicle for identifying, manipulating, and changing power relations between people' (1999: 14). According to Corson, schools are never neutral:

> Either they contribute to the disempowerment of culturally diverse students and their communities, or they enable teachers, students and communities to challenge the operation of unwanted power structures. (1999: 14–16)

If schools are not neutral, but in fact do affect power relationships, it is then doubly important to know how schools in all types of settings enable or disempower burgeoning language minority populations throughout the US.

Mill Creek, Arkansas

In Arkansas in the 1960s, there were few language minority children in schools. By 1998, the census estimated that the total number of Hispanics living in Arkansas had increased to about 50,000 persons or 1.95% of the total population. Relative to the previous census count, Arkansas was leading the nation in the growth of its language minority population. The state numbers for language minorities had increased in the 2000 census by 343% (US Census Bureau, 1991–8). Demographers expect that trend to continue.

Mill Creek (pseudonym) is located in a part of Arkansas that does not have a history of educating minorities. This region has traditionally been largely homogeneous and isolated from other centers with more experience in dealing with diversity. The state, as a whole, has had little linguistic diversity; therefore, there is as yet no established system for training or preparing educators to meet the needs of language minority students. Any school district faced with new language minority populations will find it a challenge to meet the needs of its students, but in a district such as Mill Creek the difficulty is compounded by regional isolation and lack of resources.

Additionally, Mill Creek is located in a mountainous region four hours' drive from the state capital (the state's only urban center). The Mill Creek area is experiencing a phenomenal population growth due to various factors. These factors include the influx of industries such as agricultural processing, motor freight companies, and manufacturing firms; the selection of Mill Creek as the international headquarters for several major corporations; and tourism created by the attraction of the area's numerous state and national parks and the recreational facilities of a nearby lake.

This region of the state has had recent influxes of language minorities who are attracted to the region by agricultural industry (poultry processing and rabbit processing in particular). The largest poultry processor in the US has its headquarters in that region[1] and the four largest poultry concerns employ approximately 13,000 people in this area according to a Chamber of Commerce brochure. That industry has attracted other related industries such as trucking and packaging plants. Several language minority populations have moved into the region and the largest minority population is Spanish-speaking (Mexican, mostly, but other Central American countries are represented as well). In addition, there are numbers of Marshallese (people from the Marshall Islands in the Pacific) and a residual number of Laotians and Vietnamese who came to the US during periods of violence in their countries. There is good evidence (the continued growth of industries and population) to indicate that the language minority student numbers in the district are only a fraction of the number to be educated in the future.

A Case of Four Students

The following case study of two language minority students and two language majority students in the Mill Creek school district distills findings from ethnographic research there. I spent six months in the district, engaging in participant observation and interviewing in six or seven schools, with students, teachers, parents, and community members (Lincoln, 2001).

My research used the continua of biliteracy to examine and understand the experience of language minority students in the Mill Creek school district in two ways: first, to help understand language minority students' academic struggles and sometimes academic failure, even in situations where there was evidence of adequate dual language facility; and second, to predict ways to enhance their agency and allow their voices to inform and impact their own educational experiences.

Three of the students described here were interviewed at the same time. They are Juan (all student names are pseudonyms), who refers to himself as both Mexican and Mexican-American; Rose, a Salvadoreña who was adopted when she was four by an Anglo Arkansas family; and Sue, a member of the language majority, who is less well known to the researcher. The fourth student is Roger, an Anglo, who was in English as a Second Language (ESL) for a year. He was not present during the above conversation but is included here because of the interesting and useful data elicited during his own individual interview.

The interview with Sue, Rose, and Juan took place on 6 May 1994, my last day in the field. It was also the last day of the regular school year. The three were hanging out in the ESL classroom at the high school. There was no one else there. Most of the students had gone on a field trip. These three had decided not to spend the money, or else did not have the money. They were in the ESL classroom that all the language minority students professed to love, evidently even when there was no one else there. I had actually planned to run in quickly and say goodbye, but when we began to talk, their words just spilled out. I ran to the car for the tape recorder; they waited patiently, and then just continued to talk.

Sue

Sue said little during this interview. She wanted to work in a day care center after graduation. She had attended Latino church once. That was her only experience with Latinos out of the school setting. She really enjoyed the Latino students, but seldom ever spoke Spanish. Of the three students here who were taking Spanish, only she claimed to be comfortable in the Spanish class. She had an A in the course. Other data concerning her are limited and she is included primarily because she was present at this encounter.

Juan

Juan went to school in Texas before coming to northwest Arkansas. At the time of the interview, he was 18 years old and a junior. He was completely fluent in spoken English. He had a slight intonation and stress pattern that identified him as Latino, but every word was intelligible. When he spoke English, however, he put his hands on his face in a gesture of mild dismay. He made no grammar errors, although he used a few non-standard structures (e.g. double negatives). However, most of the non-standard forms he used are commonly heard among language majority student populations as well.

During the interview conversation he told me:

> I don't talk in any class, but in here (the ESL classroom) and in the Spanish class. I don't know about the preterite and future. The Spanish teacher won't let me say 'selva' for jungle. She wants another, Costa Rican word or something.

The Spanish teacher's rejection of his word choice for *jungle* troubled and confused him. The ESL teacher's explanation of English, on the other hand, had helped him with understanding the syntax of his first language ('the preterite and future'), presumably by allowing him to transfer understanding of syntax in the L2 back to the L1. I asked him what he did in other classes 'like math' if he didn't understand something. He said:

> I don't ask questions, because of my English. I'm too shy to ask. When I'm here (in the ESL classroom) . . . whatever I say they'll understand. Whatever I say to the ESL teacher, she'll understand. Over there in the main building, I can't say what I'm thinking; I have to say what I'm trying to say. You understand? When I'm speaking to Maria or someone, I can talk, but I get nervous talking when I'm making conversation with someone else, with an American, with a gringo.

Juan said that in the US (not just in Mill Creek), he had been called names:

> Yeah, they call me names, but they can just call me names. Yeah, it's only partly because they see us alone, because if they see us with someone else, they won't say nothing. . . . It's all America, Central, South . . . we're Americans too, but they don't see that, because we're brown. They don't see that because they're white.

I asked him what he called Americans. He grinned and said, 'Gringos.' I asked if he played any sports or belonged to any clubs. He said he wanted to play soccer but couldn't maintain the grade point. He did not belong to any clubs. I asked what he did on weekends. 'Nothing. I just go to school and go to work.' He didn't go to the lake; he had no American friends (evidently, including Sue who was present). He told me that in Texas he had done pretty well in school where both languages (Mexican Spanish and English) were acceptable and 'even the gringo teachers' spoke Spanish. When I asked him what the future held, he said he wanted to be a mechanic. He rejected my suggestion of being a teacher (even a

Spanish teacher), because his English was not good enough and he spoke the 'wrong kind' of Spanish.

Rose

Rose was fascinating as a disparate case. Until recently, she had not spoken Spanish since she was four or younger. She was adopted by Americans and brought from El Salvador to Arkansas by her new parents, who spoke only English. Of all the students I interviewed, she seemed to have done the most grappling with questions of identity and social loyalties or at least she was able to articulate the struggle most clearly. '[Before her time in ESL class] I always spent time with Americans, which I have no problem with.' She had started learning Spanish again when she started going to the ESL teacher's class 'to help.' She seemed to have been liberated by the struggle to learn who she was. However, she said that, when she first came to the ESL classroom, they had looked at her as if she were 'different, and it was *hard*' (emphasis hers). She had felt as if she did not completely belong in either place.

She was having difficulty in Spanish class, as was Juan. When Rose first started the class, the teacher said, 'I don't know why you forgot it [Spanish].' Rose said the teacher called her a 'native speaker of Spanish . . . I feel like a dummy in her class.' Now, however, after a year or more of associating with the ESL class and socializing with the Spanish-speaking students outside of school, she wanted nothing more than to speak Spanish. Some day she wanted to help the ESL students, perhaps become a teacher. She seemed to have settled the identity question. It was a solution that she seemed to find satisfying. When I asked her, 'Which are you? Hispanic or American?' she made it a declaration. She was ambiguous, but not ambivalent, 'I am both.'

Roger

It was during the first week of class that I met Roger. He was a blond, Anglo boy who had been placed by mistake in the ESL classroom the previous year and had stayed (see below for explanation). This interview took place in the high school ESL classroom when there were no other students present (28 April 1994). He was in a work/co-op program with the school, going to school in the morning and working an internship/job in the afternoon. He had a full, busy life, but had found there was room for more.

In his eleventh grade year, he was short an English credit and his schedule was full because of his co-op program. His counselor suggested putting him in the ESL classroom so he could get the necessary English credits. He was worried at first. He had seen how the language minority students were treated (ostracized). He said the language majority students treated the language minority students 'terrible.' He told me his thoughts about his first day in the ESL class:

> Well, ain't nobody gonna talk to me. . . . If you're not like them, they push you away. And these people [pointing to the desks in the ESL room], they took me in like I was one of them and I appreciate that. . . . And I admit at first I was a little racist at first. . . . They changed my whole way of thinking. And I guess I kinda helped them because I don't speak the best English, but I speak better than some people. There ain't nothing different in um. If we went over to there, where they're from, we wouldn't fit in. I got in there with them, and they're all going off in different languages I'm trying to catch on, you know, but it was fun.

He said that 'to tell the truth' he was better in his senior English classes this year because the ESL teacher could relate to how he learned. He said his senior English teacher this year had talked to his previous ones. She told them that he had improved a lot. His former English teachers told her that he was a slow learner. However, after the ESL class, he had improved 'tremendously':

> The whole class are just around me looking at it [the group assignment]. The pressure is on, man. I'm writing things. They watch my every move. I mean, you wouldn't believe there's nights I go to bed early so I can get up and do good the next morning. . . . And the teacher I have this year she says I'm doing great. I've got an A in her class.

The next two sections discuss these language minority students' experiences in light of the continua of biliteracy. The continua are used to understand these students' academic failures and successes.

Continua of Media and Content

One commonly held tenet in second language acquisition is that students are better motivated and able to learn language when the affective domain is considered (Celce-Murcia, 1991; Krashen, 1982). Certainly respect for minority and vernacular content might have offered Juan (and quite possibly Rose) a foothold into a majority context that often limits the access of the language minority student by honoring their word choices and vernacular usage. The continua model predicts that, for language minorities to have agency and voice, planners and educators must pay more attention to the typically less powerful ends of the content and media continua, that is, minority ways of knowing, vernacular ways of speaking and writing, and contextualized language use, as well as non-standard or 'mixed' language varieties and orthographies.

The irony of Juan's frustration in Spanish class is poignant. He felt his vernacular was inferior to Rose's Spanish and yet knew he was the native speaker. Rose, on the other hand, told me she had felt bad in Spanish class because the teacher called her a 'native speaker' (of Spanish) and she was sad to have 'lost' her Spanish. Sue, alone, felt comfortable there and she had had no exposure to Spanish before. However, in fact, having now gotten to know the Latinos through Spanish class, she had come to be interested in them and their minority culture, even going so far as to go to church with them on at least one occasion.

Juan's revealing statement about his ESL class, 'whatever I say, they'll understand,' is an accolade, coming from any high school student. If classroom teachers truly want to create a classroom atmosphere that lowers the affective filter, then it appears that they may learn from the ways the ESL teacher used to provide those positive conditions and by implication created a microlevel context for risk-taking in language learning. The valuing of the ESL classroom by students was one of the great successes with the language minority students throughout the district. All the ESL professionals in the district were receiving these endorsements from students. The ESL teachers at the lower levels seemed to be able to create safe places for students anywhere they happened to be, including cafeteria and playgrounds; secondary teachers did the same with their classroom spaces apparently even when there were neither students nor teacher present.

The Spanish teacher's choice of reading material was another success with regard to the content and media continua. Juan referred to this book often. The reading in his first language (L1) seemed to offer a view into things unfamiliar (the Jaguar), through use of the comfortably familiar (Spanish). Part of Juan's willingness to talk in the Spanish class in spite of some of the ambivalence he exhibited toward the class lay in the content of the curriculum. In fact, the content was meaningful enough to him that he was willing to persevere despite what was to him some adversity to be able to participate. This certainly seems to be support for the argument that curricular attention must be paid to minority and vernacular content. It is possible that some of his academic struggles were rooted in content choices that excluded his own identity, experiences, and vernacular word choices.

The successful reading assignment in Spanish class and scaffolding from English grammar structures to Spanish grammar systems in the ESL classroom were two positive educational experiences Juan described to me. The ESL teacher was able to use the structures of English to aid Juan's understanding of the metalanguage of structures in his own L1.

In contrast, an emphasis on prescriptive standard language (media) and majority content (Spanish word choice) in Spanish class contributed to feelings of failure and may possibly have contributed to Juan's F in the class. Part of Juan's lack of success in Spanish[2] may be attributed to feelings of loyalty or solidarity with his own minority culture. The teacher's rejection of Juan's own native-speaker word choices (*selva* for jungle) left Juan an outsider in what should have been his area of expertise. It may be important that educators not only provide meaningful, relevant content, but content as well which represents the vernacular varieties within language groups. To state it another way, attention to minority and vernacular content might help Juan and students like him to feel less disloyal in moving towards target standard in their L1 or L2. In fact, use of their forms as teaching resources might give language minority students access to two or more forms of their L1.

In the Spanish class where Juan enjoyed the content and wanted to participate, there were few opportunities provided for him to use his L1 freely. The Spanish teacher's refusal to accept his word choice for jungle is a classic example of the devaluing of vernacular content and non-standard language varieties. He seemed puzzled in the interview when he talked about kinds of Spanish – Costa Rican, Colombian, and his own. He was the native speaker, yet his vernacular (and possibly he himself) was somehow wrong.

Where the media of biliteracy allowed for simultaneous exposure to the learners' multiple varieties, Juan acquired voice, literally in the case of the ESL classroom, one of the only places he talked at all. Conversely, in a setting where exposure was successive and exclusive of multiple varieties, he sounded disenfranchised. His example of the ESL class having helped him understand the Spanish preterite, a case of simultaneous exposure, is interestingly one where his second language supported his first. In this case, he did seem to feel successful and empowered.

Rose's deliberate positioning of herself with the language minority and the Mexicans in particular is interesting. Besides being attracted to the opportunity to revive her first language, Rose also seemed to be drawn to Latino culture. She told me, '[Before her time in ESL class] I always spent time with Americans, which I have no problem with,' a fascinating piece of discourse. She had been raised by Americans presumably to think of herself as American, yet there is evidence in this sentence of a distancing or positioning of herself not with Americans but with Other. The phrase 'which I have no problem with' seems to indicate efforts to be open, ostensibly to something that she could be closed to and to something she might possibly have a problem with. She said 'they' looked at her as if she were 'different.' 'They' seems to mean the language majority culture, which had for most of her life been her own home culture. As she learned about being Latina, Rose seemed to find liberation.

It would be interesting to know how use of the minority content in the classroom (ESL or regular education) might further continue that liberation process for Rose and other language minority students. Rose's comment that it is 'hard' to be seen as different and Juan's 'we're Americans too' both seem to be examples of feeling excluded from mainstream majority content that both troubled and confused these language minority students, not to mention positioning them as outsiders in their own learning environment. Sue had been to Hispanic church once. She really enjoyed the Latino students, but seldom ever spoke Spanish outside the classroom. On the other hand, she experienced success in Spanish class, in part, presumably *because of* her access to the language majority and school literary ends of the continua. The Spanish class setting provided ample exposure to familiar majority and literary content. The Spanish language was in many ways just another American school content area with its emphasis on production, writing and English. The actual grade assessment in Spanish for the three students was almost a bilingual education cliché. Sue had an A in the class. Juan, the native speaker, had an F. Rose was truly mid-way between the two, a C. ('I'm both,' she had told me when I asked her which she was, Hispanic or American.) Sue excelled. Rose coped. Juan struggled.

There is evidence for the belief that valuing a person's first language vernacular provides opportunities for learning that language. It comes oddly enough from language majority student data. Roger's previous English teachers thought him slow. His time in the ESL classroom had positioned him as the language 'expert.' In that role, he had become engaged with learning his first language. He had an A in senior English.

Continua of Development and Contexts

Hornberger and Skilton-Sylvester contend that 'Looking closely at biliterate contexts, and specifically at multilingual, oral interaction at the microlevel, allows us to see how measures of intelligence have ignored those ways of speaking and knowing that have not been valued inside of school contexts' (2000: 196).

While many of the issues described in Juan's case seem to come from classroom teacher choices regarding content and media, some discussion of context and development is called for. Juan did not seem to understand the complexities of his struggles with Spanish. It appears that he connected his problems with the fact that he did not know how to put the 'accent on top and stuff like that.' The development continua, in particular the oral–written continuum, are useful in understanding Juan's school failure in Spanish. American public schools in general and this setting in particular place heavy emphasis on the written and literate ends of the development and context continua. If more attention were paid to the oral ends of both the development and context sets, Juan might find ways to succeed in his coursework. In a setting such as a Spanish class, those times when the curriculum includes language arts and minority students seem to engage with the text are prime moments for allowing students to be the experts. Viewing language minority students as resources at these moments could help shape the mainstream view of these students and give them voice at the same time. According to Roger, his view of language minority students had been positively defined by his time in the ESL classroom.

Where structures such as word choices diverge, lesson plans could include differences in varieties of languages (their own and a standard included). Because it seemed so important for Juan to know how to 'put the accent on top,' his receptive skills were not encouraged. He missed a chance to be the expert, and the Anglo children were denied access to an authentic speaker of Spanish. This setting could provide opportunities for language majority students in a largely monolingual setting to have interaction with native speakers of Spanish who could provide rich language input and interaction, luxuries often difficult to provide in a foreign language teaching setting.

This context, that is the school district itself, with its emphasis on monolingual English literacy, does not allow for recognition of Juan's native Spanish oral skills. The de-emphasis of the bilingual and oral ends of the context continua fostered Juan's belief that he could not succeed academically in this monolingual school context. Even in a class where he was a native speaker and could possibly have been a vital resource, he did not feel heard because the variety of Spanish he spoke was devalued. In addition, the focus on the productive, written, and L2 ends of the development continua rather than on Juan's personal strengths (oral, L1 fluency) again reinforced his sense of being silenced even in a class whose content was a variety of his own L1.

Juan's case suggests that reluctance by language and education planners at the microlevel context to provide post-high school bilingual education and training limits the possibilities for language minority students in these settings. This is an example of power weighting in one set of continua influencing and affecting the power weighting along the other sets in the continua. Administrators affect and influence the microlevel context and policy through the types of curriculum and programming they provide for students. They must look for ways to encourage the use of minority and vernacular content to enable language minority students to become productive members of the local community. Attention to the literary rather than the vernacular meant that, in a situation in which Juan could have been a resource (to use Ruiz's 1984 model), he was, in fact, again viewed as problem, because there was no place for his kind of Spanish.

Not surprisingly, then, language minority students expressed feelings of isolation from the mainstream. Power weighting solely on the monolingual, L2, majority ends of the continua does not merely silence, but sets up conditions for separation and perhaps even racism: 'It's all American . . . they don't see that cause they're white . . . we're brown.' Even racism at the level of student–student discourse may be in part at least a result of power weighting on the majority content, L2 English development, and monolingual context ends of the continua, as evidenced by Juan's comments about his own identity and the names he is called.

Name-calling may be a reflection at the microlevel context of macrolevel policies that seem to devalue diversity and bilingualism. Students mirror their parents and, to some extent, policy makers respond to their perceived desires of their constituency when generating macrolevel policies. The English Only Movement with its emphasis on monolingualism and majority interests appears to communicate to those at the microlevel context a disregard or devaluing of diversity. Still, the dialogue with Juan concerning racism is in some ways both hopeful and endearing. He grinned when he used the word *gringo* and that took some of the 'sting' out of it as well as revealing an understanding of the complexities of the situation. Juan was perceptive and thoughtful enough to recognize the irony and humor in his own use of stereotyping when discussing North Americans while he spoke with disapproval of stereotyping his own culture by others.

Despite feelings of exclusion, it is also true that many of the language minority students observed and interviewed for this study did not want to be mainstreamed. They felt more comfortable where they were. The irony was that the very success that the ESL professionals had, in creating safe places for risk-taking and language learning, seemed to contribute to the language minority students' continued isolation from the mainstream.

Juan believed he could not succeed in the Spanish class because he did not know about putting the 'accent on top' and because he did not speak the right kind of Spanish. He was overwhelmed by classroom teachers' acceptance of only those written literary and literate ends of the continua of media, development, content, and context, respectively. In Texas, he said, he 'did well' where both languages (Mexican Spanish and English) were acceptable.[3] 'Even the gringo teachers' spoke Spanish, he said. That phrase is telling. He understands that the US context requires him to move to the L2 and literate ends of the continua. He recognized that, in this greater context, there was no pressure for American teachers to be bilingual. However, there is wistfulness to the statement. He knew that he could be more successful in a bilingual educational context and understood that it would not come to him.

Juan saw himself as unsuccessful in school in ways other than just grade assessment. He did not plan to go to college. He was going to go back to Texas to Vo-tech and a school that understood his 'type of Spanish.' I asked him if he thought about teaching Spanish some day. He said, 'No, because they didn't speak his kind.' The *they* here is provocative. It could refer to the local context of Mill Creek schools, but more possibly it implies the context of the American school setting. When I asked him how he might feel about being a Spanish teacher, he said he would not consider teaching Spanish in Waco, or anywhere else. His Spanish was not good enough. He did not seem to see biliteracy as an asset in any US setting. Some might question whether the public school experience often excludes language minority students; Juan did not have to pause to consider. Bilingualism did not seem to Juan to give him any advantage at all.

Corson talks about native language development classes being used to inform students that the variety of the L1 they spoke was not acceptable. While this did not seem to be a goal of the placement of language minority students in Spanish class in Mill Creek, it seems to have been a by-product.

It is sometimes hard to explain public schools' reluctance to use minority and vernacular content. It is possible that, when the macrolevel context does not encourage bilingualism or promote and value the bilingual and oral ends of the context continua, that viewpoint is echoed in the microlevel context. In other words, if the US and state contexts (e.g. through legislation and funding decisions) discourage simultaneous exposure to and acceptance of dissimilar structures, that view may be evidenced in microlevel classroom practice that inhibits use of vernacular, minority, and contextualized content. Those decisions may, at an even more micro level, provide a context at the level of student-to-student interaction that allows racism and distrust to continue (e.g. name-calling and isolation).

Inclusive and supportive educational contexts can create opportunities for language minority and language majority students to commingle on equal footing. The ESL classroom that had made a place for Roger, an Anglo, had created friendships. Roger had expected ill-treatment from the language minority students in the ESL class because he had seen how language minorities were treated by the language majority: 'Well, isn't nobody gonna talk to me. . . . If you're not like them, they push you away. . . . I was very surprised, cause I mean, you see the way they're treated out in . . . .' Roger had had a change of thinking regarding other races and ethnic groups. He had found that the [ESL kids] were 'no different.' It was in this context where he saw himself as leader and 'expert' that he began to succeed in English himself.

Conclusion

Participants' location at any given moment on a particular point on the continua is not static. Where on the continua they are positioned in terms of power weighting often correlates with the presence or lack of student voice. In all my interviews with language minority students (and to a lesser degree with language majority students as well), there was little evidence of students' empowerment. Most students interviewed expressed at least some frustration with school and their limited ability to affect their own futures. However, as with other categories, the language minority groups showed less movement toward the power-weighted end of the continua than did the majority students.

One example of this was that, while language minority students viewed language majority students as English language experts, they did not express the same opinion of themselves in their own L1. While Roger reported no dearth of friends or social life in the Anglo community, language minority students told a different story. The language minority students did not see the microlevel context (at the levels of their particular school building, anyway) as providing them access to change or providing help when they needed it. They expressed frustration at being unable to use their own language even in Spanish class and at being judged as having lost or become deficient in their first languages.

In addition, the weighting of the continua toward a monolingual English context, majority content, and development through successive exposure to English in their present school settings limited these language minority students' belief in their future career possibilities. Juan repeatedly revealed obvious reluctance to participate in mainstream settings because of his English. The ESL teacher and others said this persisted in spite of reassurances by her and others that his English was quite good. She said he showed no eagerness to make the transition from ESL support to mainstream course work. If Juan and others like him do not learn to participate in the mainstream during their public school experience, they may be further limited in their access to language majority content, and written and literary development in the L2. Limited exposure to majority language content may curtail their access to points along the more powerful ends of the continua. Without the benefit of mainstream course work and interactions, language minority students may well be ill prepared for life in the larger language majority context, whether in Arkansas or in any other part of the US. The irony is that, instead of promoting integration and assimilation into the mainstream, limiting students' use of their L1 appeared to restrict access to the mainstream culture. Insistence on emphasizing and valuing the majority, written, and literary ends of the continua reinforced the isolation students felt and limited their pursuit of the content and curricula that they need for success in a larger, primarily monolingual context.

The microlevel context in Waco, Texas, however, appealed to Juan as a comfortable place to continue education after high school. It is unlikely that regions of Middle America such as northwest Arkansas that have small numbers of any one minority language group and have had little success in getting funding for language minority education from the state and federal sources will be able to develop post-high school training centers that encourage second language use or that attract ESL users. We can, however, through inclusion of minority, vernacular content and through emphasis on simultaneous exposure to two or more languages, provide language minority students with a public school curriculum that offers greater access to educational parity. Many of these findings, both positive and negative, are better understood in light of the continua of biliteracy. There is evidence in this case study that attention to all points on the continua does, in fact, provide benefit for students in both the language minority and language majority.

The ambivalence toward the mainstream classes and programming demonstrated by the language minority students seems likely a reflection of the same ambivalence evidenced in the mixed messages sent from the greater state and federal contexts. Laws passed to protect and assist language minority student education are often followed by cuts in spending and, sometimes, a reversal of those same laws, or the development of policy that countermands them.

It may in fact be Rose and Roger's voices that offer educators the most hope. Of all the students (both language minority and language majority) talked to, they had the most liberated and powerful story to tell. By returning to her inheritance language and persisting in becoming bilingual, Rose seemed to have found voice. Rose had been able to turn her ambiguity about her identity into something positive. As predicted by Hornberger (1989), in embracing all points on the continua, this participant found voice and agency. Rose had found a liberating identity: 'I am both.'

Roger, the Anglo mainstream student, through being included in the minority setting, had learned that his stereotypes about language minorities did not hold. He made friends across cultural 'boundaries.' In addition, from helping others, his own academic and L1 language skills had improved. He was eager to tell about his involvement with the ESL students in his English class. He was amazed at what he learned of the content and what he learned from the students: 'They changed my whole way of thinking.'

Educators looking for ways to improve relations between and among ethnic groups in schools might well listen to his story. By associating with the language minority, he learned lessons about acceptance and the unreliability of stereotypes. Through preparation to be a role model in English, he was motivated to study to be ready for students who were looking to him for help. Inclusion and acceptance of language minority culture and language may be the only way to stem the phenomenon of negativity toward Other to something more appropriate and hopeful in US educational contexts. The data here suggest that it is critical that we give voice and agency to language minorities (and to all participants) in creating their own particular educational settings. If education is the key to the future, then language is the vehicle to that future. We must see to it that language minorities in this country have access to education through language practices that enable and empower. In the US, researchers in the fields of ESL and bilingual education have for some time sought to understand language minority educational needs in those places where language minority populations are most heavily concentrated, but there must also be better understanding of language minority children's educational experiences in all types of educational settings, including this seldom studied one.

Notes

1. Tyson Industries.
2. It is important to acknowledge the part individual learning differences can make in the academic success of any student. However, this student was chosen because I had spent many hours observing him in the classroom. He did his work, he paid attention, he attended class. His teachers thought he was capable and conscientious.
3. It is possible that his Spanish teacher, who was a native speaker of English, might not have understood Juan's Spanish vernacular and was not rejecting his word choices outright. In addition, she may have been uncomfortable with her subject matter, which could produce insecurity (personal communication with Schrock, 30 November 2000).

References

Celce-Murcia, M. (ed.) (1991) *Teaching English as a Second or Foreign Language* (2nd edn). Boston: Heinle & Heinle.

Corson, D. (1999) *Language Policy in Schools: A Resource for Teachers and Administrators.* Mahwah, NJ: Lawrence Erlbaum Associates.

DeYoung, A.J. (1991) Preface and introduction. In A. DeYoung (ed.) *Rural Education: Issues and Practices*. New York: Garland Publishing, Inc.

Faltis, C. (1998) Case study methods in researching language and education. In N. Hornberger (ed.) *Research Methods in Language and Education*. Vol. 8 of the Encyclopedia of Language and Education. The Netherlands: Kluwer Academic Publishers.

Fillmore, L.W. and Valadez, C. (1986) Teaching bilingual learners. In M. Wittrock (ed.) *Handbook of Research on Teaching* (3rd edn, pp. 648–85). New York: MacMillan.

Fishman, J. (1979) Bilingual education, language planning and English. *English Worldwide* 1 (1), 11–24.

Holm, A. and Holm, W. (1990) Rock Point, a Navajo way to go to school: A valediction. *The Annals of the American Academy of Political and Social Science (English Plus: Issues in Bilingual Education)* March, 170–84.

Hornberger, N.H. (1989) Continua of biliteracy. *Review of Education Research* 59 (3), 271–96.

Hornberger, N.H. and Skilton-Sylvester, E. (2000) Revisiting the continua of biliteracy: International and critical perspectives. *Language and Education: An International Journal* 14 (2), 96–122.

Jensen, L. and Eggebeen, D. (1994) Nonmetropolitan poor children and reliance on public assistance. *Rural Sociology* 59 (1), 45–65.

Krashen, S.D. (1982) *Principles and Practices in Second Language Acquisition*. Oxford: Pergamon Press.

Lincoln, F. (2001) *Language Minority Populations Twice Neglected: A Critical Ethnographic Study of Language Education Policy and Practice in Middle America.* Ann Arbor: UMI Dissertation Services.

Morison, S. (1990) A Spanish–English dual-language program in New York City. *The Annals of the American Academy of Political and Social Science (English Plus: Issues in Bilingual Education)* March, 160–9.

Ruiz, R. (1984) Orientations in language planning. *NABE: Journal of the National Association for Bilingual Education* 8 (2),15–34.

Sherman, A. (1992) *Falling by the Wayside: Children in Rural America*. Washington, DC: Children's Defense Fund.

Theobald, P. (1991) Historical scholarship in nineteenth century rural education. In DeYoung, A. (ed.) *Rural Education: Issues and Practices*. New York: Garland Publishing, Inc.

Thomas, W.P. and Collier, V. (1997) *School Effectiveness for Language Minority Students*. Washington, DC: National Clearinghouse for Bilingual Education.

US Census Bureau (1991–8) Report WP/91 to WP/98, *World Population Profile: 1991–1998*. Washington, DC: US Government Printing Office.

Chapter 7

Biliteracy Development among Latino Youth in New York City Communities: An Unexploited Potential

CARMEN I. MERCADO

Introduction

Contrary to what has been said and written about the undervaluing of Spanish among Latino children and youth, and I do not doubt that that is true, my work in non-bilingual classrooms leads me to other conclusions. Spanish, in its infinite varieties, *is* a vital presence in the lives of Latino youth. Despite the low status that social (and more recently, academic) uses of Spanish have had historically in schools and in US society in general, its influence is ineradicable, in the same way that the influence of English is pervasive in the world. For those of us who come from bilingual/multidialectal communities in the United States, Spanish is in our English and English is in our Spanish and both are an inextricable part of who we are. Sometimes both languages are intertwined in complex ways and sometimes they have distinct identities, and many variants are possible within the same person.

Although some attention has been given to examining the influence of this sociolinguistic reality on the development of communication strategies (Zentella, 1997) and oral virtuosity (Flores, 1993) among Latino youth, negligible attention has been given to its influence on the development of literacy in English, in Spanish, and in both, even though literacy is integral to language development. Greater attention has been given to the study of emergent biliteracy within the context of dual/second language learning; for example, both Edelsky (1983) and Hudelson (1984) have examined for close to two decades emergent biliteracy in the primary grades. However, recently researchers have begun to examine the written expression of Spanish/English bilinguals at the intermediate (Reyes, 1991) and secondary levels (Valdés, 1991). Reyes (1991) found 'stark differences' in the written expression of incipient bilinguals (learners in bilingual/ESL programs) by language whereas Valdés (1991) found that even the writing of functional bilinguals (learners in mainstream, non-bilingual programs) evidenced non-native qualities that distinguished them from monolingual peers. McKay (1989) refers to these non-native features as written discourse accent, which she defines as a lack of proficiency in grammar, word choice, cohesion, rhetorical organization, and topic development.

In part, the problem is one of complexity, as Hornberger (1989) and Valdés (1991) emphasize. The complexities of biliteracy need to be disentangled, and this demands equally complex, interdisciplinary frameworks for locating and understanding the social practices in and around community uses of literacy in Spanish, in English, and both. Hornberger developed such a framework, 'using the notion of continuum to provide the overarching conceptual scheme for describing biliterate contexts, development, and media' (1989: 273).

This analysis is important as ongoing research on literacy as a social practice is beginning to shed light on how living in economically and politically marginalized communities leads to the development of multiple forms and uses of literacy that allow children and families to survive in hostile environments (see the work of Moll *et al.*, 1992 on funds of knowledge). Vélez-Ibáñez and Greenberg argue that 'it is the shift from Spanish to English that interrupts or "fractures" an extended development of Spanish comprehension and literacy in reading and writing' (1992: 327). Although translation practices have been of major interest, these form but one of the many categories of practices that reflect how social needs create social practices in and around the symbolic representation of meaning and the presentation of self.

Understanding the incipient forms of biliteracy emerging from social uses of literacy in homes and communities moves us toward unraveling the dormant potential that home/community practices have for learning in school and which may be harnessed to promote the development of literacies in and for academic purposes in English and Spanish, and to shape individual and collective destinies. To paraphrase Labov (1987), the community is a powerful educator for the school. In this chapter, after presenting background information on the context of the city and the school where I carried out my study, I will present three comparative cases of middle-school Latino students which give glimpses of spontaneous biliterate development that is either invisible or misinterpreted in school – all too often, the latter. These cases hint at the untapped potential for intellectual development in formal learning contexts such as schools that resides in bilingual/multidialectal communities.

The Sociohistorical, Sociolinguistic Context

The phenomenal growth and diversification of the Latino community in the United States is strengthening the influence of Spanish in our lives. Each new wave of immigrants from Latin America introduces new varieties of Spanish into established communities. Falcoff (1996) observes that 'in raw statistical terms, the United States is more important in the constellation of Spanish-speaking countries than Uruguay, Ecuador, or Chile or the five Central American republics and Panama combined.' Davis states it more dramatically: 'US Latinos are already the fifth largest nation in Latin America, and in a half century they will be third only to Brazil and Mexico' (2000: 15).

In addition, circular migration combined with the social and linguistic isolation resulting from residential segregation also contribute to the revitalization of Spanish. When Latinos live within geographical proximity in barrios or neighborhoods that form distinct sociolinguistic communities, as many do, the mutual influence and accommodation that results from this contact produces variations or hybridizations in cultural practices, language, and resources. However, when Latinos (and low status social groups in our society) live in disenfranchised communities, language (as does ethnicity) also emerges as a powerful marker of identity. This explains why the Puerto Rican communities, the oldest of all Latino communities in New York City, also evidence the greatest degree of bilinguality. As one scholar asserts:

> Though not a socially recognized asset, bilingual discourse and continued access to Spanish have been a major element in the reinforcement of Puerto Rican cultural identity and in the self-definition of a group demonstrating the full range of Spanish–English language contact. (Flores, 1993: 190)

However, the influence of languages in contact affects more than community sociolinguistics; in a capitalistic society such as ours, it also influences the uses of language in commerce, especially in the booming entertainment and publishing businesses where Latinos recently have come of age.

The growth in the Spanish-speaking media market is producing a change in the treatment of Spanish by the business community, and, therefore, in the public domain. Davis (2000) reports that there are 500

Spanish-language radio stations and two Spanish-language television networks. Even the mainstream media is beginning to program events intended for Spanish-speaking audiences on the major networks and, increasingly, commercials appearing on the major television networks are peppered with Spanish. Falcoff (1996) emphasizes that some of the most important television and radio transmissions in the Spanish language originate in the United States:

> There is a vigorous daily, weekly and monthly Spanish-language press. The importance of books in Spanish is growing rapidly, and some major American publishers are starting to print Spanish-language novels, essays, and works of nonfiction. (Falcoff, 1996: 14)

This instrumental treatment of Spanish in the media and in commerce stands strangely at odds with Propositions 227 in California and 203 in Arizona (which establish the primacy of English in public schooling), putting into question univocal representations of its status and value in public life in the United States. Spanish is, after all, the first European language of the continental United States and an undeniable and integral part of our nation's history. Its status and power, as history also demonstrates, is neither fixed nor immutable.

With eight million inhabitants and more than a million school-age children and youth, New York City is the nation's largest and most diverse urban center and school district. The city has a long history of ethnic and linguistic diversity, which has been traced to its origins as the nation's center of commerce and finance, and its first capital. Commenting on the PBS documentary based on the Pulitzer Prize-winning history of New York called *Gotham*, Times reporter Dan Berry (1999) states it bluntly: New York City was 'largely founded on the premise of making a buck.' As the documentary also explains, 'these commercial roots contributed to a kind of no-nonsense tolerance that continues to this day' (Berry, 1999: 52). This tolerance may be read in the instrumental use of Spanish by local businesses (many hiring Spanish-speaking laborers) in Spanish-speaking communities.

The city continues to be the destination for large numbers of immigrants, as evidenced by the dramatic changes New York City has experienced over the past decade, specifically the growth and diversification of its Latino population, which now constitutes 25% of the total population and 38% of the school-age population (surpassing the African-American student population which has been dominant for the past 50 years). It is noteworthy that a full one-third of the city's school-age population has been Latino for the past 30 years, primarily Puerto Rican

(American citizens by an act of Congress in 1917), who have outnumbered all Latino groups since the turn of the century. However, over the past two decades, the influx of immigrants from the Caribbean and Central America, overwhelmingly from Santo Domingo and Mexico, is changing the face of the city, making it the largest Latino city in the United States (Davis, 2000).

Because of the power of English and the revitalization of Spanish, New York City has a distinctive Latinized bilingual character. Zentella documents how this dynamic affects the use of Spanish and English found in these heterogeneous communities, which she describes as a 'bilingual/multidialectal repertoire, that is, a spectrum of linguistic codes that range from standard to non-standard dialects in English and Spanish, one of which an individual may speak the best and others which s/he may speak with specific interlocutors or for specific purposes' (1997: 41).

Zentella identifies at least seven dialects of English and Spanish as comprising this bilingual/multidialectal repertoire in the Puerto Rican community she studied, which suggests that there is a potentially even broader range of dialects that are rising from the Latinization of New York. Among the dialects Zentella found in the Puerto Rican community of East Harlem are Popular Puerto Rican Spanish, Standard Puerto Rican Spanish, English-Dominant Spanish, Puerto Rican English, African-American Vernacular English, Hispanicized English, and Standard New York City English. She cautions, however, that these dialects are more overlapping than a discrete listing conveys, thus her use of the term multidialectal repertoire, a term in keeping with Hornberger's notion of the continua of biliterate media. More importantly, Zentella adds that this repertoire is dynamic and in constant flux to reflect the influence of kinship, friendship, and collegial networks in our lives. From this perspective, language development is a life-span phenomenon that reflects and results from socialization processes. In addition, as both Hudelson (1986) and Valdés (1991) point out, community language norms and usage may also have an effect on written expression. Thus, membership in these bilingual/multidialectal communities influences not just the way the language is spoken, but also how it is written.

Even so, the bilingual and biliterate potential of Latino youth remains, for the most part, invisible or discredited in settings where students' bilingualism and biliteracy is neither understood nor valued by bilingual and non-bilingual educators. As a result, many Latino students may have endured long-term disparagement and denial of access to their mother tongue as a valued resource which is vital to learning and self-making (Suarez-Orozco & Suarez-Orozco, 1995). This denial, in turn, affects students' beliefs about who they are, how they use language, and what they know (Altwerger & Ivener, 1994). As Cummins (1994) explains, when school personnel reject students' identities (by punishing them for using their native language, for example), they force students to make an unnecessary and potentially traumatic choice between their two cultures, and the resulting conflict may actually interfere with learning and, more importantly, with their sense of self. Students' biliteracy, however, is visible in settings outside of school, elicited when the need arises, to accomplish personal and social goals, and to survive. However, we know more about how living in bilingual/multidialectal communities shapes language use than about its influences on the writing practices of school-age children and youth (Valdés, 1991).

Transforming School Learning Contexts

Presently, Latino students in New York City are likely to attend under-achieving, segregated schools – possibly the most segregated in the nation. By the time they enter high school, these youngsters are far behind others in terms of academic achievement (Reyes, 1994), a serious problem at a time when a college diploma is essential for economic survival. Schooled literacies, writing in particular, play vital gatekeeping functions in creating or limiting access to a post-secondary education which is essential to increase the life chances of these students. Latino students are not usually exposed to the forms and functions of literacy (especially writing) that are likely to increase those chances.

Motivated by the seriousness of this situation, I collaborated with a middle-school teacher (now director of a welcome center for parents) for five years to address this inequality. Ours was a modest effort to craft a version of quality instruction that addressed concerns associated with being a member of this stigmatized 'minority' during the middle-school years, a time when these students are most vulnerable in their schooling. First- and second-generation children of Spanish-speaking immigrants from countries such as the Dominican Republic, Ecuador, El Salvador, and Honduras, and second- and third-generation Americans of Puerto Rican ancestry experienced a range of literacy practices associated with the work of social scientists. More importantly, they applied these practices to locate, document, and legitimize local knowledge on social issues that were of concern to them but which did not form a part of the required curriculum. It was in this specific context of use that students engaged in and harnessed the power of the strategic application of literacy to learn and to participate in a scholarly community that typically devalues who they are and what they know. In terms of the continua, these practices were directed toward the minority, vernacular, and contextualized ends of the continua of biliterate context.

Guiding students to locate the local knowledge, i.e. vernacular, minority, contextualized content, embedded in their daily lives enabled them to re-experience the ordinary, transforming routine activities into unusual opportunities to practice forms and functions of literacy associated with academic pursuits. Thus interacting with family members, going to medical appointments, visiting a hospitalized relative, running errands, attending church services, or watching television became opportunities to do school work instead of being distractors or obstacles to it. In redefining students' social worlds as sources of knowledge, wisdom, and emotional support which could be drawn on to accomplish challenging academic activities rather than as problems or obstacles to be overcome or avoided, students' social identities were also redefined. They did not have to stop being who they were (that is, put aside one identity to assume another) as a condition for acceptance into our special community of learners.

In all of these activities, Spanish had an undeniable presence. Using Spanish was a vital means of lessening the social distance between Latino students and teachers. It allowed us to make discoveries about the strengths and capabilities of learners that would not have been as readily transparent in English. In their study of community-based organizations for Latino and African-American youth, Heath and McLaughlin found that creating a sense of belonging or community:

> depends much more on how those in one's immediate environment ask questions, give directions, frame time and space, and reflect expectations than it does on verbal declarations of collectivity or acceptance. (1993: 8)

We agree that creating community occurs in subtle ways during ordinary, face-to-face interactions and in our community both Spanish and English played important roles in accomplishing this sense of belonging.

Separate from its use to create social/pedagogical relationships, Latino youth had exposure to learning in Spanish in ways that served to elevate the status of Spanish among youth for whom Spanish is often a disparaged language in school settings, even in bilingual programs. When a Latino epidemiologist was invited to give a lecture on Aids-related diseases, it gave access to expert knowledge on a topic of vital concern (at the time this borough had the highest incidence of Aids nationally), but it also elevated the status of Spanish among students who have little exposure to Latino professionals who use their bilingualism to help others learn. Contrary to popular belief, most Latino students have not attended bilingual programs, and in these non-bilingual settings the teachers are likely to be non-Hispanic white. Similarly, when students attended state and national conferences for bilingual educators they had exposure to a large professional community who use Spanish in their personal and professional lives to learn and to connect to others, and to improve the conditions for learning in school. In effect, Latino youth gained entry into a social network that valued and used their bilingualism, including their biliteracy, in their personal and professional lives. This, in turn, elicited students' biliterate potential because bilingual individuals, as Hornberger (1989) reports, key language choice to the characteristics of the situation.

As important, students had exposure to non-Latinos (and future teachers) who valued the importance of Spanish, as did Carolyn and Monique (pseudonyms), pre-service graduate students who volunteered to learn from and work with the young adolescent learners in the low-performing middle school where these activities occurred. Although Monique was initially more fluent in Spanish than Carolyn, eventually Carolyn's resolve to learn Spanish led her to gain sufficient competence in Spanish to give a talk at an invitational exchange held at the University of Puerto Rico. The five and a half-page manuscript Carolyn prepared to guide her talk at this exchange was dedicated to the students who contributed to her biliterate development. Clearly, encounters with future teachers and esteemed adults who also value the learning of Spanish and the linguistic resources that define Latino youth are not the norm in school contexts.

This description of our inquiry-oriented approach is intended to make clear the intellectual and emotional context which gives rise to the biliterate potential of Latino youth and which is the focus of this chapter. Clearly, the context we organized shifted the value we attached to Spanish in this mainstream setting, as Spanish was used, when appropriate, in combination with English to establish social and pedagogical relationships, to access information, and to re-present ourselves through the written and spoken word. Analyzed from the perspective of the continua framework, it is clear that, in our micro-level school learning context, we inverted the power relationships of the macro-level wider societal context to create a context where multilingualism rather than monolingualism, and oral as well as literate language use were privileged. Students' use of Spanish, which never detracted from the primacy of English, was evident in face-to-face interaction with peers and adults and in the substantive body of writings that were collected over a four-year period.

The written texts produced by students as they engaged in inquiry were, in effect, a means of representing themselves within the various social worlds in which they interacted and in all of these worlds Spanish had an undeniable presence.

Comparative Cases of Biliterate Development

It must be understood, however, that the texts produced by students do not reside in the written word alone as the written and spoken word were seamlessly interwoven. Hornberger refers to 'any and all instances in which communication occurs in two or more languages around writing' as biliteracy (1990: 2). This view is consistent with Wells' (1990) notion that all modes of symbolic representation constitute texts, including oral discussions and conversations. Further, although Spanish may be more transparent in the presence of others who are similarly bilingual, it is always present in ways that are more difficult to discern. It must be read in the symbolic representations that are products of students' expressive capabilities, even of those who are long-term Americans.

Spanish is evident in the code students use to clothe their ideas, i.e. the biliterate media (formal and informal varieties of Spanish, English, or a combination of the two). Reyes (1991) even found differences in the handwriting of students when writing in English as compared to Spanish, another aspect of biliterate media. Spanish in the students' bilingual/multidialectal repertoire is also evident in what they choose to write about (e.g. the family, relationships, school experiences, cultural practices, human agency), their rhetorical strategies (e.g. a conversational tone, giving advice, using humor), and the genres and modalities they prefer to frame their ideas (e.g. an oral performance such as a speech or rap, storytelling, a letter), all of these latter relating to biliterate content.

While Valdés (1991) argues that differences in students' written expression reflect multiple influences, e.g. bilingualism, length of exposure to writing, and writing conventions in English and the primary language, others emphasize cultural influences on writing (Grabe & Kaplan, 1989; Smitherman, 1994). In studying the writings of multidialectal African-American students (a form of bilingualism/biliteracy in my estimation), Smitherman (1994) found distinctive features of students' discourse style that reflect what she considers to be a different world-view, and that is different from grammatical use (e.g. syntax and agreement). In effect, biliterate development, and specifically 'the creative application of L1 knowledge to L2 learning' (Hornberger, 1989: 284), goes beyond what is known as language transference (for example, McKay's (1989) notion of 'written discourse accent') or language fossilization (as Valdés describes).

Specifically, motivated by a need to understand the poor performance of African-American students on the writing tasks of the National Assessment of Educational Progress (NAEP), Smitherman (1994) found that there is a discernible African-American discourse style of writing that reflects a different cultural orientation and world-view, conditioned by their experiences in the world. These features include: (a) rhythmic, dramatic, evocative language; (b) reference to color–race–ethnicity; (c) use of proverbs, aphorisms, Biblical verses; (d) sermonic tone reminiscent of traditional Black church rhetoric; (e) direct address–conversational tone; (f) cultural references; (g) ethnolinguistic idioms; (h) verbal inventiveness; (i) cultural values–community consciousness (or concern for welfare of entire community, not just individuals); (j) field-dependency (or lack of distance from topics and subjects). I have found many analogous features in the writings of the Latino students I have worked with in non-bilingual settings, some that reflect students' identities as members of bilingual communities.

The three comparative cases featured in the following narrative are of biliterate youths who have lived in bilingual/multidialectal communities most, if not all, of their lives. Thus, they are best described as circumstantial, functional bilinguals (Valdés, 1991), that is, they are 'members of a group of individuals who as a group must become bilingual in order to participate in the society that surrounds them' (8). Although they are different from recent arrivals who may be in bilingual or ESL programs, what they share in common is their use of their linguistic codes to express themselves in writing, and the perception of teachers that they are 'very poor in writing.'

My analysis of these students' writings over a five-year period has led me to other conclusions. Latino students evidence surprising levels of biliteracy in the sense that Hornberger (1990) suggests. It should be clear, however, that our activities were designed primarily to motivate personally meaningful writing in a variety of academic genres in English. Students' ability to process information presented through one language modality (usually spoken Spanish) and re-presented in another (usually written English) was not of immediate interest although the study of biliteracy in this context is powerful precisely because it illustrates how knowledge of Spanish is always present, but it also surfaces as a deliberate strategy when the need arises in authentic and hospitable contexts of use.

In our case, this hospitable context was an institutional setting where the functions and uses of languages other than English (Spanish, in our case) are seldom applied to broaden access to knowledge and information, particularly knowledge and information that resides in people as much as in books. Rather, it is a setting where non-standard uses of language associated with bilingualism are, at best, poorly understood or, at worst, stigmatized (Reyes, 1991; Valdés, 1991; Zentella, 1997). Even so, these cases give glimpses of how literacy knowledge and skills in one language aid (not impede) the learning of knowledge and skills in the other. However, these cases also illustrate that the written language of circumstantial Spanish/English bilinguals is qualitatively different from the written language of non-bilinguals as it reveals evidence for the continued influence of Spanish (or the home culture, as Hudelson refers to it) long after students have entered mainstream instructional settings, as Valdés (1991) observes. Lastly, these cases illustrate the individual paths to literate/biliterate development that each learner takes, thereby confirming the findings of previous studies in monolingual and bilingual contexts (see, for example, the work of Hudelson, 1986). The comparative case approach serves to highlight these individual paths as each learner's uniqueness stands out when seen in relation to her/his peers. While there is great intra-learner variability, that discussion goes beyond the scope of this chapter.

Contrastive Cases of Biliterate Development

Consistent with the continua framework, the following accounts discuss individuals' biliterate development along L1–L2, oral–written, and receptive–productive dimensions, all of this understood to be occurring in relation to the biliterate contexts, media, and content I have outlined.

Pensive Izzy

I met Izzy in September of 1990 when he was 12 years old. He was a first-grade holdover, which, as he relates to Monique, 'made [me] mad because it was just 'cause I was Spanish.' Although his mother was born in the Dominican Republic and his father in Puerto Rico, Izzy makes clear that his 'heritage is from the United States.' Although Izzy has a good sense of humor and an easy relational style, he has the maturity and seriousness of one who bears the responsibility of being the man of the house. At the time we met, he was living with his mother and two younger sisters, which also meant negotiating the English-speaking world (translating) for an adult who speaks primarily Spanish. Izzy often seeks out *consejos* (advice) and information from esteemed adults. However, while respected and liked by this year's official teacher and peers, in academic settings Izzy's hesitant demeanor suggests self-doubt more than thoughtfulness. This may be a reaction to and consequence of institutional treatment, as these quotes reveal:

> Izzy's work and study habits need improvement. He gets easily frustrated and is willing to give up. (1st grade teacher)
> [Izzy's] behavior and attitude need improvement. (3rd grade)
> [Izzy has the] ability to do better but lacks consistency. (5th grade)

In contrast, our interactions revealed extraordinary thoughtfulness, human sensitivities, and a strong awareness of self – qualities which were distinctive in comparison to his peers, as he gives voice to in his own writings:

> She (Dr Mercado) was so kind that she gave (us) a calendar and we wrote the special occasions.

> Monique (a pseudonym) and I were talking about a lot of things. She told me that I used to do more work than know (now). I think it's true. . . . We also talked about taking notes. I need help so I decided to tell Indio (a pseudonym) to help me. I think this talk help(ed) me think.

Izzy emphasizes, as the situation warrants, that he 'speaks two languages,' but it might be more appropriate to say that he is multidialectal in the sense that Zentella uses this term. His English reflects multiple social worlds; it has traces of Dominican and Puerto Rican Spanish phonology, reflecting his familial and friendship networks, and a speech style peppered with southern expressions ('ya'all') to mark solidarity with a bi-racial peer group. Clearly, Izzy's speech reflects that his social networks are distinct from those of Indio, and others in his class, suggesting the uniqueness of each student's path to oral and written language development. Izzy shifts easily between English and Spanish during casual conversations with bilingual adults, in a manner that illustrates the importance of Spanish in establishing and marking personal relationships among Latinos. Spanish is also the language of the home, and the language he uses to help his mom learn English by writing words on a blackboard for her. Although most of his school writing is in English, it is clear that, for Izzy, Spanish and English are intertwined in unusual ways, in speaking and in writing.

In writing, Izzy has a distinctive clean, clear, and engaging narrative style, as this chronicle of our trip to a statewide conference for bilingual educators ('The Conference on Saturday') demonstrates (see Figure 7.1).

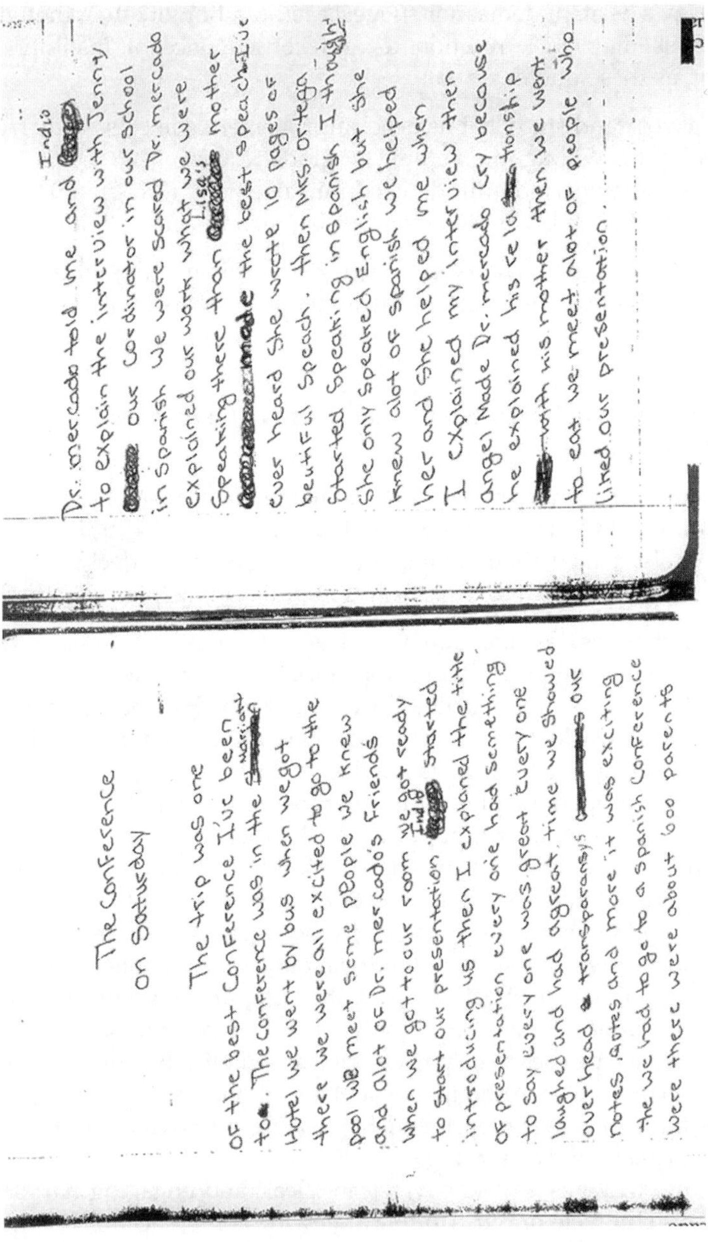

The Conference
on Saturday

The trip was one
of the best Conference I've been
to. The conference was in the Marriott
Hotel we went by bus when we got
there we were all excited to go to the
pool we meet some people we knew
and alot of Dr. mercado's Friends
When we get to our room we got ready
to start our presentation Indio started
introducing us then I explaned the title
of presentation every one had something
to say every one was great every one
laughed and had a great time we showed
overhead transparansys our
notes, notes and more it was exciting
the we had to go to a Spanish Conference
were there were about 600 parents

Indio
Dr. mercado told me and
to explain the interview with Jenny
our Cordinator in our school
in Spanish We were scared Dr. mercado
explained our work what we were
Speaking there than Lisa's mother
made the best speach I've
ever heard She wrote 10 pages of
beutiful Speach. then Mrs. Ortega
Started Speaking in Spanish I thought
She only Speaked English but she
knew alot of Spanish we helped
her and She helped me when
I Explained my interview then
angel Made Dr. mercado cry because
he explained his relationship
with his mother then we went
to eat we meet alot of people who
liked our presentation.

Figure 7.1 Izzy's essay, 'The Conference on Saturday'

At the conference the children referred to as the 'Spanish Conference,' Izzy found himself, once again, helping an adult (a paraprofessional, this time) with her Spanish. As was characteristic of Izzy, he confesses surprise and pleasure at being of help to an adult and expresses appreciation to Lisa's mother for the 'beautiful ten-page speech' she presented. In both instances, Izzy reflects how much he values the Spanish language.

Although the instructional context establishes the primacy of English, this student's primary language and culture (lived experience) continue to influence his writing in English. This ongoing influence puts into question notions that the influence of students' primary language (the L1) is a temporary phenomenon and supports Valdés' (1991) argument that language use like Izzy's (particularly his use of idioms) evidences non-native-like features which she believes characterize the writing of functional bilinguals who live in bilingual/multidialectal communities. Smitherman (1994) would probably say Izzy's language use reflects his use of 'ethnolinguistic idioms.' However, both explanations acknowledge how the lived experiences (culture) of learners shape their written language expression and development. Also, both explanations are strikingly different from the judgment that Izzy is 'very poor at writing.'

Izzy also experiments with writing in Spanish, as the need arises. When Izzy's class was invited to attend the Aids lecture given by a Spanish-speaking epidemiologist, Izzy used his understanding of Spanish to gain access to technical information from an expert (information on an important topic not likely to be available in English), and he uses his communicative competence in two languages to translate what he has learned (in Spanish) to present it within the genre of lecture notes (in English), as presented below (see Figure 7.2). What is interesting is how Izzy incorporates technical terms such as *fiebres, diarreas, pulmonía, trastornos del sistema central,* at the end of these notes (which I assume he copied), possibly to emphasize the legitimacy of the information he has received and his self-worth as a learner capable of receiving information in technical Spanish. Clearly this unusual school experience made transparent the untapped potential that students such as Izzy have using his Spanish language competence to augment his learning opportunities – even for a student who has been born and raised in the Bronx. It illustrates, as well, how deceptive it is to assume that Izzy's English competence will be on a par with native-born speakers of English who do not live bilingual lives, as Hudelson (1986) and Valdés (1991) maintain.

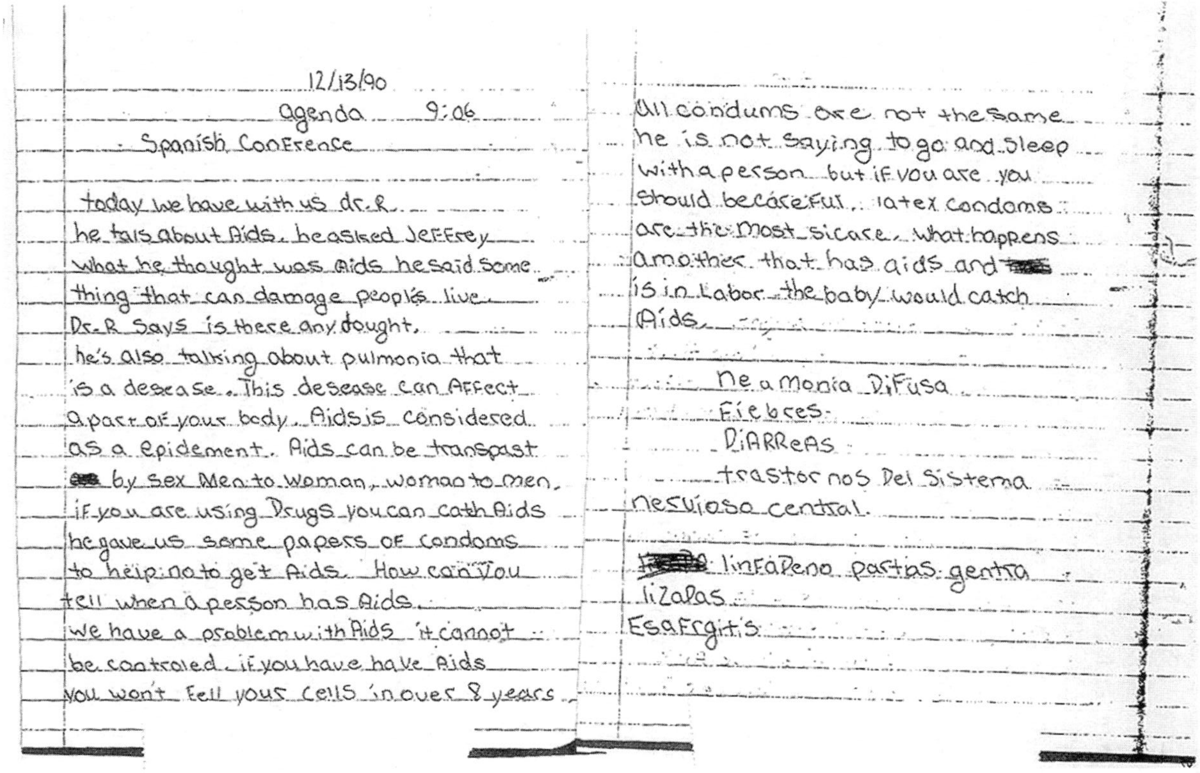

12/13/90
agenda 9:06
Spanish Confrence

today we have with us dr. R
he tals about Aids. he asked Jeffrey
what he thought was Aids he said some
thing that can damage peoplés live.
Dr. R says is there any dought.
he's also talking about pulmonia that
is a desease. This desease can Affect
a parr of your body. Aids is considered
as a epidement. Aids can be transpast
by sex Men to woman, woman to men.
if you are using Drugs you can cath Aids
he gave us some papers of condoms
to heip no to get Aids. How can You
tell when a person has Aids.
we have a problem with Aids it cannot
be controled. if you have have Aids
you won't fell yous cells in over 8 years

All condums are not the same
he is not saying to go and sleep
with a person but if you are you
should be careful. latex condoms
are the most sicure. What happens
a mother that has aids and
is in Labor the baby would catch
Aids.

Ne a Monia DiFusa
Fiebres.
DiARReAS
trastornos Del Sistema
nesvioso central.

linfaDeno partas genta
lizaDas.
EsaFrgitis.

Figure 7.2 Izzy's essay, 'Spanish Conference'

Indio, a performer

Indio was 12 years old when we first met in the fall of 1989. He was born in Puerto Rico of a New York City-born mother. He entered school in New York City at the age of five. After he was held over in the first grade, his mother agreed to place him in a (transitional) bilingual program. He says with a tinge of anger that he was held back 'because he was Spanish,' but writes that his 'favorite school subjects are reading and Spanish.' Indio often spends his summers with his grandfather in Puerto Rico. This constant contact with the island is evident in the 'Hispanized English' he speaks which, according to Zentella's term, is marked by a transfer of Spanish phonology and grammar, 'common among those who have been reared in Puerto Rico' (1997: 47). Interestingly, his mother does not appear as verbally facile in Spanish as Indio is, however this assessment is based on limited interactions. What is especially distinctive about Indio is that he accomplishes complex relational work through writing, as he has discovered its potential to elicit the attention, approval, and encouragement of respected adults (this proved to be an important function or use of writing for these learners). However, because Indio often wrote in response to face-to-face conversations, the spoken word (often in Spanish) was always intertwined with the written word (usually in English).

In speaking, Indio is a performer. We grew to depend on him to moderate our presentations at professional gatherings. Indio displayed oratorical virtuosity in crafting speeches, a literacy practice he introduced to the group, and in assuming the role of moderator, which also included fielding questions following our presentations. This was a role Indio performed with the skill and confidence of a professional, even though we had never prepared him for it. As social scientists tell us (see Flores, 1993), the oratorical skills (e.g. improvization, performance, and playfulness with language) that are evident among Latino youth are forms of human expression that represent sociocultural adaptations tied to self-affirmation and survival in hostile environments.

Indio harnesses his expressive abilities in Spanish and English as the need arises. Our participation at 'The Spanish Conference' brought out the incredible potential that resides in Indio. His attentiveness to language and the ease with which he can re-present ideas and experiences, particularly ideas presented in 'professional' varieties of Spanish (that is, Spanish that reflects the influence of the printed word) took us by surprise. In his written reflections (in English) following this event (in Spanish), Indio accurately re-presents the central message of the lengthy speech (10 pages of literate Spanish prose) delivered by Lisa's mother:

> The 'Save' Conference was very nice. ... Before we went to the presentation, Dr M. show us some of her researcher friends. In the conference, the student researchers were doing fine and spoke so professional. ... After the questions, the researchers went to another one but the difference was that the conference was in Spanish. That conference was nice and experenceful to me. CM did lovely in her speech the only thing I remember was the word 'L.E.C.T.U.R.A.' I also forgot what it meant. After CM finish, Lisa's mother went up to talk. She had said to the parents in the audience that when parents hear and let their kids talk and express themselves that the parents then will understand their kids problems. ... At the end Indio took the stand and talk to the parents about how the program 'Research' has help him and his mother get closer. ...
>
> Comments: CM you did great!!! Mrs G. I think you did a wonderful speech! I love it! ... Student researchers you all did wonder, marvelous, great ... !!!! (Indio's fieldnotes, 3 September)

For Indio, Spanish remains an unexploited potential as it is primarily used as an adjunct text that gives rise to or enhances the written word. It would, however, be deceptive not to think that Indio is biliterate, in the sense that Hornberger uses this term.

Lisa the masquerader

Lisa turned 11 in November of 1990, making her the youngest member of her class. Her mother celebrated Lisa's birthday in class, bringing rituals of the home into the school at a time when pre-adolescent learners commonly turn away from their parents. Lisa wrote that she was named for a character in a book her mother read before she was born, most likely as a Spanish translation of the original. She was born in the Dominican Republic, as were her older brother and parents. Lisa's family left her in Santo Domingo when they first ventured to New York City because they were unable to obtain a visa for her. Her uncle brought her to New York at the age of two-and-a-half to reunite Lisa with her family. Thus far, Lisa's schooling has alternated between the Dominican Republic and New York City. She attended bilingual programs in kindergarten through second grade in New York City and, due to a death in the family, she returned to the Dominican Republic for third grade, at a school where her mother was a close friend of the principal. She came back to New York for fourth grade where, once again, she was placed in a bilingual class because she 'needed to learn more English.' This is her second year in a mainstream class, and the first time with a teacher who happens to be bilingual.

Lisa was often hesitant and shy to speak in class (even in small groups), but her writing reveals a playful personality, sharp wit, and independent thinking, depending on her mood. Thus writing provides a mask (or safe space) which allows her to give voice to ideas she is often reluctant to express publicly. Newkirk (1997) tells us that all forms of 'self-expression,' all of our ways of being personal, are forms of performance – in Erving Goffman's terms, 'a presentation of self' (Newkirk, 1997: 3). Her writing also evidences heightened awareness of language (metalinguistic awareness) as a tool for thinking, unusual in comparison to her peers and possibly a reflection of her strong bilingual background, as this excerpt reveals:

> I wrote this note because I didn't understand some of the words. . . . The words I wasn't friendly with was promptly and dissatisfied. I had never heard of those words so I'm going to search for it in the dictionary.

In one of her first writing pieces, a letter in which she introduces herself to a potential pen-pal, Lisa displays her knowledge of local demographics when she assumes her pen-pal is likely to be Puerto Rican. Lisa uses codeswitching appropriately to describe a favorite meal (*arroz con mollejaz*), a cultural referent that defies translation, and interjects humor effectively to diffuse any potential tensions commonly associated with inter-ethnic relations, as this pointed commentary reveals:

> My culture is from the Dominican Republic but don't worry. I like Puerto Ricans. All my best friends I have are Puerto Ricans so you don't have to worry about it. Dominicans are just like you guys. They just want to be your friends so the world could be together. I kind of like Puerto Ricans alot. OK lets just forget about that know let's know talk about me.

Lisa's multifaceted personality comes out strongly in her writing; in contrast, her soft spoken manner and her bilingualism are revealed in her softly accented speech in English. She speaks fairly Standard Spanish phonology and grammar, perhaps the product of her mother's background in education. However, what is distinct about Lisa's situation in comparison to her peers is that she probably has had the greatest exposure to literate Spanish at home, by way of a mother who loves to read and to write ('*Soy amante de la escritura, lectura, y matemáticas*'), as she revealed to us in solidarity with the students in the class. Even so, we suspect Lisa may not fully understand or appreciate its potential, as yet. She was as surprised as we all were to learn about her mother's oratorial and writing skills in Spanish, as she describes in a chapter she titled, 'A Conference My Mother Made':

> This was in Westchester. My mother was making a conference in Spanish. She wrote 10 pages of what she was going to say in the conference. I was shocked because I didn't know she was going to write all those pages. I thought she was only going to write a brief speech.

Even so, as is the case with Izzy and Indio, Lisa's biliterate potential is an untapped potential, as these notes from the Aids conference reveal.

Conclusions

The cases of biliterate development among Latino youth presented in this chapter illustrate how students harness the power of biliteracy to affirm themselves, to relate to others and to gain access to a broad range of intellectual and emotional resources that are beyond the walls of their classrooms. Furthermore, all of this is accomplished as the valuing of English is also strengthened. Although what is represented as the dominant ideology (I am not convinced it is, considering that both New York City and New York State have policies promoting the use of students' linguistic resources for learning in school) emphasizes the negative impact that the vernacular (in this case Spanish) has on school achievement and the learning of English, these comparative cases suggest otherwise.

Even so, these cases also illustrate missed opportunities to broaden students' use of their bilingualism as intellectual, social, and economic resources in strategic ways. We need to go beyond valuing Spanish to become more strategic in our efforts if we are to broaden the communicative repertoires and the learning and career opportunities of Latino students. This also means that all educators, including researchers, need to understand the vital connection between language, community, and identity, and that language has deep affective roots. When teacher education programs emphasize the role of language in learning from purely linguistic, psycholinguistic, or psychological models, teachers are not being prepared to understand the important role that language plays in the formation of self. This, in turn, has dangerous consequences for perpetuating existing social and educational inequalities.

These understandings are especially important at this historical juncture given that the growing Latino presence is altering the dynamics of power in interesting ways. In our free-market economy, producers of goods and services are paying close attention to the Latino community and the competition for the huge profits that are at stake, evident in the wide assortment of products and services specifically targeted at this community and the need for professionals who are bilingual and biliterate and who give access to these communities and to global markets where Spanish is the language of commerce. Because schools are the mirrors of society, the societal curriculum may yet emerge as a powerful positive educator in ways that we have yet to imagine and it may yet play a decisive role in unleashing the dormant potential that resides in bilingual/multidialectal communities for the benefit of our youth and our communities. Such an unleashing of biliterate potential would be for the benefit not only of our youth, but also our communities.

References

Altwerger, B. and Ivener, B.L. (1994) Self-esteem: Access to literacy in multicultural and multilingual classrooms. In K. Spangenberg-Urbschat and R. Pritchard (eds) *Kids Come in All Languages.* Newark, DE: International Reading Association.

Berry, D. (1999) A metropolis made by greed. *New York Times.* 21 November.

Cummins, J. (1994) The acquisition of English as a second language. In K. Spangenberg-Urbschat and R. Pritchard (eds) *Kids Come in All Languages.* Newark, DE: International Reading Association.

Davis, M. (2000) *Magical Urbanism.* New York: Verso.

Edelsky, C. (1983) *Writing in a Bilingual Program: Habia Una Vez.* Norwood, NJ: Ablex.

Falcoff, M. (1996) North of the border. The origins and fallacies of the 'Hispanic' threat to the United States. *Commentary, The Times Literary Supplement,* No. 4859 (pp.14–15). 17 May.

Flores, J. (1993) *Divided Borders. Essays on Puerto Rican Identity.* Houston, TX: Arte Publico Press.

Grabe, W. and Kaplan, R.B. (1989) Writing in a second language: Contrastive rhetoric. In D.M. Johnson and D.H. Roen (eds) *Richness in Writing* (pp. 263–83). New York: Longman.

Heath, S.B. and McLaughlin, M. (eds) (1993) *Identity in Inner-city Youth.* New York: Teachers College Press.

Hornberger, N. (1989) Continua of biliteracy. *Review of Educational Research* 59 (3), 271–96.

Hornberger, N. (1990) Creating successful learning contexts for biliteracy. *Penn Working Papers in Educational Linguistics* 6 (1), 1–21.

Hudelson, S. (1984) Kan yu ret and rayt en ingles: Children become literate in English as a second language. *TESOL Quarterly* 18 (2), 221–38.

Hudelson, S. (1986) ESL children's writing: What we've learned, what we're learning. In P. Rigg and D.S. Enright (eds) *Children and ESL: Integrating*

Perspectives (pp. 23–54). Washington, DC: Teaching English to Speakers of Other Languages.

Labov, W. (1987) The community as educator. In J. Langer (ed.) *Language, Literacy, and Culture: Issues of Society and Schooling* (pp. 128–46). Norwood, NJ: Ablex.

McKay, S.L. (1989) Topic development and written discourse accent. In D.M. Johnson and D.H. Roen (eds) *Richness in Writing* (pp. 253–62). New York: Longman.

Moll, L.C., Amanti, C., Neff, D. and Gonzalez, N. (1992) Funds of knowledge for teaching: Using a qualitative approach to connect homes and classrooms. *Theory into Practice* 31 (2), 132–41.

Newkirk, T. (1997) *The Performance of Self in Student Writing*. Portsmouth, NH: Boynton/Cooke Publishers/Heinemann.

Reyes, L.O. (Chair) (1994) *Making the Vision a Reality: A Latino Action Agenda for Educational Reform*. Final report of the Latino Commission on Educational Reform, 23 March (Available from New York City Board of Education, 110 Livingston St., Brooklyn, New York).

Reyes, M. de la Luz (1991) Bilingual student writers: A question of fair evaluation. *English Journal* 80 (91), 16–23.

Smitherman, G. (1994) The blacker the berry, the sweeter the juice: African American student writers. In A.H. Dyson and C. Genishi (eds) *The Need for Story. Cultural Diversity in Classroom and Community* (pp. 80–101). Urbana, IL: National Council of Teachers of English.

Suarez-Orozco, C. and Suarez-Orozco, M.M. (1995) *Transformations: Immigration, Family Life, and Achievement Motivation among Latino Adolescents*. Stanford, CA: Stanford University Press.

Valdés, G. (1991) *Bilingual Minorities and Language Issues in Writing: Toward Profession-wide Responses to a New Challenge. Technical Report No. 54.* University of Berkeley, Berkeley, CA: Center for the Study of Writing.

Vélez-Ibáñez, C.G. and Greenberg, J.B. (1992) Formation and transformation of funds of knowledge among US–Mexican households. *Anthropology & Education Quarterly* 23 (4), 313–35.

Wells, G. (1990) Creating the conditions to encourage literate thinking. *Educational Leadership* 47 (6), 13–17.

Zentella, A.C. (1997) *Growing Up Bilingual*. Malden, MA: Blackwell.

Chapter 8

To Correct or Not to Correct Bilingual Students' Errors is a Question of Continua-ing Reimagination

MELISA CAHNMANN

Introduction

One of the most frequent questions I receive from teachers in the multilingual and multicultural foundations courses I teach is how to respond to students' written and spoken language errors. Increasingly, in critical theories of language education there has been a movement away from the rigid enforcement of standard English and the eradication of students' nonstandard dialects and toward a more sociolinguistic view of language – one that accepts and promotes the use of standard *and* nonstandard varieties of language and one that advocates bi- or multi-dialectalism. This shift in thinking requires teachers to examine their own language biases and change their role from that of 'language police' to 'linguist,' one who studies, tolerates, and appreciates variety while still teaching – but not enforcing – the language of power. Such a shift toward more critical practice is tremendously challenging for any teacher, but especially so for bilingual educators working with urban Latino populations. These bilingual teachers often work with students who negotiate standard/marketplace and vernacular varieties of both Spanish and English. Little is known about how this negotiation takes place in the day-to-day practice of critical bilingual educators. In analyzing my data I have sought to understand how the classroom teacher, the students, and myself, the researcher, addressed the use and value of marketplace and vernacular varieties of language within bilingual development. What can such an analysis reveal about the limitations and possibilities for bilingual education?

My goal as a researcher and educator in the field of bilingual education has been to voice critique of bilingual education from a position of advocacy. My underlying assumption is that public school support for literacy in two languages can promote a more socially just, aware, and, as a consequence, better educated citizenry. Another assumption is that any attempt to implement effective bilingual education in a society that, for the most part, views other languages as threats to national unity or as impediments to social and economic efficiency, will not be without struggle and contradiction. In this chapter I will use the core aspects of the continua of biliteracy to understand the struggle and contradiction that are involved in the assessment of students' biliteracy production. My aim is to highlight *struggle* as an essential part of biliteracy teaching and learning, that is, the simultaneity of success and failure inherent in any attempt to challenge the status quo and promote literacy in two languages, particularly among Latino youth.

Defining Biliteracy

I have used the continua of biliteracy to explore the relationships between language, identity, culture, and power in this study. For my analysis of student errors and correction I have highlighted three core continua – monolingual–bilingual (norms), oralcy–literacy, and macro–micro – that I felt best captured the comprehensive meaning of the original 12. I have used these three core continua to build on Hornberger's (1990: 213) definition of biliteracy and propose another working definition:

> *Biliteracy*: any and all micro instances of communication that take place along a continuum of bilingual–monolingual norms within oral–literate modes and traditions that can change and be changed by macro social structural contexts.

At the most fundamental level biliteracy concerns two language codes. Decades of sociolinguistic research have concluded that there are two distinct norms (i.e. attitudes, beliefs, and practices) for using and valuing two codes that exist in a community. The first, *monolingual norms*, are values, attitudes, and uses of biliteracy that emerge from a one language = one nation = one literacy paradigm (Anderson, 1991; Heller, 1999). For example, one may have bilingual abilities in more than one language but may have a monolingual orientation that maintains more or less firm separation between the use of one code and another. In contrast, *bilingual norms* are values, attitudes and uses of biliteracy where the boundaries between codes are blurred, where there is such extensive and sanctioned use of code-switching that at times the two codes appear to merge into a new variety of language altogether. For example, when I recently prepared to teach (28 January 2002) a lesson on the events of 11 September in Spanish, I called one of the Puerto Rican students' families from this study to ask how one would refer to the 'World Trade Center' in Spanish. I spoke with a bilingual adult male in the household, asking '*¿Cómo se dice el lugar dónde pasó los eventos del 11 de Septiembre?* (How does one say the place where the events of 11 September occurred?),' careful not to use any of the words in English that I was looking for in Spanish, so as not to influence his answer. He replied, '*nosotros decimos (we say)* los buildings, *o los* twin towers, *o el* World Trade Center.' Eventually, I found '*las torres gemelas*' (the Twin Towers) on a Spanish website (where '*el* World Trade Center' also appeared). However, this exchange made it clear that for this bilingual adult, and many bilingual youth and adults in the community, questions of language separation do not make sense.

Language spoken along bilingual norms (i.e. using a Spanish article with an English noun as in '*los* buildings') is rarely a sanctioned or privileged variety. Rather, as Hornberger and Skilton-Sylvester (2000) suggest, monolingual norms are currently the most powerful, institutionally-sanctioned variety of language use. This is especially so in the case of transitional bilingual education (TBE, the most common variety) in the United States where schools seldom recognize widespread bilingual norms (except to forbid them), preferring only to acknowledge students' shift from a non-English monolingual norm (i.e. Spanish) to an English monolingual norm in the shortest amount of time possible. To recognize monolingual–bilingual norms as part of the definition of biliteracy is to recognize the distinction between knowing two languages and the ways these languages are used, valued, and privileged in different communities in a single society.

A related consideration is that biliteracy is also centrally about two *written* language codes. An ongoing debate questions the degree to which the written, literary, and standard varieties of a single code and the skills involved in receiving (reading) and producing (writing) the written code can be distinguished from the skills involved in receiving (listening/understanding) and producing (speaking) the spoken, vernacular varieties of the same code. The concept of biliteracy recognizes the continuum between *oralcy* and *literacy* in one language and across more than one language where one may have different speaking, listening, reading, and writing abilities in multiple codes. Nonetheless, power is often placed on the ability to comprehend and produce standard, literary texts as opposed to comprehension and production in spoken vernacular forms (Hornberger & Skilton-Sylvester, 2000). Education for powerful biliteracy involves the ability to critique standard literacy texts and produce more inclusive alternatives.

Finally, any definition of biliteracy must consider the immediate moment of an interaction (i.e. person to person around text or person to text) within the surrounding minority–majority power relations. Thus, the *micro–macro* continua frame any single moment of biliteracy as always nested within larger local and local-removed (i.e. national and international) considerations. This study has understood micro–macro relationships as central for understanding that perceived 'success' and 'failure' in the bilingual education classroom must be contextualized within the surrounding socio-political context that supports the relative success of some communities more than others.

Below I use this definition of biliteracy (as composed of monolingual–bilingual norms, literacy–oralcy, and macro–micro considerations) to explore the following aspects of biliteracy and correction: (a) the individual and community *development* of biliteracy and standards for 'correct' or appropriate language use; (b) the language codes, scripts, and grammatical structures (i.e. *media*) involved in producing appropriate language; (c) the *context* where biliteracy errors and correction take place; (d) the *content* through which errors and correction are or are not explicitly discussed. My findings, as presented in the section below, have also helped me to further define what the development, media, context, and content mean in terms of biliteracy relevant to this study and possibly others. Below I introduce some background to this study and working definitions of biliteracy development, media, context, and content as they pertain to correction.

Background

This study is part of a larger critical ethnography of bilingual education. I spent one academic year in Ms Maria's ninth-grade classroom, a site that was recommended to me as a place of best practice in the school district. It was also recommended because it represented a successful, grass roots effort to expand bilingual education from the middle school into the high school grades. I immediately sensed Ms Maria's professionalism when I scheduled my first visit for an afternoon in September 1999. I arrived while she was modeling descriptive writing with her students and she did not stop instruction when I entered her classroom or introduce herself formally until the students left for lunch. At first I felt a little awkward – after all most teachers I'd met stopped teaching entirely to talk when I arrived! But Ms Maria's respect for her own work and that of her students, her homey classroom environment with lace table cloth book displays, a sofa and 'reading' pillows, and her immediately apparent love of literacy and bilingual/biliteracy instruction, kept me coming back for more. As a former bilingual teacher myself, I felt an immediate connection with this teacher's work, and after a few months of observation, I was certain this was a challenging and engaging environment within which to understand the constraints and possibilities of critical practice. This impression was further supported when I learned Ms Maria has been a long-time revolutionary. She was born and raised in Nicaragua and joined the Sandinista forces through the late seventies and eighties, and became an international journalist, and an important part of the Sandinista Literacy and Women's Rights Movements.

I believe that Ms Maria's classroom was an ideal environment to study the possibilities for bilingual education as well as to observe the challenges to successful implementation. It was from Ms Maria and her students that I learned to *re-imagine* or think anew about bilingual education in ways that revitalized original 1968 bilingual policy intentions for 'new and imaginative' programs (United States Commission on Civil Rights, 1975) to meet the needs of youth for whom language proficiency was only one of many obstacles. Ms Maria and her students engaged in re-imagination insofar as they also 're-cognized' in Schmidt's (2000: 51) terms, the relationship between language, identity, culture, and power, reclaiming the possibility of a coherent bilingual, bicultural identity (Owens, 1992: 157).

The Approach

In order to understand the moments of correction involved in full biliterate development, I became a participant observer in Ms Maria's classroom over a school year and I used two kinds of interviews. The first were narrative interviews to get background information on the teacher and students' personal and family histories, and attitudes toward language use, ability, and status. The second were process interviews that took place during classroom literacy activities. I observed, asked questions, and audio-recorded while students were by themselves, with other students, with me, or with the teacher and engaged in writing activities. In this way I used an ethnography of writing approach to understand students' written products in the context of the process they experienced (Szwed, 1981).

Findings

My central purpose in this study has been to understand when and why bilingual students accept or resist participation in biliteracy practices. I found that a focus on correction and assessment sheds light on larger issues of language, literacy, and power in the classroom and local community. Below I examine the development, media, context, and content of biliteracy in relationship to oralcy–literacy and monolingual–bilingual norms, drawing from micro–macro findings in this study and pedagogical implications to be considered. First, I begin with my own understanding of development, adapted and expanded from Hornberger and Skilton-Sylvester (2000):

> *Development*: An understanding that moment to moment micro aspects of bilingual/biliterate development are deeply connected to macro-developmental oralcy–literacy processes which take place over an individual speaker's lifetime as well as community language development processes and monolingual–bilingual norms within and across generations. Individual and Community language developmental processes and norms can change and be changed by moment-to-moment aspects of learning that take place in face-to-face interactions.

One finding from this study is that Latino students use bilingual oral and literacy norms as they develop standard monolingual Spanish and English literacy skills required in their bilingual education program. Before placement in Ms Maria's bilingual classroom where emphasis was placed on standard literacy development in both languages, many students had been previously placed in classrooms with monolingual English-speaking teachers. Though students said they relied on bilingual norms in these classrooms, they also stated these applications to English literacy were mostly invisible. For example, in the following transcript bilingual student, Marilyn, responds to my question as to whether and how bilingual education might be helpful to students:

1 **Marilyn:** It helped me a lot. 'Cause it helped me 'cause I had problems in English spelling and I was a real slow reader. I'm getting better.
2 **Interviewer:** Yeah? You can tell?
3 **Marilyn:** I can tell myself 'cause I, now like, like, I used to give the teacher work in English we have to do spell check, all these words. Now it's less, it's a lot less.
4 **Interviewer:** Hm, I wonder how that happened.

5 **Marilyn:** And you know what? You know how I really learned – I remember this so clearly. I was in Fairhill with Miss Marshall. I was in fourth or fifth grade, and, um, she was always giving us quizzes. I was in a, it was a little bilingual. I don't know if it was bilingual but she was always giving us quizzes. And I never knew how to spell like real good so what I did was, instead of learning the word in English I read it in Spanish. And I learned it in Spanish and I wrote it like that, and it's ALL right.
6 **Interviewer:** So a word like, um/
7 **Marilyn:** People, I used to say (uses Spanish pronunciation) PE-O-PE-LE [English = pay-oh-pay-lay].
8 **Interviewer:** Oh!
9 **Marilyn:** That was the first word (laughing), yup.
10 **Interviewer:** Pe-o-pe-le.
11 **Marilyn:** That's the first word I ever did that with. Pe-o-pe-le. I remember that CLEARLY. And that that was a word that they made me stand up and spell it too.
12 **Interviewer:** Wow, and did you ever get in trouble for doing that. Did the teacher ever say what are you doing? You know, it's not pe-o-pe-le, it's people. No one ever said that?
13 **Marilyn:** *They never knew that I was doing it.*

Studies of second language acquisition have referred to this application as 'transfer' resulting in the study of errors (negative transfer), facilitation (positive transfer), and the avoidance or overuse of target language forms (Ellis, 1994: 341). These distinct forms of transfer are important for the study of second language acquisition; however, for the practicing teacher and student, *all* forms of transfer may be considered positive in so far as they shed light on students' bilingual development strategies. In other words, errors in student output that might be categorized theoretically as 'negative' or 'avoidance' are more appropriately labeled 'positive' and 'opportunistic' in terms of teacher practice, as errors indicate students' strengths and zones of proximal development (Vygotsky, 1978), i.e. areas where teachers can have the most potential impact on student learning. In the above example Marilyn spoke proudly of her unique L1–L2 strategy which made use of Spanish grapho-phoneme (sound-letter) connections, applying them to English where such connections are much less consistent. Her last comment in turn 13, that no one knew she was doing it, reveals the frequent silence in schools about such strategies and their undercover implementation by student language sleuths like Marilyn.

Marilyn's comment is evidence of sophisticated metalinguistic reflection. She articulated a bilingual norm: the ongoing and successive (L1 to L2) connections bilingual students make between oral and written varieties of both languages throughout their experiences with school literacy and throughout lifetime literacy development. Szwed (1981: 15–16) discussed this type of lifetime literacy development in terms of 'literacy cycles' where individuals vary in literacy – in this case biliteracy – abilities and activities that are conditioned by one's stage and position in life. This explains why students like Marilyn also talk about 'losing their Spanish' as they increase the amount of time they spend reading, writing, listening, and speaking in English (Cahnmann, 1997, 1998). Therefore, a definition of biliteracy development must also account for the continuum of monolingual–bilingual norms associated with a range of oralcy and literacy practices over the context of one's lifetime experiences with literacy in more than one language. Similarly the bilingual learner's lifetime developmental processes must be understood within the context of whole community bilingualism and biliteracy. Teachers, often engaged in assessing students' development, must consider a student's placement on developmental continua when making decisions about when and how to correct students' learning strategies and the effect of these strategies on student output. For example, 'pe-o-pe-le' may be a strategy that enables success, but, without effective and timely correction, applying Spanish grapho-phoneme connections might, at another point in her literacy cycle, result in spelling errors that produce an image of student failure, especially on high-stakes standardized assessments, college entry exams, and job applications. For this reason, bilingual teachers and students themselves must explicitly recognize and negotiate this contradiction to enable biliterate development that takes power and *context* into consideration. An understanding of the similarity and differences between the *media* of the multiple codes being developed will enable this explicit recognition. For this reason, a discussion of media is necessary, followed by a discussion of context.

> *Media*: An understanding that micro-linguistic structures such as phonemes, morphemes, syntax, and scripts are interconnected to larger macro-level applications of linguistic knowledge for oralcy–literacy in specific contexts of use governed by monolingual–bilingual norms (Scribner & Cole, 1981: 236; Hornberger, 2001: 10).

> The micro aspects of bilingual–biliterate language use can slowly change and be changed by macro institutions that prescribe macrolinguistic norms of communication.

In order to fully appreciate the kinds of dynamic problem-solving strategies bilingual students use developmentally within the monolingual English literary activities expected of them at school (as discussed earlier), it is helpful to analyze the microlinguistic structures of the varieties of language involved. Many of Ms Maria's ninth-grade students had greater literacy production in English because, for years prior to this classroom, even those students that had consistently been enrolled in bilingual programs experienced greater emphasis placed on English literacy skills. Despite several students' spoken English dominance these bilingual youths made a number of errors in their spoken and written English production. At first, I tried to characterize their errors in English as the result of transfer from students' knowledge of spoken and written Spanish. However, careful analysis of the media of these errors indicated that students were applying bilingual developmental norms to their English literacy assignments that could not simply be characterized as linear applications of L1 to L2. Rather, the media involved in student output shed light on their 'zig-zag' development (Hornberger, 1989: 286), the non-linear, back-and-forth relationship between students' receptive (listening and reading) and productive (speaking and writing) competence in Spanish, English, and both languages.

An example of this zig-zag process took place when student, Marta, was writing about her classmate, Mario, for her autobiography. She wrote, 'He think he look good but he didn't. But somebody mosted told him wrong.' When the media are understood from an L1–L2 transfer perspective, one might view errors in the student's use of third person singular (i.e. 'He think(s) he look(s) good,'), tense and spelling (i.e. 'he think(s) ... he didn't,' and 'mosted (must've)), and translation of idiomatic expression (i.e. 'told him wrong (gave him the wrong idea)).' Each one of these errors can be characterized by features in Spanish structure being transferred to English. For example, the third person singular morpheme is not expressed in Spanish by 's' but rather by the verb itself as in 'piensa' (s/he thinks). The word 'mosted' rather than 'must've' may be connected to overgeneralization, a common feature found in second-language learners' writing (Garcia, 1999). In this case, Marta may have overgeneralized the morpheme 'ed' for past tense and applied it to the word 'most' to indicate past, as in 'must have.' In comparing the contraction 'must've' and Marta's version, 'mosted' she used a shwa-sounding phoneme 'e' /ə/, and /d/, a voiced consonant, similar to the shwa+voiced+fricative found in standard spelling and phonology of 'must've' /mΔstəv/. Similarly difficult for Spanish speakers is the shift between vowels in the two languages. For example there is no distinction in Spanish between /o/ as in 'most' and /Δ/ as in 'must,' phonemes that change a word's meaning in English.

However, a transfer perspective overlooks other influences on the media of students' output. For example, the influence of Black English vernacular in this student's written production and the influence of this variety of English in her largely Puerto Rican and African-American community life. Marta's written production, 'He think he look good' is a statement that is correct in Black English vernacular where third person singular 's' also does not appear. Likewise, overgeneralization of 'ed' for past tense represents an appropriate English developmental stage among native English speaking youth. Thus, there are multiple influences on Marta's written output including Spanish, Black English, and English-as-an-L1 literacy development. In other words, analysis of the media of the students' output illustrated the complex interplay of sounds, meanings, and bilingual–bidialectal language processes that bilingual educators must simultaneously be aware of during literacy instruction (Cahnmann, 2001: 144). An effective instructional approach to error correction must make every effort to explicitly address the varieties of language media present in students' local communities and the *contexts* where the use of spoken and written vernaculars are more or less appropriate. Following is a discussion of *context* as related to instructional *content*. First, a definition:

> *Context*: An understanding that *where* biliteracy (a continuum of oralcy–literacy within a range of monolingual–bilingual norms[1]) takes place in moment-to-moment interaction is intricately connected to the socio-economic and historic context, including relations of power between the speakers themselves and the identity groups they represent (i.e. representation along a number of social variables, including but not limited to ethnicity, race, gender, language, sexual orientation, etc.). Macro social structural contexts and (bi)literacy practices can change and be changed by micro interactions.

Thus far, I have noted how the media of students' written output can shed light on the bilingual–bidialectal norms students' use as they develop biliteracy, often requiring a shift to monolingual literacy norms. I have advocated a resource perspective (Ruiz, 1984), one which views students errors as windows of opportunity to appreciate students' rich and varied linguistic backgrounds and the creative problem-solving strategies they utilize to negotiate monolingual literacy activities required of them in school. However, appreciating students' resources is not enough. Effective biliteracy instruction must take into account a sociolinguistic communicative competence approach that makes explicit how varieties of standard and vernacular language are used, when, with whom, and for what purposes. Effective validation of students' norms must also include an understanding of the relationship between context and power, structured inequality and opportunities to challenge that structure through individual and group agency. In other words, students must be aware of the choices they have about what variety to speak as well as an understanding of the consequences of their choices for providing or denying access to a variety of socio-economic relationships and political power.

The following is an example from this study of an occasion when a student shed light on the struggle she experienced when contexts for standard and vernacular language use overlapped. Two students were at the printer and one of them, Minerva, asked the classroom teacher if she could print her paper from the computer, '*¿Puedo printear el papel?*' The student used the English lexicon 'print' with a Spanish infinitive morpheme, 'ear.' This form, derogatorily referred to as Spanglish, is commonly used throughout Spanish–English bilingual communities in the United States. Ms Maria corrected Minerva, saying '*imprime*,' (Spanish for third person singular 'print') and did not answer Minerva until the student repeated her question using the standard Spanish form.

Later I asked Minerva and her peer, Wilma, who was also present during this exchange if they understood why Ms Maria had corrected Minerva's word choice, '*printear*.' When they indicated they didn't understand, I explained that this was a word only bilinguals would understand. Wilma responded:

> Oh yeah Miss I know a bunch of those words like roofo (roof) and parkea (park). One time I was home and my mom used parkea and I said no Mom it's *estaciona el carro* (Standard Spanish, 'park the car'). She told me *no te pongas como mierda* – don't get all high class on me! (Field Notes, 18 April 2000: 3)[2]

Table 8.1 Third person singular of 'to print' across three varieties

Marketplace Spanish	*'Spanglish'*	*Marketplace English*
Imprime	Printea	Print

As I began to analyze the data I was talking often to Wilma on the phone. I reminded her of this exchange and she added the following: 'No matter what, your family comes first before you do what the teacher says. Especially your parents' (Field Notes, 26 August 2000).

Wilma's statement reminds critical educators and theorists that correction will not be effective if it goes against family and community norms. She also reminds us how difficult it is to become bidialectal, to make sense of competing norms depending on the linguistic and cultural context. Heller (1999) captured the dilemma facing language minority youth for whom loyalty to community norms can often contribute to their own failure in demonstrating marketplace proficiency:

> To abandon their own practices for those of the others or of the school is to betray not only values, but also people who are important in their lives, whether family or friends. . . . Nonetheless, as has so often been noted with respect to marginalized groups, these students tend one way or another to collaborate in their own marginalization. (Heller, 1999: 273)

The critical educator's role is no less difficult, fraught with tensions and contradictions – how to both identify and accept community norms in the school context (challenging the status quo) while training students to be fluent in standard codes of power. Ms Maria recognized that nonstandard varieties of Spanish and English were feasible, possible, and done throughout the community (Hymes, 1971). However, she appeared to struggle with the appropriateness of alternative, nonstandard norms in the classroom as compared to their legitimacy in the local community. In this case, the classroom teacher was caught between roles in conflict. On the one hand, Ms Maria, a bilingual advocate, supported students' bilingual norms as legitimate and a resource for standard biliteracy acquisition. On the other hand, she wanted to use classroom time to demonstrate and support students' use of standard monolingual norms, as these norms are required and rewarded in school and are seldom available to students outside classroom time. This analysis helps us to make sense of how and why certain types of correction take place and perhaps leaves the educator with more questions than answers. To correct or not to correct, how, why, for what purposes, with whom, in which varieties of language, and at which stage in the individual and community biliteracy cycle? – these are only a few extensions of the original question. I believe that how educators structure the biliteracy *content* of their lessons can help educators and students find answers, collaborating to develop biliteracy for empowerment:

Content: An understanding that whatever content is being taught to bilingual students (i.e. mathematics, literature, high school graduation requirements, test-taking exercises, etc.) is inextricable from the micro–macro, contextual content of both students' lives and official curriculum framework expectations at the district, state and national levels. Institutional expectations for curriculum content (often focused on English monolingual literacy) can change and be changed by bilingual students' lives (often lived in Spanish–English, bilingual oralcy).

Throughout this study there were many examples of the ways in which Ms Maria skillfully tapped into the content of students' lives as a way to connect and transfer (Hornberger, 1990: 227) their background knowledge and interests to more traditional curriculum content with monolingual literacy expectations. For example, at a staff meeting with other bilingual teachers Ms Maria explained how the writing process enabled her to find a middle ground between accepting students' language varieties and teaching them standards. In regards to the nonstandard Puerto Rican Spanish spoken by the schools' majority student population, Ms Maria said: '*tenemos que homonizar sin perder respeto, es legítimo*' (we have to homogenize without losing respect, it [the nonstandard Puerto Rican variety of Spanish] is legitimate) (Field Notes, 16 December 1999: 2). How to homogenize without losing respect for the legitimacy of students' nonstandard Spanish varieties is not an easy matter.

When asked about her practice she explained the writing process had also allowed her to emphasize content over form, guiding students to first find their voice to say what they have to say. For example, as students were about to interview each other on the film *Amistad* (Field Notes, 8 December 1999: 2), Ms Maria referred to her philosophy, using code-switching to emphasize her point:

> Who cares if the word is written correctly? I don't want you to stop the interview because you don't know the spelling. Don't worry about it, that's not the important thing. The important thing is the meat of the picture. Es como la hamburguesa: yo quiero la carne (It's like hamburgers: I want the meat).

Through the writing process Ms Maria found a middle ground between accepting students' vernacular and developmental language norms and guiding students toward standard literacy. Further, she taught students history through Puerto Rican and Caribbean literature such as *House on the Lagoon* by Rosario Ferré and *When I Was Puerto Rican* by Esmeralda

Santiago as a way to hook students into reading and writing. Having spent time as a journalist and vacationer in Puerto Rico, Ms Maria was familiar with cultural and linguistic references that would earn her students' trust and interest. For example, when teaching a unit on poetry and metaphor, she incorporated '*piropos*' and '*bombas*,' rhyming lines that are an important part of oral Caribbean culture, similar to the kind of verbal repartee displayed in playing the dozens in Black English vernacular.

On another occasion she read a story by Sandra Cisneros called 'Me no speak English' to the class (Field Notes, 14 April 2000). In the story Cisneros' character, Mamacita, an older immigrant woman, expresses feelings of displacement and frustration through her refusal to speak more than eight words of English. Ms Maria and her students discussed at length the following passage:

> Somebody said because she's too fat, somebody because of the three flights of stairs, but I believe she doesn't come out because she is afraid to speak English, and maybe this is so since she only knows eight words. She knows to say: *He not here* for when the landlord comes, *No speak English* if anybody else comes, and *Holy smokes*. I don't know where she learned this, but I heard her say it one time and it surprised me. (Cisneros, 1991: 77)

Ms Maria talked about the first English words she learned in this country, 'give me money' and 'I'm hungry.' Students chimed in with their stories, like Raul who energetically recalled: '*yo aprendí* (I learned) chicken, Missy! Chicken!'

Ms Maria drew her point to a close by connecting Cisneros' stories to the students' lived experiences. She encouraged them to observe their own lives carefully, to reflect on defensive strategies and give creative voice to their own stories:

> *Tu puedes ir a casa hoy y observa. Observa lo que pasa en ese camino a tu casa. ¡Ustedes podrían escribir! ¿Que cosas te han pasado a ti en el camino a tu casa? . . . Entonces observe, observe. ¿Cuantas veces pasan cosas que uno ni cuenta se da? Vayan a ver en su familia cuanta gente hay que prefiere no salir de la casa con (?) que lo pasara al bochorno de 'I don't speak English.' O cuanta gente usa la excusa porque para alguna gente es una excusa.* (You can go home today and pay attention. Pay attention to what happens along the way home. You all can write about it! What things happen to you on the way to your house? So pay attention, pay attention. How many times do things happen that you don't even realize? Go

> and see how many people there are in your family who would rather not leave the house and stay all day because 'I don't speak English' or how many people use it as an excuse because for some people it really is an excuse. (Field Notes, 14 April 2000: 7)

The above examples illustrated some of the many culturally contextualized (Cahnmann & Remillard, 2002; Remillard & Cahnmann, in press) teaching strategies Ms Maria used with her Spanish-dominant students to change the terms of student reaction from *resistance through desistance* (when students show a preference to drop out of participation in official school discourse when it is perceived as requiring the assimilation of a white, monolingual English-speaking identity), to helping students explicitly articulate *multiple choice resistance*, one where there were participation and non-participation alternatives, including *resistance through insistence* on student voice and story telling (Cahnmann, 2001: 156–9). As I discuss elsewhere (Cahnmann, 2001), Ms Maria's skill in the area of biliteracy content helped her foster an environment of trust and respect where students learned to resist in productive and varied ways.[3]

Conclusion

I have proposed that three core continua – monolingual–bilingual norms, oralcy–literacy, and macro–micro – provide a specific definition of biliteracy that is useful for understanding issues of power involved in the development, media, context, and content of biliteracy error correction among Latino students in the US bilingual classroom. I argue that any attempt to teach biliteracy in a way that recognizes the complexity and power dynamics involved will be full of contradiction and struggle. Teachers and students are simultaneously challenged to validate, maintain, and further develop bilingual norms while teaching or acquiring monolingual norms that will help students access the signs and symbols of power (good grades, diplomas, jobs, college degrees, etc.). Bilingual education provides a unique opportunity to examine the continua of biliteracy because the explicit focus on language choice as well as language use, practices, values, and influences renders visible the social processes that might otherwise remain invisible (Heller & Martin-Jones, 2001: 7).

In conclusion, I echo the memorable words of Monica Heller (2001) that bilingual teachers *and* students need to be prepared 'to take flack.' Any teacher, school, or district that has aimed to follow through on the implications listed above for the development, media, context, and content of biliteracy already knows that the path toward full biliterate development is not easy as it interferes with taken-for-granted processes or 'hegemonic practices' that 'without malevolent intent, nonetheless systematically limit the life chances of members of stigmatized groups' (Erickson, 1996: 45). To promote bilingual students' full biliterate development and provide more equitable access to power implies micro–macro levels of co-responsibility to re-imagine school as a place that can do a better, more equitable job of distributing educational resources to all students. Accepting the struggle is a crucial part of re-imagination.

A critical theoretical and practical approach implies the necessity of ongoing reflexivity on what's working with whom and how and the flexibility to know that what 'works' will be subject to ongoing change and adaptation to the diverse needs of a changing student population. An approach to the correction of bilingual students' literacy errors will be more successful if it eliminates the dichotomy between 'yes, one should correct' and 'no, one should not correct,' and understands the multiple and nested considerations on a continua, re-imagining possibilities for language and content instruction to simultaneously validate students' bilingual norms and provide students with the context to use and critically understand these norms as well as monolingual codes of power. Additional 'tales of the field' (Van Maanen, 1988) are needed to help teachers and students appreciate the poetic contradictions of their lives, and to validate the work of bilingual teachers and students, an ongoing struggle that is too challenging for any one person or community to overcome.

Notes

1. Hornberger (1990: 213) gave the following definition for biliteracy: 'any and all instances in which communication occurs in two (or more) languages in or around writing.'
2. Wilma used a more diplomatic rather than direct translation of her Spanish, roughly: 'Don't act like a little shit.'
3. Ms. Maria's impressive culturally relevant curriculum and respect for and from students helped her maintain students trust when she critiqued their vernacular language practices.

References

Anderson, B. (1991) *Imagined Communities.* London: Verso.

Cahnmann, M. (1997) What's behind door number one, two and three? The meanings and values that early adolescent Mexican Americans attach to Spanish, English, and bilingualism. Master's thesis, University of California, Santa Cruz.

Cahnmann, M. (1998) 'Like three doors – Spanish, English, and both; I'm going to both': Language attitudes of early adolescent Mexican Americans. *Proceedings of the Sixth Annual Symposium about Language and Society (Salsa).* Austin, Texas.
Cahnmann, M. (2001) Shifting metaphors: Of war and reimagination in the bilingual classroom. Ph.D. dissertation, University of Pennsylvania.
Cahnmann, M. and Remillard, J. (2002) What counts and how: Mathematics teaching in culturally, linguistically, and socioeconomically diverse urban settings. *Urban Review* 34 (3), 179–205.
Cisneros, S. (1991) *The House on Mango Street.* New York: Vintage Books.
Ellis, R. (1994) *The Study of Second Language Acquisition.* Oxford: Oxford University Press.
Erickson, F. (1996) Transformation and school success: The politics and culture of educational achievement. In E. Jacob and C. Jordan (eds) *Minority Education: Anthropological Perspectives* (pp. 27–52). Norwood, NJ: Ablex Publishing Corporation.
Garcia, O. (1999) Educating Latino high school students with little formal schooling. In C.J. Faltis and P. Wolfe (eds) *So Much to Say: Adolescents, Bilingualism, and ESL in the Secondary School* (pp. 61–82). New York: Teachers College.
Heller, M. (1999) *Linguistic Minorities and Modernity: A Sociolinguistic Ethnography.* London: Longman.
Heller, M. (2001) Talk on bilingualism at Temple University, 1–2 Febuary.
Heller, M. and Martin-Jones, M. (2001) *Voices of Authority.* Norwood, NJ: Ablex Publishers.
Hornberger, N. (1989) Continua of biliteracy. *Review of Educational Research* 59, 3, 271–96.
Hornberger, N. (1990) Creating successful learning contexts for bilingual literacy. *Teachers College Record* 92 (2), 212–29.
Hornberger, N. (2001) Biliteracy. To appear (cited with permission) in R. Beach, J. Green, M. Kamil and T. Shanahan (eds) *Multidisciplinary Perspectives on Literacy Research* (2nd edn). Cresskill, NJ: Hampton Press.
Hornberger, N. and Skilton-Sylvester, E. (2000) Revisiting the continua of biliteracy: International and critical perspectives. *Language and Education: An International Journal* 14 (2), 96–122.
Hymes, D.H. (1971) Competence and performance in linguistic theory. In R. Huxley and E. Ingram (eds) *Language Acquisition: Models and Methods.* New York: Academic Press.
Owens, L. (1992) *Other Destinies: Understanding the American Indian Novel.* Norman, OK: University of Oklahoma Press.
Remillard, J. and Cahnmann, M. (in press) Researching mathematics teaching in bilingual-bicultural classrooms. In T. McCarty (ed.) *Language, Literacy, Power, and Schooling.* Hillsdale, NJ: Erlbaum.
Ruiz, R. (1984) Orientations in language planning. *NABE Journal* 8 (2), 15–34.
Schmidt, R. Sr (2000) *Language Policy and Identity Politics in the United States.* Philadelphia: Temple University Press.
Scribner, S. and Cole, M. (1981) *The Psychology of Literacy.* Cambridge, MA: Harvard University Press.

Szwed, J.F. (1981) The ethnography of literacy. In M.F. Whiteman (ed.) *Writing: The Nature, Development, and Teaching of Written Communication* (Vol. 1: 13–23). Hillsdale, NJ: Lawrence Erlbaum.

United States Commission on Civil Rights (1975) *A Better Chance to Learn: Bilingual-bicultural Education*. Clearinghouse Publication No. 51. Washington, DC: National Clearinghouse for Bilingual Education.

Van Maanen, J. (1988) *Tales of the Field: On Writing Ethnography*. Chicago: The University of Chicago Press.

Vygotsky, L.S. (1978) *Mind in Society: The Development of Higher Psychological Processes*. Cambridge, MA: Harvard University Press.

Part 4: Empowering Teachers

Chapter 9

Biliteracy Teacher Education in the US Southwest

BERTHA PEREZ, BELINDA BUSTOS FLORES, AND SUSAN STRECKER

As the number of Spanish-speaking children increases in public schools throughout the United States, the shortage of bilingual teachers becomes more acute. Public schools and universities are turning to a variety of strategies to meet the demand for bilingual teachers. In San Antonio and other communities in the Southwest, consortiums have formed between schools, universities, and community organizations to identify the linguistic and intellectual capital available within the community. Two groups who have the linguistic skills and potential but who have only marginally participated in teacher preparation programs are paraprofessionals in public schools and persons with teacher training or university studies from Mexico.

At the University of Texas at San Antonio, two cohort groups of students, one group composed of paraprofessionals and the other a group of women with Escuela Normal (Normal School) or Universidad Pedagogica Nacional (National Pedagogical University) training in Mexico, are participating in the bilingual teacher preparation program. The two cohorts of students participate in the same classes, fieldwork, and program activities. The paraprofessional cohort, funded through a Title VII grant from the Office of Bilingual and Minority Language Affairs (OBEMLA), is a group of Chicanas/os or Mexican Americans who are working in local schools and are members of the communities in which they work. The second cohort, funded through a private foundation,[1] received training in either normal schools or post-secondary institutions in Mexico; and they now legally reside in the United States as citizens or permanent residents. This cohort of students is referred to in this chapter as *Normalistas*. While the State of Texas, like most other states, does not recognize non-US schools' teacher certification programs, the pool of persons with post-secondary education in Mexico who now reside within communities throughout the Southwest represent a potential pool of candidates for bilingual teacher preparation.

While on the surface the two cohorts share some characteristics, they also diverge on certain dimensions of language, discourse, culture, schooling, history, class, and power. In this chapter we examine the convergence and divergence of these dimensions along the continua of biliteracy model (Hornberger, 1989; Hornberger & Skilton-Sylvester, 2000) for participants from each of the two cohort groups. Through these seven participants, complexities of literacy and biliteracy use, power relationships, access to cultural and symbolic capital, style of social interaction, and privilege/ power distribution within and across the groups are examined.

The Bilingual and Biliteracy Continua as a Theoretical Framework

The continua of biliteracy (Hornberger, 1989; Hornberger & Skilton-Sylvester, 2000) serve as a framework for beginning to deconstruct the complexities of behaviors, competencies, relations, and products of the participants as individuals and as members of the distinct cohorts. The framework allows us to examine the layers of behaviors and purposes inherent in selected literacy and biliteracy events and to develop a more complete understanding of the uses of language and literacy. Like all bilingual persons, prospective bilingual teachers are products of their own cultural upbringing, schooling, and professional preparation; thus, the moment-to-moment decisions they make about first and second language use emerges from these sociocultural contexts.

The notion of development, content, media, and context as a set of nested relationships allows us to investigate language in contexts of situation as proposed by Hymes (1974). Hymes suggested that communicative events may be studied through examining components of the event where such an event might be an activity, or aspects of activities, that are rule- or norm-governed and that consist of one or more communicative acts. This heuristic analysis of the communicative acts helps define the dimensions within the frame of the event, situation, or community, and would include participants, settings, and topics (Hymes, 1974). The biliteracy continua provide ways of uncovering both the contextual frames and the items within the frames for specific communicative and literacy events. The notion of context permits examining biliteracy in terms of situated discourse, i.e. language use in context, and recognizes the multiple and alternative social roles and identities available for participants. For the purposes of this chapter, we explored more specifically the areas of the continua that focus on cultural context; on vernacular to literary and contextualized content; and on vernacular to standard structural, scriptural, and code switching media all as they relate to oral to written L1 to L2 development.

Community, Culture and Identity: Biliteracy Context

Many studies of schooling in the United States suggest that an individual's literacy attainment is more closely linked with community membership or social class than any other factor. This is not to say that the community membership per se determines or contributes to the attainment of literacy but that, because of living in a low-socioeconomic or a middle-class community, the process of schooling will either provide or inhibit access to the development of literacy. Community membership has not been as extensively linked to school literacy performance in Mexico, nor has it been as extensively studied. However, in both Mexican and United States schools, students demonstrate a disparate range of literacy attainment.

Roberts, Jupp and Davies (1991) suggest that critical reflection and discourse analysis are important in understanding sociopolitical context. Critical reflection and discourse analysis provide a way of examining language in terms of its role in maintaining or challenging existing social class and power relations. Power and power relations are constructed through language and in social interactions. The exercise of power as reflected in language can challenge power relationships. Studies of university counselor and student relations (Erickson & Shultz, 1982) and university students tutoring elementary children (Gutiérrez *et al.*, 1999) have found that situational social identity that emerged from the interactions rather than static social identities had the strongest influence on the communication and the outcomes of the interchange. Gutiérrez *et al.* (1999) found that university tutors and the elementary students engaged in problem solving and writing using the Internet developed co-membership in a social identity that involved changing attributes of status shared by the student and tutor. The situationally emerging co-membership had an overriding influence on social status differences. In other words, the ability to 'co-cognize' and 'co-problem-solve' (Gutiérrez *et al.*, 1999: 7) in various learning and literacy tasks depended on the degree to which the tutor and the student were able to mediate a sense of co-membership based on shared attributes of their social identities. The situated discourse and multiple and alternative social roles and identities created and sustained the successful learning activities over time.

Cazden (1988) describes how in bilingual classrooms where teachers and students share ethnic identities the status relationship between teachers and students was mediated and adapted to the children's community interaction styles. She reports on a study that demonstrated a way of relating and teaching that adapted to the students. Teachers used what can be categorized as a cultural personalized style, using 'in group' forms of address, diminutives, code switching into Spanish, and reminders of norms of interpersonal respect found in the children's cultural group, that overrode the differences in power and status.

One's identity as a member of a defined culture determines the world-view perspective and the symbolic systems used to encode and interpret the world. Culture is the way of thinking or the way of life that is represented by the symbolic systems shared by members of a group and is socially organized and constructed. This symbolic mode is shared by a community, but also conserved, elaborated, and passed on to succeeding generations that, by virtue of this transmission, continue to maintain the cultural identity and way of life of the group.

Interpretation of symbolic systems, such as language and literacy, is situated in social encounters that use and reproduce cultural contexts. Thus, in order to know what a tool or a communicative act is about, one must know the symbolic systems and the cultural context. All literacy events have their origins and their significance in the culture in which they are created. The cultural situatedness of meanings assures their negotiability and, ultimately, their communicability. For however much individuals may seem to operate on their own in attempting to make meanings, no one can do it without the help of the culture's symbolic systems. Culture provides the tools, including language and literacy, for organizing and understanding our worlds. Thus, learning and thinking are always culturally situated and dependent upon cultural resources. Individual variation in language and literacy use can be attributed to the varied opportunities that different cultural settings provide (Ferdman, 1990; Heath, 1983). When we seek to understand learners (individuals), we must seek to understand the cultural contexts within which they have developed, learned to interpret who they are in relation to others, and learned how to process, interpret, or decode their world (Weis, 1988).

Cultural knowledge and cultural identity are further defined by socioeconomic status, religion, family educational history, gender, ethnicity, and sociopolitical status. All of these sociocultural factors intertwine and interact to result in individual cultural identities. A recent study of preservice teachers' self-identity along a continuum from Mexican to Hispanic (Flores & Clark, 2000) demonstrates the relative nature of ethnic or cultural identity; for some individuals ethnic identity may represent their sociopolitical awareness as a minority group within the US society. For example, legally-residing *normalistas* aspiring to be bilingual educators were more likely to ethnically identify as Mexicano or with their country of origin rather than as US Mexicans or Mexican Americans. Flores and Clark indicate that these *normalistas* may lack the sociopolitical awareness of what it means to identify as an ethnic individual within a society in which their group is not the majority power holder. On the other hand, Mexican American preservice teachers' ethnic identity labels demonstrated a continuum from Mexicano to Hispanic. Thus, these Mexican American preservice teachers may choose their ethnic identity label based on their personal affiliations and experience of being a minority power holder within a sociocultural-political context.

Vernacular,[2] Standard, and Literary Language: Biliteracy Media and Content

Schooling takes place in schools, and 'schools are powerful places that create and sustain meanings and values' (Freeman & Johnson, 1998: 409). Understanding the sociocultural terrain and the powerful environment of schooling in which some actions and ways of being and talking are valued and encouraged whereas others are downplayed, ignored, and even silenced is critical to biliteracy development. Heath 'demonstrated how differences among group's experiences and expectations about schooling and differences among the groups are not so much along the lines of oral versus literate culture as along the lines of which literacies most closely resemble those of the school' (1983: 386).

The familiarity with structures and scripts (media) as well as with vernacular and literary forms and written discourse styles (content) in L1 and L2 may depend on experience with schooling in Mexico and the United States. As young adults begin to work or continue in post-secondary education, the institutional systems in which they previously participated will further encourage or delimit literacy development. In the case of paraprofessionals who begin working in schools without any higher education, the employer provides and encourages the continued development of job-specific skills but may do little to encourage or assure the continued development of higher levels of literacy attainment (Pérez, 1998).

Numerous studies have been conducted on the use of vernacular and standard forms of English and Spanish in South Texas schools and communities (Jacobson & Faltis, 1990; Schecter & Bayley, 1998). Jacobson and Faltis's study of bilingual teachers' use of the vernacular documents how bilingual teachers reflect the language and literacy used in the community. Thus, becoming a bilingual teacher requires the development of multiple literacies that can be used to accomplish specific purposes, e.g. teaching a formal lesson in L1 or L2, writing a letter to parents in L1 or L2, and speaking informally with children. Teachers' knowledge of and level of comfort with the vernacular of both languages, as well as knowledge of the standard and literary forms of both languages, will contribute to learning success. All the levels of context must be nuanced and understood by prospective teachers, for example, whether a child is using L1 vernacular to communicate a community experience, or L1 'standard' to write a letter of invitation, or L2 to read and write during an examination must be understood and defined with each instance of its particulars (Milk *et al.*, 1992).

Within the use of the vernacular as biliterate medium, code switching has been a language and social marker. Recent studies (Jacobson & Faltis, 1990; Zentella, 1982) of code switching show that code switching historically was stigmatized because it was believed to reflect the bilingual's lack of complete knowledge and control of the two languages. Zentella found that code switching, in fact, reflected a response to contextual factors and represented competent use of context-specific language.

Gumperz (1982) also found that code switching was used to convey social meaning, to emphasize situational changes, or to acknowledge salient role relationships. Zentella (1982) examined the context of interactions to illuminate the multiple social roles and identities expressed through the use of code switching. In Zentella's study individuals conveyed social and cultural meanings in the process of interaction and they recognized the multiple social roles and identities in situated language use. The social roles and meanings are what are crucial to understanding the use of code switching.

Gumperz (1982) defined the contextualization cue as 'any feature of linguistic form that contributes to the signaling of contextual presuppositions. ... The code, dialect and style switching processes, some of the prosodic phenomena ... as well as choice among lexical and syntactic options, formulaic expressions, conversational openings, closings and sequencing strategies' (Gumperz, 1982: 131–40). By means of contextualization cues and drawing on background knowledge that they bring to the interaction, which can be characterized as frames, schemata, or scripts, participants make their way moment by moment through an interaction, making situated inferences as to what is going on and what is their own role and identity as they interact in literacy events.

Literacy across languages and cultures can also be examined through the written products. Grabe and Kaplan (1996: 179) put forth the notion of 'contrastive rhetoric' to account not only for notions of language structure, learning, and use but also to describe ways in which written texts operate in larger cultural contexts. Thus cultural-use preferences can be examined through written texts. This notion is useful for the examination of genres of the same language and the study of differences between similar genres in different languages. According to Grabe and Kaplan, contrastive rhetoric can go beyond the superficial differences of word order, tense, aspect, or mode conveyed in a written text by providing a way to examine matters relating to topicalization, ways of achieving cohesion, and to the combination of surface linguistic features which reflect identifiable discourse functions, and to the mechanism through which coherence is achieved. Of particular interest is how the notion of coherence-making in written texts operates in different languages or is signaled by second language learners in both their native and second languages.

A number of studies have pointed to the notion that writers whose first language was Spanish used a more 'elaborated' style of writing; that is, whether writing in Spanish or in English, these writers will typically make greater use of both coordination and subordination in clause structuring. Montaño-Harmon (1991) compared two groups of students writing in their own first languages: secondary school Spanish writers in Mexico and English first language writers in the United States; and observed that Spanish writers wrote longer sentences, used fewer simple sentences, and used more coordinating clauses. Lux and Grabe (1991) compared university-level Ecuadorian Spanish writers and university English students in the United States and also found that Spanish writers wrote longer sentences. They also made greater use of subordinate clauses, but there was no difference in the use of coordinate clauses.

Other areas of investigation in contrastive rhetoric examine multiple textual parameters derived from linguistic feature analysis to understand the functional/textual dimensions of text. There is considerable evidence that different cultures have different rhetorical preferences for the organization of written text and these preferences not only shape written text in distinct languages and cultures, but tend to manifest themselves consistently, if subtly, in the writing of students learning a second language.

A Study of Seven Biliterate Teachers-in-preparation

Two primary questions guided our study, both related to the oral to written, L1 to L2 development continua, and the contexts, media, and content through which they develop. First, would the *normalistas,* who had sophisticated Spanish literacy attainment as evident by informal and formal measures, be able to demonstrate English literacy attainment at a level appropriate for university work? And would their literacies assist them to situate themselves when a full range from vernacular to literary language skills in both languages was required in the context of bilingual teacher preparation activities? Second, in the case of the paraprofessionals, would the level of literacy development in Spanish be more on the vernacular end of the continuum and how would that knowledge and the knowledge of more standard and literary forms of English situate them within the context of bilingual teacher preparation activities?

This study employed qualitative case study methods to explore the research questions. Seven participants were conveniently selected (Miles & Huberman, 1994): four *normalistas* and three paraprofessionals. It is important to note that one *normalista* employed as a paraprofessional was classified as a *normalista* for the purpose of this study. To establish trustworthiness, the researchers employed triangulation and team debriefing (Lincoln & Guba, 1985). Confidentiality and anonymity were maintained by coding and erasing all tapes once the study was completed (Rubin & Rubin, 1995). Each participant signed and was offered a copy of the consent form as is suggested by Miles and Huberman (1994).

Data sources

Language samples for seven participants, three *normalistas,* and three paraprofessionals, and one *normalista*-paraprofessional, in both English and Spanish were collected from multiple sources. Both verbal and written data were collected in both English and Spanish. The genres of writing included in the analyses were personal narrative, description of personal literacy acquisition, reflective essays on various topics of literacy instruction, and essays that accompanied the students' applications for admission to the bilingual teacher preparation projects. Verbal data included transcribed audiotapes of tutoring with elementary school children and verbal interactions with these children. Additional verbal data included the oral interviews conducted by the project's selection committee. Students' performances on the Bilingual Prochievement Test (González-Pino, 1991) provided additional information regarding students' proficiencies in Spanish. Observational notes of two teaching episodes per student that captured gesture and ambience provided an additional data source.

Interview process

Each of the grants requires interested individuals to apply to the respective program and to meet selective criteria. For example, paraprofessional applicants had (a) to have a minimum GPA of 2.5 and (b) to be nominated by the cooperating school district. In addition to these criteria, preference was given to paraprofessional applicants who had passed all or portions of the state-mandated entry test, Texas Assessment of Skills Proficiency (TASP) and had a minimum of 30 completed hours of college course work. For the *normalistas*, the same grade point average standards applied if they had attended a community college; if not, applicants were screened based on the course work completed in the normal school. *Normalista* applicants with a high grade point average and having completed a *licenciatura* (licensure equivalent to Bachelor's degree) were given preference. Both groups submitted written responses to questions and these were also used as part of the screening process. The final screening consisted of a 30-minute taped oral interview of the most qualified applicants.

Interviews were conducted in two parts. First, the applicants were interviewed in the non-dominant language and each committee member assigned an individual score on the non-dominant language. Second, using the applicants' dominant language, they were asked a number of questions based on their prior experiences, such as their philosophy of teaching and bilingual education, their view of the native language and a description of their approaches to teaching reading and mathematics. After the completion of the interview, each applicant was rated on his/her responses and was given an overall global score. This overall global score assisted in the final selection process. The non-dominant language score was also used as an informal indicator of potential needs in that target language. These data were cross-validated with the formal assessment in the target language and assisted in the advisement process and course development for each group.

For the *normalistas* applying to Project Alianza, an additional formal interview was conducted. The applicants were asked a series of structured questions during a one-hour interview in Spanish. A Spanish-speaking graduate student administered and recorded the structured questionnaire (Miles & Huberman, 1994). These data were transcribed and also assisted in triangulation.

Prochievement test

The Bilingual Prochievement Test (Gonzalez-Pino, 1991) was developed for the purpose of measuring the four language domains of reading, writing, listening, and speaking in Spanish. The test was designed for group administration in a foreign language lab or alternate settings. Each language domain is rated from low to advanced based on the scale of the American Council of Teaching Foreign Languages and the Educational Testing Services; an overall score is also given. The test has been used to determine appropriate placement for university-level Spanish course work and to determine the level of Spanish proficiency of preservice bilingual education teachers at the university. The Bilingual Prochievement Test acts as a predictor of future performance on the state-mandated Texas Oral Proficiency Test (TOPT). All of the paraprofessionals were required to take this test. Some *normalistas* also took this test as well.

Tutoring sessions, verbal interactions, and field sites

Although both groups had experiences within school settings, one of the requirements for the participants as preservice bilingual education teachers was to complete 24 hours of field experience in a bilingual classroom every semester. The school sites were chosen based on the type of bilingual education programs; a number of the sites have dual language programs, while other sites have transitional bilingual education programs. The selection of the bilingual classrooms was based on the following minimal criteria: Spanish must be spoken at least 60–70% of the time. The cooperating teacher must be (a) a fully certified bilingual education teacher, (b) an effective teacher nominated by the school principal, and (c) a willing mentor for the preservice bilingual teacher. An effort was made to insure that the preservice teacher had a variety of experiences across grade levels and in different types of bilingual settings.

During the period of the study, the seven participants were placed in five different schools in the inner city, Westside and Southside of San Antonio. All the schools serve economically underdeveloped communities and have a mix of public housing and low-income single-family homes. Two schools, Emma Fry and Coronado/Escobar Elementary, are in the Edgewood Independent School District (EISD). Two other schools, Herff Elementary and J.T. Brackenridge are located in San Antonio Independent School District (SAISD). One school, Wright Elementary, is located in Harlandale Independent School District (HISD). The student populations in each of these schools are predominately Mexican American and each school has a large number of children whose first language is Spanish. Nearly one-third of these schools' populations are classified as being limited English proficient.

Data analysis

To analyze the multiple written language samples, a rubric was developed. Researchers examined existing rubrics in both the ESL literature and in the area of writing. From these models, a rubric was developed relevant to the particular context. All written texts were analyzed using a four-category rubric that included: (1) literacy in context for cultural referents; (2) the influence of first language forms and vocabulary on the second language; (3) syntactic text structures; and (4) functional communication of genre. Category one examined the cultural, personal historical, social, or school-related references within the content of each piece of text. Category two examined the influence of L1 on L2 or L2 on L1, especially in the use of syntactic elements, discourse styles, and evidence of code switching. Category three examined the cohesiveness, coherence, complexity, and lexical loading of each piece of text. Category four examined the overall function of the text in terms of communicating, purpose of genre, and global content. Each category was evaluated on a five-point scale. (See Appendix for scoring rubric.)

Transcripts of oral interviews and tutorial tapes were examined for cultural referents, dominance of language used, and evidence of L1 and L2 influence, in particular code switching. Each oral language category was evaluated on a five-point scale, with 5 being the highest level of references/uses/evidence and 1 the lowest.

To establish inter-rater reliability, written work and transcripts of oral language of students not in the study were scored jointly by raters using the rubric. When inter-rater reliability reached 90%, three raters independently scored the language samples of participants. Those scores were later compared. No score differed by more than one point, and all scores were negotiated to 100% agreement.

Findings

In order to show how each group was initially situated and is moving along the biliterate continua during their teacher preparation program, each group's informal and formal language samples were analyzed.

During the interview process, the admissions committee rated the three *normalistas* as Spanish dominant with a low overall rating in English; the Bilingual Prochievement advanced scores for all *normalistas* validated their Spanish dominance. The admissions committee rated Martha, the participant who was both a *normalista* and a paraprofessional, as being bilingual.

In the case of the paraprofessionals, two out of the three were rated as being bilingual and one paraprofessional was rated as being more English dominant with intermediate proficiency in Spanish. The Bilingual Prochievement Test validated the admissions committee ratings with only two of the paraprofessionals scoring at the advanced level. The admission committee ratings and scores on the Bilingual Prochievement scores demonstrate where each participant and where each group was initially situated prior to commencing their respective program of study.

The scores of the written text samples indicated an increasing English writing proficiency for both *normalistas* and paraprofessionals over the course of their participation in the teacher education program. Table 9.1 provides an overview of the means of their scores on all the English and Spanish written texts collected for the study.

Contextual situatedness: Context and content in biliterate writing development

Contextual literacy included participants' cultural references and references to personal historical and social events, including their own schooling experiences. Each written and oral text sample in English was evaluated for these contextual literacy elements on a score of 1 (no references) to 5 (highest number of references). Both the *normalista* and paraprofessional groups placed literacy in rich contexts. The *normalista* group averaged 4.5 (with 5 being highest number of references), and the paraprofessional group averaged 4.7 on the scale of 5. All written genres elicited contextual references.

The highest numbers of cultural and personal references were found in essays on personal acquisition of literacy and in reflective essays about aspects of literacy learning and instruction. The professor encouraged participants to apply their own knowledge and experiences to the reflective essays, and they did so. The lowest number of contextual references were found in the application essays, the most formal of the written genres.

The following are samples of cultural and personal contexts referenced in the participants' writing. The first is from Martha who was the only participant to be categorized as both a *normalista* and a paraprofessional:

> I am able to relate it [course content] to what I learned going to school in Mexico. I am able to see the relation with what some teachers do in the school that I work at. I am even able to put to practice some of the things I learn during your class. What I have a problem with is organizing my thoughts, and tell you how much I have learned, and the insecurity that I get when I write in English.

Table 9.1 Means of English and Spanish texts for *normalistas* and paraprofessionals

Name	***English context***	***Spanish context***	***Influence Spn–Eng***	***Influence Eng–Spn***	***English syntax***	***Spanish syntax***	***English function***	***Spanish function***
Normalistas								
Yolanda	4.67	3	4	1	2.91	4	4	4
Irene	4.58	4	3.78	1	3.14	4.5	3.71	4
Laura	5	5	3.78	1	2.96	5	3.60	5
Martha	3.71	3.5	3.56	1	3	3.5	3.5	4
Group means	4.5	3.87	3.78	1	3	4.25	3.7	4.25
Paraprofessionals								
Karina	5	1*	1.16	1	5	1	4.91	1
Teresa	4.2	5	2.83	2	3.87	3.5	4.58	4.5
Diana	5	5	1.14	1	3.75	4.5	4.92	4
Group means	4.7	3.6	1.7	1.3	4.2	3	4.8	3.1

Note: *Written in English

In this sample Martha makes references to schooling in Mexico and compares it to schooling in the United States. While she does not compare the cultural contexts, it is embedded in her reference to the two distinct educational systems. She is able to look at both worlds, as her form of prior knowledge, to socially construct meaning of the task in her present context. She also reflects on her practice and mental processes that may lead her to self-regulation as a learner and expresses 'insecurity' with her language abilities. This awareness of her mental processes and questioning of her language may lead to self-regulation as a learner in future tasks.

The example from a reflection by a *normalista*, Yolanda, further explores cultural and contextual references:

> But the focus of literacy is different because in my country [Mexico] when you read a book in kindergarten is more like to relax activity. . . . Usually in my country [Mexico] we begin the strong emphasis of literacy in first grade. . . . Here [US] we have a lot of good books that use for prediction, for teach colors and numbers.

Yolanda makes a reference to Mexico ('in my country') while discussing the kindergarten literacy practices found in the classroom where she is doing her fieldwork. She demonstrates her developing sense of multiple identities by referring both to Mexico and to US schooling in the personal plural pronoun 'we.' Her strong experiential base developed in Mexico allows her to compare literacy practices, but also to contrast them as she begins to take ownership of the practices that she is being exposed to in her preparation program.

Cultural and personal references are also explored by paraprofessional Teresa, but she voices an awareness of the power relationship dimension:

> I would just do it [read aloud] the way she [teacher] wanted me to do without asking questions. At time I felt like I was like a parrot just saying or copying what other people do. The sad part is that the teachers never took the time of explaining what was the hidden purposes of teaching the way they do. Now I know that I should always ask why things are done in the manner that they are.

Teresa's transcript reveals her reflection and perhaps developing understanding of social relations, class standing, and power relations in her reference to parroting and copying school practices that were not questioned. Through the analysis of her own schooling and experiences within her work as a paraprofessional and perhaps her university class discussions, she begins to voice a critical position in which she is feeling empowered to question the status quo. Her references to 'hidden' purposes might also refer to the schools' power position demonstrated in their not making visible the curriculum and methodology to the students and community, which she also begins to question.

These examples suggest the confluence of power within cultural and personal identity, and the ways in which biliterate learners negotiate the power-weighting of the context and content continua. As the two *normalistas* and the one paraprofessional reflect on issues of personal identity, they also begin to analyze issues of power and school practices. As in Gutiérrez *et al.*'s (1999) study, Martha, Yolanda, and Teresa are beginning to redefine their co-membership through reflection on their interactions and discourse with their peers, their professors, and their students in their fieldwork.

Influence of L1 on L2 in biliterate development

Examination of the influence of L1 (Spanish) on L2 (English) revealed significant differences between the *normalista* and the paraprofessional groups. In the analyses of the influence of Spanish on English in the oral language samples, the *normalistas* averaged 4 (with 5 as the highest level of influence of first language). The paraprofessionals averaged 1.3 revealing a much lower influence of Spanish on their spoken English. Similar differences were found in participants' writing. Across the multiple English written samples evaluated on a scale of 1 to 5, with 5 showing the highest level of influence of Spanish on English, the *normalistas* scored 3.8, while the paraprofessionals scored 1.7, see Table 9.1. Thus, the paraprofessionals, who attended high schools in the United States, showed less influence of Spanish on their written and spoken English than did the *normalistas* who completed both secondary and post-secondary work in Mexican schools.

The influence of L1 on L2 is evident in the syntactic complexity of the texts as well as in transfer of specific phrases and structures or syntactic collocations, for example, as in the use of elaborate introductory sentences in this excerpt from a reflective essay by *normalista* Irene:

> I never knew if the teacher knew about my problem, because in front of the group I was reading well, but my reality was that if I did not practice, I will not had a good fluency in my reading.

Irene uses a construct from Spanish that could be a literal translation, i.e. 'but my reality' could have been expressed in Spanish as '*mi realidad es que*' which is a common usage among native-educated speakers of

Spanish. Another of the numerous examples comes from a personal narrative by the same author:

> When she returned to the house after class, her mother gave her lunch, and all the family took a place *on* the table.

Irene uses a brief introductory clause but also uses a literal translation for 'took a place on the table' from the Spanish '*tomar su lugar en la mesa.*'

The influence of L1 on L2 in the choice of lexical items and the use of code switching in written text were also evident. Laura, a *normalista,* shows the influence of her dominant Spanish language in her choices of lexical items, syntactical forms, and the evidence of code switching in written text:

> My mother have a own specialty at literacy in Spanish in *iniciación a la lecto-escritura,* (initial literacy) in fact today the work that my mother do it is *reconocido* (recognized) between the parents and the community and schoolars as a district scholar.

The lexical items 'schoolars' and 'scholar' may be influenced from the Spanish knowledge of the word 'escolar' which is the item for both schoolchild and scholar. In English most students would not refer to the public school context as a place for scholars. Her elaborate explanation of the topic of her mother's specialty, '*iniciación a la lecto-escritura,*' illustrates the influence of the syntactical forms of Spanish. Her use of code switching in the written text illustrates her lack of biases for language purity and perhaps her higher priority need to communicate her ideas about her mother's specialty. She demonstrates the acceptable standard usage for code switching and the code switching contributes contextually to the meaning. The reference to the initial reading process was part of a reflection text written as part of a reading class assignment. Her exposure to the class discussion or 'way of saying' this may have influenced her decision to write '*iniciación a la lecto-escritura*' in Spanish, perhaps to signal a difference of cultural schemata for her understanding of the initial reading process.

The influence of L1 on L2 was also seen at the phonemic level. The following excerpt from Laura's application shows this influence of Spanish on her English. In Spanish, words with multiple consonant clusters at the beginning of the word normally are preceded with a vowel; thus, for the word 'stimulate' she writes 'estimulate':

> I'm be able to work in teams, to accept mistakes, and to *estimulate* the student in achieving new and best goals.

The *normalistas* and paraprofessionals began at different starting points on the continua of biliterate development and drew from different resources across the continua. The above examples of syntactic, lexical, and phonemic transfer from Spanish to English show how the *normalista* group drew on the resources of their L1, oral, and receptive language skills to accomplish productive, written communicative purposes in their L2.

Syntax and function: Media in biliterate writing development

The syntactic analysis of text structures included four subcategories: (a) cohesiveness, (b) coherence/clarity, (c) complexity/variety of sentences, and (d) lexical loading (richness and preciseness of language used). Each written and oral text sample in English was evaluated for these syntactic elements on a score of 1 (poorest) to 5 (highest). There were differences between the paraprofessionals and the *normalistas*. The paraprofessionals' average score was 4.2; while the *normalistas'* average score was 3.

This example with a syntactic score of 3 is from a reflective text written by a *normalista* and shows lack of full control over English syntax:

> Unfortunately, on my own experience I don't had the opportunity of to teacher read and write at this level (elementary) because I always worked with the most little in kindergarten years (ages 3–4).

Contrast the above example with an excerpt from a reflective text with a syntactic score of 5 written by a paraprofessional who has lived all her life in the US and is very comfortable with English language structures:

> As one of the oldest children on both sides of my family, I have always assisted my younger cousins with their schoolwork. . . . I loved reading all sorts of stories aloud to them, as well as making up my own bedtime stories for them. After reading a story together, my cousins and I would draw pictures and write our own story relating to the one we had just read.

All English texts were also scored for overall 'function.' That is, raters scored the language samples on how well the text communicated its message and how well the text fit the genre. The function ratings were from 1 (low function) to 5 (high function). There were differences between the paraprofessional and *normalista* groups in this category. The paraprofessionals averaged 4.8 and the *normalistas* averaged 3.7.

This excerpt, with a function score of 2.5, is from a *normalista's* reflective text about her own acquisition of literacy. It shows the writer's understanding of the genre and while the meaning is comprehensible, understanding of the communication requires effort on the part of the reader:

> Thanks God I have only good memories about the way that I learned to write and to read, because I born in a family that the major parts are teachers. When I was born my mother and my older sister start a kindergarten and I grew up with this (literacy) environment surrounded all my life.

Here again, the different starting points of the *normalistas* and paraprofessionals on the continua of biliterate development meant that they drew differently on the continua of biliterate media. The paraprofessional group had greater facility with English language structures, while the *normalistas* were still acquiring them.

Code switching and cultural genre: Media and content in biliterate oral interaction

The tutoring fieldwork data gives us evidence of the use of language and literacy in the work of the *normalistas* and paraprofessionals in the sociocultural interaction with Mexican American Spanish-speaking children within the contexts of schools and schooling. All participants were required to tape two lessons and they could choose the language of the lesson.

In this excerpt from a tutoring session, Karina, a paraprofessional, code switches and uses colloquial words in Spanish and English to encourage the students:

> *Pon una moneda de one cent sobre* (place a coin of one cent over) . . . okay . . . *ándale* (way to go) . . . *coloca en cada frasco la misma cantidad de monedas* (place in each jar the same amount of coins) . . . ready? . . . *¿está bien?* (Is it right?) . . . *ándale* (way to go) . . . ya'll did so good all of you, alright, *muy bien, ándale* (very good, way to go).

In another tutoring session she uses code switching as part of the math content instruction and for control:

> Four y four bears *es ocho* (are eight) . . . *dame tu* (give me) teddy bear.

On the other end of the continuum, a *normalista*, Yolanda, maintains her use of Spanish in spite of the students' code switching during a tutoring session. In the examples that follow the tutor is identified with the T and the child's response is identified with a C.

T: *Lo último que dijimos . . . Se-mi-lla, la ultima silaba es lla . . .* (the last thing we said . . . se-mi-lla, the last syllable is lla).
C: I know what's that one.
T: *¿Cuál es?* (Which is it?)

Here she acknowledges the child's contribution but continues the session in Spanish. In another episode, she asks the child to say the word in Spanish:

T: *Ahora, ¿qué es esto?* (Now, what is this?)
C. Egg.
T: *¿En español? huevo, huevo,* (In Spanish? egg, egg).

In the tutoring sessions, the paraprofessionals were more likely to code-switch. On the other hand, the *normalistas* were more likely to maintain their interaction with the children in Spanish. As expected, *normalistas* were more likely to conduct their lessons in Spanish. Conversely, paraprofessionals were more likely to teach one lesson in English and the other in Spanish. While the one English-dominant paraprofessional code-switched the most, her interactions with the children were often reflective of the children's and community discourse. Even when teaching in English, paraprofessionals would code-switch into Spanish to praise, clarify, and express diminutives. Within this community, bilingual children tend to employ code switching as a form of social interaction. Thus, as Escamilla (1994) has argued, depending on the usage of the child's discourse within the bilingual classroom, bilingual education teachers' use of code switching can create a more equitable learning environment in which the minority language is viewed as having a majority status.

Although the paraprofessionals' cultural referents were more evident than the *normalistas'* in their writing samples (as we saw above), evidence of cultural situatedness was present for both cohorts during the field experiences. Throughout the taped tutoring sessions, both groups tended to use a great deal of praise and diminutives when speaking to the children. The *normalistas* were more likely to use cultural referents in the form of traditional children's verses or rhymes as cues for turn taking:

T: *A ver, a ver,* ***tin Marín de don pingüe cucara macara títere fue, yo no fui, fue tete pégale pégale con el pie, que este mero fue,*** *ándele le toco a usted. Una donde este 'ba,' la combinación de la 'b' con la 'a' 'ba' la combinación de la 'b' con la 'a' 'ba' localice una en las palabras.* (Let's see, let see . . . okay, it is your turn. Where is (ba), the combination of the 'b' with the 'a' 'ba' the combination of the 'b' with the 'a' 'ba' locate one in the words.)

Irene uses a traditional turn-taking verse, *tin Marin de don pingüe . . . ,* to keep the children actively engaged and also exposes them to the symbolic cultural tools within the context of literacy:

T: *¿Cómo suena 'be' bebiendo, o-kay, vamos a ver quien quiere pasar?* (How does it sound, 'dr' drinking, okay, who wants to be first?)
C: *Yo! Yo!* (Me! Me!)
T: *A ver, **tin Marín de don pingüe cucara macara títere fue, yo no fui fue tete, pégale pégale con el pie, que este mero fue** – le toco a usted, ándele no pues es la suerte – es el tin Marín.* (Let's see . . . it is you, come on it's the luck of the draw – it's *tin Marín.*)

Laura, a *normalista,* who had specialized in early childhood in Mexico, uses a repetitive cultural story form that is introduced with '*¿Quieres que te cuente un cuento?* (Do you want me to tell you a story?),' has a verse, and usually ends with '*¿Quieres que te lo cuente otra vez?* (Do you want me to tell it again?).' Here she uses this rich cultural genre to keep the children engaged while learning the concept of five. She begins with the children having their hands open and counting down from pinky to thumb making a wave of the hand (as in greeting) and continues with variations:

T: *¿Quieres que te cuente un cuento?* (Do you want me to tell you a story?)
C: *¡O, si!* (Oh, yes!!)
T: *Vamos a practicar, son cinco. Según yo conté cinco. ¿ Si? Practicamos todos. ¿Las hacemos las cinco? Saben cual primero para que sea hola como hola de un saludo. ¿La de las manitas, si?* (We will practice with five. According to me, I count five. Yes? Let's all practice. Shall we do the five? Do you know which one first, so that it's like a wave, like a hello wave. One with the hands, yes?)
C: *¡Si!* (Yes!)
T: *Bueno, todo el mundo con sus manos por enfrente . Listos, manos aquí enfrente. Una, dos, tres . . . .* (Good, everyone with your hands in front. Ready, hands in front. One, two, three . . . .)
T and C: (in unison) *Hola mano. ¿Qué tal mano? ¿A qué jugamos? ¿A los gigantes? ¿O a los enanos? No, ya sé mejor a caminarte. Tan tatan tatan tan tanan tan tan tantan. No, ya sé mejor a la baraja. No ya sé mejor al sube y baja. Sube y baja riendo y saltando toda la tarde los vi jugando. Sube y baja, sube y baja.* (Hello hand?

How are you hand? What shall we play? The giants? Or the midgets? No, now I know how [to play] walking. . . . No, now I know how [to play] cards. No, now I know how to see saw. Up and down, laughing and skipping all afternoon long, I saw you playing. Up and down, up and down.)

T: *¡O!, un aplauso – que barbaros que inteligentes. ¡No, porque no lo hemos hecho tantas veces y ya se la saben!* (Oh, applause – what marvels [you are], how intelligent! No, because we have not done it many times and you already know it!)

Evident from our observations was that these genres of traditional verse and cultural referents within a context of literacy were very much enjoyed by the children in the different settings. For some children, these literacy forms, although in their native language, were something novel, while for others they were a reflection of prior home literacy experiences. The social interaction between teacher and student also demonstrated how cultural knowledge (content) is socially distributed within the situated context of literacy lessons.

Dimensions of the Continua in Developing Biliterate Teachers' Texts and Interaction

The seven participants studied exhibited varying degrees of contextual situatedness and multiple social roles and identities in their texts and discourses, as revealed through both the media and content of their biliterate expression. Although the participants in this study shared a broadly defined Latino ethnic culture, the context of their cultural upbringing varied significantly and their use of more formal discourse in written language and formal interviews was more similar within group than across the groups. However, during the tutoring work with children, all exhibited aspects of situationally emergent language and social identity. That is, through co-membership with their students they created a shared social identity and adapted their communicative style to what was going on during the lesson presentation. Both groups worked equally well within the schooling context and neither challenged schooling expectations. On the one hand, there appeared to be a certain privileging of the paraprofessionals due to their knowledge of schooling in the United States. On the other hand, the *normalistas* may have had more positive experiences with schooling in Mexico although they were less knowledgeable about schooling in the United States.

Cultural experiences may be seen as ranging along the continua of literary-to-vernacular, majority-to-minority content, especially for members of the same ethnic group who are divided by a national border, as is the case of Mexicans and Mexican Americans in South Texas. The situatedness along these cultural content continua was most obvious from the data of the tutoring sessions as both *normalistas* and paraprofessionals adapted their cultural references to the cultural context of the children. In other words, they contextualized the content for the children. These social interactions with children show how cultural knowledge (content) can be both socially situated and distributed within a literacy context from teacher to student, from expert to novice.

To understand the dynamic of the biliteracy continua in the very diverse language and literacy skills that the *normalistas* and the paraprofessionals had and were developing, we had to first see the interrelatedness of the media, content, and context continua. The *normalistas* from Mexico can be theorized to have a certain level of Spanish literacy attainment, and that level of attainment assisted them in situating themselves in the formal university context, but when a full range of vernacular to standard language skills were required in the context of tutoring they appeared to be less adaptive than the paraprofessionals. In the case of the paraprofessionals, the level of literacy development in Spanish was more on the vernacular end of the continuum and that knowledge and the knowledge of more standard and literary forms of English assisted them in the university classes conducted in English and in the tutoring. However, they were less adaptive in the Spanish interview and university classes conducted in Spanish. Because the bilingual preparation program offers some classes in Spanish and some in English, the shifts in the comfort, control, language dominance, and discourse were dynamic and, in some cases, dramatic. Additionally, other factors such as level of literacy, knowledge of the culture of schooling in the US, or knowledge of the history and culture of Mexico also contributed to the social and power relations dynamics among students and between the two cohort groups as well as between the students and professors.

The acceptance of the use of the vernacular by speakers of English and Spanish within the teacher preparation program, and in particular in the tutoring sessions, provided opportunities for all to understand the community use of the vernacular. This context also provided opportunities for development of standard speakers of English and standard speakers of Spanish – which is the ultimate goal of the teacher preparation program.

Furthermore, assuring that bilingual educators have these tools as they enter the bilingual classroom can assist in the acquisition of ethnic and linguistic self-determination of the learner as described in the literature (See Ricento & Hornberger, 1996). Consistent with Hornberger & Skilton-Sylvester's (2000) argument for the need to contest the traditional power-weightings of the continua of biliteracy, this type of preparation of bilingual education teachers addresses language policy and power issues within the bilingual education field and assures that language minority students' native language is used as a mediation tool in the acquisition of equity and power.

Notes

1. Project Alianza is funded by the W.R. Kellogg Foundation and is a collaboration of the Intercultural and Developmental Research Association and the Mexican and American Solidarity Foundation. The views presented here are those of the authors and not of these organizations.
2. 'Vernacular' in our usage refers to both the content and media of biliteracy, the former specifically to vernacular discourse styles or genres and the latter to vernacular or 'nonstandard' structures and scripts, i.e. nonstandard grammatical, phonological, lexical, and orthographic usages.

Appendix

Analysis of language usage

Subject name ____________ **Language used** ____________

Rater ____________________ **Form** ____________________
(interview, written reflection, narrative, classroom interaction, etc.)

______ 1. Literacy in context (references within content)
(5 = highest number of references 1 = no references)
cultural
____ personal historical
____ social
____ school related

______ 2. L 1 and L 2
(5 = much influence of L1 on L2 1 = no influence of L1 on L2)
____ evidence of code switching
____ syntactic elements
____ discourse styles

______ 3. Syntactic analysis of text structures
(5 = high 1 = low)
____ cohesiveness (logical development; paragraph flow)
____ coherence/clarity (complete thoughts/ideas conveyed)
____ complexity within/between sentences (variety)
____ lexical loading (richness/preciseness of language)

______ 4. Function of text
(5 = high function 1 = low function)
____ functional in terms of communicating
____ purpose of genre
____ global content

References

Cazden, C. (1988) *Classroom Discourse: The Language of Teaching and Learning*. Portsmouth, NH: Heinemann.

Erickson, F. and Shultz, J. (1982) *The Counselor as Gatekeeper: Social Interaction in Interviews*. New York: Academic Press.

Escamilla, K. (1994) The sociolinguistic environment of a bilingual school: A case study introduction. *Bilingual Research Journal* 8 (1–2), 21–47.

Ferdman, B.M. (1990) Literacy and cultural identity. *Harvard Educational Review* 60 (2), 181–204.

Flores, B.B. and Clark E.R. (2000) Retooling normalistas as bilingual teachers: Who are they and what resources do they bring? Paper presented at National Association for Bilingual Education Annual Conference, San Antonio, Texas.

Freeman, D. and Johnson, K.E. (1998) Reconceptualizing the knowledge-base of language teacher education. *TESOL Quarterly* 32 (3), 397–415.

González-Pino, B. (1991) *The Bilingual Prochievement Test*. San Antonio, TX: Editorial Interamerica.

Grabe, W. and Kaplan, R.B. (1996) *Theory & Practice of Writing*. New York: Longman.

Gumperz, J. (1982) *Discourse Strategies*. Cambridge: Cambridge University Press.

Gutiérrez, K.D., Baquedano-López, P., Álvarez, H.H. and Chiu, M.M. (1999) Building a culture of collaboration through hybrid language practices. *Theory into Practice* 3 (2), 87–93.

Heath, S.B. (1983) *Ways with Words*. New York: Cambridge University Press.

Hornberger, N.H. (1989) Continua of biliteracy. *Review of Educational Research* 59 (3), 271–96.

Hornberger, N.H. and Skilton-Sylvester, E. (2000) Revisiting the continua of biliteracy: International and critical perspectives. *Language and Education: An International Journal* 14 (2), 96–122.

Hymes, D. (1974) *Foundations in Sociolinguistics: An Ethnographic Approach*. Philadelphia, PA: University of Pennsylvania Press.

Jacobson, R. and Faltis, C.J. (eds) (1990) *Language Distributions Issues in Bilingual Schooling*. New York: Multilingual Matters.

Lincoln, Y.S. and Guba, E.G. (1985) *Naturalistic Inquiry*. Beverly Hills, CA: Sage.

Lux, P. and Grabe, W. (1991) Multivariate approaches to contrastive rhetoric. *Lenguas Modernas* 18 (2), 133–60.

Miles, M.B. and Huberman, A.M. (1994) *Qualitative Data Analysis: An Expanded Sourcebook* (2nd edn). Thousand Oaks, CA: Sage.

Milk, R., Mercado, C. and Sapiens, A. (1992) *Re-thinking the Education of Language Minority Children: Developing Reflective Teachers for Changing Schools*. NCBE Focus: Occasional Papers in Bilingual education 6. Washington, DC: National Clearinghouse for Bilingual Education.

Montaño-Harmon, M. (1991) Discourse features of written Mexican Spanish: Current research in contrastive rhetoric and its implications. *Hispania* 74 (4), 417–25.

Pérez, B. (ed.) (1998) *Sociocultural Contexts of Language and Literacy*. Mahwah, NJ: Lawrence Erlbaum Associates.

Ricento, T.K. and Hornberger, N.H. (1996) Unpeeling the onion: Language planning and policy and the ELT professional. *TESOL Quarterly* 30 (3), 401–27.

Roberts, C., Jupp, T. and Davies, E. (1991) *Language and Discrimination: A Study of Communication in Multiethnic Workplaces*. New York: Longman.

Rubin, H.J. and Rubin, I.S. (1995) *Qualitative Interviewing: The Art of Hearing Data*. Thousand Oaks, CA: Sage.

Schecter, S.R. and Bayley, R. (1998) Concurrence and complementarity: Mexican-background parents' decisions about language and schooling. *Journal for a Just & Caring Education* 4 (1), 47–64.

Weis, L. (ed.) (1988) *Class, Race, and Gender in American Education*. Albany, NY: State University of New York.

Zentella, A.C. (1982) Code switching and interaction among Puerto Rican children. In J. Amastae and L. Elias-Olivares (eds) *Spanish in the United States: Sociolinguistic Aspects* (pp. 354–85). Cambridge: Cambridge University Press.

Chapter 10

Content in Rural ESL Programs: Whose Agendas for Biliteracy are Being Served?

JOEL HARDMAN

Content had been a long-neglected feature of language education before thankfully being reassigned an increasingly higher level of importance over the last two decades (see Brinton *et al.*, 1989; Grabe & Stoller, 1997). However, accepting the importance of content in language teaching and learning leads to more complex questions: How should that content be presented? Whose content? Whose purposes should content serve? Hornberger and Skilton-Sylvester's (2000) revision of Hornberger's original (1989) continua of biliteracy addresses the content question directly by examining the power relations inherent in the control of knowledge and meaning in a social context such as a school. As they describe the content continuum, there is on one end what might be thought of as school-centered content (majority, literary, and decontextualized), and on the other learner-centered content (minority, vernacular, and contextualized).

The content continuum intersects, according to their model, with the continua of media and context. The media continua cover the mode of exposure to the two literacies, the types of scripts involved, and the types of structures (for example standard or nonstandard structures). The context continua relate to the social situation in which biliteracy occurs – for example, the language policies of the school, and how they affect teacher practice. These two intersections will be exemplified by examining two tensions I have observed in my work with ESL/bilingual[1] teachers in the rural US Midwest: one between content and language and another between two types of content – mainstream classroom-centered content and more learner-centered content.

I will discuss in this chapter the differing roles of English language learners, ESL/bilingual teachers, mainstream classroom teachers, and other school personnel in the control of content in ESL/bilingual programs in a rural area in the Midwestern United States. This discussion is based on a year-long involvement with four area ESL/bilingual teachers in three different school districts who are engaged in action research addressing questions of content in their programs. During the year I interviewed the teachers, observed their teaching, attended meetings of their action research group, and exchanged notes/questions/responses to observations.

Based on this research I would like to highlight some distinctions relevant to the control of meaning and knowledge in ESL/bilingual programs, particularly programs in rural areas where the role of the teacher in curriculum decisions is marked by a lack of institutional direction and professional support. To begin with, in the ESL/bilingual teaching situations described in this chapter, there is a point of tension at the intersection of the continua of media and content between 'content of the school's (or mainstream classroom teachers') choosing' and 'no content at all' (language-only). Under the latter option, the 'medium' of language instruction may be language structures themselves (words, rules, sounds, scripts) or particular mainstream school content. Both learners and teachers are disempowered in a system where this tension is left unaddressed – neither group having much say in the choice of knowledge and language competencies deemed important for ESL/bilingual learners to have.

When ESL/bilingual teachers *do* exert a choice of content, another distinction can be made between content which the ESL/bilingual teacher perceives to be in the students' best interests aside from mainstream classroom needs, and content they think will support the students' mainstream classroom success. This tension exemplifies the intersection of the continua of content and context (e.g. the language policies of the school system). Whose agendas for biliteracy are being served by the system (McKay, 1993)? The teachers'? The school's? The learners'?

The answer to these questions is complex. One could argue that the students' interests are being served whichever way one looks at it. However, the schools, mainstream classroom teachers, and ESL/bilingual teachers each have their own agendas. The extent to which these agendas are in conflict will also be explored in this chapter. The nested nature of Hornberger and Skilton-Sylvester's continua provides a clear framework for exploring how these conflicts relate to the full socio-political environment in which biliteracy develops. Every biliteracy event can be examined according to the 'what' (content), 'how' (media) and 'who/where' (context) of communication. Content is being used here as the primary analytic lens because it is a link between the material of instruction (the media) and the socio-political context.

The notion of 'content' as it is used in Hornberger and Skilton-Sylvester's continua model provides a tool for examining various aspects of the use of texts in classrooms. Textual content, and the *use* of that content, is integral to the construction of knowledge and identity in the classroom. 'Content-Based Instruction' (CBI) as discussed below is one particular way of framing content in the classroom. There is at one level *always* content in a language classroom, if one considers the form of language itself a kind of content, and the random bits of meaning encoded in the lexicon 'content.' When a student learns to say 'Mary drank the milk' or 'John saw the pony,' have they learned something about milk? About ponies? To know that a pony is a small horse – is that content knowledge or linguistic knowledge? It is obviously unwise to make a simplistic and dichotomous distinction between the two. However, the ESL/bilingual teachers themselves frequently make a distinction between language and content, as that distinction is encoded in mainstream curricula and program design.

In the more widespread use of the term 'content' in language teaching, it refers to matters other than language and specific vocabulary items. It is this 'other' that I discuss here, the math, science, social studies, geography, etc., which form the basis of most content-based language curricula. From the perspective of the ESL/bilingual teachers I have worked with, teaching 'content' typically refers to teaching the subjects covered in mainstream classrooms.

Using Hornberger and Skilton-Sylvester's terms for discussing content, CBI *tends* to foreground majority, decontextualized content, what I'm referring to here as 'mainstream classroom content,' which is tied to a context which empowers schools over teachers, and media which are dominated by standard English. However, I do believe there is space within the CBI construct to privilege more vernacular, contextualized content, space that empowered teachers *can* stake out in their classrooms. To the extent that CBI is intended to be motivating and student-centered (Snow *et al.*, 1989), the latter perspective is certainly compatible.

One way of looking at how CBI enmeshes teachers in relations of power is by way of Rampton's (1999, 2000) notion of ritual. He argues that the practice of language teaching displays aspects of ritual (Rampton, 1999, 2000), meaning that there is a sense of stepping outside the normal flow of events and modes of interpretation, and reliance on a special set of 'formulaic content' (Rampton, 2000: 328). There should be an identifiable structure to the ritual (here called 'Content-Based Instruction,' or CBI) and differing relations of power regarding participation in and control of the particulars of the ritual.

The ritual of CBI has been articulated in numerous sources (Brinton *et al.*, 1989; Met, 1994; Snow *et al.*, 1989). I will focus on one aspect of CBI that is particularly ritualized and reflects its conceptual core – the distinction between content-compatible and content-obligatory language structures (see particularly Met, 1994: 162–4 and Snow *et al.*, 1989: 30–2). This distinction has been ritualized in language-teacher education programs, with teachers being trained in explicit detail how to perform the tasks involved in the selection of language structures for instruction. It is an interesting distinction because it also points to the tensions in relations of power under discussion here – that is, there are certain structures teachers *must* teach (content-obligatory) and certain structures they *can* teach (compatible). The tension between the obligatory and the possible is both a prescribed feature of the CBI ritual *and* points toward teacher-empowerment within the ritual – the possible. Snow (1998: 257) identifies these issues of power and status concerning the relationship between ESL and content-area teachers as an ongoing challenge.

CBI is ritual, in Rampton's terms, in how it tries to explicitly 'step outside' the normal flow of either the language or content classrooms, utilizing formulaic content. ESL/bilingual teachers can be seen as following this formulaic content to varying degrees, indicating different stances toward content and to one mode of its representation, the CBI ritual. Seeing CBI as ritualized helps describe the intersection within Hornberger and Skilton-Sylvester's continua framework of content and media. Having formulaic content means the content is encoded in certain kinds of language – certain media (the standard academic English of classrooms, most especially).

CBI can also be seen as a kind of discourse practice or discourse event (Fairclough, 1992; Gee, 1990). As Fairclough defines the term:

> Discursive events . . . are analysed linguistically as texts, as instances of discourse practice, and as instances of social practice. By 'discourse practice' I mean the practices of producing, distributing, and consuming texts. (1992: 269)

The productivity of texts, their ability to reform discursive practices, 'is not in practice available to people as a limitless space for textual innovation and play: it is socially limited and constrained, and conditional on relations of power' (Fairclough, 1992: 270). Gee's notion of Discourse (capital 'D') itself entails the participation in certain practices and ways of thinking (1990: xix). Such a notion of discourse can clearly add to an understanding of CBI. As Fairclough argues, 'A discourse is *a particular way of constructing* a subject matter,' a notion which emphasizes that 'contents or subject matters – areas of knowledge – only enter texts in the mediated form of particular constructions of them' (1992: 286).

CBI, then, lends itself to analysis as a discourse practice because it is explicitly a ritual for 'constructing subject matter,' a ritual with a linguistic form which is itself a discourse practice. That is, there is the discourse practice which can be labeled 'CBI' and there are the discourses which are the focus of that practice, the discourse of geography, the discourse of social studies, and so on. The discourse practices of CBI most relevant here are those of obligation and compatibility. These discourses communicate to the teacher, and learner, that certain things *must* be known and others *may* be known. In practice the 'must be known' tends to be the majority, decontextualized language and content, while the 'compatible,' and therefore more marginalized knowledge, is more contextualized, vernacular, and minority.

One final aspect of the notion of discourse practices needs to be discussed before moving on to an examination of CBI in practice. Fairclough (1992) uses Kristeva's (1986) concept of 'intertextuality' (which was itself largely based on her analysis of Bakhtin [1986]) to describe how texts are constructed and interpreted within certain social contexts, and how the texts themselves then produce/transform discourse conventions needed for future textual construction and interpretation (270). Such intertextual chains 'often become lines of tension and change: the lines, or channels, through which text types are colonized and invested, and along which, relationships among text types are contested' (Fairclough, 1992: 289–90). This tension is central to the problematic and varying ways in which the ESL/bilingual teachers participate in the CBI ritual.

In the discussion that follows, the experiences of the four ESL/bilingual teachers will be examined using the above frameworks of ritual and discourse to understand how they are caught up in the power relations surrounding the distribution and validation of content/knowledge in ESL/bilingual programs. The practices and beliefs of each teacher can be seen as exemplifying tensions at the intersections of the content continua of biliteracy with media and context, respectively.

'Media and Content': No Content (Language Only) ↔ Mainstream Classroom Content

The following is an excerpt from an interview with Penny[2], who teaches children whose first language is Spanish in a predominantly African-American school district:

How do you go about deciding what to do in a given meeting?

With the non-speakers it's just basically body parts and classrooms and school and environment, so there are survival skills to get their vocabulary built up, and do some phonics and things like that. With the limited-to-fluent we take their story that they're reading in their basal that week, and we do a picture walk first. And then we go through and I read it to them. Then they go back and look at it themselves and pick up vocabulary that they don't know and write that down. They each have one of those little pocket notebooks that they carry around with forever. Then we go through and decide what categories to put them in. If they are older students we'll put them in nouns, verbs, adverbs, adjectives. If they are younger students we'll put them in people, places, things. After we put them in categories we'll decide synonyms for them. I have tons of thesauruses, and those little Franklin dictionaries. So then we write down the synonyms. If they're younger they make a picture with that. And then there's a couple games we play – true/false questions, other questions, it's like a game to them. And they point to the word, say it, give the definition, or the synonym, and then the category.

Do you meet with their teachers with any regularity?

Not real formally. Just when I go pick up the kids or drop them off. If they have something to say to me, or I to them.

So you don't negotiate with them about what you're going to be working on or teaching?

With the older students, yes, I can. But with the younger students it's really pointless. I'd be more like somebody giving them the answers in Spanish. But yeah, with the older students sometimes if they have something that they're really working on, like a skill, I can take that skill out of the lesson that we're doing from the basal and work on those individual skills.

Do the other teachers ever tell you things, like 'could you teach them about the civil war, or the names of the countries of Europe,' something like that?

I think I did have one teacher say they were working on a social studies unit and we did go over some of those countries that the students had to know. But mostly it's like, 'we're working on compound words this week, or suffixes this week.' They know how my lessons go, and they know what kind of things to put in there, and what kinds of things are on the state tests that the students need to work on.

So you really do stick to the language issues rather than content?

Unless content is pertinent. I just think they learn quicker sticking on the language.

Penny's strong commitment to teaching language skills, not content, is quite evident in this excerpt. This stance is also evident in other work I have seen Penny do, discussed below.

Later in the year as part of an action research project that some of the ESL/bilingual teachers were conducting, Penny circulated a survey to the mainstream content-area teachers in her school to find out what they think L2 students need most. Below is the complete list of responses that she collected (it is important to see the entire list in order to fully interpret her response to it):

Following and understanding directions
Science-writing-reading
Oral language skills and auditory picture clues
Oral language skills
Letters and spelling
Develop reading skills – strategies, attack
Vocabulary knowledge and definitions
Speak more English
Letter to sound (vice versa) analyses [response of Spanish reading recovery teacher]
Comfort speaking in their own language, in own classroom for confidence
Phonics
Sounds
Alphabet in English
More teachers or aides
Lots of phonics and reinforcement in sounds, English at home and school
Phonics
Vocabulary
Reading
Reading and spelling
Vocabulary
Decoding and encoding

Penny's own interpretation of these results was that the 'compassionate' teachers think students need more language, while the 'strict' teachers think they need more reading and writing. Interestingly, she perceived the results in terms of language skills only, and seemed to use the phrase 'reading and writing' when she talked about the results as a cover term for both literacy skills and content (see 'science-writing-reading'). Her reading of the survey may speak to how she defines her relationship to the mainstream classroom teachers – how they divide roles and responsibilities. Those teachers with whom she shares an understanding of her job being centered on language skill development she views as compassionate, and the others, who don't share this view, she sees as strict. They are strict not only with the children but also with her because they try to get her to work in ways she doesn't want to.

Within the context of the school as a whole, the 'no-content (language only)' and 'mainstream-classroom content' options exist side-by-side, but compartmentalized (departmentalized). But for Penny, is the 'language only' stance simply a capitulation to the status quo, or can it be interpreted as a kind of resistance to mainstream classroom/teacher demands, as if she is saying, 'language is my thing, and content is yours'? When she is done with what she considers to be her job in support of the children's needs, only then will the interests of the other classroom teachers and school be entertained. Though her rejection of the ritual and discourse of Content-Based Instruction would be easy to criticize as 'traditional' or pedagogically out-of-date, one can also interpret her stance as a kind of self-empowerment within the institution, a rejection of a status subservient to the mainstream content classrooms implied in some CBI.

The experiences of Georgia, an ESL/bilingual teacher working with children who have many different native languages, reveals what can happen when a teacher emphasizes the 'mainstream-classroom content' aspect of the intersection between content and media. Below is a description of a short geography lesson she did with a dozen middle school students:

> 9:30 Georgia hands out sheets of paper for a quiz. The students have to write down state capitals that she reads out loud. The students complain that it's too easy.
>
> 9:36 Georgia talks about 'mid-Atlantic' and distributes a handout about Maryland. The class is working through all 50 states. She asks questions that require reading straight from the handout, nominating students. She draws pictures on the board to explain certain facts in the reading. Her questions gradually become more complex. 'What are the industries in Maryland? Why do you think there would be fishing?'

9:45 She begins reading the whole passage out loud, then nominates students to read sections. She explains concepts and vocabulary items as they read. She makes an off-hand comment about studying students' home countries in a similar manner, and the students get very interested, but the idea is not pursued.

10:00 Worksheets are handed out for Maryland. Students work at their desks on it, on their own. They occasionally ask each other for help.

Georgia is enacting a standard CBI ritual, embedding the study of language within the study of content, content which she explained the students were supposed to know in their mainstream classrooms, content which she felt no great affinity for but covered out of a sense of obligation. That is, she was working with what she perceived to be 'content-obligatory language' (state names, industry labels). After I observed the lesson I gave Georgia the above notes and asked her the following questions: What is your reaction to the lesson? Did it go as planned? What do you think in particular worked well or went wrong? She responded:

> Unless they have something personal to add (if they have experienced some of the geography first-hand, for example) it seems that they are only doing the work to get it done. I am trying to get some work together that they can work on in a group, to help with communication. As exhibited in the reaction to studying other countries, it has to be personal for them to be particularly interesting. I also try to have pictures or movies to give them some idea of what the area looks like.

She responds to the experience by analyzing it within the discourse of CBI – it is supposed to be motivating and student-centered. In my interview with Georgia a few months previous, she explained to me her beliefs about motivation and content:

> I think that people pay attention to what they are interested in, for whatever reason. You have to *use* the language to learn it. . . . You have to use it, you have to start thinking in the language. That's achieved by immersing yourself in it.

Later in the interview she commented:

> I took a human origins class. We had to know all the bones in the body. It wasn't even hard for me because it was so much fun. I mean, it was just like going out and doing the gardening. It must be the same way with language. If it's something you really want to know, and you're really interested in, you're going to learn it a lot better, a lot faster. And it's going to stick with you. And if it's totally obscure,

you have no idea what someone's trying to tell you or what you're supposed to be doing, you're not going to learn it.

On one level there does seem to be a certain match between what Georgia says about content and motivation and what she does in her classroom; she believes content motivates learners and motivation drives language acquisition, so she follows the CBI ritual in the hopes that the content will motivate her students. But on another level there seems to be a great mismatch – the content *does not* motivate or interest her students, and she seems to sense that. Her lesson is mainstream content-centered, not learner-centered. She sees this, but seems to feel a bit powerless in the face of the demands of the ritual. She, and the teacher she works with, complained throughout the year about the content they felt required to cover in their classes (a complaint familiar to all teachers). Georgia can be seen as attempting to shoulder the content responsibilities given her, even when they conflict with her own stated beliefs about language acquisition. That is, even when there seems to be no intrinsically motivating way of covering certain content-obligatory language, it must still be covered.

Georgia distributed the same survey as Penny concerning mainstream classroom teachers' opinions of English Language Learner needs, and made an interesting comment about a math teacher's response: 'I was interested in the math teacher's comment about vocabulary: "math is a symbolic language." Duh . . . you still need the words for multiply, divide, etc. Just shows how uninformed some of the teachers are.' Despite her feelings of obligation to cover the content required by the schools, she can still oppose their authority. As much as the math teacher does, she feels she can say what it takes to know math.

Georgia and Penny can both be seen as sharing a space within the institutional context which marginalizes more learner-centered, vernacular content, either by rejecting content entirely, in the case of Penny, or working with the standard English-medium, majority content. However, ESL/bilingual teachers can also position themselves in neither a subservient nor oppositional stance to mainstream content, as discussed below.

'Content and Context': Content-for-classroom ↔ Content-for-learner

Anne teaches in a district where she has to travel from school to school pulling children out of their mainstream classrooms. Below are my notes addressed to Anne, describing a piece of a lesson about spiders which she put together for a group of four children from five to seven years old:

2:25 You engage in various schema-activation activities related to spiders. When you all count the number of legs a spider has, the Bulgarian girl silently mouths the numbers.

2:30 You read 'The Very Busy Spider.' While reading, you try to prompt the kids to call out words, but it only works sometimes. For one example:

You: 'Baa baa said the . . .' ('Sheep' is the word in the book)
Boy: 'Lamb?'
You: 'Lamb?'

Anne is committed to CBI, and for these elementary school children she typically chooses content on her own, such as spiders and math. When I interviewed Anne, I tried to get a sense of where her approach to content and language comes from:

You say you're trying to get away from textbooks when you teach. How do you go about putting together a typical lesson?

There's all different kinds of things that I do. In some situations with kids I work one-on-one, and I might do a tutorial program with whatever subject they're having difficulty with. For example, like social studies or science if they're having problems with the vocabulary or the concepts. I do a lot of pre-teaching, with introducing the vocabulary words, trying to explain them on a more simple level, I guess. So that way, when they go back into the classroom they have some exposure to some of the concepts. It'll probably be a little bit easier for them to understand what's going on.

How do you find out what their difficulties are?

I talk with the teachers. It's a lot of communication with the teachers, constantly. In some situations, *when the kids first come here, I kind of do my own thing*, whether it's focusing on a particular theme that they're doing in the classroom, or whether it's just doing simple vocabulary, talking, TPR, things like that to just get them, you know, taking them on tours in the school so they start understanding, 'this is the bathroom, that's the classroom.' Things like that. I do a lot of communication with the teachers. If they're new arrivals, then I know I need to start on just the simple basic things, just survival English. *But if they are verbally fluent, usually I will kind of go along with what the teacher's doing in terms of the theme, but then I pick my own things I want them to work on. . . .* I think what I do in terms of a pull-out is maybe provide them with extra attention or maybe support in terms of the whole ESL/language/culture thing that they might not get in the regular classroom. . . . My job is to help them function in the regular classroom. (italics added)

Anne is clearly making content decisions based on her perceptions of student needs related to classroom success. She enacts the CBI ritual because she feels it will best support what is going on in the students' mainstream classrooms. The discourse she displays a preference for when describing what she does foregrounds this 'support' relationship. However, she is also in control of what she does, 'doing her own thing' – she is making the decisions about what she believes students need to know.

Irene teaches in the same site as Georgia, her students representing numerous language backgrounds. Below is a description of part of a social studies lesson for some of the same middle-school students Georgia worked with on geography:

> 10:30 Irene reviews information about Martin Luther King from a previous lesson. She leads an open-ended discussion of what a minority is. She opens today's lesson by asking one of the Hispanic students how to pronounce 'Cesar Chavez' correctly. Chavez is the subject of the new chapter they are reading. She repeats his model pronunciation a few times.
>
> 10:40 Irene begins reading aloud the chapter on Chavez, asking questions as she goes, constantly linking the content of the reading to her students' lives. She links a comment about Chavez's father's farm failing to the Chinese restaurant one of her student's parents run. She asks both simple comprehension questions and high-inference questions about the reading.
>
> 11:10 Following a reference to 'outhouses' in the reading on Chavez, Irene leads a *long* funny discussion of the meaning.

The way that Irene enacts the CBI ritual differs from Georgia and Anne. The classroom discussion seems at times to be more about her students than the content they are studying. That is, her approach to this content is highly learner-centered and vernacular, more toward the contextualized end of the content continuum. It is more important to her for her students to reflect on their own lives than to acquire specific knowledge of Cesar Chavez. In an interview a few months earlier I had asked Irene about her approach to language and content:

> *Do you work on language issues rather than content issues?*
>
> No, no. Content within language. When it comes up, language comes out through all of the content things that we do, where they

wouldn't in regular class. They wouldn't spend time on vocabulary as much.

Do you think at all levels you work with the same proportion of language and content issues?

For the upper groups, we meet with them for three hours. The first hour is for language, and the second two hours is for content. I would say we do more content than language.

Her focus does seem to be on the language development, and the content is simply a means. In terms of the CBI ritual, she is working mostly with content-compatible language. This focus can be seen in an interesting light based on her stated attitudes regarding language: 'I say, "this is what you'll hear, but this is what's correct" . . . (laughing) I think standard English is best, myself. Just for everybody's continued comprehension. Since we're getting more global, there has to be an English that everyone understands.' She is aware of how content is related to (intersects with) the continua of media, specifically the standard and non-standard forms of language. Irene grew up in rural Illinois and tends to portray her family as linguistically 'non-standard,' which she brought up when I asked her where her beliefs about language came from:

> Probably from school. Because, I taught myself to speak differently than my family speaks, because people thought I was dumb by how I spoke. So I changed how I spoke so I could fit in better, appear different than . . . which is kind of bad, but . . . . I know that the big controversy is bilingual versus ESL, and we just don't have a choice here. I'm not fluent in Spanish. I do speak Spanish, but I'm not fluent, and the majority of our kids do not speak Spanish. . . . Our kids speak all different languages. . . . I sit through the conference, I go to the bilingual conference cause they have the best ESL stuff. . . . So I started going to the bilingual one, and they give their bilingual speeches, you know. And I see the point, but I still think that English is the way to go. And I don't think the United States should be bilingual. I think it should be English only.

These are opinions Irene frequently brings up – part of a firm belief in what it means to her to be 'American.' Interestingly, she is able to rely on a discourse typically associated with disempowerment (assimilationism, the standard-English-only movement) to explain her vision, which she achieves through an empowering pedagogy (e.g. linking the work/life of Cesar Chavez to the lives and knowledge of her students). Also in contrast to her stated beliefs, her classroom is stocked with multiple bilingual dictionaries, and she speaks a little Spanish at times.

Despite being most outspoken regarding the overall goal of cultural and linguistic assimilation, Irene makes decisions in her classroom that are based entirely on her perceptions of what learners need for a good life in the US, regardless of what they are doing in their mainstream classroom. This stance is perhaps related to her lack of contact with the schools her students attend. They are bussed to her ESL center from throughout the county, and she rarely, if ever, has contact with their other teachers. Her participation in the CBI ritual is not motivated by mainstream classroom teachers' needs, or the needs of her students in those classrooms, but by a vision of what she perceives to be the 'right' sociolinguistic future for her students.

Conclusion

Austin tells a story about the christening of a nautical vessel:

> Suppose, for example, I see a vessel on the stocks, walk up and smash the bottle hung at the stem, proclaim 'I name this ship the *Mr Stalin*' and for good measure kick away the chocks: but the trouble is, I was not the person chosen to name it. (1962: 23).

When doing CBI, teachers are saying to students 'this is what you need to know – this is school knowledge.' But if teachers are not the official 'christeners' of school knowledge, is it in fact important school knowledge? In enacting the ritual of CBI in various ways and to varying degrees, these ESL/bilingual teachers are demonstrating how various lines of power run through them, lines of tension and change (Fairclough, 1992) which situate them vis-à-vis the school system and other teachers. The lines of tension and change vary from teacher to teacher, and are strung out in different directions. The same ritual empowers some teachers, and seems to disempower others.

The discourses at the heart of CBI (e.g. 'geography,' and the discourse of CBI itself) are, in Bakhtinian terms, intertextual chains – discourse practices which 'set the tone . . . to which one refers, which are cited, initiated, and followed' (1986: 88). These traditions 'are expressed and retained in verbal vestments' (Bakhtin, 1986: 88) which can sweep up a teacher, or sweep them aside. The discourse of content-obligatory and content-compatible language itself represents an intertextual chain, and it opens up spaces for resistance and change.

Hornberger and Skilton-Sylvester's continua framework provides a way of examining how teachers' content decisions are also tied to decisions about language media (e.g. standard classroom English) and the full context of language acquisition – from the classroom, to the school, to the community. Despite the complexities of intersecting and nested continua, the framework 'describes, not a kind of web in which teachers and learners are trapped, but rather the possibilities inherent to a language-rich environment, wherein reflective practitioners can take on the power to 'christen,' along with learners, the knowledge relevant to biliterate development.

Notes

1. I use the term 'ESL/bilingual' here and throughout because I work with teachers labeled as one or the other, though that labeling seems to be unrelated to the work that they do. Some ESL teachers in this area use as much of students' native languages as they know, while some 'bilingual' teachers use only English. This is the topic for another paper, or book.
2. The names of the four teachers are pseudonyms.

References

Austin, J. (1962) *How to Do Things with Words*. Cambridge, MA: Harvard University Press.

Bakhtin, M. (1986) *Speech Genres and Other Late Essays*. Austin: University of Texas Press.

Brinton, D., Snow, M.A. and Wesche, M. (1989) *Content-Based Language Instruction*. New York: Newbury House.

Fairclough, N. (1992) Intertextuality in critical discourse analysis. *Linguistics and Education* 4, 269–93.

Gee, J. (1990) *Social Linguistics and Literacies: Ideology in Discourses*. Bristol, PA: The Falmer Press.

Grabe, W. and Stoller, F. (1997) Content-based instruction: Research foundations. In M.A. Snow and D. Brinton (eds) *The Content-Based Classroom: Perspectives on Integrating Language and Content* (pp. 158–74). New York: Longman.

Hornberger, N. (1989) Continua of biliteracy. *Review of Educational Research* 59 (3), 271–96.

Hornberger, N. and Skilton-Sylvester, E. (2000) Revisiting the continua of biliteracy: International and critical perspectives. *Language and Education: An International Journal* 14 (2), 96–122.

Kristeva, J. (1986) Word, dialogue and novel. In T. Moi (ed.) *The Kristeva Reader* (pp. 34–61). Oxford: Basil Blackwell.

McKay, S. (1993) *Agendas for Second Language Literacy*. Cambridge: Cambridge University Press.

Met, M. (1994) Teaching content through a second language. In F. Genesee (ed.) *Educating Second Language Children* (pp. 159–82). Cambridge: Cambridge University Press.

Rampton, B. (1999) Dichotomies, difference, and ritual in second language learning and teaching. *Applied Linguistics* 20 (3), 316–40.

Rampton, B. (2000) Instructed foreign language rituals in and out of class. Presentation at the American Association of Applied Linguistics Conference, Vancouver, Canada.

Snow, M.A. (1998) Trends and issues in content-based instruction. *Annual Review of Applied Linguistics* 18, 243–67.

Snow, M.A., Met, M. and Genesee, F. (1989) A conceptual framework for the integration of language and content in second/foreign language instruction. *TESOL Quarterly* 23 (2), 201–17.

Chapter 11

Enabling Biliteracy: Using the Continua of Biliteracy to Analyze Curricular Adaptations and Elaborations

DIANA SCHWINGE

There is a growing trend in American education to use centrally controlled comprehensive school reform, academic standards, scripted curricula, and high-stakes achievement testing to attempt to create educational equality and provide a better education for low-income students. However, while a more standardized school curriculum is being adopted, the school children studying the curriculum are often ethnically and linguistically diverse. This diversity can be seen as a disadvantage and a difficult complication for those who wish to see a uniform curriculum adopted. However, bilingual and bicultural home and community environments can also be viewed as a resource (Ruiz, 1984) to help students learn new academic content and be able to express their ideas in a larger variety of languages, genres, and semiotic modes. Even in situations where the classroom curricula and activities are specified in great detail, some teachers are able to act as bottom-up language and literacy planners (Ricento & Hornberger, 1986) by modifying and adapting the curricula and suggested activities to better enable their students to become bilingual, biliterate, and bicultural. Thus, the purpose of this chapter is to use ethnographic data to provide examples of how two elementary school bilingual education teachers who teach a mandated curriculum utilize the various linguistic, cultural, and textual resources that are available in their bilingual classrooms to help ensure that their classroom instruction is comprehensible, draws upon the community's local funds of knowledge, and enables students to successfully become bilingual and biliterate.

These curricular adaptations and elaborations are analyzed using the model of the continua of biliteracy as a framework, focusing especially on the content continua and the development continua. The continua of biliteracy (Hornberger, 1989; Hornberger & Skilton-Sylvester, 2000) form a framework that can be used as a model for analyzing teaching, research, and language planning in multilingual settings. The framework is composed of four nested sets of continua, each of which captures a significant aspect of the learning contexts that are essential for developing biliteracy. These four sets of continua are the media, contexts, development, and content of biliteracy. Each continuum consists of weaker and more powerful ends, and the continua thus recognize that all modes of expression and types of knowledge are not viewed as equally powerful by society. However, while the modes of expression and content represented by each end of the continua are not usually accorded equal time and respect in school, the model of the continua of biliteracy suggests that the more the learning context allows learners to draw from across the whole of each and every continuum, the greater the chances for the full development of biliteracy. Thus, this framework is based on the assumption that, by integrating the weaker and stronger ends of the continua when they plan lessons, teachers can create a more appropriate and more effective learning experience that is more likely to draw on the large variety of different alternatives and options that are available in bilingual literacy events.

One of the strengths of the framework of the continua of biliteracy is that while the sets of continua are interrelated to one another, each set is stated independently. Although it is possible that using the continua of biliteracy to examine a single aspect of a literacy event may not capitalize on the multidimensionality that is one of the strengths of the theoretical construct of the continua of biliteracy, using the framework as a heuristic to focus on individual aspects of literacy events may also have certain advantages. For example, while classroom literacy events have the potential to be modified in many aspects, during my research I noted that the teachers who I observed usually focused on adapting one aspect of a particular literacy event.

This chapter focuses on the content and the development continua because incorporating local minority content into lessons and developing proficiency in an increased number of languages, semiotic modes, and language skills appeared from my observations to be the most frequently used ways of adapting and elaborating on the literacy curriculum. Of course, since each aspect of the continua is interrelated with all of the others, all the various aspects suggested in the continua as a whole can also be identified in each literacy event described. For example, the literacy events described in the section on the development of biliteracy are also closely related to the media of biliteracy. Thus, the development of two linguistic codes can also be viewed as the simultaneous and successive acquisition of two languages, and communication in different semiotic modalities could be interpreted as related to the use of divergent and convergent scripts.

While the examples presented in this chapter are positive ones, the purpose of this analysis is not to hold up these teachers as perfect models of bilingual instruction. As is true in many urban schools serving low-income language minority children, the two teachers who were observed during this study face many challenges. However, this chapter does hope to suggest that it is possible for teachers to adapt and elaborate the structured curriculums that they are often mandated to teach in their classrooms, and to explore how the continua of biliteracy could be used as a model for analyzing certain aspects of classroom instruction so that curricular adaptations and elaborations could be shared with other classroom teachers, administrators, teacher trainers, and curriculum designers.

Research Methodology

The elementary school where this research was conducted is located in the heart of the Puerto Rican community in Philadelphia. Located just a block away from a major Puerto Rican shopping area, a cultural activity center, and a local public library with a section of Spanish language children's books, the school is able to draw upon a variety of cultural resources. The school educates approximately 770 students; 92% of these students have a family income low enough to qualify for a free or reduced school lunch. The Pennsylvania System of School Assessment Data for the school presents a mixed picture of student achievement. While students at this school generally do well compared to schools with similar levels of poverty, overall levels of achievement are low as measured by these tests. More positively, there are several special programs at the school that seek to raise the students' level of academic achievement. These include participation in the district's literacy intern program, which provides an extra teacher for kindergarten and first grade classes, materials and training in balanced literacy, an after school program, Saturday school, and an extensive summer school program. The school also has a maintenance bilingual education program for limited English proficient students in grades K–5.

The school was an early implementer of *Éxito Para Todos,* a Spanish language adaptation of a nationally known comprehensive school reform program Success for All. In fact, one of the early studies done on the success of the Success for All reading program with bilingual students was conducted at this school (Slavin & Madden, 1999). The *Éxito Para Todos* curriculum for grades 2–6 is called *Alas Para Leer,* and consists of several features that are similar in all classes that use the program, including the two classes reported on here. The first 20 minutes of the 90-minute reading period is used for a read-aloud and discussion of books that have been selected by the teacher. Then, students read stories using a specific sequence of activities that include explicit vocabulary instruction, silent and paired reading, discussing stories and making story maps, and answering written comprehension questions. During the last 15 minutes of the class, or when the students finish their written work, students are allowed to read independently from books of their choice. Students are also assigned nightly homework to read independently for 20 to 30 minutes. As part of the program, the students take weekly written tests on the stories they have read, and the teachers assess the students every eight weeks. These assessments are used to place students into appropriate reading groups across grade levels. In addition, students in the fourth- and fifth-grade class studied here were transitioning into English instruction, and thus sometimes also used the Success for All English materials for grades K–1. While there have been several studies that evaluate the *Éxito Para Todos* reading program or the use of Success for All by English language learners by comparing the progress of matched comparison groups (Calderon *et al.*, 1998; Livingston & Flaherty, 1997), little long-term ethnographic research has been done to determine how the program is actually implemented in bilingual classes (for an exception see Prado-Olmos & Marquez, 2001).

The data presented and analyzed in this paper were collected over a two-year period between 1999 and 2001 in an ethnographic discourse analytic study of one second-grade and one combined fourth- and fifth-grade classroom. The teacher of the second-grade class, Ms Santiago, is Puerto Rican, and the teacher of the fourth- and fifth-grade class, Ms Smith, is an African-American who is a fluent speaker of Spanish. Both of the teachers had taught at least five years in the school, finished their graduate degrees in elementary education and received state certification during the period in which the study was conducted. The majority of the students in these two classes were Puerto Rican, but there were also small numbers of students from several Latin American countries including the Dominican Republic, Honduras, and Venezuela. Most of the students' parents were born outside the continental United States, and the classes had a high rate of mobility in part due to circular migration to Puerto Rico.

In these classrooms, I took the role of a participant observer. During the two-year study I spent one or two days each week at the school, and had several periods of intense study where I collected data at the school every day for several weeks. Field notes, audio and video tapes, documents, and interviews were used to attempt to gain an understanding of the way that literacy events in the classroom were planned and conducted from the viewpoint of the participants. While the primary focus of the study was on the classroom read-alouds that were done as part of the Success for All reading program, additional classroom activities were also observed.

The Content of Biliteracy

According to the framework of the continua of biliteracy, the content of biliteracy includes three contrasts: minority–majority content, vernacular–literary content, and contextualized–decontextualized content. Traditionally, schooling has primarily drawn upon a restricted body of academic knowledge and literacies, but recent research has suggested that the knowledge that individuals gain from participation in their families and communities can also be successfully used as a basis of learning in school. This minority, vernacular, and contextualized content is sometimes referred to as 'local funds of knowledge' (Moll *et al.*, 1992). This section gives examples of how the two teachers observed have adapted and elaborated on their classroom lessons by using minority content, vernacular texts, and contextualizing texts.

Minority and majority content

While most of the curricular content that was utilized in the two classes observed could be classified as majority content, both of the teachers also carefully adapted class activities so that students could also use local (minority) funds of knowledge to complete assignments. One area where the teachers particularly incorporated minority content into their instruction was in the written projects that they assigned. For example, in the fourth- and fifth-grade class, the teacher selected popular children's chapter books and expository texts to use for the daily read-alouds that are mandatory as part of the Success for All reading program. She then had students write in genres similar to those suggested in these texts, but she encouraged students to utilize the local funds of knowledge as a basis for their written work. The result of these assignments was projects that were presented in a formal school-related genre, but that contained content that was related to the students' minority community. This type of activity was valuable in giving students practice in writing in majority genres and in recording the important knowledge of their local community so that their friends and outsiders to their community could better understand these cultural practices.

For example, as a read-aloud done as part of the Success for All reading program in the fourth- and fifth-grade class, Ms Smith selected the book *Amber Brown Wants Extra Credit* (Danziger, 1996). In the book, the main character Amber has to complete a school assignment to create a 'how-to' project. In the text, Amber does her project by teaching her class how to make a special type of brownies with treats such as gummy bears or jelly beans inside. The day after the class had finished reading the book, Ms Smith read the class an announcement from the principal that there would be a school fair and that people from the community could rent a table in order to sell things. The students figured out that they could rent a table if each student in the class brought in 25 cents. The students collected the money to rent their table, spent an afternoon reading the brownie boxes, cooked brownies with interesting treats inside, and then sold the brownies at the fair. With their profits, they had a pizza party. After their enjoyable experience selling brownies, the students expressed interest in learning about other things that they could make to sell.

However, instead of using 'how-to' books or other sources of majority content information, Ms Smith suggested to the students that their families and their neighbors probably knew how to make and do a lot of different things that the other students in the class would like to know about. Ms Smith designed a class writing assignment based on the project that was described in the read-aloud book. Over a four-week period, each student learned how to do something, wrote out detailed directions for their how-to project, made a poster or a video that described the steps of their project using visual images as well as words, and gave an oral presentation to the class.

For this assignment students were free to decide how best to explain their how-to project, and the class had discussions about the best ways to communicate different types of information. For example, when Marisa brought in a video of a cooking project, she initially taped herself describing what to do. After watching the video, the class had a discussion about how it would be easier to understand the process if she actually filmed herself making the food using the utensils and ingredients that were needed. Then, Marisa went home and redid her video incorporating the class suggestions. Also, after getting feedback from their teacher about what parts of their instructions were unclear, students used a variety of resources to get additional information. One student supplemented her recipe with additional English language cooking hints that she found on a web site, while another student went home and quizzed his mother about techniques for model building. In addition, the students were also allowed to choose whether English or Spanish or both languages would best convey the directions for the projects to their bilingual classmates. After the presentations, the posters were displayed in the hallway where they were read by members of the community, a group of student teachers, and even foreign visitors to the school who were often genuinely interested in learning how to make the foods, games, or handicrafts displayed in the posters.

The fourth-grade 'how-to' project is one example of how teachers can help students to link majority and minority content successfully. While the project drew on content from the majority culture for its form and genre, it also allowed students to use various resources to draw on the local minority community's funds of knowledge. Through the 'how-to' project, the local funds of knowledge of the community were granted greater status as an important resource that can be used as the basis of a school project, and as helpful knowledge that could be of interest to others in the classroom and beyond.

Vernacular and literary content

Another aspect of biliteracy content that is suggested by the continua of biliteracy is the vernacular–literary continuum. This continuum draws a contrast between the more frequent use of standard literary texts versus the less frequent use of vernacular texts as the content of instruction in literacy development. Certainly, in bilingual classrooms formal school texts such as basal reading stories, science and social studies texts, and children's literary picture books were the most frequent texts utilized for classroom instruction. However, teachers in these two classes also used vernacular texts such as the information located on food labels, the backs of seed packets, and traditional Puerto Rican songs as a basis for literacy instruction. In addition, the students in this community had been exposed to a wide variety of vernacular texts in their life outside of school such as Bible stories and Hispanic fairy tales. Thus, when attempting to utilize the content of vernacular texts, the teachers could also draw on the students' knowledge of vernacular texts that they had developed outside of school.

The use of vernacular content for literacy instruction was often highlighted in the second-grade classroom during periods of vocabulary instruction. One important element of the Success for All curriculum that was implemented in these classrooms was a daily period of vocabulary instruction. In this part of the day, the teachers presented vocabulary words explicitly to the students and had the students give sentences using the words. In general, these sentences primarily involved content from the texts that the students were reading in class. However, the second-grade teacher also frequently encouraged students to share information with the class about instances when they had seen the vocabulary words in texts outside of school. This adaptation of the curriculum helped the students to make connections between the use of the vocabulary words in the literary content of the basal stories and the encounters that students have had with these words in their own lives.

The students in the second grade were able to use the vernacular texts that they had seen outside of school to provide additional information to the class about additional contexts in which the classroom vocabulary words could be used. For example, one day the teacher was preparing the students for read-alouds and a basal reading story about farming by introducing the word *cosecha* (harvest). One student, Rosa, said that she had seen that word printed on the fruit sacks that her family had used in Puerto Rico. She further explained that the sacks had listed the dates when it would be good to pick a variety of crops. Another frequent source of additional information about vocabulary words came from the Bible stories that were familiar to the students in the class from vernacular story telling in their homes and churches. While the Bible could definitely be considered a literary text, it is clear from the students' comments that they have often heard these stories told orally by their relatives or pastors as part of the vernacular oral heritage of their community. When the class was preparing to read a basal reading story about some animals that had flown in the basket underneath a helium balloon, the teacher asked the students if they had seen the word *canasta* (basket) before. One student, Marta, suggested that her aunt had told her a story about how Moses' mother had placed him in a basket so that he would float down the river in Egypt. These examples show that it was possible to use vocabulary knowledge from vernacular texts to enhance instruction in the bilingual classroom, even when those particular vernacular texts were not even present in the classroom.

Contextualized and decontextualized content

One of the difficulties elementary school students have is in reading and understanding decontextualized text, defined here as a text that explains phenomena without the use of examples, concrete explanations or reference to the readers' experiential knowledge. Rather than eliminating decontextualized texts from the curriculum, teachers can help students understand them by using related contextualized texts in conjunction with them. There are two ways in which the decontextualized and contextualized texts can be linked. First, students can read a contextualized text first and then use the information or examples to understand a decontextualized text. Conversely, the students can struggle to understand the content of a decontextualized text and then be exposed to a contextualized text that clarifies the meaning of the decontextualized text.

In Ms Santiago's second-grade class, students often asked questions about the content of the read-aloud stories. Ms Santiago took their inquiries very seriously and would search her classroom book collection or the teacher resource room to find textbooks, encyclopedias or non-fiction trade books that contained the answers to their questions. Many of these texts were either written in the students' second language or were more complex than the texts that would usually be read to second-graders. However, since the content of the decontextualized texts was related to examples from the contextualized texts that the students had already listened to and understood, the decontextualized texts were comprehensible.

For example, one day Ms Santiago was reading the second-grade students the book *Isla* (Dorros, 1995), a story about a child and a grandmother who dream that they have flown to the island of Puerto Rico. The story presents common experiences of Puerto Ricans such as eating tropical fruits or swimming in salt water by using the detailed dream of the child and his grandmother. Since many of the students in the class have visited Puerto Rico with their family, they were able to tell their own stories about their experiences swimming in the ocean. Several of the students discussed their own experiences in salt water, such as crying when they got salt in their eyes, having to take a shower after swimming in the water to get the salt out of their hair, or being able to float better in salt water.

However, Fernando noted in his comments about the book that he had also been swimming in lakes and there wasn't any salt there. He wanted to know what made the water in the sea salty. Ms Santiago told Fernando that she wasn't exactly sure why there was salt in salt water, and the class would have to hear about that from another book. Later that afternoon, I went to the teacher resource room and found a volume of a Spanish language scientific encyclopedia entitled *Jovenes Cientificos: Todo Acerca del Agua* (World Book, 1995) that had a two-page spread that explained about solutions and other scientific principles that were related to why the sea was salty.

The next day, Ms Santiago read to the students the explanation. While this decontextualized text presented scientific principles in a genre appropriate for a science encyclopedia, it was still comprehensible to the students because the contents of the text related to their own experiences swimming in the ocean and their own questions about the sea. Thus, the lesson moved from a highly contextualized text about a child swimming to a reading of a decontextualized formal science reference text. One advantage of making connections between contextualized and decontextualized texts is that this type of connection may prepare younger students for the decontextualized texts that they will have to read in their textbooks in higher grades. Through their initial exposures to these texts during the read-alouds, they are learning about their format and how to begin to use the process of research to answer the questions they ask when they read.

In a contrasting situation, the curriculum in Ms Smith's fourth- and fifth-grade class often included decontextualized texts that provided few examples or concrete explanations of the phenomena that they discussed. Since by the fourth and fifth grade many texts used in the science and social studies curriculum were also only in English, the students' second language, there was a strong possibility that the texts would not be understood if additional texts and experiences were not used with them. However, Ms Smith suggested that it was still important for the students to be able to read and understand the concept in the texts. Thus, she often adapted a strategy of having students attempt to read the decontextualized text first, and then she provided additional contextualized texts, pictures, and experiences.

For example, in conjunction with their basal reader stories and as part of a service learning project in which the class created a community garden, the fourth-grade students studied a unit about how plants grow and reproduce. Part of the unit was based on reading the children's book *From Seed to Plant* (Gibbons, 1991) that included a few pages of text about the parts of a flower and how plants reproduce. The passage was in English and after the students read the pages together in class, they could not explain how the process of plant reproduction worked to their teacher. In order to increase the students' comprehension of the text, Ms Smith taught a series of lessons based on worksheets that provided detailed, annotated drawings of plant reproduction. First, Ms Smith had the students name what each part that was listed on the drawings was called in Spanish, and then the students wrote in the more familiar Spanish names below the English names. This helped the students make connections between their prior knowledge and the parts of the plants. For example, one student noted that one of the parts of the flower, the ovary, was the name of a part of the human body too. Then, the next day, Ms Smith brought into class many different types of cut flowers. The students looked at the different types of flowers, dissected them to identify and label their parts, and then created their own annotated diagrams of plant reproduction using the actual parts of the different flowers. The teacher then had the students explain the process of reproduction that the plants used by pointing out the dissected parts of their flower while they discussed them. At the end of the lesson, the students got out their reading books to match the actual parts of the flower with their worksheets and the written description in the book. By using the diagram and the labels on the actual dissected flowers, Ms Smith was able to increase her students' understanding of the decontextualized text that was part of the school curriculum.

The Development of Biliteracy

In addition to looking at how local funds of knowledge are drawn upon in classroom instruction, it is also useful to consider how different combinations of the four language skills, semiotic modalities, and linguistic codes can be used together in the classroom to help students attain biliteracy. This principled, purposeful, and organized mixing can be referred to as 'hybridization' or 'hybrid literacy practices.' As Gutiérrez *et al.* state:

> hybrid literacy practices are not simply code-switching as the alternation between two language codes. They are more a systematic, strategic, affiliative, and sense-making process among those who share the code, as they strive to achieve mutual understanding. (1999: 88)

Research studies have shown that hybridization can be structured as an essential aspect of the design of certain literacy teaching methods. An example of this is given in Moll and Diaz's (1985) explanation of how they changed the teaching methods that were used in an English reading class. While Moll and Diaz did not discuss their design of their new method of teaching literacy as a hybrid practice, it is quite clear that their approach involved a strategic mixing of language skills, semiotic cues, and linguistic codes in order to help enable students to understand a text that would otherwise be beyond their reading level. This section provides additional examples of how teachers can use the four language skills, varying semiotic modes, and multiple linguistic codes in order to create more productive paths to biliteracy for their students.

Development of receptive and productive language skills

The two teachers who were observed for this study selected their own books for the classroom read-alouds, and in the eight-week assessments required for the Success for All program only an evaluation of the students' oral responses to the read-alouds was required. In contrast, the receptive–productive continuum suggests that it would aid students' development of biliteracy to create responses to the books that they had heard by using listening, speaking, reading, and writing. The two teachers that were observed in this study achieved this by elaborating on the classroom read-alouds by requiring students to use all four language skills to provide creative and aesthetic responses to the stories that they had heard.

For example, in the second-grade class, the daily picture book read-alouds were often used as an inspiration for projects that involved utilizing all four language skills in an integrated way. Ms Santiago often read students several variations of the same fairy or folk tale, and she also encouraged the students to write their own variations of their favorite stories. Right before Thanksgiving, Ms Santiago read the students the book *Gracias, El pavo de Thanksgiving* (Cowley, 1998) that tells the story of a boy named Miguel who receives a live turkey to raise in his New York City apartment and eat for Thanksgiving dinner. However, Miguel becomes attached to the bird, and in the end of the story the family sends the turkey to a petting zoo and eats chicken for Thanksgiving instead. During the discussion of the book, many of the students gave examples of turkeys that they had seen being raised in Puerto Rico in anticipation of a special dinner, and two students even named people in their own urban neighborhood who were currently keeping a live turkey in their basement.

After listening to the students' enthusiastic responses to the story, Ms Santiago suggested that the students produce their own version of the story that they had heard, but that the class should set their version in their own community. The class worked together with the students taking turns telling parts of their new version of the story, listening to their peers' suggestions, writing the story down, and reading their version out loud to the other students. When the new version of the story was finished, Ms Santiago typed out each line of the story onto a different page. The students then worked cooperatively in pairs or small groups to illustrate the line that they had been given, again reading parts of the story to their classmates, writing comments or speech bubbles in two languages in the pictures, suggesting to their partners what they should illustrate in their drawings, and listening to the suggestions of their classmates. When the class book was assembled, it became one of the students' favorites to look at during independent reading time, when its details often became the focus of heated discussions. From the students' work and their discussions, it was possible to evaluate the students' literacy skills in a complex task in a more complete way than would have been possible if one had only considered their initial responses during the discussion of the original book.

Development of oral and written language skills

In general, schools give greatest emphasis to the development of reading and writing and encourage students to get information from formal written sources such as textbooks, basal readers, and encyclopedias. However, this aspect of the continua suggests that students can be instructed to use information from many semiotic means of communication to create a deeper understanding of the information that is being studied. While the continuum highlights 'oral' means of communication such as listening and speaking, this continuum can also be expanded to other semiotic means such as visual images, music, or physical movement. One of the ways that the two teachers observed developed more complete biliteracy in their students was to incorporate many sources of information in their lessons and encourage students to use a variety of ways to learn about a topic.

One example of the use of a variety of semiotic resources is a unit of instruction that the second-grade teacher used to communicate information about the geography, history, and culture of China. Since she was unable to find sufficient resources in Spanish about China, she used oral conversations in Spanish and English about the pictures in English language books to convey the information that she wanted the students to learn. For example, during the read-aloud time in the Success for All program the class looked together at the pictures of the Great Wall and other Chinese symbols in the English language book *Eyewitness: Ancient China* (Cotterell, 2000). Then, one of the students went to the library and borrowed an English copy of the folk tale *Lon Po Po: A Red-Riding Hood Story from China* (Young, 1989), and the teacher also had the students look at the pictures and then she told the students the story in English and then in Spanish. In both of these cases, the semiotic cues from the pictures in the books were used as important sources of information. The students also participated in a school arts program to learn how to do Chinese dances using props such as ribbons, and went to watch a professional performance of Chinese dance at a local university. When the students returned from the performance, they drew and wrote about what they had learned about Chinese culture by learning about its dances.

Months after the unit was finished, the students were still making connections between the information they learned about China and new texts that they encountered. For example, during the unit on China, Leticia had used phonological similarities between words she knew in English and new words learned in Chinese to remember the foreign vocabulary words. In one case, she remembered the Chinese word for 'hello,' *nihao*, by remembering that to her it sounded almost like the English word for the sound that a cat makes, 'meow.' Later in the year, after reading an English book entitled *City Cats, Country Cats* (Shook Hazen, 1999) that includes fanciful descriptions about what different types of cats can do, she used her phonetic connection in a piece of creative writing that she shared with the class. 'Chinese cats speak Chinese. Nihao, hello. Nihao, goodbye.' Thus, students were able to use the information that they learned through multiple types of semiotic cues in their written work.

In addition to encouraging students to use a variety of different semiotic means to gather information for their written work, the teachers also encouraged the students to use written texts as references to help the students to remember vocabulary words or concepts that they wanted to use in oral discussions. One way that the students used these textual resources was to help them remember and review vocabulary that they had forgotten, thus ensuring that they could use just the right word in an oral discussion. The teachers encouraged students to do this by leaving out the basal textbooks that the students had completed, read-aloud books that had previously been read to the students, and independent reading books that the students had previously read in class. An example of how students utilized the written texts in order to help them in oral discussion occurred one day when one of the students, Michael, and I were discussing one of the books in his independent reading folder, *Ideas Sobre el Espacio* (Walker, 1993). The first page of this book showed a picture of three men from long ago looking up at unexplained things in the night sky. Michael pointed to and gave the names of some of the things in the picture like stars and the moon. However, he hesitated when he put his finger on the picture of a shooting star. I suggested to him that the red ball being shown heading toward Earth was *una cometa* (a comet). However, he wasn't satisfied with that answer and replied, '*Espera un momento. Nosotros tenemos este tipo de cosa en un cuento en "El sol y la luna"*' (Wait a moment. We have this type of thing in a story in *The Sun and the Moon*. [*The Sun and the Moon* is a basal textbook the students had read in a previous semester.]) Then, Michael went over to the shelf where the basal readers are kept and got a copy of the book. He carefully searched through each story in the book until he got to one story, *La lluvia de estrellas* (Herrera, 1987), that had a page that showed shooting stars in the night sky. He immediately started to read the story aloud, and he didn't stop until he read the part on the second page where it gives the name of the astronomical phenomenon that was in the original picture '*una lluvia de estrellas*' (meteor shower). He said the term '*una lluvia de estrellas*' several times, his voice climbing from a whisper to almost a shout. Then, he got up and put away the basal reading book. He came back to his chair, sat down, opened the little book back to the first page and named each object in the picture while pointing to it, '*Los hombres miran las cosas extrañas en el cielo: la luna, las estrellas, y* (with emphasis) *una lluvia de estrellas.*' (The men looked at strange things in the sky: the moon, the stars, and a meteor shower.) This is an example of how students could use written sources in order to increase their oral vocabulary and reinforce content that they had learned in written texts.

Development of L1 and L2

One of the aspects of biliteracy that is highlighted in the continua of biliteracy is the development of literacy through the medium of two languages. In the United States there is a well-documented pattern of language shift among bilingual students. While many students begin school fluent only in their first language, they quickly begin to show a preference for reading in English. This pattern of language shift is reinforced in the program structure of the Success for All reading program as it is implemented in this school because the 90-minute reading block is all conducted in a single language. Thus, in the second-grade classroom only Spanish is used for reading instruction, while in the fourth-grade classroom English is the sole language used during the Success for All reading period. While it is possible that students can continue to practice reading in their first language during periods other than those designated for reading instruction, this type of program design would seem to encourage the pattern of language shift from Spanish to English that is predominant in transitional bilingual education programs in the United States.

However, part of the plan for Success for All reading instruction is a suggestion that students read independently every day for approximately 15 minutes during the school day and for 20 to 30 minutes at home. Since most of the students in this low-income neighborhood do not have easy access to appropriate books from libraries or other sources, the teachers have a large amount of control over the books that students use for independent reading. Instead of only giving students books in the language in which they were conducting classroom reading instruction, both the teachers found ways to use the mandated independent reading time that is part of the Success for All program to encourage the students to read independently in both Spanish and English.

In the second- and the fourth-grade classrooms the students each had folders where they stored the books that they were using for independent reading. In the second-grade classroom, a system was developed where the students would receive a new bag of three guided reading books in Spanish and an English book at their reading level in their reading folder each week. The students then selected two additional books from the class book rack which included picture books that the teacher had read aloud to the students, series books such as *Clifford* and *Franklin* books that Ms Santiago and I had purchased from the Scholastic book club or local bookstores, and books that had been left at the school as samples by textbook publishers. In order to provide sufficient time for the students to read independently in both languages, the second-grade teacher generally provided the students with about 10 additional minutes of daily reading time in addition to the time that was scheduled as part of the Success for All reading program. The fourth- and fifth-grade teacher usually used the reading folders as part of the students' homework. Ms Smith had the students take home both the English books that they had already read in class as part of the Success for All reading program and some Spanish science readers. Thus, the fourth- and fifth-graders were also able to read independently at home in both English and Spanish.

In addition to the gains in biliteracy that may have been made by providing students with independent reading books in two languages at school, the experience of reading books in two languages in school appeared to also change students' habits of book selection outside of school. For example, near the end of the year when I went to the library with one of the second-grade students, Maritza, I noticed that she was checking out two books at a time rather than her previous habit of checking out a single book. When I asked her why she was taking out two books instead of one, she told me 'Of course I have two books now. It's like in school. One book in Spanish and one book in English.'

In addition, on the last day of school when the second-grade teacher gave out extra poster board and construction paper, I asked Leticia what she planned to do with her paper over the summer and she answered, 'I'm going to have my older brothers use the paper to make Spanish books for me because I don't have any Spanish books at home and I like to practice reading in both my languages.' Thus, perhaps the most important aspect of providing students with independent reading books in two languages is that it suggests to students that reading regularly in two languages is normal and appropriate.

Conclusion

While a large number of students in the United States are enrolled in bilingual programs in elementary schools, there are many challenges in achieving the simultaneous development of full literacy in two languages. One of these challenges is adapting the activities and texts used in mandated curricula to make sure that the instruction provided in class is appropriate and draws upon all the resources available in a bilingual and bicultural environment. This study suggests that teachers who are using a mandated curriculum like Success for All to instruct language minority students can adapt and elaborate on the content knowledge and the communicative practices suggested by incorporating local funds of knowledge and hybrid literacy practices in their instruction, and that these practices can be analyzed using the framework of the continua of biliteracy. While individually each of the curricular adaptations and elaborations that are provided by teachers who act as bottom-up language and literacy planners are small changes to classroom literacy activities, in the long run they may have a large effect on the ability of students to increase their knowledge of the content of the texts they read and to develop biliteracy.

References

Calderon, M., Hertz-Lazarowitz, R. and Slavin, R.E. (1998) Effects of bilingual cooperative integrated reading and composition on students making the transition from Spanish to English reading. *Elementary School Journal* 99 (2), 153–65.

Gutiérrez, K., Baquedano-López, P., Alvarez, H. and Chiu, M. (1999) Building a culture of collaboration through hybrid language practices. *Theory into Practice* 38 (2), 67–93.

Hornberger, N.H. (1989) Continua of biliteracy. *Review of Educational Research* 59 (3), 271–96.

Hornberger, N.H. and Skilton-Sylvester, E. (2000) Revisiting the continua of biliteracy: International and critical perspectives. *Language and Education* 14 (1), 18–44.
Livingston, M. and Flaherty, J. (1997) *Effects of Success for All on Reading Achievement in California Schools.* Los Alamitos, CA: Wested.
Moll, L. and Diaz, S. (1985) Ethnographic pedagogy: Promoting effective bilingual instruction. In E. Garcia and R.V. Padilla (eds) *Advances in Bilingual Education Research* (pp. 127–49). University of Arizona Press.
Moll, L., Amanti, C., Neff, D. and Gonzalez, N. (1992) Funds of knowledge for teaching: Using a qualitative approach to connect homes and classrooms. *Theory into Practice* 31, 132–41.
Prado-Olmos, P. and Marquez, J. (2001) Ethnographic studies of *Éxito Para Todos.* In R. Slavin and C. Margarita (eds) *Effective Programs for Latino Students.* Mahwah, NJ: Lawrence Erlbaum.
Ricento, T. and Hornberger, N. (1996) Unpeeling the onion: Language planning and policy and the ELT professional. *TESOL Quarterly* 30 (3), 401–27.
Ruiz, R. (1984) Orientations in language planning. *National Association for Bilingual Education Journal* 8 (2), 15–34.
Slavin, R.E. and Madden, N.A. (1999) Effects of bilingual and English as a second language adaptation of Success for All on reading achievement of students acquiring English. *Journal of Education for Students Placed at Risk* 4 (4), 393–416.

Children's books

Cotterell, A. (2000) *Eyewitness: Ancient China.* New York: DK Publishing.
Cowley, J. (1998) *Gracias, El pavo de Thanksgiving.* New York: Scholastic.
Danziger, P. (1996) *Amber Brown Wants Extra Credit.* New York: Little Apple, G.P. Putnam's Sons.
Dorros, A. (1995) *Isla.* New York: Dutton Children's Books.
Gibbons, G. (1991) *From Seed to Plant.* New York: Holiday House.
Herrera, S. (1987) *La lluvia de estrellas.* In J. Flores *et al.* (eds) *El Sol y la Luna* (pp. 90–101). New York: Macmillan Publishing Company.
Shook Hazen, B. (1999) *City Cats, Country Cats.* New York: Golden Books Publishing Company.
Walker, C. (1993) *Ideas Sobre el Espacio.* Cleveland, OH: Modern Curriculum Press.
World Book (1995) *Jovenes Cientificos: Todo Acerca del Agua.* Chicago: World Book.
Young, E. (1989) *Lon Po Po: A Red-Riding Hood Story from China.* New York: Philomel Books.

Part 5: Sites and Worlds

Chapter 12

When MT is L2: The Korean Church School as a Context for Cultural Identity

HOLLY R. PAK

Introduction

Each Saturday, five cars and a van bring about 25 children and ten adults to a small church building in a suburb of Philadelphia. The children that arrive first mill around in the large room of the church or run to their classrooms to finish copying their homework sentences or to review the words they will have to know for a quiz in a few minutes. They are getting together for Korean language school, an ethnic mother tongue school similar to the many Korean language schools run by Korean churches in the Korean community of Philadelphia and in other parts of the US.

These schools are not unique to Koreans. Alongside mainstream education in the US, there exist numerous schools set up by minority language groups for culture and language education of their children. These schools fill an important identity-forming and identity-providing function for millions of Americans, and according to Fishman (1989: 454) should not only be studied but also appreciated. Like other ethnic groups, Koreans in the US attempt to pass on cultural and linguistic behavior and values to their children.

In this paper, I will describe the Korean church and school (KCS) as a context that foregrounds Koreanness; how this context is perceived differently by the adults and children; and how, in this context, manipulation of the continua of development, media, and content of biliteracy reveals the students' negotiation of their Korean identity.

I begin with a short description of the KCS and its goals; then discuss how in each of the four continua – context, media, development, and content – the power relations between English and Korean are reversed from outside the Korean church context; and how the tension from this reversal is revealed through the children's expression of cultural identity.

Biliterate Context

Korean churches are one of the places in an English-dominant society where Koreans meet with Koreans and, depending on the speech situation, use Korean. Many researchers have cited Korean churches as one of the backbones of Korean culture in the US (Byun, 1990: 122–4; Kim, 1988: 265–7). As such, many Korean churches have language policies that attempt to strengthen the chances for language maintenance by the younger generations. In some churches these goals are made explicit with language schools set up for their implementation.

The site of this study, the Korean Baptist Church located in the suburbs of Philadelphia, averaged an attendance of 100, including children, and the school was held on Saturday mornings during the public school year. Most of the schoolchildren's parents were members of the church. During my five years at the church, there were 25 to 35 students who attended the school. In addition to being a participant observer, I collected data through informal and formal interviews with adults and children, and through classroom observation and recording.

Throughout the interviews with the adults in the church, most of whom were parents of children who attended the Korean school, when adults talked of Korean language and what they wanted their children to be able to do with Korean, they inevitably talked of culture or of 'being Korean.' Questions about language maintenance were answered with the adults' opinions about what it meant to be Korean, demonstrating that the issue of language maintenance for the next generation was tied to Korean identity maintenance. When a mother was asked why she was teaching her boys Korean, she simply restated the irrefutable connection between being Korean and knowing the language:

> Mrs Lee: I'm sure that there is an aspect in which we want them to learn [Korean] so that we can communicate with them. But more important, since they are Korean, I think perhaps that they should learn Korean. (18 February 1996: 1)

The adults wanted the children to identify themselves as Korean and not to lose their Korean identity. The children were taught or pressured into using Korean as a means to the larger goal of preserving Korean identity. Several times, the adults stated that certain things about Korean behavior and being Korean required the use of Korean language. Note the following in response to the question, 'The reason for the importance of the Korean school is your desire to instill Korean nationalism/ heritage?':

> Mrs Lee: Well, it may be nationalism may be a little too much. I think it's difficult to teach them the whole history of Korea. They have a difficult time with American history even. It is difficult to teach them Korean history in English. But through Korean language and Korean ways, we can tell them a little bit about what Korean is. And maybe they will find out that they are Korean. (18 February 1996: 6)

It was as if the children could not learn about Korean behavior and being Korean apart from the language. The teaching of Korean was related to the goal of learning to be Korean.

In the context of the Korean church, the Korean adults attempt to cultivate in their children a sense of who they are as Koreans in America. In terms of the continua of context, the KCS inverts the usual power relations in the US society (where English monolingualism and literacy are dominant at the macro level); here, instead, the KCS seeks to define its own (macro) context where Korean monolingualism and literacy are privileged.

In the US the usual power relations between Korean and English put English on the right-hand, more powerful side of each continuum and Korean on the left-hand, less powerful side. My argument here is that the Koreans have created a context within the church where the roles of the languages are reversed with regard to power. At the church, the Korean language is on the right-hand side on the more powerful end of each continuum, while English is on the left-hand side, occupying the less powerful position. Figure 12.1 illustrates the switch.

Consider the continuum of multilingual/bilingual–monolingual. Outside of the church English monolingualism was privileged, and inside the church Korean monolingualism was dominant. The adults used Korean for the functions of the church. All of the adults in the church, except for two non-Korean members, were native speakers of Korean. In the adult functions of the church, English was the marked language, used only occasionally in sermons for terms not easily translated into Korean and in conversations between adults as humorous asides.

The adult who did not speak Korean would find being at the church uncomfortable and awkward. Although he/she spoke the dominant language of the society, English, this gave no advantage in the church activities. The shift in the language of power between the context of the Korean church and the context of American society was most evident both

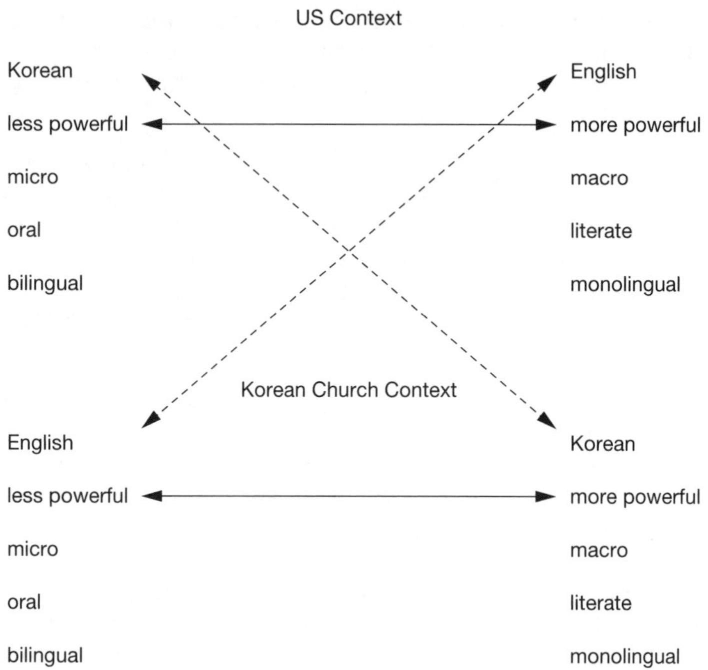

Figure 12.1 Switch of power between English and Korean in the Korean church context

when a non-Korean-speaking adult attempted to participate in the church, and when the monolingual Korean-speaking adults of the church tried to learn the language of the American society, English.

As participant observer, I attended this church for seven years with my husband who was an assistant pastor. I served in several capacities and personally experienced the discomfort of being a non-Korean-speaking adult in this Korean church context, as illustrated by the following:

> When I went to the adult services, not only did I feel faint from having to sit so long without understanding what was being said, but I felt uncomfortable when I couldn't smile or laugh in response to the speaker at the appropriate moments, or I felt frustrated at often being wrong in my guesses as to how long the rest of the sermon would be, based on the intonation of the speaker. I was out of place largely because of my inability to understand Korean. The same could be said for most other adult gatherings. I can recall times when as a children's

> Sunday school teacher, I would be called to a quarterly meeting with one or two other teachers. The assistant pastor, who could speak English and Korean, would lead a devotional and discuss upcoming events all in Korean, with a word or two in English for my sake. I had to smile and try not to feel like I was wasting my time. My English language skills were of little use to me in those situations. By contrast, however, I was asked to lead an English language class for the adults to improve their English language skills. In this setting, I was in charge, and the members (many of them deacons and elders) had to (at least pretend to) follow my ideas of how to learn English. I did not feel quite as powerless in these situations due to a lack of Korean language skills. (Journal entry, 23 May 1997)

What is noteworthy in this excerpt from my recollections at the church is the dramatic shift in power as relates to language when the context was opened up to include the norms of the US context. Within the context of the church, Korean monolingualism was dominant, yet there was constant interplay between the church as an isolated setting, and the church as a minority setting within the larger American society.

Much of the interplay between Korean language as the dominant language versus English as the dominant language became apparent in the contrast provided by another group in the church made up of children and teenagers who spoke English. Among the children, there was little advantage to speaking Korean. During the service, if the children's pastor led songs in Korean, and if the children needed to sing in Korean in front of the adults, then there was a disadvantage to not knowing Korean. However, outside of these adult-initiated activities, the children and teenagers were comfortable in English. Interaction with adults during the time at church was limited and, beyond an initial greeting, could generally be avoided. Children who had recently come from Korea and who didn't speak English had a difficult time adjusting until they learned English. Teenagers who didn't speak English wanted to be and were encouraged to be with people their own age, but during the services felt an ambivalence toward where they could avoid feeling the most uncomfortable – in the adult service which was held in Korean, so they could understand the language but perhaps not the content; or in the youth service, which was shorter and more geared for their age, but held in English, and so little understood.

All of this is to state the obvious: that the advantages that come from speaking a society's dominant language do not hold in a setting where a minority language is the norm. However, even within that minority language setting, the weighting of power for the minority language is not a constant, but depends on subgroups' shared values.

The difference between the adults' and children's perception of the norms for language behavior is illustrated in the following excerpt. A boy, SJ, had arrived from Korea as a second grader just eight or nine months earlier than this episode. He was still quite dominant in Korean and struggled with learning English, and yet he often used English in situations where he was expected to use Korean. One such example happened on the church van. He was riding with his mother and several other adults, including the Korean youth pastor. He spoke in English to the youth pastor and was immediately chastised by his mother for being disrespectful by using English with a Korean adult. He retorted in English, 'Why should I speak in Korean, we're in America now.'

In this encounter, I see the contrast between perspectives of adults and children. Though in a Korean church setting, the adult and child subscribed to different rules – American norms vs Korean norms. The mother was saying, 'because of the participants involved, this is a Korean setting. You have to respect your elder by using his language.' The child was saying, 'No, this is America, where English is dominant. I don't have to use Korean; I don't have to abide by Korean rules, because Korean rules are not the norm.'

SJ was obviously looking at the Korean language from the perspective of the US context where English monolingualism was more desirable, whereas his mother adhered to the values of the Korean church context where the rules of Korean monolingualism should be followed. While the mother was adhering to the norms of the immediate context, SJ preferred to see their immediate context as a micro one within the larger US society macro context.

With regard to the context of the church along the oral to literate continuum, it is interesting to point out the value placed on printed material in Korean and the transfer of this value to materials printed in English and Korean for the children. Most of the children carried their own Bibles. Many of their Bibles were bilingual, printed in both English and Korean. The church had purchased these Bibles in large quantity and then sold them to the parents for their children or gave them as rewards for contests. Inside the cover of the Bibles the children carried were collections of bulletins. These bulletins, which publicized the events in the worship service and who was responsible for leading each event, were typed in English, copied and folded. One bulletin was handed out each Sunday for the children's worship service, and they seemed to be an important part of the service. The service could not begin until each child was given one. The children were encouraged to keep their bulletins and bring them to church. Periodically there was a prize for the one who had the most collected. The children's bulletins mirrored the adults' version in format and informational categories, but they differed in language and amount of information. The adults' service bulletins were in Korean, and the information was much more detailed and lengthy.

Other uses of printed materials made me aware of the value of written Korean. Korean words printed decoratively on banners often hung at the front of the sanctuary where the adults' services were held. These announced a worship theme or part of a verse from the Bible; or they announced the title of a special service, such as a revival, or a religious holiday, such as Easter or Christmas. Pride was taken in the ability to write beautifully in Korean, and the members of the church knew who had that skill of good handwriting.

In connection with the church, there were other instances that highlighted the value of written Korean. In the homes of the church members, the walls were often decorated with framed Bible verses written in traditional Korean script from top to bottom and right to left. We were given bath towels as guest favors for ordination ceremonies, and celebrations of significant anniversaries of the church. These towels were professionally embroidered or printed with the significant names and dates of the events. In addition, messages of sorrow or congratulations along with the donors' names were printed in glue and glitter on ribbons that hung over huge flower arrangements at funerals and weddings. Obvious care had been taken in the beauty of the lettering. The color of the lettering was also important, as I found out when a mother kindly asked me to not use red crayon when writing the preschoolers' names on the crafts they made each week during Sunday School. She told me that some mothers felt that using red to write someone's name could be a bad omen.

So we see that the interpretation of the context of the church differed according to the participants. For most of the adults, the context was defined as (a) monolingual Korean as opposed to bilingual in Korean and English or monolingual in English; (b) a macro setting distinct and often seemingly set off from the American setting; and (c) broadly concerned with both oral and literate Christian Korean traditions. For the children, the church setting was (a) bilingual in Korean and English; (b) at the micro level, embedded in the larger church context, which in turn was embedded in the larger American context; and (c) marked by both oral and literate practices, with an emphasis on the oral.

The Korean church and school emphasized the macro, literate, and monolingual sides of each of the context continua. But Korean took the side of power as opposed to English in wider society. In this context, the children were aware of the power of English and in rare cases insisted on the appropriateness of English as opposed to Korean. In the conflict, we see negotiation of identity. As illuminated by the continua of the context of biliteracy, even within one church, the contexts were distinct for the adults and the children. It's as if the walls of the church were a little thinner for the children than for the adults.

Now, I would like to show how, in this context, the development, media, and content of biliteracy are all re-framed in keeping with this space for Korean identity.

Biliterate Development

As with context, in the continua of development of biliteracy, we can place Korean on the right side of each continuum. In this section, I show that in the KCS the emphasis is on production, written L2 (Korean). However, the teachers and students draw from both ends and the entire length of each continuum as a means of learning. We can also see the negotiation of identity in cases of disagreement over where the teacher assumes the students' knowledge of L1 and L2 to be.

Hornberger and Skilton-Sylvester note that society has traditionally given more power weighting to the productive, written, and L2 ends of the continua of biliterate development (2000: 105). The same was true in the Korean school, but because of the context, in the Korean church school, the L1 was English and the L2 was Korean. The students, nearly all of whom were dominant in English, were learning Korean, their mother tongue, as if it were a second language.

The children used the terms mother tongue and native language to refer to Korean, but they also used first language to refer to English, thus problematizing the typical meanings of the terms native speaker, mother tongue, and first and second language. Rampton (1995: 337) criticizes the use of the term native speaker because it fails to distinguish between language ability and loyalty, or 'expertise,' 'allegiance,' and 'inheritance' (342). This is exactly the case in this setting, where the students have internalized a sense of failure, for while claiming native speakerhood, they have to go to Korean school because their level of ability does not match that of their native speaker peers in Korea. In this paper, I use mother tongue to reference the sense of allegiance and/or inheritance, and the terms first and second language to reference language expertise.

During the spring semester of 1994, there were four levels of Korean classes held on Saturday mornings at the church building. The classes were arranged according to age and Korean ability of the students. Level One had the youngest students and Level Four had the oldest students.

Although the teachers and students incorporated the receptive, oral, L1 (English) in classroom discourse to aid in learning both language and the inescapable elements of culture that accompany language learning, the emphasis in the Korean school classes was on production, the written, and of course, Korean, the L2. Activities in the classes were primarily teacher-led and emphasized literacy skills; almost all of the activities depended in some way on written Korean.

Illustrative class sessions from each level (from among those I observed and recorded) give an idea of the emphasis on literacy events. In one Level One class session, the students were involved in reading aloud a page copied from a Korean textbook, calling out the names of Korean letters that the teacher wrote on the board, and writing on the board and in their textbooks. In one Level Two class session, students read aloud a paragraph from a handout in both English and Korean, read aloud from their texts, and read aloud from vocabulary flash cards. They wrote words on the board and copied sentences from their textbook into their notebook. At Level Three, students read aloud Korean words other students had written on the board, read aloud from their texts, and read comprehension questions as they did individual work assignments. They wrote vocabulary on the board and on their own paper during a quiz. In one Level Four class session, the students wrote sentences that the teacher dictated, read aloud a story from their texts, located vocabulary chosen from the text, and wrote their own sentences using the vocabulary from the story. All of these activities involved literacy skills and represented the function of literacy in these classes, at the primarily productive, written, and L2 (Korean) ends of the continua.

With the exception of a few instances that required the students to respond orally to the teacher's oral cues, all of the rest of the teacher-led activities involved some writing or reading of the written L2 (Korean). However, although the focus was on learning the skills associated with the written end of the continuum of oral to written, the students needed to listen and to understand Korean, to be able to speak Korean, and to be able to use English to show their understanding of Korean. They had to draw from both ends of each continuum in their development of biliteracy.

The teachers also worked along the entire length of each of the continua. They used English, the L1, to explain Korean, the L2, both by translating Korean words into English and by using English grammar to explain Korean grammar. For example, the Level Four teacher used English grammar to explain a similar rule in Korean: the 'er' morpheme that

English uses on the end of verbs changing the verb to a person noun – 'swim' to 'swim-(m)er.' While rereading a Korean text, the teacher stopped to explain the structure of 'errand' and 'runner of errand,' which is loosely translated as 'message' and 'messenger':

Teacher:	…심부름인데. 심부름꾼이라는 것은, 너네, 너네도 영어로도 있잖아. 뭐 이렇게 하면, or 이나 er 을 부치면 사람이 되잖아. 예를 [illegible]이봐.	*Errand [message]. [Messenger] is. You, you have it in English too. Like this. If you put 'or' or 'er,' it becomes a person. For example.*
Student SY:	It's like men.	It's like men.
Student MJ:	No.	No.
Teacher:	아니.	*No.*
Student SY:	Like whoever.	Like whoever.
Teacher:	그래. 맞아. swim 그러면, 여기다 er 을 부치면, 사람이 되지…	*Right. If you add* 'er' *to* 'swim,' *it becomes a person . . .*

This example portrays the teacher's use of the students' L1 (English) to bring them to an understanding of the L2 (Korean). The teacher assumed that the students knew English better than Korean, and demonstrated that she thought of them as closer to the L1 than the L2 on the continuum of L1 to L2 in the development of biliteracy. The teacher assumed that an explanation that involved a comparison between English and Korean would help the students learn Korean. While the overall goal of the language class was for the students to learn Korean, the teachers and students both knew that use of English was advantageous to learning Korean. So there was a judicious use of English in trying to reach the overall goal of learning Korean.

Biliterate Media

As the children go about acquiring biliteracy through the media of Korean and English, they negotiate across rather divergent scripts and dissimilar language structures, as well as negotiate issues of identity and personal language allegiance as they acquire English and then Korean in succession. Here I will talk briefly about the former, but focus more on the children's expressed allegiance to Korean and English. The subsequent section, on content, will take up their negotiation of identity.

With regard to divergent and convergent scripts, Korean and English are very much divergent. However, the children are expected to be able to learn the Korean script and use it for various functions in the church services as well as the classes. The children were expected to be able to speak Korean, since their parents spoke Korean, and this same expectation carried over to literacy in Korean. The children were expected to learn the Korean alphabet, put the sounds together, and read for understanding. The teachers in the school did not spend any time apologizing for the differences between English and Korean script. If anything, Korean script was considered easier than English, with its simple correlation between sound and symbol (Korean uses a phonetic alphabet). The participants took for granted that the script could be learned and used.

English and Korean are also more on the dissimilar end of the continuum in terms of structure, and the structure of Korean was taught explicitly most often in relation to the narratives presented in the texts, as in the 'messenger', '–er' transcript. But the dissimilarities of English and Korean, interestingly, were not the issue most encountered by the teachers. Rather, the teachers had to contend more with the differences between how the students used Korean orally and how it should be written. The salient dissimilarity was between oral and written Korean. Because the students mostly could understand and respond in at least simple Korean, they used that type of Korean when they wrote. For example, in the Level Four class, the students were assigned a final project to write a letter of thanks to one of their parents. Each student was preparing his/her letter to read aloud at the closing program held at the end of the school year, which coincided with parents' day, an important Korean celebration. The students worked on their letters at home, and the teacher edited them at school. The teacher instructed her students to change the sentence-final verbs from a simple form used when talking to friends to a more polite form customarily used when writing deferentially.

With regard to simultaneous or successive exposure to English and Korean, I need to briefly explain the children's language experience outside of the Korean church as well as their language use in the classes. Each child differed in his/her language experience and background, but there were commonalities. Korean surrounded most of the children, from birth to the time they started attending a public school. They spoke Korean as a native language with their parents and relatives. The preschoolers at Korean church could produce only a few English words.

Korean was, for most of the children, a first language and mother tongue. At home the parents generally taught their preschoolers the Korean alphabet. However, once the children began public school, they began to speak and write in English. The parents still spoke to their children in Korean, but the children began to speak to their siblings and peers in English. Korean became the language for communication with adults and little preschoolers, and the children generally became more proficient in English literacy and oral production than in Korean. At about this same time, the children began attending Korean language classes at the Korean church.

Except for the youngest students and a couple of older Korean dominant children, English became in effect the students' L1, and Korean was their L2, by the time they started Korean school. Korean was the language of learning, the target language in the classrooms. Using Rampton's (1995) terms, Korean was no longer their language of expertise. In interviews with the children many of them spoke of Korean as both their second language and their mother tongue, and spoke of learning Korean as similar to learning any other second language, like Spanish or French. They felt it would be good to learn as many languages as possible. On the other hand, they also explained to me that their parents wanted them to learn Korean because it was their mother tongue. Their mother tongue had become their second language.

Despite the successive exposure to Korean then English, then relearning Korean, the children maintained a strong connection between being Korean and speaking the language. In my interviews with the children and adults, the children shared the adults' assumption that Korean language is tied to Korean identity. For example, when asked in a group interview (led by the youth pastor, Ken) why they needed to learn Korean, the children answered, 'because we're Korean.' The children assumed that Koreans, who naturally inherit Korean language, should necessarily have both affiliation with and expertise in Korean:

Ken: OK. What do adults tell you?
Child: To speak in Korean.
Ken: Why?
Child: So you can learn more//because we're Korean people. (29 October 1994: 1)

The children were well aware of the fact that many Koreans did not speak Korean. But there was a label for these people. If you didn't follow the expected 'Koreans speak Korean', then you were labeled 'Americanized.' How well you spoke Korean was a marker of how Korean you were.

Or conversely, how poorly you spoke Korean was a marker of how Americanized you were. This was true for Korean behavior as well as for the ability to speak Korean. Language expertise was a marker for cultural affiliation.

During one teenaged girl's talk about Koreans who were Americanized, in which she said that Koreans from Korea were impressed by how much Korean she knew, she boasted that no one would think of her as Americanized since she could speak Korean:

Holly: What about Koreans who can't speak Korean?
Grace: They are usually more Americanized. Friends from Korea are amazed that I can speak Korean. No one thinks I'm Americanized.
Holly: Why do they think of you as not Americanized?
Grace: Usually they think that American Koreans wouldn't be able to speak Korean so well, so .... (16 October 1995: 10–11)

There seemed to be a continuum from Korean to 'Americanized Korean.' It wasn't a question of being Korean or not, but of 'how' Korean you were. Kids knew how to go back and forth on this continuum with language and behavior depending on the situation. They knew the different expectations and acted on them. The children were aware of the stigma that could be attached to using English with people they should use Korean with, and struggled with not being labeled as 'Americanized'.[1]

This unquestioned connection between being Korean and knowing Korean produced frustration in children who knew how they were supposed to talk or act, but didn't feel capable. Susan, a teenager expressed her worries; she knew she should respond to a Korean adult's questions in Korean, but worried that she wouldn't understand enough or remember enough Korean to respond without mistakes:

Susan: If I couldn't speak at all I would feel really stupid if I were even talking to my grandmother. I mean if she doesn't know English at all and so, even with talking to her I feel uncomfortable because I'm afraid I won't know the answer that she's going to ask me a question to, and I'm going to have to say it in English, then she won't understand it and .... Or I'm going to pronounce 'ten' wrong. I feel like even with my grandmother. But you shouldn't be like that with your grandmother ... and so like ... just in that way ... I wish I could just speak really good. (13 August 1995b: 13)

Susan acknowledged that she didn't feel that Korean was her language of expertise, or as she called it 'her first language,' and in certain situations felt that using English was more natural than using Korean, even though her parents would have wanted her to use Korean. She said that she used English with her siblings, because it felt natural. She had been speaking English all day with her classmates, and it was too much to expect her to change to speaking only in Korean when she went home:

Susan: It's just hard to all of a sudden go home and, 'OK, well, it's time to talk in Korean,' you know. You can't just turn that off. Like, like the fir

Holly: You can't turn off English?

Susan: Turn off Korean, I mean. Yeah, can't just, I mean, the first first language that comes out of my mouth is English. (13 August 1995b: 10)

There was conflict when what children expected did not match what adults expected. And the children individually worked it out. The parents told them to use Korean with their siblings, but the children felt it was not natural. So when the parents were around, in hearing distance, the children used Korean or (more likely) were silent. For example, there are honorific terms for older brother/older sister in Korean that some children were taught to use instead of their older sibling's first name. I never heard younger brother, David, and younger sister, Susan, use these terms for their older sister, Sharon. Instead, they just did not call out to Sharon. They avoided both using her name and using the Korean title. However, when they were talking with their mother or father in Korean, they would use the title to refer to their older sister.

In summary, most important for the continua of the media of biliteracy is the sequence of exposure to English and Korean. The feelings students express about Korean as mother tongue and their connection with their language yet their inability to speak Korean – the disparity between inheritance/affiliation and expertise – resulted in constant juggling so as to not be perceived as too Americanized sometimes or too Korean at other times. We can see that language use relates directly to identity.

Biliterate Content

Similar to the negotiation of language allegiance along the media continua, there was negotiation of identity along the continua of content. There were often instances of negotiation between teachers and students in terms of vernacular to literary content, contextualized to decontextualized content, and minority to majority content.

As seen with the other continua, here, too, Korean is on the more powerful side of the continua of content in the KCS, but not outside. The students reveal their relation to being Koreans in America within disputes over their knowledge of Korean majority or American minority content. Teachers and students draw from both ends of and all along each continuum, but students sometimes correct the teacher on how much content they know of majority or minority and in doing so reveal their connection with being Korean/American. The discourse serves as a way to test out who they are and where they stand.

Teachers and students did not just negotiate meaning of texts, but also how the students' identify themselves on the continuum of Korean (majority) to American (minority) identities. Sometimes the teacher overtly expressed her view that the children were Korean as opposed to American. Sometimes the teachers placed the students on the Korean/majority end of the minority – majority continuum, as in the following example which occurred within a literary speech event.

The Level Two teacher opened her class with a prayer in which she asked God to help the children learn Korean well and to love 'our country,' Korea:

> 하나님 아버지, 감사합니다. 오늘도 좋은
> 날씨 주심을 감사하며, 한국말 잘 배위시 한국
> 이린이로 우리 나라를 사랑하는 착한
> 이린이가 다 되게 해 주시고, 하나님도
> 사랑하고 나라 사랑하는 귀한 어린이들이
> 되게 인도해 주세요. 예수님의 이름으로
> 기도합니다. 아멘.

> Lord, Father, thank you. Thank you for giving us a nice weather. Let us learn Korean well; and as Korean children, to love our country; let us become good children; guide us to become precious children who love God and love [our] country. In the name of Jesus, Amen.

This prayer reinforced the connection inherent even in the class's physical surroundings – the connection between being lovers of God and lovers of Korea, or being good Christians and good Koreans, as well as between being good Koreans and learning Korean well.

Prayer is a literate genre, in that it is a formalized, recognizable piece of text, even though it is not written. As such, we can think of this speech event much as a literacy event. And the teacher uses the prestige and seriousness of the prayer event to encourage the children in her overall goal, namely, that through learning Korean, the children would affiliate with their God and with their Korean heritage. Through the prayer and its emphasis on the Korean homeland, she situated the children on the Korean end of the minority–majority continuum in the US context.

The students often contributed to the classroom discourse in order to help other students understand, sometimes by helping the teacher explain to other students, by adding personal experiences that related to the topic, or by questioning the meaning the teacher offered. The students used both English and Korean to negotiate meaning. By incorporating their own experiences or knowledge into the class discourse, the students were contextualizing an otherwise decontextualized exercise.

An example of students contributing to the class discourse to negotiate identity and contextualize content was when the teacher in the Level Two class discussed Korean manners and ways of greeting. She had brought with her a supplemental page of Korean text that already had the English translation printed below in a separate paragraph. Each student was given a copy of the page. The text explained the superiority of Korean manners envied by Korea's neighboring countries and gave examples of the respect shown to elders in the description of Korean greeting bows, both the common everyday bow, and the special bow reserved for relatives on special occasions.

The content of the paragraph on Korean greetings was idealized, from a Korean perspective and apparently intended for a Korean audience with a shared knowledge of Korean greetings. In this church/school context, from a majority/Korean perspective this text was perfectly understandable and would not be questioned. The teacher apparently assumed that the students were at the same place as her and the text on the minority–majority continuum, because she did not see the need to explain either the ethnocentric tone in the text of thinking of Korean manners as being enviable by all other peoples/cultures, or the description of Korean bows. The English translation part of the text certainly sounded strange to me in its overt expression of cultural superiority, and in the description of the special bows. The English text says, 'whenever one sees his parents or elders, he makes a special bow to the floor.' The wording of 'whenever' is simply not correct, since Koreans do not bow to the floor every time they see their parents. They do this only on special occasions and/or after a long separation. When compared with the Korean text, however, the English version is not a bad translation. It just has a slightly heavier emphasis on the word 'whenever.' The Korean is not objectionable, either, since the audience would presumably locate the words in their shared knowledge and experiences.

On the content continua, this text was on the majority end in viewpoint, but the teacher and students negotiated the meaning. One boy, Student J, reacted to the text with the comment, 'sounds weird-ya,' which may be interpreted as his ideological move away from the strongly biased majority content. In calling attention to the weirdness of the text, Student J positioned himself away from the majority slant. The teacher brought them back, though, by incorporating the students' own experiences into her explanation of the text, thereby helping her students identify themselves with this traditional Korean activity that embodies a fundamental Korean value – respect for elders.

The students were asked to read aloud in unison, first the Korean paragraph, then the English translation paragraph. Then the teacher asked them to share with her their experiences of when they bow to the floor, and the students responded quickly with a description of their bows on New Year's Day, but added the other important aspect of what they get in return for their respectful bow – an envelope with money from their elders:

Teacher:	OK. 자. 그 다음에, 인사, 인사.	*OK. Now, next. Greeting, greeting.*
Student J:	Welcome.	Welcome.
Student SJ:	Welcome.	Welcome.
Teacher:	Greeting. 인사. 또, 보통 인사는 어떻게 해 ?	Greeting. *Greeting.* *How do you greet normally?*
Student J:	보 ?	*Norm . . . ?*
Teacher:	보통 인사.	*Normal greeting.*
Student J:	안녕하세요 ?	*Hello* (lit. 'Are you well?')
Teacher:	Regular. 응. 그냥 보통 인사.	Regular. *Uh huh. Just normal greeting.*
Student MR:	Hi.	Hi.
Student J:	안녕하세요 ?	Hello.
Teacher:	이렇게. 이렇게. 굽히고 하지 ?	*Like this, don't you bend like this?*
Student MR:	Yeah.	Yeah.
Teacher:	그 다음에. 큰 절. 큰 절. 큰 절.	*Next, the special bow, the special bow, the special bow.*
Student MR:	I go like that like you go you put your head down you put your head down.	I go like that like you go you put your head down you put your head down.

Teacher:	그렇게 하는 거 응.	*Right, doing it that way.*
Student J:	Say something. Then go like that. Then money 줘..	Say something. Then go like that. Then *they give* money.
Student MR:	Xxx 할머니..	xxx *grandmother.*
Teacher:	언제 해 ?	When do you do it?
Student H:	New year. Korean new year.	New year. Korean new year.
Teacher:	Korean new year 때 큰 절 했이 ?	*Did you do the special bow on* Korean new year?
Student J:	네.	*Yes.*

Through their contributions the students show first a move away from the teacher's placement of them on the Korean side of majority–minority content, then agreement with the teacher on how to relate to the majority content.

Sometimes, however, students disagreed with the teacher on where they were being placed. In the story they were reading aloud, the Level Four teacher stopped the reading to highlight the use of the honorific particle 'nim,' a particle used in Korean to show respect when addressing someone.

Teacher:	자, 봐봐. 여기서 "님"이 나오잖아, 님.	*Now Look.* *Look here you have 'nim' [an honorific marker].*
Student SH:	높은	*For higher.*
Teacher:	높은 말 하는거야. 그래서 "고래군요"가 아니고 그냥 동화속에서 "고래님이군요". 이것 봐. 선생님. 목사님. 여기님. 알지	*It means higher.* *So it's not 'it's you whale' in the story rather it's 'it's you Mr whale'.* *Look teacher-'nim'.* *Pastor-'nim'* *It's 'nim' ok?* *Boss-'nim'.* *Right?*
Student SY:	전도사님.	*Assistant pastor-'nim'.*
Teacher:	전도사님.	*Assistant pastor-'nim'.*

As seen in the transcript, the students already knew about the usage of the Korean honorific particle 'nim.' (It is a student who contributed a definition of 'nim' as 'higher.') They showed the teacher that they were not as ignorant of Korean usage as she assumed. So the students positioned themselves closer to the Korean end of the continuum than the teacher did. In this way they negotiated their relative social identity through their expressed knowledge of Korean language norms.

The teacher could also have been emphasizing the relatively higher degree of respect shown in Korean language and in Korean culture as opposed to American culture and English. I think she may have wanted the students to be better at showing respect; to be good Koreans, and not to be as disrespectful as she was observing in American culture and language, to which she was just then adjusting in her own life. None of the teachers had any qualms about teaching morality in class. After all, they were situated in a church building, but more than that, they shared a common Korean background, which was differentiated from American ways. In the classes, the teachers implicitly and explicitly taught Korean behavior rules. Although this wasn't explicitly language instruction, it was part of the reason for the founding of the school and for the parents' sending their children to the school.

Conclusion: Church as Haven for Koreanness

Thirty to 35 years ago in the US, Korean immigrant adults pushed their children to learn English to the point of even forcing the children to speak English in the home. At the time of this study from 1991 to 1997, Korean language skills in the next generation were no longer considered a given. The adults now realized that the children would not automatically hold on to their Korean language skills. Korean language now needed to be protected actively.

Korean was also needed for the children's future as Koreans in America. The adults reasoned that, because of appearance differences, the children would not be totally accepted in the mainstream culture, and so would need to rely on the Korean community to get ahead financially. According to Hurh (1998), they were right in assuming that they would not be socially accepted into the mainstream culture, and as Koreans would need to keep ties with the Korean-American community.

According to Hurh (1998), there is a distinction between cultural assimilation and social assimilation. Cultural assimilation is when the immigrant group learns the ways of the host country, but social assimilation only occurs when the members of the host society socially accept the members of the immigrant group. Social assimilation for non-whites in American society has been particularly difficult because of racial barriers. Hurh writes:

> For instance, Korean immigrant physicians may become highly acculturated into the American way of life by virtue of their good command of English, conversion to Protestantism, and high professional status; but they may not be socially assimilated into the mainstream of the American social structure due to their immutable racial status. (1998: 69–70)

The Korean church served as a kind of refuge from lack of social integration. Chong writes in her article about the role of religion in the construction of ethnic identity and boundary among second-generation Korean-Americans:

> the strong sense of ethnic identity and exclusivity observed among second-generation church-goers reflects a form of defensive ethnicity against their perceived 'marginal' status within American society as a nonwhite minority group. Thus, despite its role as a vehicle for the cultural interests of the first generation, the paradoxical appeal of the Korean ethnic church for many second-generation members lies in its capacity to provide a kind of 'refuge' from this sense of marginalization, and along with it, positive social identity and group empowerment. (1998: 261)

Cut off from full participation in American society, the second-generation children in the church that I observed would need Korean language skills to successfully negotiate the Korean American network.

While situated within the American society, the church offered the adults a social setting where Korean rules of behavior were the norm. This was in contrast to involvement with American society in which Korean norms were marked. Their involvement in the Korean church allowed them to relax, to be themselves for a while. It was a kind of haven for being Korean in the language with which they are most comfortable.

The children, too, as opposed to feeling conspicuous outside of the Korean church/school context, reported feeling at ease in the church. Susan, a teenaged girl, did a good job of summarizing most of the distinctions that the other children also mentioned. These were distinctions that she noticed between being with Korean children at church and American children at school. She expressed her feelings of being different and feeling conspicuous when talking in Korean around Americans:

Holly: You said it was different with the kids that were Korean and your friends from school.

Susan: Yeah, well because . . . they could speak Korean too, and . . . they ate Korean food, so . . . it was . . . just a different experience when I was with my friends at school and then when I was at church with my friends there. At church . . . I guess I didn't feel like I had to . . . like I mean the food we eat is different uhm you know like everyone talked like that to their parents and it was I think it was . . . we spoke English to each other as kids but it was still a different experience than when I was at school with my friends.

Holly: You talked like that to your parents? What do you mean everyone talked?

Susan: Like cause . . . we talked to parents in Korean, so we spoke Korean. And . . . I think, well, especially when I was younger, I would feel uncomfortable talking . . . Korean in front of my friends at school, but it was OK at church, cause everyone else did it too. So . . . in those ways it was different. Like I didn't feel like I had to hide anything . . . I felt Korean at church. At school I was just like everyone else. I don't know if you understand. Like I didn't feel any different [at school], cause I mean I did everything the same. But at church I guess it was kind of different because everyone there was Korean. I don't know (laugh) I feel like I'm confusing myself too. (13 August 1995b: 1)

In contrast, the children reported a feeling of being 'comfortable' at church. Everyone spoke Korean, so it was 'OK' to use Korean at church; to be Korean at church. No one was going to make fun of you for having parents who didn't speak English. The church and the church language school provided a locale for the children to be with others who looked like them, who ate the same kinds of foods, and whose parents spoke Korean, without feeling conspicuous. Church was one of the few places outside of home where being Korean was the norm.

Even in this Korean context, the adults and children differed in their perspective of how much the US context played a part within the church and school. Korean identity was renegotiated through each person and each interaction. So, we see in the KCS the making of the micro–macro. There is a change in the power relations from within the church to without, yet the high status of English as society's majority language still makes itself felt and obvious through the negotiation of Korean identity. For the children and the adults, the church and school is a dynamic, permeable haven of Koreanness.

Note

1. In Korean, the word for American, '미국사람' (mi guk sa ram), translates as 'America person'. But it was obvious that this term only referred to white Americans, not Americans of other races, and thus not Korean-Americans. There were other terms for people of other races. This is why there was some confusion with the word 'American' in English. 'American' could be used to refer to the 'white race' or it could refer to a nationality. Korean children, then, could refer to themselves as American, if they were talking about nationality or citizenship; or they could refer to themselves as 'Americanized,' meaning 'like white Americans.' In addition, the term 'American' was also used instead of 'English.' The Korean word for English is '미국말' (mi guk mal), translated as 'America language.' It shares the syllables 'mi guk,' meaning 'America,' with the word for 'America person.' So when translated directly from Korean, the word 'American' was used as the shortened form for both 'American person' and 'American language.' The children repeatedly referred to white people as 'Americans,' so I use their terminology here.

References

Byun, M.S. (1990) Bilingualism and bilingual education: The case of the Korean immigrants in the United States. *International Journal of Sociology of Language* 82, 109–28.

Chong, K. (1998) What it means to be Christian: The role of religion in the construction of ethnic identity and boundary among second-generation Korean Americans. *Sociology of Religion* 59 (3), 259–86.

Fishman, J. (1989) *Language and Ethnicity in Minority Sociolinguistic Perspective.* Clevedon: Multilingual Matters.

Hornberger, N.H. and Skilton-Sylvester, E. (2000) Revisiting the continua of biliteracy: International and critical perspectives. *Language and Education* 14 (2), 97–122.

Hurh, W.M. (1998) *The Korean Americans*. Westport, CT: Greenwood Press.

Kim, B.L. (1988) The language situation of Korean Americans. In S.L. McKay and S.L. Wong (eds) *Language Diversity: Problem or Resource* (pp. 252–75). New York: Newbury House Publishers.

Rampton, B. (1995) *Crossing: Language and Ethnicity among Adolescents*. London and New York: Longman.

Chapter 13

'Be Quick of Eye and Slow of Tongue': An Analysis of Two Bilingual Schools in New Delhi

VINITI BASU

As one walks into the SKV there is a signboard outside the principal's office which reads 'Thought for the Day.' On this board is written the quotation in the title of this paper, 'Be Quick of Eye and Slow of Tongue,' a saying literally translated from Hindi, which explains why it sounds so odd. On the principal's desk is a sign which says '*Kripya Hindi kaa prayog Karen*' meaning 'Please use Hindi.' These are indications of the unique and fascinating bilingual program in Hindi and English which is currently in place at the SKV. Comparing it with the bilingual program in the NNBV reveals a rich landscape where one can explore issues brought out in Hornberger and Skilton-Sylvester's Continua of Biliteracy.

Before embarking on a discussion of the Continua, readers should familiarize themselves with the educational environment from which this discussion emerges. The following three sections offer a concise description of the two schools and brief history of literacy and language planning in India. Once these contexts are introduced, the remaining sections take up the Continua of biliterate media and content, respectively, in each case comparing across the two schools. It should be emphasized that the analysis is based on ongoing, as yet incomplete, ethnographic research in the two schools, and that conclusions presented here should therefore be considered tentative at this time. This ethnographic research started in November 1999 as part of my Ph.D. in Educational Linguistics at the University of Pennsylvania and is still ongoing.

Sarvodaya Kanya Vidyalaya (SKV)

This is part of a chain of SKVs run by New Delhi Administration. There are a total of 1019 schools under New Delhi Administration and of these

343 are SKVs. These schools are located all over New Delhi, in both privileged and poor neighborhoods. The SKV studied here is located in East Vinod Nagar which is a relatively poor neighborhood in New Delhi. These schools charge a minimum fee of Rs15 per term (US $1 is equivalent to Rs48). Usually these children buy their own textbooks and uniforms. However, starting 1 July 2000 the New Delhi Administration has allocated Rs400 per child. Now these children get free textbooks and school bags.

Kanya means girl and the SKVs are mainly girls' schools, but many of them have boys from class 1 till class 3. These schools are currently up to class 9 and are in the process of adding classes 10, 11 and 12. In each class the children go through three tests. The session begins in July and they have the first test in September. The second is in December and the third in May. In classes 1, 2 and 3 promotion is automatic as long as the student shows 75% attendance. After class 3 the weak students may be retained. All the SKVs have two sections for each class, thus for class 1 there will be a 1A and a 1B. One section is Hindi medium and one is English medium. For the English medium classes, Science, Math and English are in English. Hindi and Social Studies are in Hindi. For the Hindi medium sections all the subjects are in Hindi and they study English as a second language. The home language of most of these children is Hindi. Their fathers are government employees and may have secondary school educations. The mothers are illiterate. Some of the teachers told me that when they want to speak to the parents they always ask for the father. The children speak practically no English at home.

Nagar Nigam Bal Vidyalaya (NNBV)

This is also part of a chain of schools which provide only functional literacy as they are from nursery to class 5. These schools are run by the Municipal Corporation of New Delhi or MCD. There are a total of 1800 such schools under MCD which service 900,000 children. The nursery is a recent addition. Before that the NNBVs started from class 1. Most of these schools are located in 'clusters,' which is Indian-English for 'slums.' Thus they cater to children from very poor families. These are children of migrant workers who come to New Delhi from the adjacent villages and work in unskilled jobs. Many are children of domestic workers. These schools are totally free; the children receive textbooks, free uniforms, including shoes, socks and sweaters in winter, and they are also supposed to get a midday meal. In the NNBV that I am observing there have not been any midday meals. These schools run two shifts, one in the morning and the other in the afternoon. The morning shift is for girls with an all-female staff. The afternoon shift is for boys with an all-male staff but this currently has a very cooperative female principal. My research focuses on the afternoon shift. The medium of instruction is totally Hindi, except that from 1 July 2000 the MCD has introduced a basic textbook for English. All the classes from 1 to 5 are taught only this one textbook. These children speak various dialects of Hindi at home, many of which are very closely related to Hindi.

Linguistic Context

In describing the linguistic history of India this author is cognizant of the micro–macro Continua of biliterate contexts. In her 1989 article Hornberger writes:

> At the macro–macro level are the insights that there may exist domains associated with one or other language in bilingual societies ... or that a language may fulfill one of a range of functions in the society. These functional roles include the high and low variety in a diglossic situation ... a second language of wider use ... a foreign language ... or a language of wider communication. (p. 279)

All these aspects of the macro–macro level are covered in the following discussion.

The institutions which provide literacy in India are fairly well organized for a developing country. India spends 6% of its Gross Domestic Product on education and 50% of this sum is earmarked for primary education. The Central Government tries to provide free and compulsory education to all children up to the age of 14. There are various chains of literacy providers throughout the country. For instance the Kendriya Vidyalayas (Central Schools) were established in 1962 and there are currently 877 such institutions in India. These schools use Hindi and English as media of instruction. The Navodaya Vidyalayas are a chain of schools for talented children from rural areas. There is one Navodaya Vidyalaya in every district in the country. The city of New Delhi has two other chains, namely the Sarvodaya Kanya Vidyalaya and the Nagar Nigam Bal Vidyalaya, which are the two schools where my research is based. The teachers for these schools are trained in various types of institutions, the most common being the District Institute for Educational Training. The government tries to ensure that there is at least one DIET in every district (MIB, 1999). Besides these there are numerous private schools in India which are English medium and teach the mother tongue as a second language. Before the 1990s it was these elite private schools (in India these are called 'public' schools and the public schools are called 'government schools') which were the sole distributors of English literacy. Since the lower middle class did not have access to these schools they were kept outside the gates of English literacy. In the 1990s a profound change has come in education in India in that the government schools too are now providing English literacy to the masses and thus opening the gates to upward mobility.

The Indian government is committed to the idea of universal literacy and its policies show a leaning towards both language as problem and language as right (Ruiz, 1984). The government promotes the idea of national literacy through the chain of NNBVs. These schools promote literacy only in Hindi, the national language. Fishman (1971) sees this type of literacy as 'nationalism,' which creates sociocultural integration and 'nationism,' which in turn creates efficient politicogeographic integration. Since the home dialect of the children in the NNBV is not taught in the school, this policy does not support mother tongue literacy or local literacies and, using Ruiz's (1984) terminology, sees language as problem. From a different perspective, most of the 18 standard languages in the constitution are well represented in the school system, with Hindi and English as second and third languages. Annamalai writes that there are 'forty-seven languages used in education as medium' (2001: 35). This shows the government's commitment to multiple literacies and language as right.

A discussion of literacy in India is not possible without an understanding of its complex linguistic terrain. Khubchandani (1983) estimates that there may be 3000 mother tongues in India; however, the Constitution recognizes 18 of these as major languages (see Table 13.1). These are listed in the Eighth Schedule and are often referred to as scheduled languages. Note the languages and their relative strengths (from MIB, 1999: 17, Table 1.13):

As Brass states:

> A listing in the Eighth Schedule carries symbolic and material advantages: a presumptive right to recognition as a minority language in states where other languages are dominant, including a presumptive right to recognition as medium of instruction in both primary and secondary school classes in such states, a right to the protection of the President of India (i.e. the central government) on the advice of the Commissioner of Linguistic Minorities against discrimination in use of the language, and representation on language development committees appointed by the central government. (1990: 154)

Table 13.1

Language	*Percentage to total population in 1991*	*Language*	*Percentage to total population in 1991*
1. Hindi	39.85	10. Oriya	3.32
2. Bengali	8.22	11. Punjabi	2.76
3. Telegu	7.80	12. Assamese	1.55
4. Marathi	7.38	13. Sindhi	0.25
5. Tamil	6.26	14. Nepali	0.25
6. Urdu	5.13	15. Konkani	0.21
7. Gujerati	4.81	16. Manipuri	0.15
8. Kannada	3.87	17. Kashmiri	n.a.
9. Malayalam	3.59	18. Sanskrit	0.01

Thus these 18 languages have some place in the educational system of India, if not as medium of instruction, then as second or third languages.

According to the 1991 census, there are 96 other languages which are not specified in the Eighth Schedule (see Appendix). Being represented in the Eighth Schedule is largely a matter of political resourcefulness by language groups. This is because some languages not in the Eighth Schedule have more speakers (languages like Santali and Bodo) than those in it (Manipuri, Kokani). It is interesting to note that the L1 of some children at the NNBV was said to be Kumaoni, Pahari or Garwali (shown in italics below). These languages appear in neither the Eighth Schedule nor the list of non-scheduled languages. These are considered dialects of Hindi which the Indian census subsumes under the Hindi speakers. According to the 1981 census (Census of India, 1981: 4–5) the following dialects are reclassified under Hindi:

Awadhi	Bagheli/Baghekhandi	Banjari
Bhadrawhi	Bharmauri/Gaddi	Bhojpuri
Braj Bhasha	Bundeli/Bundelkhandi	Chambeali
Chhattisgarhi	Churahi	Dhundhari
Garhwali	Gojri	Harauuti
Haryanvi	Jaunsari	Kangri
Khariboli	Khorta/Khotta	Kulvi
Kumaoni	Kurmali Thar	Lamani/Lambadi
Laria	Lodhi	Magadhi
Maithili	Malvi	Mandeali

Marwari	Mewari	Mewati
Nagpuria	Nimadi	Padari
Pahari	Panchapargania	Pangwali
Pawari/Powari	Rajasthani	Sadan/Sandri
Sondwari	Sugali	Sujapuri
Surgujia		

As explained in the previous section the fact that the children of the NNBV are speakers of these dialects of Hindi has direct bearing on education. These dialects are very similar to Hindi, the language of instruction in their school, and this is one of the reasons why the children of the NNBV become fluent in Hindi.

Of the scheduled languages, the two most important in India today are English and Hindi. English came to India with the British colonizers. When the British were formulating India's educational policy there was a debate between the Orientalists who wanted education in the vernaculars and the Anglicists who wanted the medium of instruction to be English. Many far-sighted Indians like Raja Ram Mohun Roy (1772–1833) advocated English literacy so that Indians would be part of the modern world of science and technology. Finally it was this view that was accepted by the British government, though for different reasons. On 7 March 1835, the seal of approval was stamped on Macaulay's minute which advocated English education to create 'a class who may be interpreters between us and the millions whom we govern, a class of persons, Indian in blood and colour, but English in taste, in opinion, in morals and in intellect' (Kachru, 1985: 68).

In keeping with its elitist origins, English remained a resource only for the elite until recently. It was and still is the medium of instruction in all the elite schools and is taught as a second language in many other schools. Nearly all the tertiary educational institutions use English as a medium of instruction. In the 1991 census, 178,598 people listed English as their mother tongue (Bose, 1998). Though this is a small number out of one billion, which is the total population of India, a much larger number of people know English as a second or third language at varying levels of competence. Today there is a massive demand for literacy in English and it is common to see all types of billboards advertising courses in English to the public. In keeping with this demand, many government schools like the SKVs and the NNBVs, which are the non-elite schools, provide English education.

At the time of independence (1947) it was decided that Hindi would be the national and official language. Since Hindi was not adequately developed, English would be a co-official language till 1962 when it would be displaced by Hindi. However, in the early 1960s there was major agitation by non-Hindi speakers who felt safer with English than Hindi as the sole official language. Thus the plan of displacing English was shelved and the Indian government passed the Official Languages Act (1963) according to which English would continue to be an additional official language indefinitely (Brass, 1990: 143).

Educational policy regarding medium of instruction was codified in 1961 with the adoption of the Three Language Formula. The Education Commission (1964–6) improved on this and recommended that children should study:

(1) mother tongue or the regional language;
(2) the official language (Hindi) or the co-official language (English); and
(3) a modern Indian language not covered under (1) and (2), and different from the one used as medium of instruction. (Sridhar, 1996: 334)

This formula is implemented with flexibility in the various schools in India. For instance, in the SKV, both Hindi and English are media of instruction. Those in the Hindi medium are taught English as a second language and those in the English medium are taught Hindi. However they are not taught another modern Indian language; in the NNBV the children are taught only Hindi, both as a medium and as a subject. Now, though, they are also taught basic skills in English.

Against this complex linguistic background the following sections analyze two relevant sets of continua: the Continua of biliterate media and the Continua of biliterate content. The all-pervasiveness of the Continua of biliterate contexts, though it is not discussed separately, is evident in each of the subheadings. This pervasiveness emphasizes the nestedness of the four continua and shows that they are all interlinked rather than linear events which can be discussed discretely. Throughout, the analysis seeks to answer the question: Why is the NNBV more successful in making its students proficient in Hindi while the SKV is not so successful in doing the same in English?

Continua of Biliterate Media: Relationship Between Mother Tongue (MT) and Medium of Instruction (MI)

This set of continua is made up of three sub-continua:

- Convergent and divergent scripts.
- Similar and dissimilar structures.
- Successive and simultaneous exposure.

The following discussion touches on all these issues in varying degrees of importance, depending on how they impinge on the relationship between MT and MI. A major aspect of this relationship between MT and MI is whether there is transfer or interference between the two. Related to this are questions like: Is lower proficiency the result of interference between MT and MI? If not, then what are the other variables which could be responsible for this lower proficiency? The following discussion tries to explore possible answers to these questions.

Hornberger writes that the more a learner can access all points on the continuum the more easily can he/she acquire literacy. For instance, on the Continua of biliterate media, the children of the NNBV are very close to the similar structures (between dialect and Hindi) and successive exposure ends (as they start learning Hindi after the age of three). In fact, due to the similarity of structures between the dialect and Hindi, the Indian census does not include these dialects in either the Eighth Schedule or the list of non-scheduled languages. These dialects are subsumed under Hindi as discussed in the section on the linguistic background of India. The dialect does not have a script and thus this aspect of the continua is not applicable. Given the context of education in India, being close to the similar structures (between dialect and Hindi) end helps the children of the NNBV to acquire the L2.

The children of the SKV, on the other hand, are close to the dissimilar structures (between English and Hindi) end of the continuum and this, coupled with other variables about their English usage, causes interference between L1 and L2 and results in poor acquisition of L2.

The relatedness of mother tongue (MT) and medium of instruction (MI) is a key concern in bilingual education. Some scholars give evidence for the fact that in later stages in a child's school career he/she has ease of learning if the MT is related to the MI. According to Corder, the traditional position has been 'that the relative ease or difficulty in acquiring some feature of the target language crucially depended on the similarity or difference it bore to the mother tongue. Similarity implied ease of learning and difference difficulty' (1983: 32). He goes on to say that empirical evidence had displaced this traditional view. However, empirical research has also shown that in the later stages of development there is ease of learning a similar language. Thus 'some languages are more readily learned than others by speakers of a particular mother tongue' (1983: 32).

On the other hand there is no such similarity between Hindi and English, which are the two languages of instruction in the SKV. The idea that similarity between languages leads to ease of learning is contradicted by a study conducted in India and published three years before Corder's essay. In this study Jayaram and Misra (1980) compared the achievement in Hindi language and Social Studies taught in Hindi between two groups of students: group A consisted of students whose mother tongue was Punjabi, Marathi, Urdu and Sindhi (Indo-Aryan languages like Hindi), and group B consisted of speakers of Tamil, Telegu, Kannada and Malayalam (Dravidian languages unlike Hindi). Their conclusion was, 'there is no initial advantage for the child whose mother tongue is nearer to Hindi, over the child whose mother tongue is not' (30). However, Jayaram and Misra leave the idea open that in later stages there may be some advantages for learners of similar languages. In my opinion the similarity between MT and MI is an advantage for the children of the NNBV because they do not have any reinforcements at home. In the NNBV the children come from a very print-poor environment. All the language learning that takes place for them happens in school and this might not have been adequate had the two languages been very different. Similarly for the SKV children, there is no reinforcement at home of English, and the vast difference between English and Hindi does not help these children to master the language.

Cummins' (1981) theory of the Separate Underlying Proficiency (SUP) vs Combined Underlying Proficiency (CUP) presents an interesting contradiction in understanding the relationship between MT and MI in the Indian context. Cummins explains SUP as the assumption that the L1 and the L2 are different skills in the brain and unrelated to each other. The supporters of SUP do not think that teaching the L1 will lead to improvement in L2 acquisition. On the other hand the CUP model assumes that the two skills are related and the best way of acquiring L2 is through instruction in the L1. This theory, because of the unique contexts of education in India, does not hold true for the two schools where I am conducting participant observations. For instance, the children of the NNBV are not offered any instruction in the L1 but they become fluent in Hindi. However, the children of the SKV are given intensive instruction in their L1, Hindi, but they do not become proficient in the L2, English. This chapter will unfold some of the contexts that create this unique educational phenomenon.

I approached the question of whether positive transfer from the dialect to Hindi is one of the reasons why the children of the NNBV are able to acquire their L2 more fluently than their counterparts in the SKV, through interviews. At the SKV the teachers told me that they do not think interference between Hindi and English is the reason why the children are not able to become fluent in English. The reasons they listed for poor proficiency in English are as follows:

- Motivation of the child.
- Involvement of the parents.
- Home environment.
- Poverty.
- Difficult text books.
- Fluency of the teachers in English.
- Corporal punishment.

It was interesting to note that not one of the teachers felt that language interference was a reason for the SKV child's poor proficiency in English. Amarjeet, one of the senior teachers at the SKV, told me that if the child is a '*padhne wala bachcha*' or a studying child he/she will be able to learn English very well. However, the non-studying child will be weak in both English and Hindi. Also, many of the mothers are illiterate, although the fathers may have secondary school educations. I asked Amarjeet what kind of help she expected from the parents given the fact that their own educational backgrounds were so limited. She said it is not important for parents to be highly educated. The parents should sit with the child for at least an hour every day and make sure the child goes over the work done in school. Some of the other teachers told me that the home environment of these children is not conducive to good study habits. In most cases a family of six or more members is living in just one room and there is no place for the child to study. One teacher pointed out a child to me who has eleven siblings. Poverty and lack of resources are other factors that impede the learning of these children.

A teacher told me about a child who has only one copybook for all the subjects. When the book has no pages left the child erases the pencil marks and starts writing again. Amarjeet showed me the science textbook for grade 5 and said that this is a very difficult textbook for the children. Pointing to the questions after the lesson on the human body, she said the material in the lesson is difficult enough, and the children find it nearly impossible to handle the questions. However, Amarjeet felt that the English and Math textbooks were not difficult for these children.

The lack of fluency of the teachers requires extended analysis. Many of the teachers commented honestly on their own lack of fluency in English. Some commented on their lack of training for teaching in an English medium school. Government school teachers are trained in the District Institutes of Educational Training (DIETs), which are located in most major towns in India, or in Teacher Education Institutes (TEIs). There are two types of TEIs: ones that prepare teachers for general stages of education and those which orient teachers for special streams. The latter include (Yadav & Lakshmi, 1999):

(1) Technical Teachers Training Institutes, which prepare teachers for polytechnics;
(2) National Institutes, which prepare teachers for teaching children with special needs;
(3) Central Institute of English and Foreign Language;
(4) H.M. Patel Institute of English, which prepares teachers for teaching English.

These training institutes have many problems. Nagpal (1999) reports that many of the DIETs suffer from 'poor perception of training needs' and 'shortage of staff.' Also, in many parts of India, secondary school teachers are training elementary school teachers. Yadav and Lakshmi, reporting on the TEIs, write that the teacher educators here are drawn from various disciplines and may be training teachers who are working in a discipline different from their own (1999: 29). These problems are apparent from what the teachers told me. They do not feel that they have received adequate training for teaching in an English medium environment. Some of them felt that they would like to attend courses which could improve their English.

So far we have discussed home environment, difficult textbooks, parental involvement and poverty as variables which affect the acquisition of proficiency in the L2. To this should be added a brief note on corporal punishment, since some teachers considered this a factor in the children's poor English acquisition. I noticed an extensive amount of corporal punishment in both the schools, but it was far more pervasive in the SKV. Here the teachers would pinch the child's ears, slap the child or shout at him/her. In both schools children were often punished by being made to stand in a corner. In one case a teacher at the SKV asked the child to 'become a rooster.' This meant the child had to squat and hold his ears. In some cases the child would start crying. Many would look extremely upset and embarrassed when punished. Corporal punishment is not looked at negatively in this environment. One time at the SKV I observed a mother discussing her child's performance with a teacher. The mother encouraged the teacher to hit the child if he was not behaving properly as she herself was having discipline problems at home. Also, when I talked with Ram Niwas, a driver whose son is in the SKV, he said that one of his sons is beaten every day, yet it has no effect on him and he still does not study.

In the NNBV, as in the SKV, the teachers did not think that there was major interference between the dialect and Hindi for those few children who did not become fluent Hindi speakers. The teachers are aware that most of their students show a language shift from dialect to Hindi. One of the teachers told me that, when the children come to this school at the age of five or so, they can only speak the dialect. After a few years their Hindi becomes better than their dialect and they speak Hindi in the playground and even with their siblings, reserving the dialect only for the home domain. For those children that lag behind, the teachers listed many of the same factors listed by the teachers of the SKV. When I probed the teachers about what kind of interference they see, some told me that the home dialect can affect:

- Accent.
- Spelling.

To show me the interference in accent a teacher in grade 5 made one of the boys read from the Hindi text book. The boy read fluently and without any accent that I could detect. In spelling the teacher said that these children often get confused with '*matraas*.' Hindi uses a system of '*matraas*,' which are symbols that represent vowel sounds in a word. The vowel sound may be written as a letter or as a '*matraa*' along with the consonant next to which it comes.

The discussion above shows that the relationship between the MT and the MI is not perceived as an influential variable in language acquisition by the teachers. It is the macro and micro contexts in which language acquisition takes place that are more important. This idea reinforces the nested nature of the Continua of Biliteracy and shows that the media of biliteracy cannot be seen as discrete from the contexts of biliteracy.

Continua of Biliterate Content

'Whereas the media continua focus on the forms literacy takes, the content continua focus on the meaning those forms express' (Hornberger and Skilton-Sylvester, 2000: 20). This new aspect in the revised Continua of Biliteracy is crucial in analyzing what exactly is being taught in the classroom.

Majority vs minority

One reason why the children of the SKV are not able to master English and those at the NNBV become fluent in Hindi is the status of Hindi and English, which can be better explained by seeing how these languages fit into the content continua. The languages of instruction in both the schools, English in the SKV and Hindi in the NNBV, are the L2s of the students.

In the case of the NNBV, Hindi is the majority language of New Delhi, while Pahari, Kumaoni, Bihari etc. (which are dialects of Hindi and the L1s of these students) are the minority languages. In the SKV, Hindi is a majority language. However, English is in a way both 'majority' and 'minority' language; it is 'majority' because it is a language of prestige, and 'minority' because it is spoken only by a small group in India:

SKV			NNBV		
English L2	:	Hindi L1	Hindi L2	:	Dialect L1
majority/minority	:	majority	majority	:	minority

One of the reasons why the children of the NNBV are able to master Hindi is that, in addition to the Hindi they are exposed to in school, they also hear Hindi all around them as it is the majority language of New Delhi. Of the nine million people who live in New Delhi, 7,690,631 speak Hindi (Bose, 1998). Though many of these children are too poor to have TVs they all hear Hindi on the radio. Most of them listen to songs from Hindi films, which are extremely popular. Since there are so many dialects that the children speak at home in the NNBV, they use Hindi to communicate with each other in the playground and while chatting on the way home. One of the teachers at the NNBV told me that, though these children speak the dialect with their parents, they speak Hindi with their siblings. Thus, though the children of the NNBV do not have any Hindi books or newspapers at home, Hindi is very much part of their lives.

Also, in the NNBV the children and their parents are keen to replace their dialect with Hindi – the language of education. In fact their support of Hindi goes against the idea that the mother tongue is the best medium of instruction. The 1953 UNESCO report recommends mother tongue as medium of instruction because, 'psychologically, it is the system of meaningful signs that in his [the student's] mind works automatically for expression and understanding. . . . Educationally, he learns more quickly through it than through an unfamiliar linguistic medium' (11). Indian scholars like Pattanayak strongly recommend mother tongue instruction in the early stages of a child's career and then a smooth transition to the school language. Pattanayak argues for 'a conscious bilingual bidialectal transfer model of education for those whose home language is different from the school language which will exploit the resources of their home language . . . and will ensure a smooth transition to the standard or the language of school' (1981: 60). However, mother tongue as medium of instruction is not possible in India because there are too many mother tongues and many of them have no script. Besides, the speakers of these minority languages themselves do not support their mother tongues, like the NNBV community. In another example Sridhar conducted a survey in the state of Bihar and found that 93% of students in that survey chose Hindi as medium of instruction even though their mother tongue was not Hindi (Sridhar, 1996: 339). Agnihotri also observes, 'there is no motivation among either the elite or the local groups themselves to pursue literacy in the local languages' (1994: 48). My own field work reinforces this view.

There is bound to be language shift due to the education policy followed by the NNBV as the students here are not reading and writing in the L1. However, there is no sign of the Reverse Language Shifters described by Fishman (1991) in 'Why try to reverse language shift and is it really possible to do so?' He describes RLSers as language loyalists who campaign for the preservation of minority languages which are being eroded by a majority language. Marilyn Martin-Jones (1989) uses the term 'conflict perspective' to categorize studies which support the rights of linguistic minorities. She cites scholars like Gal and others who have been working on minority languages of Europe and situates herself in the conflict perspective where scholars, many of whom tend to be Marxist, see a class struggle between the speakers of minority languages and their counterparts who speak the standard. Even scholars who do not situate themselves in this perspective argue for the maintenance of minority languages. For instance Hornberger in 'Continua of biliteracy: Quechua literacy and empowerment in Peru' writes that 'the promotion of Quechua literacy' in a country where the majority language in Spanish, 'increases the potential for full literate development and fuller social participation of hitherto marginalized sectors of Peruvian society' (1994: 237). Though I agree with Martin-Jones and Hornberger regarding the importance of minority languages, I do not see much community support for them in the Nagar Nigam Bal Vidyalaya (NNBV). Here the community is being empowered despite the loss of the dialect.

In the SKV, where the children should be doubly empowered as they are learning two languages of prestige, they are actually being short-changed. For these children being at the dissimilar ends of the Continua of biliterate media proves to be a disadvantage because the only English they hear is in school. As mentioned at the beginning of this discussion, English is both a majority language in terms of its status and a minority language because it is spoken only by an elite minority. Since these children come from a low-income background they are not exposed to much English. If they have TVs they do not have most of the English channels. On radio most of the programs are in Hindi. They live in very print-poor homes.

Decontextualized vs contextualized

There are some specific literacy practices which are the root cause of denying the children of the SKV full mastery of the English language. In particular 'an exclusive emphasis on decontextualized parts of language makes it so that students do not learn how to construct wholes with academically appropriate parts' (Hornberger & Skilton-Sylvester, 2000: 23). Skilton-Sylvester tells the story of Chamran who for three years of schooling was only copying from the board or from a work-sheet. When Skilton-Sylvester asked her to write a story, she wrote 'spelling test' on top of the page and numbers on the left hand side from 1–15. Similarly, I learned that the grade 5 children of SKV are not taken beyond word recognition. In a long conversation, Amarjeet, the class teacher of grade 5, told me that the Science textbook is very difficult for these children. She showed me a chapter on the human body. At the back of this lesson were some questions. She told me that these questions are very difficult because the answer cannot be copied from the lesson. Thus in the exam she only chooses those questions which have one-word answers.

A large part of the work that children do is copying from the textbook without understanding the meaning. For instance, in the English copybook of a class 3 student I read the following fill-in-the-blanks exercise:

> Last year there was no rain <u>at all</u> m our district. Th wells and <u>ponds</u> were dry. The. fields <u>dried</u> too and the farmers have plenty of water.

I asked the class 3 teacher of the SKV if the students could fill in the blanks by themselves. She said only one or two can in a class of about 30. She usually makes them write the answers in the textbook first and then they copy the exercise in the copybook, which she checks. It is clear that the child whose book I looked at had copied without understanding the meaning of the sentences.

These literacy practices are grounded in what Street (1995) calls the 'autonomous model,' which sees literacy as the necessary condition for social mobility and economic take-off. On the other hand the 'ideological model' of literacy recognizes the 'culturally embedded nature of such practices' and 'stresses the significance of the socialization process in the construction of the meaning of literacy for participants, and is therefore concerned with the general social institutions through which this process takes place and not just the "educational" ones' (29).

It was interesting to note that the English textbooks do culturally contextualize the lessons. The lessons are set in an Indian context to which the children can relate. Some of the lessons, like 'Birbal Finds the Thief' and 'Ramalinga and His Two Servants,' from *Lets Learn English: Book Three*, are based on folk-tales. There are colorful pictures and many of the lessons have a humorous quality. Most of the other stories like 'Sita Finds Her Way Home' in *Book Two* have Indian characters. The pictures show figures in a very Indian setting. Thus these books are not alien to the children. At the same time, some of the textbooks also have a few traditional English poems like 'Mary Had a Little Lamb.'

However, the exercises after each lesson are created mainly around word recognition. They consist of fill-in-the-blanks, matching words with pictures and who or what questions. The questions are written such that the student can pick the key sentence from the text and copy it as an answer. The reason why this is so was revealed to me in an excellent interview with Dr K.K. Vashishtha, professor and head of elementary education at the NCERT (National Council for Educational Research and Training). The NCERT is responsible for writing most of the textbooks used in India. In an hour-long interview, Dr Vashishtha told me that these English textbooks are written for second and third language speakers, thus the language is controlled. The purpose of the textbooks is to teach reading, writing, listening and speaking in English. He said that he is aware that these goals are not being met in the classroom and his department is in the process of revising these textbooks. He said that for the poor children of the SKV 'textbook is curriculum,' i.e. that is all they have in terms of tools for studying. Thus the textbook must provide the means for passing the exams without much help from the teachers who do not speak English well, and parents who do not speak English at all.

In the SKV I observed that the grade 5 children were made to bracket the answers in the textbook and then memorize them for the exam. I observed a class studying 'Rumpelstiltskin' from their English textbook. The teacher, Nirmal, was well liked and she had the full attention of the class. She began the class by asking a student to read the whole story, which the student did without much difficulty. Then Nirmal explained the story in Hindi to an enthusiastic audience. She translated the key words, like spinning wheel, into Hindi. Subsequently she began working out the questions with the class.

'What did the king ask the girl?' Nirmal asked and there were many volunteers. I felt that many students in this class found these questions quite easy. She then made them bracket one sentence in the text which was the answer to this question and reminded them to memorize it. Because of these decontextualized literacy practices the children of the SKV are not able to become fluent in English, despite the fact that the textbook is written in keeping with Street's ideological model of literacy.

The term 'decontextualized' also has cultural implications. Hornberger and Skilton-Sylvester write:

> If students' whole contextualized texts, with all of their imperfections, could be used as a starting point, meaning would be insured and students could intrinsically see the links between contextualized and decontextualized language, and between the literary and the vernacular. If minority texts could be chosen as a part of the literary content of the classroom, links could also be made between the content students bring with them to school and the content they encounter at the school door. (2000: 26)

In this case the inclusion of the 'vernacular' has a different context because Hindi is not a vernacular. It is a language of great prestige with a very ancient tradition that comes from Sanskrit. Using the Continua model the dichotomy here is between literary and literary not between literary and vernacular. In this competition between Hindi and English, Hindi wins out because the children of the SKV are more exposed to it. On TV and radio there are numerous excellent Hindi programs geared towards children. Entire Disney movies are aired which have been dubbed in Hindi. The hugely popular Ramayana and the Mahabharata, epics comparable to Homer's Odyssey and Iliad, are aired on weekends and are watched by the whole family. When the traffic-choked streets of New Delhi are clear one can be sure that it is the Ramayana slot on TV. The language in these TV serials is dense and formal but the children still enjoy them.

The children from the NNBV, who speak a dialect of Hindi at home, are not faced with any competition from their home language. The dialects they speak do not have a literature or script of their own. Most of these dialects are used in Hindi literature merely to provide humor or local color. In fact, by the time the children of the NNBV reach grade 5, they are more familiar with Hindi, in which they can read and write, than with their home dialect in which they can only speak. Also, they sense that their dialect is stigmatized and that by becoming fluent in Hindi they are upgrading themselves.

Conclusion

The underclass in India has not had access to English, which until about 10 years ago was reserved only for the elite and transmitted to them through elite schools. Now the government schools, like the SKVs, which service the poor sections of society, are offering this language as a medium of education. Through interviews with policy makers at the Ministry of Education I learned that English is being offered in the government schools due to demand from the parents. They would rather pay more and send their children to a private school which is English medium or to a school where English is taught as a second language, than to an all-Hindi government school which is free. Thus the Ministry of Education was forced to make many of government schools English medium, otherwise they would lose a lot of students.

It is unfortunate that, despite an excellent program at the SKV, which aims to bring elite education down to the grassroots, the children are not becoming proficient in the L2. They do not become fluent in English because they are not able to access many of the points on the Continua of Biliteracy. For instance, they are too close to (a) the dissimilar structures end of the continuum in the Continua of biliterate media and (b) the decontextualized end in the Continua of biliterate content. This is coupled with the fact that the teachers in the SKV do not have fluency in English, the children come from poor families and their parents do not speak any English. In the case of the NNBV children, who become very fluent in Hindi, their literacy practices are located such that they are able to access more points on the Continua of Biliteracy. This, coupled with several other contextual factors described in the foregoing sections ensure that the children of the NNBV become fluent in Hindi.

Appendix

Languages not specified in the Eighth Schedule

	Language	*Number of persons speaking*		*Language*	*Number of persons speaking*
1.	Adi	158,409	12.	Chakru/Chokri	48,207
2.	Anal	12,156	13.	Chang	32,478
3.	Angami	97,631	14.	Coorgi/Kodagu	97,011
4.	Ao	172,449	15.	Deori	17,901
5.	Arabic/Arbi	21,975	16.	Dimasa	88,543
6.	Bhihnupuriya	59,233	17.	Dogri	89,681
7.	Bhili/Bhilodi	5,572,308	18.	English	178,598
8.	Bhotia	55,483	19.	Gadaba	28,158
9.	Bhumij	45,302	20.	Gangte	13,695
10.	Bodo/boro	1,221,881	21.	Garo	675,642
11.	Chakesang	30,985	22.	Gondi	2,124,852

23.	Halabi	534,313
24.	Halam	29,322
25.	Hmar	65,204
26.	Ho	949,216
27.	Jatapu	25,730
28.	Juang	16,858
29.	Kabui	68,925
30.	Karbi/Mikir	366,229
31.	Khandeshi	973,709
32.	Kharia	225,556
33.	Khasi	912,283
34.	Khezha	13,004
35.	Khiemnungan	23,544
36.	Khond/Khondh	220,783
37.	Kinnauri	61,794
38.	Kisan	162,088
39.	Koch	26,179
40.	Koda/Kara	28,200
41.	Kolami	98,281
42.	Kom	13,548
43.	Konda	17,864
44.	Konyak	137,722
45.	Korku	466,073
46.	Korwa	27,485
47.	Koya	270,994
48.	Kui	641,662
49.	Kuki	58,263
50.	Kurukh/Oraon	1,426,618
51.	Lahauli	22,027
52.	Lahnda	27,386
53.	Lakher	22,947
54.	Lalung	33,746
55.	Lepcha	39,342
56.	Liangmei	27,478
57.	Limbu	28,174
58.	Lotha	85,802
59.	Lushai/Mizo	538,842
60.	Malto	108,148
61.	Mao	77,810
62.	Maram	10,144
63.	Maring	15,268
64.	Miri/Mishing	390,583
65.	Mishmi	29,000
66.	Mogh	28,135
67.	Monpa	43,226
68.	Munda	413,894
69.	Mundari	861,378
70.	Nicobarese	26,261
71.	Nissi/Dafla	173,791
72.	Nocte	30,441
73.	Paite	49,237
74.	Parji	44,001
75.	Pawi	15,346
76.	Phom	65,350
77.	Pochury	11,231
78.	Rabha	139,365
79.	Rengma	37,521
80.	Sangtam	47,461
81.	Santali	5,216,325
82.	Savara	273,168
83.	Sema	166,157
84.	Sherpa	16,105
85.	Tangkhul	101,841
86.	Tangsa	28,121
87.	Thado	107,992
88.	Tibetan	69,416
89.	Tripuri	694,940
90.	Tulu	1,552,259
91.	Vaiphei	26,185
92.	Wancho	39,600
93.	Yimchungre	47,227
94.	Zeliang	35,097
95.	Zemi	22,634
96.	Zou	15,966

References

Agnihotri, R.K. (1994) Campaign-based literacy programs: The case of the Ambedkar Nagar experiment in Delhi. In *Language and Education: An International Journal. Special Issue: Sustaining Local Literacies* 8, 1–2.

Annamalai, E. (2001) *Managing Multilingualism in India: Political and Linguistic Manifestation* (Vol. 8: Language and Development). New Delhi: Sage Publications.

Bose, A. (1998) *Demographic Diversity of India: 1991 Census, State and District Level Data*. New Delhi: B.R. Publication Corporation.

Brass, P.R. (1990) Language problems. *The Politics of India since Independence.* Cambridge: Cambridge University Press.

Census of India (1981) Series 1, Part IV B(I), 'Population by language/mother tongue' (Table 7): Part A: 4–5.

Central Institute of English (1997) *Let's Learn English: Book Two Special Series.* Hyderabad: National Council of Educational Research and Training.

Central Institute of English (1998) *Let's Learn English: Book Three Special Series.* Hyderabad: National Council of Educational Research and Training.

Corder, P.S. (1983) A role for the mother tongue. In L. Selinker and S. Gass (eds) *Language Transfer in Language Learning* (pp. 30–42). London: Newbury House.

Cummins, J. (1981) The role of primary language development in promoting educational success for language minority students. In California State Department of Education (ed.) *Schooling and Language Minority Students: A Theoretical Framework* (pp. 3–49). Los Angeles: Evaluation, Dissemination and Assessment Center, California State University.

Fishman, J.A. (1971) The impact of nationalism on language planning. In J. Rubin and B. Jernudd (eds) *Can Language be Planned? Sociolinguistic Theory and Practice in Developing Nations* (pp. 3–20). Honolulu: University Press of Hawaii.

Fishman, J.A. (1991) Why try to reverse language shift and is it really possible to do so? *Reversing Language Shift* (pp. 10–38). Philadelphia: Multilingual Matters.

Hornberger, N.H. (1989) Continua of biliteracy. *Review of Educational Research.* Fall, Vol. 59 (3), 271–96.

Hornberger, N.H. (1994) Continua of biliteracy: Quechua literacy and empowerment in Peru. In L. Verhoeven (ed.) *Functional Literacy: Theoretical Issues and Educational Implications* (pp. 237–56). Philadelphia: John Benjamins Publishers.

Hornberger, N.H. and Skilton-Sylvester, E. (2000) Revisiting the continua of biliteracy: International and critical perspectives. *Language and Education: An International Journal* 14 (1), 18–44.

Jacobson, R. (1990) Allocating two languages as a key feature of a bilingual methodology. In R. Jacobson and C. Faltis (eds) *Language Distribution Issues in Bilingual Schooling* (pp 3–17). Philadelphia: Multilingual Matters.

Jayaram, B.D. and Misra, J. (1980) *Bilingual Achievement in Schools* (edited by E. Annamalai). CIIL Occasional Monograph Series – 19. India: Central Institute of Indian Languages.

Kachru, B.R. (1985) Indian English: A sociolinguistic profile. *The Indianization of English: The English Language in India* (pp. 65–95). New Delhi: Oxford University Press.

Khubchandani, L. (1983) *Language Diversity in India*. Simla: Simla Institute of Advanced Studies Press.

Martin-Jones, M. (1989) Language, power and linguistic minorities: The need for an alternative approach to bilingualism, language maintenance and shift. In R. Grillo (ed.) *Social Anthropology and the Politics of Language* (pp. 106–25). London: Routledge.

MIB (Ministry of Information and Broadcasting, Government of India) (1999) *India 1999: A Reference Annual*. Compiled and edited by Research, Reference and Training Division. New Delhi: Aravali Printers and Publishers.

MIB (Ministry of Information and Broadcasting, Government of India) (2001) *India 2001: A Reference Annual*. Compiled and edited by Research, Reference and Training Division. New Delhi: Aravali Printers and Publishers.

Nagpal, S. (1999) Human resource development climate in improving quality management in teacher education: A study on DIETs. *Journal of Indian Education* 24 (4). New Delhi: NCERT.

Pattanayak, D.P. (1981) *Multilingualism and Mother Tongue Education*. New Delhi: OUP.

Ruiz, R. (1984) Orientations in language planning. *NABE Journal* 8 (2), 15–34.

Sridhar, K.K. (1996) Language in education: Minorities and multilingualism in India. N. Labrie and S. Churchill (eds) *International Review of Education. Special issue: The Education of Minorities* 42 (4), 327–47.

Street, B.V. (1995) Literacy and social change: The significance of social context in the development of literacy programmes. In *Critical Approaches of Literacy in Development, Ethnography and Education* (pp. 28–47). London: Longman.

Swain, M. (1982) Immersion education: Applicability for nonvernacular teaching to vernacular speakers. In B. Hartford, A. Valdman and C.K. Foster (eds) *Issues in International Bilingual Education: The Role of the Vernacular* (pp. 81–97). New York: Plenum Press.

UNESCO (1953) *The Use of Vernacular Languages in Education*. Monograph on Fundamental Education. UNESCO.

Yadav, M.S. and Lakshmi, T.K.S. (1999) Equipping teacher educators. *Journal of Indian Education* 25 (1). New Delhi: NCERT.

Part 6: Conclusion

Chapter 14

Multilingual Language Policies and the Continua of Biliteracy: An Ecological Approach*

NANCY H. HORNBERGER

Introduction

Two scenes from the year 2000:

18 July 2000, Johannesburg, South Africa. In the course of my two-week visit at Rand Afrikaans University, I meet early this Tuesday morning (7.30 a.m.) with a group of young pre-service teachers enrolled in a one-year Diploma in Education program. The university has been bilingual from its founding, offering instruction in Afrikaans and English in a parallel dual medium format; in the post-apartheid period, rapidly expanding numbers of speakers of diverse African languages have enrolled.

About 20 students attend this English Language Pedagogy class where I have been invited to speak about bilingual education. Their teacher Judy is present, as is my host Elizabeth. At one point, I mention my dissertation research which documented 'classroom success but policy failure' for an experimental bilingual education program in Quechua-speaking communities of Puno, Peru. The policy failure, I suggest, was at least partly due to some community members' resistance to the use of Quechua in school, which they had always regarded as a Spanish domain. Taking off from this, Judy asks what one can do about negative community attitudes which impede top-down language planning, citing the case of Black African parental demands for English-medium instruction in the face of South Africa's new multilingual language policy.

Later, when the discussion turns to the importance of the teacher's recognizing and valuing students' languages and cultures even if they're not the teacher's own, Elizabeth takes the opportunity to demonstrate one such practice. Students are instructed to break into small groups to talk to each other about bilingual education for two–three minutes in their own languages. The result: four Nguni speakers (one Zulu, one Xhosa, two Swati), two Gujarati-speaking women, three Afrikaans speakers, and one Portuguese speaker (who talks with me) form groups, while the rest of the class members chat to each other in small groups in English. The students clearly enjoy this activity and it generates lively whole-class discussion.

17 August 2000, La Paz, Bolivia. On the first day of a three-day *Taller de reflexión y análisis sobre la enseñanza de castellano como segunda lengua* (Workshop of reflection and analysis on the teaching of Spanish as a second language), the Vice-Minister of Education welcomes workshop participants, emphasizing to us that the key to the Bolivian Education Reform is Bilingual Intercultural Education, and the key to *that* is Spanish as a Second Language. In recent months, she tells us, questions have been raised about the Reform's attention to indigenous languages, and indigenous parents have begun to demand that their children be taught Spanish. Perhaps the Reform erred, she says, in emphasizing the indigenous languages to such a degree that bilingual education appeared to the public to be monolingual indigenous language education.

There are approximately 45 participants in the workshop: 15 technical experts from the Curricular Development Unit of the Ministry, a half-dozen representatives from PROEIB, the Andean regional graduate program in bilingual intercultural education at the University of San Simón in Cochabamba, Bolivia, another 8–9 Bolivian pedagogical experts, and about a dozen international specialists in bilingual and second language education (from Brazil, Chile, Ecuador, Mexico, Peru, Belgium, Germany, USA, and Sweden). Many of us had participated five years earlier in a similar workshop on the curriculum and materials for the teaching of the indigenous languages, principally the three largest languages, Quechua, Aymara, and Guarani. The materials we reviewed then have been under implementation in the schools for a couple of years now.

Our charge this time is to review the Spanish as a Second Language curriculum and materials developed by the Curricular Development Unit and to make recommendations for improvement in design and implementation. Among the materials available for review are curricular guides, teaching modules for Spanish, bilingual modules for the content areas, cassette tapes and laminated posters, an 80-book class

> library, a literary anthology, and a series of six big books in Spanish, three of them based on traditional Quechua, Aymara, and Guarani folktales.
>
> In the ensuing three days of intensive work across long hours (8 a.m. to 9 p.m.), discussions are remarkable for the honesty and integrity with which the Curricular Development Unit experts welcome critical scrutiny of their work. These experts worry about how best to teach Spanish to a school population which in many cases has little to no exposure to oral Spanish or to print media outside of the classroom, and so have opted for a richly communicative and literature-based curriculum design. Some of the second language experts are concerned that there is not enough explicit grammatical and lexical instruction and that the syllabus is not sufficiently incremental. Concerns from those who have seen the materials in use in the field are of a different nature. They ask questions like: What are the implications for second language learning of teachers' frequent code-mixing in class, code-mixing prompted by the desire to communicate with the students in a language they understand?; By the same token, what are the implications for maintaining and strengthening the indigenous languages if one and the same teacher teaches in both the indigenous language and Spanish?

As these scenes readily show, the one language–one nation ideology of language policy and national identity is no longer the only available one worldwide (if it ever was). Multilingual language policies which recognize ethnic and linguistic pluralism as resources for nation-building are increasingly in evidence. These policies, many of which envision implementation through bilingual intercultural education, open up new worlds of possibility for oppressed indigenous and immigrant languages and their speakers, transforming former homogenizing and assimilationist policy discourse into discourses about diversity and emancipation. This paper points to two broad sets of challenges inherent in implementing these new ideologies, as they are evident in two nations which undertook these transformations in the early 1990s.

Post-apartheid South Africa's new Constitution of 1993 embraces language as a basic human right and multilingualism as a national resource, raising nine major African languages to national official status alongside English and Afrikaans;[1] this, along with the dismantling of the apartheid educational system, has led to the burgeoning of multilingual, multicultural student populations in classrooms, schools, and universities nationwide. The Bolivian National Education Reform of 1994 envisions a comprehensive transformation of Bolivia's educational system, including the introduction of all thirty of Bolivia's indigenous languages alongside Spanish as subjects and media of instruction in all Bolivian schools. Yet, to transform a standardizing education into a diversifying one and to construct a national identity that is multilingual and multicultural constitute ideological paradoxes which are a challenge to implement.

Recently, scholars are increasingly turning to the metaphor of ecology to think and talk about language planning, teaching, and learning in multilingual settings. In the first part of the paper, I explore salient themes of that metaphor – namely language evolution, language environment, and language endangerment – and argue that multilingual language policies are essentially about opening up ideological and implementational space in the environment for as many languages as possible, and in particular endangered languages, to evolve and flourish rather than dwindle and disappear. In the second half of the paper, I use my continua of biliteracy model as heuristic to consider two broad sets of challenges facing these multilingual language policies (as exemplified in the above scenes) and suggest that there is urgent need for language educators, language planners, and language users to fill those ideological and implementational spaces as richly and fully as possible, before they close in on us again.[2]

Multilingual Language Policies, Ideology, and the Ecology of Language

The one nation–one language ideology, the idea that a nation-state should be unified by one common language, has held sway in recent Western history from the rise of the European and American nation-states in the eighteenth and nineteenth centuries on through the formation of independent African and Asian nation-states in the mid twentieth century and up to the present. Fishman wrote of the several score new members brought into the family of nations in the mid twentieth century and of the nationistic and nationalistic ideologies underlying their choice of a national language: 'nationism – as distinguished from nationalism – is primarily concerned not with ethnic authenticity but with operational efficiency' (1969: 113). In either case, emphasis was on choosing *a* national language, *one* national language, whether it were a Language of Wider Communication serving nationistic goals or an indigenous language serving nationalistic ones.

Yet the one language–one nation equation is increasingly recognized as an ideological red herring (Woolard & Schieffelin, 1994: 60–1). For one thing, it is a relatively recent phenomenon when seen against the backdrop of human history. Referring not only to the Greek, Roman, Aztec, and Inca empires of ancient times but also to the more recent Austro-Hungarian and Ottoman empires, May writes in his recent book on the politics of language that 'empires were quite happy . . . to leave unmolested the plethora of cultures and languages subsumed within them – as long as taxes were paid' (May, 2001: 6).

Furthermore, in our day, twin pressures of globalization and ethnic fragmentation exert pressures on the one language–one nation ideology. May suggests that modern nation-states have had to reassess the limits of their sovereignty as a result of the rise of globalization and the 'burgeoning influence of multinational corporations and supranational political organisations,' while at the same time minority groups increasingly exert their rights 'either to form their own nation-states . . . or for greater representation within existing nation-state structures' (2001: 7). In like vein, Freeland notes that Latin American nations are particularly prone to two frequently mentioned effects of globalization from without and within: (a) the weakening of the state from the surge of transnational phenomena and (b) the weakening of the state from social and ethnic fragmentation (1996: 168). Certainly, African nations are similarly prone to these effects.

Gal suggests what might be considered a linguistic corollary to these pressures when she notes that global processes like colonization, the expansion of capitalism, and transnational labor migration have replaced earlier processes of 'dispersion of populations and the peopling of the world,' such that: (1) the characteristic form of language change in the modern era is the coming together of languages; and (2) the former 'relatively egalitarian linguistic diversity, based on small-scale languages whose speakers believe their own language to be superior, [has been changed] into stratified diversity: Local languages are abandoned or subordinated to "world languages" in diglossic relations' (1989: 356). All of this points to two countervailing trends working together to break apart the one language–one nation ideology: the rise of English as a global language, hence infringing on national languages; and the reclaiming of endangered indigenous, immigrant, and ethnic languages at local and national levels, hence undermining the ascendancy of national languages.

Ecology of language

As the one language–one nation ideology breaks apart, so too the language planning field increasingly seeks models and metaphors that reflect a multilingual rather than monolingual approach to language planning and policy. One such model is the continua of biliteracy (to be taken up below) and one such metaphor is the ecology of language; both are premised on a view of multilingualism as a resource. Ruiz, like Fishman (1966a) before him, drew our attention to the potential of a language-as-resource ideology as an alternative to the dominant language-as-problem and language-as-right ideological orientations in language planning (1984). Mühlhäusler argues that 'language planning until the 1980s was based on the premise that linguistic diversity is a problem' (1996: 311–12), but that it is now undergoing a conceptual shift toward recognizing linguistic diversity as an asset.

Einar Haugen is generally credited for introducing the ecology of language in his 1970 paper by that title (Haugen, 1972). Haugen himself points to an earlier, 1964 paper by Carl and Frances Voegelin, who suggested that 'in linguistic ecology, one begins not with a particular language but with a particular area, not with selective attention to a few languages but with comprehensive attention to all the languages in the area' (Voegelin & Voegelin, 1964: 2).[3] For his part, Haugen defines language ecology as 'the study of interactions between any given language and its environment,' going on to define the environment of the language as including both psychological ('its interaction with other languages in the minds of bi- and multilingual speakers') and sociological ('its interaction with the society in which it functions as a medium of communication') aspects (1972: 325). He emphasizes the reciprocity between language and environment, noting that what is needed is not only a description of the social and psychological situation of each language, but also the effect of this situation on the language (1972: 334). Haugen argues for the heuristic value of earlier biological, instrumental, and structural metaphors in understanding the life, purpose, and form of languages and goes on to invoke the tradition of research in human ecology as a metaphor for an approach which would comprise not just the science of language description, but also concern for language cultivation and preservation (1972: 326–9). He concludes with a comprehensive catalogue of ecological questions which Mühlhäusler later repeats (Haugen, 1972: 336–7; Mühlhäusler, 1996: 3–4).

For my purposes here, I am primarily interested in three themes of the ecology metaphor which are salient to me in writings on the ecology of language; all of them are present in Haugen's original formulation. These are: that languages, like living species, evolve, grow, change, live, and die in relation to other languages and also in relation to their environment; for ease of reference, I will call these the *language evolution* and *language environment* themes. A third theme is the notion that some languages, like some species and environments, may be endangered and that the ecology movement is about not only studying and describing those potential losses, but also counteracting them; this I will call the *language endangerment* theme.[4]

In his 1996 book, *Linguistic Ecology*, Mühlhäusler advocates an ecological approach to languages which, like Haugen's approach, encompasses all three of these metaphorical themes. He argues that our focus must shift from consideration of 'given,' countable languages to one on human communication in a holistic sense (1996: 8–9) and proposes an approach which 'investigates the support system for a structural ecology of language rather than individual languages' (1996: 312–13); that is, he argues for consideration of *language evolution*. He 'sees the well-being of individual languages or communication networks as dependent on a range of language-external factors as well as the presence of other languages' (1996: 49) and claims that 'the focus of inquiry should be upon the functional relationship between the factors that affect the general interrelationship between languages rather than individual factors impacting on individual languages' (1996: 313); that is, he calls for a focus on *language environment*. Writing from a concern for the decline and loss of linguistic heterogeneity in the world, Mühlhäusler argues for applying ecological theory to the goal of language maintenance (1996: 311–24); that is, he writes from a concern for *language endangerment,* in the sense of both studying and counteracting language loss. He applauds the ecological metaphor for being action-oriented and prefers the partial and local explanations of an ecological approach to the complex yet ultimately mechanical explanations of a systems metaphor (1996: 2).

Others writing on an ecological approach to language planning elaborate on one or more of the metaphorical themes. Kaplan and Baldauf's work elaborates on the *language evolution* and *language environment* themes. They emphasize that language planning activity cannot be limited to one language in isolation from all the other languages in the environment (1997: 271). Their model representing the various forces at work in a linguistic eco-system includes 'language modification constructs' (1997: 289) or 'language change elements' (1997: 296), such as language death, survival, change, revival, shift and spread, amalgamation, contact, pidgin and creole development, and literacy development, all processes of what I am here calling *language evolution*. With regard to *language environment*, the model also depicts agencies such as government and non-government organizations, education agencies, and communities of speakers, all of which have an impact on the multiple languages in the linguistic eco-system (1997: 311). 'Language planning . . . is a question of trying to manage the language ecology of a particular language to support it within the vast cultural, educational, historical, demographic, political, social structure in which language policy formulation occurs every day' (1997: 13); 'language planning activity must be perceived as implicating a wide range of languages and of modifications occurring simultaneously over the mix of languages in the environment – that is, implicating the total language eco-system' (1997: 296).

Recent work by Phillipson and Skutnabb-Kangas (1996) and Ricento (2000) highlights the *language endangerment* theme of the ecology metaphor. Phillipson and Skutnabb-Kangas contrast two language policy options with regard to English worldwide: the diffusion of English paradigm characterized by a 'monolingual view of modernization and internationalization' and the ecology-of-language paradigm which involves 'building on linguistic diversity worldwide, promoting multilingualism and foreign language learning, and granting linguistic human rights to speakers of all languages' (1996: 429). The juxtaposition of the linguistic imperialism of English with multilingualism and linguistic human rights is clearly founded on a concern for the ongoing endangerment of many languages, displaced by one or a select few, and the need to counteract that endangerment and displacement. Mühlhäusler cites Pakir's (1991) term 'killer languages' in reference to the displacing effect of imperial English as well as other languages such as Mandarin, Spanish, French, and Indonesian.

In parallel fashion, van Lier (2000) argues that an ecological approach to language learning emphasizes emergent language development; learning and cognition as explained not only in terms of processes inside the head, but also in terms of interaction with the environment; and learners' perceptual and social activity as, in a fundamental way, their learning. These three emphases can be understood as micro-level, sociocultural language learning parallels to the *language evolution, environment,* and *endangerment* themes in an ecological approach to language planning. Bringing sociocultural and sociolinguistic strands together in his ecological approach to literacy, Barton (1994:29–32) provides a succinct and useful review of the use of the ecology metaphor in both psychological and social traditions in the social sciences.

Ricento argues that, as the macro sociopolitical context of language planning has moved over the last several decades from decolonization through modernization and into the new world order, and as social science epistemologies have simultaneously moved from structuralism through critical theory and into postmodernism, so too the language planning field has moved from a focus on problem-solving through a concern for access and into an emphasis on linguistic human rights. In words that evoke the *language endangerment* and *language environment* themes outlined above, he suggests that the ecology-of-language paradigm may well be the conceptual framework for language planning in the future, precisely because of its emphasis on language rights and on connecting macro sociopolitical processes with micro-level patterns of language use (2000: 208–9).

In sum, an ecology of language metaphor captures a set of ideological underpinnings for a multilingual language policy, in which languages are understood to (1) live and evolve in an eco-system along with other languages (*language evolution),* (2) interact with their sociopolitical, economic, and cultural environments (*language environment*), and (3) become endangered if there is inadequate environmental support for them vis-à-vis other languages in the eco-system (*language endangerment*). All three of these ideological themes come into play in the following consideration of challenges facing the implementation of multilingual language policies in South Africa and Bolivia.

Multilingual Language Policies and the Continua of Biliteracy: Implementation in Classroom and Community

The scenes from South Africa and Bolivia which opened this paper evoke broad sets of challenges at community and classroom levels. In the first instance, there are the challenges of confronting community attitudes favoring the language of power in the society, attitudes which are at odds with developmental evidence that children learn best from the starting point of their own language(s). There are also the challenges, at classroom level, of providing materials and interaction in multiple languages which are not necessarily spoken by all participants. In the continua of biliteracy model, the latter challenges relate to media and content of biliteracy, and the former to biliteracy development and contexts.

The *continua of biliteracy* is a comprehensive, ecological model I have proposed as a way to situate research, teaching, and language planning in multilingual settings. The continua of biliteracy model defines *biliteracy* as 'any and all instances in which communication occurs in two (or more) languages in or around writing' (Hornberger, 1990: 213) and describes it in terms of four nested sets of intersecting continua characterizing the contexts, media, content, and development of biliteracy (Hornberger, 1989a; Hornberger & Skilton-Sylvester, 2000). Specifically, it depicts the development of biliteracy along intersecting first language–second language, receptive–productive, and oral–written language skills continua; through the medium of two (or more) languages and literacies whose linguistic structures vary from similar to dissimilar, whose scripts range from convergent to divergent, and to which the developing biliterate individual's exposure varies from simultaneous to successive; in contexts that encompass micro to macro levels and are characterized by varying mixes along the monolingual–bilingual and oral–literate continua; and with content that ranges from majority to minority perspectives and experiences, literary to vernacular styles and genres, and decontextualized to contextualized language texts (see Figures 14.1 and 14.2).

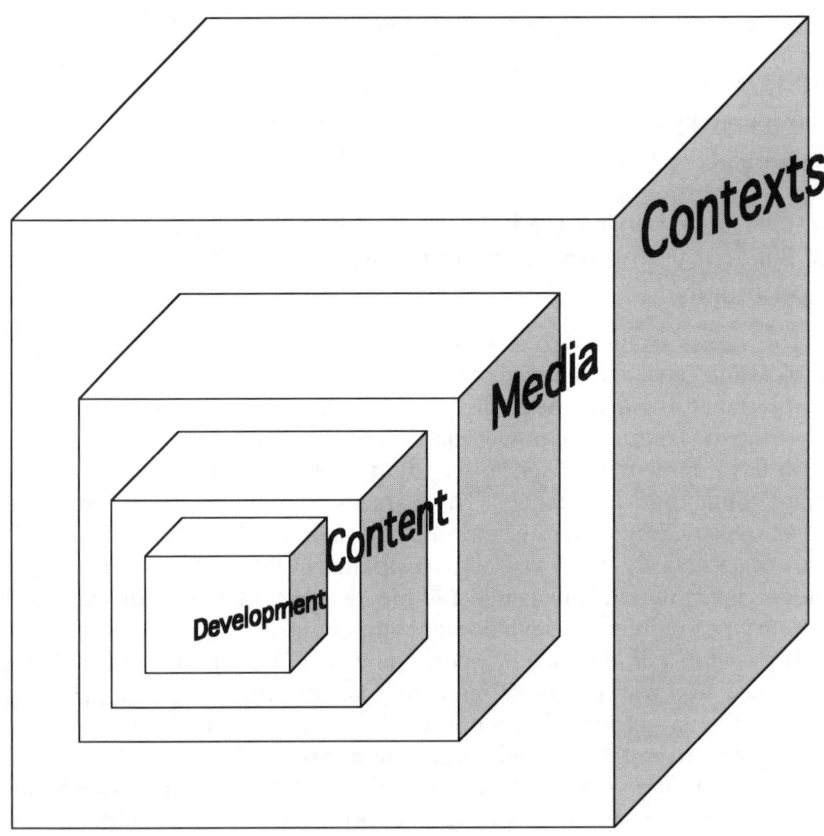

Figure 14.1 Nested relationships among the continua of biliteracy

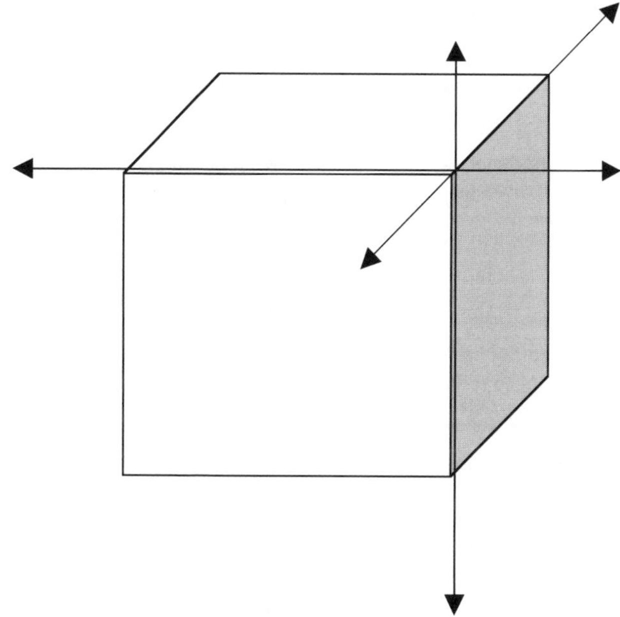

Figure 14.2 Intersecting relationships among the continua of biliteracy

The notion of continuum conveys that all points on a particular continuum are interrelated, and the model suggests that, the more their learning contexts and contexts of use allow learners and users to draw from across the whole of each and every continuum, the greater are the chances for their full biliterate development and expression (Hornberger 1989a: 289). Implicit in that suggestion is a recognition that there has usually *not* been attention to all points. In educational policy and practice regarding biliteracy, there tends to be an implicit privileging of one end of the continua over the other such that one end of each continuum is associated with more power than the other, for example written development over oral development (Figure 14.3 depicts the traditional power weighting assigned to the different continua). There is a need to contest the traditional power weighting of the continua by paying attention to and granting agency and voice to actors and practices at what have traditionally been the less powerful ends of the continua (Hornberger & Skilton-Sylvester, 2000).

As noted earlier, the continua of biliteracy model, like the ecology of language metaphor, is premised on a view of multilingualism as a

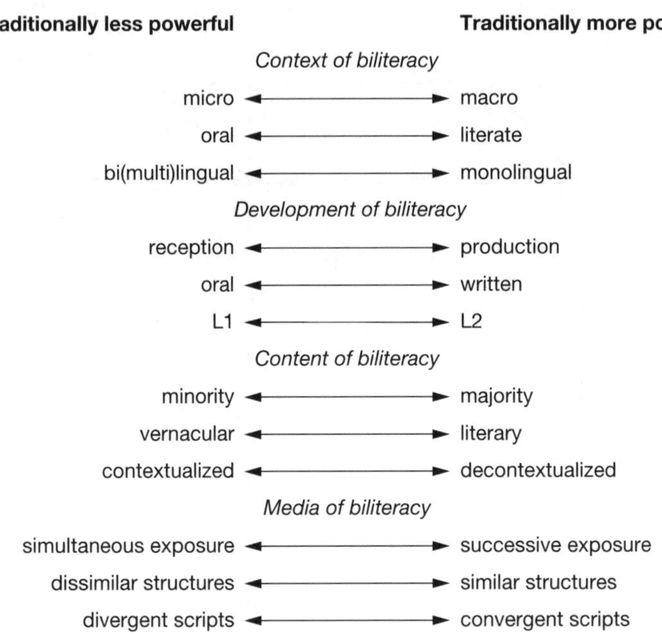

Figure 14.3 Power relations in the continua model

resource. Further, as the above overview reveals, the continua of biliteracy model also incorporates the language evolution, language environment, and language endangerment themes of the ecology of language metaphor. The very notion of bi- (or multi-)literacy assumes that one language and literacy is developing in relation to one or more other languages and literacies (i.e. *language evolution*); the model situates biliteracy development (whether in the individual, classroom, community, or society) in relation to the contexts, media, and content in and through which it develops (i.e. *language environment*); and it provides a heuristic for addressing the unequal balance of power across languages and literacies (i.e. for both studying and counteracting *language endangerment*).

Biliteracy development and contexts: Language and power in the community

Judy asked what one can do about negative community attitudes toward South Africa's multilingual language policy, referring specifically to Zulu, Xhosa, or other Black African parental demands for English-medium instruction for their children. The Bolivian Vice-Minister of Education suggested that the National Education Reform might have erred in placing too much emphasis on indigenous language instruction at the outset, while neglecting instruction in Spanish as a second language. In both cases, the zeal of educators and policy makers for teaching children literacy on the foundation of a language they already speak appears to be at odds with a popular demand for the language of power.

The challenge of popular demand for the societal language of power is a very real one in contexts all over the world, one not to be lightly dismissed. In terms of the continua model, case after case shows that societal power relationships tend to favor the macro, literate, and monolingual ends of the context continua; and national policy and school curricula tend to focus primarily on second language, written, productive skills in biliterate development.

My dissertation study in Puno, Peru in the 1980s had documented Quechua-speaking community members' resistance to the implementation of Quechua as a medium of instruction in the schools for ideological reasons, largely having to do with Spanish being seen as the language of formal education and thereby of access to socioeconomic mobility and power (Hornberger, 1987, 1988a, 1988b). I concluded that, unless the wider societal context could be geared toward valuing Quechua on a par with Spanish, 'policy failure' was inevitable; the schools, however well they might implement bilingual education, could not on their own counteract deep-seated ideologies favoring Spanish. Those same, enduring ideologies are the ones that the Bolivian Vice-Minister indexed in her opening comments at the workshop, referring to Quechua- and Aymara-speaking communities of Bolivia some 20 years after my study in Peru; these ideologies still thrive throughout indigenous communities of the Andes.

Several South African scholars have recently documented or made reference to a similar set of ideologies in Black African communities of South Africa. There, English is the language of power, undergirded not only by the worldwide hegemony of English but also by the heritage of apartheid education which left in its wake a deep suspicion of mother tongue education. Banda explores the paradox whereby black and coloured parents increasingly demand English-medium instruction even while academics and researchers agree that English-medium instruction is largely responsible for 'the general lack of academic skills and intellectual growth among blacks at high school and tertiary levels' (2000: 51); and he considers what would be needed to implement a truly additive bilingual policy. De Klerk undertook a survey and interview study in Grahamstown in the Eastern Cape Province, focusing on Xhosa-speaking parents' decisions to send their children to English-medium schools; among the reasons parents gave for choosing an English school for their children were the need for a better education, the recognition that English is an international language, and the hope that English would open the door to more job opportunities for their children (2000: 204–5).

Interestingly, both Bolivia and South Africa have opened up implementational space for popular participation in establishing school language policies, South Africa via the School Governing Boards and Bolivia via the *Comités* which are part of the Popular Participation provisions of the Education Reform. The goal is to empower parents to make their own decisions about what languages will be medium and subject of instruction in their children's schools. Yet, it would appear that the implementational space for popular participation is of little avail in advancing a multilingual language policy if it is not accompanied by popular participation in the ideological space as well.

In a study carried out in six newly integrated schools in Durban in Kwazulu-Natal Province, McKay and Chick (2001) found a pervasive English-only discourse (along with a decline of standards discourse and a one-at-a-time discourse of classroom interaction) affecting classroom teaching. English-only discourse was evident for example in principals' and teachers' rejection of the use of Zulu in classes other than in Zulu lessons, a practice for which they cited as reasons that students need to improve their English, that students need English for economic advancement, and that the African National Congress itself uses English as a means of reconciling rival ethnic groups (at odds with the ANC's publicly stated position) (Chick, 2000). Yet, the same study also found evidence of counter-discourses, namely a multicultural discourse and a collaborative, group work discourse. 'A number of teachers, primarily younger teachers, stated that they have discovered that the judicious use of Zulu in classrooms can be beneficial and are permitting the use of Zulu even when it runs counter to school policy' (2000: 7); and one teacher in a former Indian elementary school had started doing more group work since attending an in-service workshop on Outcomes-Based Education, finding it advantageous in that quick progress can be made when 'brighter and more fluent learners can explain to others exactly what is required' (2000: 12). Chick attributes the emergence of these new discourses among teachers to the ideological space which the new language policies opened up (2000: 13).

Similarly, while Bloch and Alexander acknowledge that the languages of South Africa are situated along the macro–micro context continuum with English at the most macro (powerful) end and the indigenous African languages clustered at the most micro (powerless) end, with

Afrikaans somewhere along the middle, they go on to make clear that what is at stake with the new multilingual language policy is the 'gradual shift of power towards the languages of the majority of the people, who continue in linguistic terms to be treated as a social minority' (2001: 5). They report on the work of their PRAESA[5] group at Battswood Primary School in Cape Town, where the 'intention is to develop, try out, and demonstrate workable strategies for teaching and learning, using additive bilingualism approaches'; they see themselves as working at the 'less powerful micro, oral, and multilingual ends [of the context continua] as [they] develop ways to challenge the power relations that exist at macro, literate, and monolingual English levels of the continua in the school and the wider society' (2001: 10).

What then does the continua model tell us about what to do in cases such as those depicted in the opening vignettes? The work of Chick and McKay and of Bloch and Alexander is consistent with the argument from the continua model that what is needed is attention to oral, multilingual interaction at the micro level of context and to learners' first language, oral, and receptive language skills development (that is, to the traditionally less powerful ends of the continua of context and development). It is consistent as well with the 'classroom success' story that my dissertation told alongside the 'policy failure' account referred to above (Hornberger, 1987). That is, despite the ideological privileging of Spanish for school contexts, Quechua-speaking children were seen then (and continue today) to clearly thrive from the greater participation in oral classroom interaction which receptive and productive use of their first language afforded them (Hornberger, 1988a, 1989b). In other words, what is needed is to find as many ways as possible to open up ideological spaces for multiple languages and literacies in classroom, community, and society. The continua model is a heuristic to assist in that ecological endeavor. We turn now to consideration of the media and content through which this can be accomplished and the power imbalance among languages subverted.

Media and content of biliteracy: Language and identity in the classroom

South African Professor Elizabeth encouraged her young pre-service teachers to speak and use their languages to discuss their own educational experiences and views in the classroom, thereby modeling a practice they might use with their own multilingual, multicultural students in the future. The Bolivian Curricular Development Unit experts sought to provide richly communicative and literature-based curriculum and materials for indigenous language speakers to learn Spanish, and raised questions about the implications of code-mixing practices in classroom interaction. In both cases, the negotiation of multiple languages, cultures, and identities among learners (and teachers) who bring different resources to the classroom, is at issue.

The challenge of negotiating across multiple languages, cultures, and identities is a very real one in classrooms all over the world, one not to be lightly dismissed. Yet, on the whole, educational policy and practice continues blithely to disregard the presence of multiple languages, cultures, and identities in today's classrooms. In terms of the continua model, case after case shows that majority, literary, decontextualized contents and similar, convergent, standard language varieties as successively acquired media of instruction, are the established and expected norms in educational systems everywhere.

Multilingual language policies offer a stunning contrast to these expectations, opening up a space where minority, vernacular, contextualized contents and identities can be introduced and a range of media – including dissimilar, divergent, nonstandard varieties as well as visual and other communicative modes – can be employed simultaneously in instruction. Andean teachers in a course I taught on bilingual intercultural education wrote narratives about some of their experiences along these lines. One teacher opened up a Mother's Day celebration to a child's recitation of a Quechua poem and another opened up her language class to the dramatization of a local story, using local materials and local music. In each case, the results were an impressive display of the learners' talents, accompanied by greater intercultural understanding of all those involved. These teachers made use of media and content that have historically been excluded from the school, and thereby subverted the power imbalance among the languages and literacies in the school environment (Hornberger, 2000: 191–2).

Pippa Stein writes along these lines in recounting experiences with two projects she has worked on with pre-service and in-service language teachers in Johannesburg, both of which encourage students' use of a range of representational resources in their meaning making, including the linguistic mode in its written and spoken forms, but also the visual, the gestural, the sonic, and the performative modes (paraphrasing Kress & Van Leeuwen, 1996). A reflective practitioner, she is exploring 'ways of working as a teacher using certain pedagogies which re-evaluate the value of a resource in the classroom,' specifically with the goal of ascribing equal value to resources brought by historically advantaged and historically disadvantaged students. Both the Performing the Literacy Archive

Project and the Photographing Literacy Practices Project focus on literacy because 'issues of literacy are at the heart of educational success in schools,' but in them the students 'explore meaning-making in multiple semiotic modes.' Drawing on her reflections and on written and video documentation of the students' work over the several years she has done these projects with language teachers, Stein shows how these pedagogies 'work with what students bring (their existing resources for representation) and acknowledge what [historically disadvantaged] students have lost.' As she puts it, it is 'the saying of the unsayable, that which has been silenced through loss, anger or dread, which enables students to re-articulate their relationships to their pasts. Through this process of articulation, a new energy is produced which takes people forward. I call this process of articulation and recovery re-sourcing resources' (Stein, in press).

The PRAESA group has been carrying out another effort at including practices at the traditionally less powerful ends of the content and media continua as resources in instruction in their work at Battswood Primary School with 30 Xhosa and 19 English/Afrikaans bilingual children, as they have progressed from their first days in Grade One up to the present, their third year of primary school. Bloch and Alexander report on this work in the following terms:

> Regarding the media of biliteracy, we encourage simultaneous exposure for the Xhosa and English speaking children to both languages with an emphasis on the children's first language . . . we are concentrating mainly on Xhosa and English, while at the same time not excluding Afrikaans. Our ongoing challenge, in terms of Xhosa language learning for the English/Afrikaans speakers is to try and inspire them enough, and teach the language in ways that motivate them to learn 'against the odds' of any real incentives which promote Xhosa as either necessary or even desirable in the wider society. (2001: 12)

As regards the content of biliteracy, 'the teachers have had to move from the safety of the decontextualised content of a rigid phonics-based part-to-whole skills programme to face the real evidence of what their pupils actually know and can do, thereby drawing on contextualised, vernacular, minority (i.e. majority) knowledge' (2001: 14–15).

To carry out these goals, they encourage oral, mother tongue and bilingual interaction; in Grade One, the teachers sang many songs and did rhymes with the whole class, typing up the Xhosa rhymes and songs and putting them in plastic sleeves with an English one on one side and Xhosa on the other so that the children could serve as readers to each other. They use interactive writing and journal writing, with the English- and Xhosa-speaking teachers and PRAESA staff members writing back to the children in their respective languages, a strategy which has proved to provide powerful motivation for the children's use of both languages in their writing. The teachers read daily stories in both Xhosa and English, and have collected an adequate selection of Xhosa and English picture storybooks, which they encourage the children to read in bilingual pairs. The PRAESA group has begun to identify numerous strengths which such practices develop in the children, while simultaneously confronting the fact that most scholastic assessment tools do not measure the kinds of metalinguistic and interpretive skills which particularly stand out in these children.

What then does the continua model tell us about what to do in cases such as those depicted in the opening vignettes? The work of Stein and of Bloch and Alexander is consistent with the argument from the continua model that what is needed is attention to the diversity of standard and nonstandard language varieties, orthographies, and communicative modes and the range of contextualized, vernacular, minority knowledge resources that learners bring to the classroom (that is, to the traditionally less powerful ends of the continua of media and content). It is consistent as well with the on-the-ground experience of the Bolivian and South African educators who find that multilingual interaction in the classroom is inevitable and desirable if multilingual learners are to be encouraged to participate – in the classroom, in academic success, and, ultimately, in a truly democratic society. In other words, what is needed is to find as many ways as possible to open up implementational spaces for multiple languages, literacies, and identities in classroom, community, and society. The continua model is a heuristic to assist in that ecological endeavor.

Conclusion

Bloch and Alexander express the hope that 'the window of opportunity will remain open for another few years and that the multiplication of such projects in different areas of South Africa involving all the different languages . . . will shift the balance of power in favour of those for whom ostensibly the democratic transition was initiated' (2001: 25). I share their optimism and their sense of urgency that we linguists and language educators must work hard alongside language planners and language users to fill the ideological and implementational spaces opened up by multilingual language policies; and as researchers to document these new discourses in action so as to keep those ecological policy spaces open into the future.

My sense of urgency about this is perhaps heightened because of recent accumulating events in my own country, where multilingual language policy spaces seem to be closing up at an accelerating rate and the one language–one nation ideology still holds tremendous sway. Analyzing the politics of official English in the 104th Congress of the United States, Joseph Lo Bianco writes of a US discourse which he designates *unum* and which is all about opposing multilingual excess and national disunity, i.e. about homogenization and assimilationism. Also present, he found, was a discourse of *pluribus*, about diversity and emancipation, i.e. about language pluralism (Lo Bianco, 2001). Both discourses have arguably always been present in the United States, waxing and waning with the times, an ideological tension captured succinctly in the US motto, *E pluribus unum*, 'out of many one,' from which Lo Bianco takes his designations.[6]

Though the United States traditionally has no national language policy, US language ideologies are evident in both national educational policy and state level language policies. In the latter half of the twentieth century, there have been ecological policy spaces for multilingualism and the discourse of *pluribus* in, for example, the national Bilingual Education Act, now of more than 30 years' standing, and in state language policies such as Hawaii's recognition of Hawaiian and English or New Mexico's of Spanish and English. Since 1980, however, when Hayakawa first introduced a proposed English Language Constitutional Amendment in Congress, the discourse of *unum* has been gaining ground as a growing number of states have passed English-only legislation.

Even more recently, the pace has picked up. At the state level, under the infamous Unz initiative, California and Arizona voters passed anti-bilingual education referenda in 1999 and 2000 respectively. In these states, multilingual language policies were thereby reversed (or severely curtailed) for ideological reasons before implementation could be fully realized, documented, and tested. In the debates surrounding passage of Proposition 227 in California, it became clear that (1) the public had very little understanding of what bilingual education really is; and (2) much of what passed for bilingual education in California was in fact not. The ideological discourse of *unum* prevailed over that of *pluribus*, with very little attention to the facts of institutional implementation.[7] At the national level, under the Bush administration, the Bilingual Education Act is undergoing threat of revision which would gut its potential to provide multilingual education for thousands of children who speak English as a second language. Instead, the emphasis is on 'moving them to English fluency' in a minimal number of years (National Association for Bilingual Education Action Alert, 23 April 2001; 3 May 2001). None of these trends bodes well for the pluralistic discourse of *pluribus* or a multilingual language ecology in the United States.

Happily, however, there is also a move afoot in recent years among US linguists and language educators to help solidify, support, and promote longstanding grassroots minority language maintenance and revitalization efforts in the United States, under the rubric of 'heritage languages.'[8] The Heritage Language Initiative, which has among its priorities 'to help the U.S. education system recognize and develop the heritage language resources of the country' and 'to increase dialogue and promote collaboration among a broad range of stakeholders' (http://www.cal.org/heritage/), has thus far sponsored one national research conference in 1999 with plans for another in 2002 (see Wiley & Valdés, 2000 for a selection of papers from the first conference). In the intervening years, a working group of scholars was convened to draft a statement of research priorities now being circulated to researchers and policy-makers (available in Wiley and Valdés 2000 and at www.cal.org/heritage); and a bi-national conversation on heritage/community languages between US and Australian scholars took place in Melbourne (http://www.staff.vu.edu.au/languageconf/).

This Heritage Language Initiative, supported by both the Center for Applied Linguistics and the National Foreign Language Center, is at least in part about resolving the longstanding language policy paradox whereby we squander our ethnic language resources while lamenting our lack of foreign language resources. It further seeks to draw together and provide visibility and support for the myriad and ongoing bottom-up efforts at rescuing and developing US indigenous and immigrant language resources (as documented in volumes such as Cantoni, 1996; Henze and Davis, 1999; Hornberger 1996; McCarty & Zepeda, 1995, 1998 on US indigenous languages; Ferguson & Heath, 1981; Fishman, 1966b; García & Fishman, 1997; Kloss, 1977; McKay & Wong, 1988, 2000; Pérez, 1998 on US (indigenous and) immigrant languages; Fishman, 1991, 2000; and May, 1999 on cases around the world including US indigenous and immigrant languages).

The Heritage/Community Language effort is one which, I believe, takes an ecological, resource view of indigenous, immigrant, ethnic, and foreign languages as living and evolving in relation to each other and to their environment and as requiring support lest any one of them become further endangered. As linguists and language educators, we need to fill as many ecological spaces as possible, both ideological and implementational, with efforts like these and the Andean and South African efforts mentioned above if we are to keep the multilingual language policy option alive, not only in Bolivia, South Africa, the United States, and Australia, but in all corners of our multilingual world.

Notes

* This article originally appeared in *Language Policy* 1 (1), 27–51 (2002), and is reprinted with permission of Kluwer Academic Publishers. It was first presented as a plenary talk at the Third International Symposium on Bilingualism, held at the University of the West of England, in Bristol, UK in April 2001. I am grateful to Stephen May and the members of the Organizing Committee for inviting me and providing the opportunity for me to pull these thoughts together; and I thank those present for their comments. I also thank Educational Linguistics Ph.D. student Mihyon Jeon for her thoughtful and detailed response and suggestions on an earlier version of the paper.

My gratitude goes to Professor Elizabeth Henning of Rand Afrikaans University for inviting and hosting me for a two-week visit in conjunction with the Qualitative Research in Education conference there. My thanks also go to Luis Enrique López, Director of PROEIB Andes (*Programa de formación en Educación Intercultural Bilingüe para los Paises Andinos*, Andean Graduate Program in Bilingual Intercultural Education) and to the Bolivian Ministry of Education for including me as participant in the La Paz *Taller* described in the Introduction.

1. The nine languages are: Ndebele, Northern Sotho, Southern Sotho, Swati, Tsonga, Tswana, Venda, Xhosa, and Zulu.
2. In my usage here, 'language educators' includes linguists and researchers on language education, language teachers, language teacher educators, and others; 'language planners' includes both top-down and bottom-up, organizational and individual agents of language planning; and 'language users' includes learners, parents, community members, and others. In other words, I take an inclusive view of those who should be involved in the efforts described here.
3. Van Lier 2000 cites Trim 1959 as the first reference to ecology of language.
4. In recent and forthcoming volumes (Huss *et al.*, 2001; Liddicoat & Bryant, 2001; Maffi, 2001; Nettle & Romaine, 2000; Skutnabb-Kangas, 2000), scholars posit an ecology of language in not only a metaphorical sense but also a literal one, explicitly linking the maintenance of linguistic and cultural diversity with the protection and defense of biological and environmental diversity. While I may share their views, that is not the focus of this paper.
5. PRAESA is the Project for the Study of Alternative Education in South Africa, directed by Neville Alexander and based at the University of Cape Town. The team at Battswood Primary School includes one PRAESA staff member (Carole Bloch), assisted sometimes by a post-graduate student, a Xhosa speaking teacher, Ntombizanele Nkence, and a resident Battswood teacher, Erica Fellies (Bloch & Alexander, 2001: 11).

6. Similarly, Cobarrubias identifies 'linguistic assimilation' and 'linguistic pluralism' as two typical language ideologies which have long co-existed in tension in the United States (1983: 63).
7. Similarly, May (2000), analyzing the Welsh case, writes that minority language policy must overcome both institutional and attitudinal difficulties in order to be successfully implemented at state level. That is, the minority language must be institutionalized in the public realm and it must gain attitudinal support from majority language speakers.
8. While the term 'heritage language' has been in use, particularly in Canada, since the early 1970s, a brief search in the *Linguistics and Language Behavior Abstracts* covering 1973 to 2001 shows that the term has been gaining significant ground in the US only in the last decade and in particular the last five years. Of 120 references, 100 date from 1991 or later; 68 of these from 1997 or later. While the majority of references are still to Canada's heritage languages, there is a growing number of references to US indigenous (e.g. Hawaiian, Navajo, Oneida, Siouan) and immigrant (e.g. Chinese, Korean, Italian, Spanish, Yiddish) languages. Meanwhile, as Colin Baker has noted, the term sometimes carries a negative connotation of pointing to the (ancient, primitive) past rather than to a (modern, technological) future (Baker and Jones, 1998: 509); for perhaps this reason and others, the preferred term in Australia is 'community languages' (Clyne, 1991; Horvath & Vaughn, 1991).

References

Baker, C. and Jones, S.P. (1998) *Encyclopedia of Bilingualism and Bilingual Education.* Clevedon, UK: Multilingual Matters.

Banda, F. (2000) The dilemma of the mother tongue: Prospects for bilingual education in South Africa. *Language, Culture and Curriculum* 13 (1), 51–66.

Barton, D. (1994) *Literacy: An Introduction to the Ecology of Written Language.* Oxford, UK: Blackwell Publishers.

Bloch, C. and Alexander, N. (2001) *A luta* continua!: The relevance of the continua of biliteracy to South African multilingual schools. Paper presented at Third International Bilingualism Symposium, Bristol, April.

Cantoni, G. (ed.) (1996) *Stabilizing Indigenous Languages.* Flagstaff, AZ: Northern Arizona University Center for Excellence in Education.

Chick, K. (2000) Constructing a multicultural national identity: South African classrooms as sites of struggle between competing discourses. Paper presented at Nessa Wolfson Colloquim, University of Pennsylvania, Philadelphia, USA.

Clyne, M. (1991) *Community Languages: The Australian Experience.* Melbourne: Cambridge University Press.

Cobarrubias, J. (1983) Ethical issues in status planning. In J. Cobarrubias (ed.) *Progress in Language Planning* (pp. 41–86). Berlin: Mouton.

de Klerk, V. (2000) To be Xhosa or not to be Xhosa . . . that is the question. *Journal of Multilingual and Multicultural Development* 21 (3), 198–215.

Ferguson, C.A. and Heath, S.B. (eds) (1981) *Language in the USA.* New York: Cambridge University Press.

Fishman, J.A. (1966a) Planned reinforcement of language maintenance in the United States: Suggestions for the conservation of a neglected national resource.

In J.A. Fishman (ed.) *Language Loyalty in the United States: The Maintenance and Perpetuation of non-English Mother Tongues by American Ethnic and Religious Groups* (pp. 369–411). The Hague: Mouton.

Fishman, J.A. (ed.) (1966b) *Language Loyalty in the United States: The Maintenance and Perpetuation of non-English Mother Tongues by American Ethnic and Religious Groups*. The Hague: Mouton.

Fishman, J.A. (1969) National languages and languages of wider communication in the developing nations. *Anthropological Linguistics* 11 (4), 111–35.

Fishman, J.A. (1991) *Reversing Language Shift: Theoretical and Empirical Foundations of Assistance to Threatened Languages*. Clevedon, UK: Multilingual Matters.

Fishman, J.A. (ed.) (2000) *Can Threatened Languages be Saved? 'Reversing Language Shift' Revisited.* Clevedon, UK: Multilingual Matters.

Freeland, J. (1996) The global, the national and the local: Forces in the development of education for indigenous peoples – the case of Peru. *Compare* 26 (2), 167–95.

Gal, S. (1989) Language and political economy. *Annual Review of Anthropology* 18, 345–67.

García, O. and Fishman, J.A. (eds) (1997) *The Multilingual Apple: Languages in New York City*. Berlin: Mouton.

Haugen, E. (1972) *The Ecology of Language*. Stanford, CA: Stanford University Press.

Henze, R. and Davis, K.A. (eds) (1999) Authenticity and identity: Lessons from indigenous language education. *Anthropology and Education Quarterly* 30 (1), entire issue.

Hornberger, N.H. (1987) Bilingual education success, but policy failure. *Language in Society* 16 (2), 205–26.

Hornberger, N.H. (1988a) *Bilingual Education and Language Maintenance: A Southern Peruvian Quechua Case*. Berlin: Mouton.

Hornberger, N.H. (1988b) Language ideology in Quechua communities of Puno, Peru. *Anthropological Linguistics* 30 (2), 214–35.

Hornberger, N.H. (1989a) Continua of biliteracy. *Review of Educational Research* 59 (3), 271–96.

Hornberger, N.H. (1989b) Pupil participation and teacher techniques: Criteria for success in a Peruvian bilingual education program for Quechua children. *International Journal of the Sociology of Language* 77, 35–53.

Hornberger, N.H. (1990) Creating successful learning contexts for bilingual literacy. *Teachers College Record* 92 (2), 212–29.

Hornberger, N.H. (ed.) (1996) *Indigenous Literacies in the Americas: Language Planning from the Bottom Up*. Berlin: Mouton.

Hornberger, N.H. (2000) Bilingual education policy and practice in the Andes: Ideological paradox and intercultural possibility. *Anthropology and Education Quarterly* 31 (2), 173–201.

Hornberger, N.H. and Skilton-Sylvester, E. (2000) Revisiting the continua of biliteracy: International and critical perspectives. *Language and Education: An International Journal*, 14 (2), 96–122.

Horvath, B.M. and Vaughan, P. (1991) *Community Languages: A Handbook*. Clevedon, UK: Multilingual Matters.

Huss, L., Camillen Grima, A. and King, K.A. (eds) (2003) *Transcending Monolingualism: Linguistic Revitalisation in Education*. Lisse: Swets & Zeitlinger.

Kaplan, R.B. and Baldauf, R.B. (1997) *Language Planning from Practice to Theory*. Clevedon, UK: Multilingual Matters.
Kloss, H. (1977) *The American Bilingual Tradition*. Rowley, MA: Newbury House.
Kress, G. and van Leeuwen, T. (1996) *Reading Images: The Grammar of Visual Design*. London: Routledge.
Liddicoat, A.J. and Bryant, P. (eds) (2001) Language planning and language ecology: A current issue in language planning. *Current Issues in Language Planning* 1 (3), entire issue.
Lo Bianco, J. (2001) What is the problem? A study of official English. Paper presented at the annual meetings of the American Association for Applied Linguistics, St Louis, Missouri.
Maffi, L. (2001) *On Biocultural Diversity: Linking Language, Knowledge, and the Environment*. Washington, DC: Smithsonian Institution Press.
May, S. (ed.) (1999) *Indigenous Community-Based Education*. Clevedon, UK: Multilingual Matters.
May, S. (2000) Accommodating and resisting minority language policy: The case of Wales. *International Journal of Bilingual Education and Bilingualism* 3 (2), 101–28.
May, S. (2001) *Language and Minority Rights: Ethnicity, Nationalism and the Politics of Language*. Essex, UK: Pearson Education.
McCarty, T.L. and Zepeda, O. (eds) (1995) Indigenous language education and literacy. *Bilingual Research Journal* 19 (1), entire issue.
McCarty, T.L. and Zepeda, O. (eds) (1998) Indigenous language use and change in the Americas. *International Journal of the Sociology of Language* 132, entire issue.
McKay, S. and Chick, K. (2001) Positioning learners in post apartheid South African schools: A case study of selected multicultural Durban schools. *Linguistics and Education* 12 (4), 393–408.
McKay, S.L. and Wong, S.C. (eds) (1988) *Language Diversity: Problem or Resource?* New York: Newbury House.
McKay, S.L. and Wong, S.C. (eds) (2000) *New Immigrants in the United States: Readings for Second Language Educators*. New York: Cambridge University Press.
Mühlhaüsler, P. (1996). *Linguistic Ecology: Language Change and Linguistic Imperialism in the Pacific Region*. London: Routledge.
Nettle, D. and Romaine, S. (2000) *Vanishing Voices: The Extinction of the World's Languages*. New York: Oxford University Press.
Pakir, A. (1991) Contribution to workshop on endangered languages, International Conference on Austronesian Linguistics, Hawaii (cited in Mühlhaüsler, 1996).
Pérez, B. (ed.) (1998) *Sociocultural Contexts of Language and Literacy*. Mahwah, NJ: Lawrence Erlbaum.
Phillipson, R. and Skutnabb-Kangas, T. (1996) English only worldwide or language ecology? *TESOL Quarterly* 30 (3), 429–52.
Ricento, T. (2000) Historical and theoretical perspectives in language policy and planning. *Journal of Sociolinguistics* 4 (2), 196–213.
Ruiz, R. (1984) Orientations in language planning. *NABE Journal* 8 (2), 15–34.
Skutnabb-Kangas, T. (2000) *Linguistic Genocide in Education – or Worldwide Diversity and Human Rights?* Mahwah, NJ: Lawrence Erlbaum.

Stein, P. (in press). Re-sourcing resources: pedagogy, history and loss in a Johannesburg classroom. In M. Hawkins (ed.) *Social/cultural Approaches to Language Learning, Teaching, and Teacher Education*. Clevedon, UK: Multilingual Matters.

Trim, J.L.M. (1959) Historical, descriptive and dynamic linguistics. *Language and Speech* 2, 9–25.

van Lier, L. (2000) From input to affordance: Social-interactive learning from an ecological perspective. In J.P. Lantolf (ed.) *Sociocultural Theory and Second Language Learning* (pp. 245–59). Oxford: Oxford University Press.

Voegelin, C. and Voegelin, F. (1964) Languages of the world: Native America Fascicle One. *Anthropological Linguistics* 6 (6), 2–45.

Wiley, T. and Valdés, G. (eds) (2000) Heritage language instruction in the United States: A time for renewal. *Bilingual Research Journal* 24 (4), entire issue.

Woolard, K. and Schieffelin, B.B. (1994) Language ideology. *Annual Review of Anthropology* 23, 55–82.

Afterword

BRIAN STREET

The articles in this book offer a critical exploration of the concept of 'continua of biliteracy,' enabling the reader to assess its value against a range of detailed accounts of policy and practice from different parts of the world. Since Hornberger's own work has made significant contributions to our understanding of the literacy practices of Spanish-speaking groups in both the United States and Latin America, it is not surprising that a number of the papers here continue that tradition. But we also have work from Wales, South Africa, India and 'Middle America.' The test of the robustness of the concept will depend on precisely such wide-ranging but in-depth accounts: if it holds up here, then we might predict that it will have utility even further afield. The book is topped and tailed by pieces by Nancy Hornberger herself; an original version of the 'Continua' paper (RER) and a 'revisiting' of it with Skilton-Sylvester (LE). Hornberger concludes the volume nicely with a comparison between bilingual programmes in South Africa and Bolivia and uses this to reinforce one of the natural science metaphors that sustain the original concept – 'an ecological approach.'

To remind ourselves of Hornberger's own most recent summary of the continua (in the final chapter of this volume):

> The *continua of biliteracy* is a comprehensive, ecological model I have proposed as a way to situate research, teaching, and language planning in multilingual settings. The continua of biliteracy model defines *biliteracy* as 'any and all instances in which communication occurs in two (or more) languages in or around writing' . . . and describes it in terms of four nested sets of intersecting continua characterizing the contexts, media, content, and development of biliteracy . . . . Specifically, it depicts the development of biliteracy along intersecting first language–second language, receptive–productive, and

> oral–written language skills continua; through the medium of two (or more) languages and literacies whose linguistic structures vary from similar to dissimilar, whose scripts range from convergent to divergent, and to which the developing biliterate individual's exposure varies from simultaneous to successive; in contexts that encompass micro to macro levels and are characterized by varying mixes along the monolingual–bilingual and oral–literate continua; and with content that ranges from majority to minority perspectives and experiences, literary to vernacular styles and genres, and decontextualized to contextualized language texts.

The 'continua,' then, represent an attempt at delineating the factors that need to be taken into account in understanding literacy variety across different languages. Recent books (e.g. Martin-Jones & Jones, 2000) have drawn attention to the fact that New Literacy Studies have not taken sufficient account of multilingualism, whilst multilingual studies have not taken sufficient account of the literacy dimension. We can now point out the biliteracy papers that put the two fields together: there is indeed a gap in the field and this work makes a start in showing how it could be filled. The volume is authoritative, empirically well grounded in detailed examples from diverse contexts and addresses some key theoretical issues to which it adds significantly. Most of the authors are happy to invoke the continua and to claim that it provides a helpful language of description for their own work. Some go further and suggest that the framework offers a way of 'seeing' aspects that might otherwise remain hidden, if not to themselves then certainly to policy makers. The public discourses on language planning and on literacy tend to be rooted in more traditional, functionalist and uni-dimensional frameworks that fail to bring together the complex features signalled by the continua and also fail to offer the more nuanced account provided by the continua's ability to locate a given dimension along a continuum.

In this Afterword, I will adopt the stance of a 'critical friend,' raising some questions that the model and its application may need to address. I attempt to pull together some of the threads and suggest issues that will need to be taken into account as the idea attempts to broaden its appeal. Rather than attempting a summary of the articles themselves, I briefly offer my 'take' on the way in which the chapters in this book make use of the continua framework, bringing out the principles and in some cases the problems that arise in some cases and invoking the critical questions raised.

Some Questions from a 'Critical Friend'

In all of the chapters, the question arises, how much does the continua framework add to what we already know from the variety of social perspectives on literacy, language policy and multilingualism that the authors cite? One answer is that most of the authors are attempting to use the continua to make an alliance between their own theoretical frameworks and the continua. We are exposed to language-policy ideology; New Literacy Studies; multilingualism; academic literacies; translingualism; cultural theories of reading and writing; funds of knowledge; written discourse accent; ethnography of communication; 'ritual'; critical reflection and discourse analysis; hybridization; and ecology of language. Whilst each may proceed their own way anyway, what the continua framework offers is an overall, synthesizing device, a kind of check list but also a kind of ideological frame that asserts the importance of the different 'continua' and of the different ends of each continuum. In that sense, the book offers much that is familiar to many readers whilst probably bringing to bear something new for each reader. The whole, in a sense, is greater than the sum of its parts. We should, then, be looking to the overall accounts by the various authors, rather than to the model in isolation, as the contribution of the volume.

However, questions remain regarding the relationship between the various factors and components in the model. The ways in which these factors are interrelated were, in the original account (RER), perhaps a little over elaborate and may have confused a number of readers – are they at similar levels of analysis and if not what planes are they located in and how can they be described and related to each other at an empirical level? The later article (LE) adds further 'perspectives' which are 'complementary and overlapping' – international perspectives and critical perspectives. In addition, 'content' is added to the continua. Each of the points is relevant and important – and in some senses were implicitly present in the first account, so this version is making them explicit with apt illustrative data – but in another sense this can make the elaborated model even more complex and difficult to grasp. Perhaps some theoretical position on determination is being called for – do certain dimensions of the continua override and determine others (Cahnmann suggests a possibility here, see below)? If so, on what grounds? Or is it all just a list of factors that could go on for ever? How far are the continua simply a kind of holding device for facilitating discussions around broader issues of identity, power, agency, policy, etc.? Some readers may complain that having evoked these terms the authors should develop them further at a theoretical level in the model itself. Whilst, for instance, the continua statements do indicate the importance of 'power,' what theoretical account is offered?

It is suggested that 'in every continuum, one end-point is firmly planted in a position of 'power.' The authors argue that in policy and educational circles one end of the continua is privileged over the other. They feel that making this explicit will help address power imbalances by 'paying attention to and granting agency' to 'the powerless end of the continua.' Those working in the area of power and literacy (Gee, 1999; Luke, 1994; Street, 2001; etc.) might dispute the model of power being put forward here, as though it were defined by quantity and position – at the end of continua – rather than, in a Foucauldian sense, infusing the networks of relations. In practice, many of the authors do attempt to take account of this aspect of the power dimension, invoking a range of sources such as Gee and Fairclough to do so.

With respect to stance, there is an implicit audience being addressed by addressors who are implicitly themselves in a position of power (able to 'grant agency'). In the text, the agents being called upon to 'draw on all points of the continua' and to 'pay attention and grant agency' to actors (e.g. by giving voice to oral dimensions of bilingual interaction) are presumed to be those in control of curricula and policy. But if we want to think through the continua with respect to the ethnographic realities of participants themselves, then calling upon them to take account of the 'powerless,' etc. seems odd. The question of the agent for 'taking account' may need further development – is it policy makers, theorists (in a sense the authors are talking to themselves and to academic colleagues), or participants in different cultural contexts, in each of which the relations of power will be different? This can be made explicit and the text adjusted accordingly but there remains then the theoretical question of how general is the account of power or it is just a 'factor' to be taken into account – is this a 'theory' of biliteracy or simply a prescriptive address to particular audiences of what they 'should' do? Is it a policy position or an elaboration of theory?

At the methodological level, the ethnographic sensitivity of the accounts used as illustration clearly indicates the importance for researchers of 'taking account' of multiple levels in addressing biliteracy – the difference between the 'thin' description of Solomon Islands literacies cited in LE and thick descriptions of the kind evident in this volume is certainly testimony to the value of the ethnography of communication and New Literacy Studies traditions in which the continua are rooted, with their attention to ethnographic detail and the more recent concern with power relations.

But what is being added to the already significant literature here? I think the authors are saying here that these researchers have looked at the 'less powerful' groups in a particular institutional hierarchy and that policy makers too should do so. But again there is a problem with the reification of power and its association with fixed groups: the people themselves may in other ways consider themselves to be deploying power as well as being its subjects. In fact, a number of the authors, as I indicate below, do exactly this. The question remains, though, whether the framework itself takes sufficient account of this.

Oddly, a final criticism of some of the ways that the continua of biliteracy has been taken up is that it may be applied to language relations and policies more broadly and not focus precisely on the literacy dimension. In that sense, it has a tendency to collapse into language ideology positions.

I will attempt to apply some of these questions as I briefly offer a 'take' on the chapters themselves.

A Personal 'Take' on the Chapters

Colin Baker, in his detailed account of language policy with respect to Welsh, notes that 'while the Continua does not provide an explanation [for the movement from minority language monoliteracy to biliteracy nor of the power dimensions in that movement, nevertheless], its dimensions provide the spectacles through which to seek causes and catalysts of historical change in literacy practices.' Likewise, 'simple explanations of change (e.g. changes in religious practices) need to be joined by analyzing power relations (e.g. a decline in the power of the pulpit), and a movement to similar infrastructures (e.g. mass media) supporting literacy in English and Welsh.' The continua framework, then, provides spectacles through which to observe such processes and raises questions that remain silent in dominant policy discourses. 'Whereas the standard history typically seeks to maintain differences and boundaries between Welsh and English literacies, the move to biliteracy has surely been helped by similar language scripts.' From a historical perspective, the addition of a power dimension to the account of change brings to the foreground such issues as 'the power of conformity in local chapels, the resistance to the English invader, the political marginalization of Welsh speaking miners and farmers in remote rural areas.' Likewise, in the contemporary situation, the power dimension is evident at institutional levels in, for instance, power struggles over mass communications, the rise of UK newspapers and international WWW links. 'The Continua prompts us to ask an extensive and expansive set of questions about literacy evolution, seeking re-framing and re-analysis and avoiding a standard description or a simplistic conclusion.'

With respect to curriculum issues and policy as the English National Curriculum has been adapted to take account of Welsh speaking children, attention to the continua forces policy makers to address issues of power that otherwise remain hidden. The continua, says Baker, provide the analytical apparatus for a powerful critique of the Welsh National Curriculum approach to literacy in English and Welsh. The continua indicate the very limited contexts in which Welsh National Curriculum literacy practice is situated. Indeed, there is a highly decontextualized view of literacy. For instance, while some credence is given to the oral–literate continuum, no credence is given to the monolingual–bilingual continuum. Likewise, in the complex area of 'translanguaging' and 'transliteracy,' which Baker adapts from Williams' work, the continua appear to have both anticipated some of the key concepts and to offer a way of combining the many features of this complex interplay. 'The new Continua's dimension of power relations is vital to situating transliteracy in its political reality of the majority/minority relationship in Wales. That is, when translanguaging and transliteracy engage all the dimensions of the Continua, its aims of full biliteracy in students may be more maximally achieved.' If we are to address the policy issues raised by these practices, then we need conceptual tools that address the range of components. For Baker, certainly, the continua provides such a frame.

Likewise, with respect to the situation in South Africa, *Carole Bloch and Neville Alexander* use the continua as a way of articulating a policy slide – towards the former colonial language – that they had already identified; the framework offers them a helpful language of description for developing their account of this: 'To put the situation in terms of contexts for biliteracy, it ought to be clear that what is at stake at the powerful ends of the continua is the gradual shift of power towards the languages of the majority of the people, who continue in linguistic terms to be treated as a social minority. At this level, many different political and social scenarios are possible.' They conclude that: 'The continua of biliteracy model provides a framework for reflection and action on multilingual education work in South Africa' and proceed to exemplify this with respect to their detailed account of 'one of the few biliteracy programmes in the country.' Their policy conclusion, using the language of the continua framework, is that, whilst the less powerful end is significant, we should also be addressing 'more strongly the need for movement of African languages to the powerful ends of the continua.'

Much of this comes, of course, from the New Literacy Studies on which the continua avowedly draw. Indeed, Bloch and Alexander lay the ground for their own policy interventions in these terms: 'Developing strategies for classroom literacy teaching, which view literacy as socio-cultural practice (Gee, 1990; Heath, 1983; Street, 1995), must begin from the premise that few South Africans have a well-developed culture of reading and writing in any language.' Moll and Goodman are also cited here (and by many other authors in the volume) and in some ways the programme will have a familiar ring to those working in NLS and in social and ethnographic approaches to literacy generally. What the continua adds, they claim, is the 'bi-' dimension: 'Our working definition of biliteracy concurs with Hornberger's definition of biliteracy as referring to "any and all instances in which communication occurs in two (or more) languages in or around writing" (Hornberger, 1990: 213). The children all receive simultaneous exposure to both Xhosa and English texts and to reading and writing in both languages.' In their classroom interventions, they 'encourage oral, mother tongue and bilingual interaction.' Indeed, one wonders whether some 'translanguaging' may be already going on and certainly be appropriate as policy in this context as in the Welsh one described by Baker.

Chapters by *Viniti Basu* and *Holly Pak* further challenge the standard bilingual literature with reference to the continua, addressing the relationship between mother tongue (MT) and second language (L2). In the case of Pak, her provocative title, 'When MT is L2: The Korean church school as a context for cultural identity,' questions the boundaries between these two categories, showing how what counts as MT/L2 varies with context and participant, variables brought to the fore by the continua model. She describes research in an ethnic mother tongue school, in this case a Korean language school, similar to the many Korean language schools run by Korean churches in the Korean community of Philadelphia and more generally those set up by minority language groups for culture and language education of their children in other parts of the US. She describes the Korean church and school (KCS) as a context that foregrounds Koreanness; how this context is perceived differently by the adults and children; and how, in this context, manipulation of the continua of development, media and content of biliteracy reveals the students' negotiation of their Korean identity.

Using data collected through informal and formal interviews with adults and children, and through classroom observation and recording, she shows how in each of the four sets of continua – context, media, development and content – the power relations between English and Korean are reversed from outside the Korean church context; and how the tension from this reversal is revealed through the children's expression of cultural identity that was not always in line with their parents' expectations. The adults wanted the children to identify themselves as Korean and not to lose their Korean identity, so the children were taught or pressured into using Korean as a means to the larger goal of preserving Korean identity. Pak comments that, in terms of the continua of context, the KCS inverts the usual power relations in the US society (where English monolingualism and literacy are dominant at the macro level); here, instead, the KCS seeks to define its own (macro) context where Korean monolingualism and literacy are privileged. This was brought out by the exceptional case of her own participation in the church as a non-Korean-speaking adult: 'The shift in the language of power between the context of the Korean church and the context of American society was most evident both when a non-Korean-speaking adult attempted to participate in the church, and when the monolingual Korean-speaking adults of the church tried to learn the language of the American society, English.' However, for children and teenagers who spoke English, there was little advantage to speaking Korean: 'During the service, if the children's pastor led songs in Korean, and if [these] children needed to sing in Korean in front of the adults, then there was a disadvantage to not knowing Korean. However, outside of these adult-initiated activities, the children and teenagers were comfortable in English. Interaction with adults during the time at church was limited, and beyond an initial greeting, could generally be avoided.' Her conclusion to these complex counter examples of the experience of minority/dominant status with respect to language use is that 'the advantages that come from speaking a society's dominant language do not hold in a setting where a minority language is the norm. However, even within that minority language setting, the weighting of power for the minority language is not a constant, but depends on subgroups' shared values.' It is here that the continua model adds to the general nostrums of bilingual education and research, which have tended to essentialize the relationship between minority/majority status and language use. Invoking the oral–literate continuum, for instance, Pak shows how the value of written material in each language varies for different participants and in different settings.

Across all of the continua, indeed, the interpretation of the context of the church differed for different participants: 'For most of the adults, the context was defined as (a) monolingual Korean as opposed to bilingual in Korean and English or monolingual in English; (b) a macro setting distinct and often seemingly set off from the American setting; and (c) broadly concerned with both oral and literate Christian Korean traditions. For the children, the church setting was (a) bilingual in Korean and English; (b) at the micro level, embedded in the larger church context, which in turn was embedded in the larger American context; and (c) marked by both oral and literate practices, with an emphasis on the oral.' The Korean church and school emphasized the macro, literate, and monolingual sides of each of the context continua. Whilst in the church context for adults Korean took the side of power as opposed to English in wider society, the children were aware of the power of English and in rare cases insisted on the appropriateness of English as opposed to Korean even in church contexts. In this conflict, Pak suggests, we see negotiation of identity: in her own evocative phrase, 'It's as if the walls of the church were a little thinner for the children than for the adults.' She concludes that the development, media and content of biliteracy are all re-framed in keeping with this space for Korean identity.

In another bilingual context, that of India, *Basu* explores the literacy practices regarding L2 acquisition in two government-run schools in New Delhi, basing her research on interviews with teachers and students, classroom observations and analyses of students' written work and their text books. In one of the schools, SKV, the second language of the children is English, which is also the medium of instruction, and their first language is Hindi. In the other school, NNBV, the L2 is Hindi, which is the medium of instruction, and the L1 is a dialect of Hindi. 'Thus both schools have some sort of a bilingual education policy.' These bilingual policies are represented as a great step forward in empowering the masses, but Basu notes that, despite this far-reaching goal, the bilingual education program of the SKV is not able to make its students as proficient in the L2 – English – as the NNBV school where the L2 is Hindi. As a firm believer in the values of bilingual education, Basu was drawn to investigate this discrepancy.

Calling upon the continua framework, she invokes in particular the continua of biliterate media focusing on the relationship between mother tongue (MT) and medium of instruction (MI). The biliterate media continua are made up of three sets of sub-continua: convergent and divergent scripts; similar and dissimilar structures; and successive and simultaneous exposure. A major aspect of the relationship between MT and MI is whether there is transfer or interference between the two. In relation to this, Basu uses her detailed field data in the New Delhi schools to address the questions: Is lower proficiency the result of interference between MT and MI? If not then what are the other variables which could be responsible for this lower proficiency? She notes

Hornberger's suggestion that the more a learner can access all points on the continua the more easily he/she can acquire literacy. In the present case, the continua of biliterate media for the children of the NNBV school, the similarity of structures between the dialect they speak and the L2 Hindi being taught helps the children of the NNBV to acquire the L2. The children of the SKV, on the other hand, are close to the dissimilar structures end of the continuum – in this case between English and Hindi – and this, coupled with other variables about their English usage, causes interference between L1 and L2 and may help explain poor acquisition of L2. This then speaks to the broader issue of the relatedness of mother tongue (MT) and medium of instruction (MI), a key concern in bilingual education.

However, it is not simply the closeness of MT to MI that is the key issue, so much as the other variables in the environment that the continua model enables us to see. In this case, Basu suggests that the reason why similarity between MT and MI is an advantage for the children of the NNBV is because they do not have any reinforcements at home. In the NNBV the children come from a very print-poor environment. All the language learning that takes place for them happens in school and 'this might not have been adequate had the two languages been very different.' Similarly for the SKV children there is no reinforcement at home of English, and 'the vast difference between English and Hindi does not help these children to master the language.' She concludes, in line with Hornberger's argument, that the children at SKV are not becoming proficient in the L2, English, 'because they are not able to access many of the points on the Continua of Biliteracy. For instance, they are too close to (a) the dissimilar structures end of the continuum in the Continua of biliterate media and (b) the decontextualized end in the Continua of biliterate content. This is coupled with the fact that the teachers in the SKV do not have fluency in English, the children come from poor families and their parents do not speak any English. In the case of the NNBV children, who become very fluent in Hindi, their literacy practices are located such that they are able to access more points on the continua of biliteracy.' This, coupled with several other contextual factors described in the paper, ensures that the children of the NNBV become fluent in Hindi. The continua model has enabled Basu to offer explanations for differential performance that bring in further factors than those usually considered in the bilingual literature.

Diana Schwinge's focus on recent trends in American education for schools to adopt standardized curricula, like the Success for All reading program, raises questions of policy that, again, the continua framework seems well placed to articulate. Some bilingual education teachers in the US, she suggests, act as bottom-up language and literacy planners by adapting and elaborating on the suggested activities and the content of the mandated programs to better enable their students to become bilingual, biliterate and bicultural. She examines the curricular modifications made by two elementary school teachers using the model of the continua of biliteracy as a framework, focusing especially on the content and development continua. Like other authors, she uses ethnographic data to provide examples of how two elementary school bilingual education teachers who teach a mandated curriculum utilize the various linguistic, cultural and textual resources that are available in their bilingual classrooms to help ensure that their classroom instruction is comprehensible, draw upon the community's local funds of knowledge, and enable students to successfully become bilingual and biliterate.

Again, Schwinge is calling upon a range of sources, including Moll, NLS and the multilingual literature in ways already familiar. What the framework brings, in this case, is its use as a model for analyzing teaching, research and language planning in multilingual settings, with a particular focus on the content continua and the development continua. In policy terms what the framework adds is an insistence on all of the dimensions being brought to bear: 'while the modes of expression and content represented by each end of the continua are not usually accorded equal time and respect in school, the model of the continua of biliteracy suggests that the more the learning context allows learners to draw from across the whole of each and every continuum, the greater the chances for the full development of biliteracy. . . . By integrating the weaker and stronger ends of the continua when they plan lessons, teachers can create a more appropriate and more effective learning experience that is more likely to draw on the large variety of different alternatives and options that are available in bilingual literacy events.' As in other chapters, Schwinge sees the major contribution of the framework as its synthesizing capacity: 'using the continua of biliteracy to examine a single aspect of a literacy event may not capitalize on the multi-dimensionality that is one of the strengths of the theoretical construct of the continua of biliteracy.'

The creative tension in addressing the parts or the whole comes out again here, as Schwinge attempts to isolate particular events and points out that this is the way in which teachers learn to gradually incorporate the whole framework. From this perspective she sees some hope for teachers otherwise strangled by the centralized and mandated curricula currently being imposed: by looking closely at particular literacy events it may be possible for teachers to adapt and elaborate and to build upon pupils' own funds of knowledge and local language skills, such as in the teachers' use of written projects: 'The result of these assignments was projects that were presented in a formal school-related genre, but that contained content that was related to the students' minority community.' By focusing on the content continuum and in particular the use of minority content, vernacular texts and contextualizing texts, Schwinge is able to identify those features of the teachers' practice that could provide a basis for a fuller range of the continuum: practice and theory combined. Moreover, the holistic focus offered by the framework enables Schwinge to identify aspects of the practice that have not been so strongly highlighted in earlier accounts of such work. For instance, she brings out the 'hybridization' evident in use of forms – or modes as Kress might term them – incorporating language skills, semiotic modalities and linguistic codes. The work of the teachers she describes evidently recalls that of Moll and Diaz, 'but while these authors did not discuss their design of their new method of teaching literacy as a hybrid practice, it is quite clear that their approach involved a strategic mixing of language skills, semiotic cues, and linguistic codes in order to help enable students to understand a text that would otherwise be beyond their reading level.' Again the framework adds dimensions to complementary theoretical perspectives and enables us to see the larger picture.

Mihyon Jeon's chapter depicts a comprehensive rationale for TWI (Two-Way Immersion) program policies in the United States by locating them in the context of language-policy ideologies and analyzing them through the continua of biliteracy model. The author sees continua of biliteracy as having 'predictive and explanatory powers' and tests this out with respect to a detailed account of Korean–English TWI program policy as a language policy type. As with other authors, she combines this approach with a contribution from other theoretical perspectives, in this case theories of language-policy ideology which, as we see in other chapters, are closely woven in with the continua framework. TWI programs are defined as a program type that integrates language minority and language majority students for all or most of the day, with the goals of promoting high academic achievement, bilingual development and multicultural understanding for all students. Such programmes also attempt 'to create an environment that promotes linguistic and ethnic equality and fosters a positive cross-cultural attitude.' What, then, does the continua approach add that is not already catered for in the theories currently applied to TWI programmes?

Traditional language-acquisition theories have considerable limitations in this context, says Jeon, especially with respect to the new programme goal of multicultural understanding. The continua of biliteracy and language-policy theory, on the other hand, can provide a more comprehensive rationale for TWI program policies. In particular, Jeon evokes the content and media continua in examining curriculum policy and language-acquisition policy. These two sets of continua are, she says, 'useful in examining the actual implementation process of language-acquisition policy,' but she intentionally restricts her discussion to the policy-setting level. In terms of the goals of language-acquisition policy, then, the one-language-only policy has the goal of developing only the majority language, emphasizing written language and production skills. The power weighting of the one-language-only policy is toward the right-hand end of the continua of development of biliteracy. In contrast, multilingual language policy premised on a linguistic-pluralism ideology allows equal power toward both ends of the development of biliteracy continua, aiming for learners' full biliterate development in receptive–productive and oral–written language skills. 'Transforming the traditional power weighting of the continua of biliteracy makes a difference not only in learners' biliterate development, but also in types of power relationships between majorities and minorities within a school and broadly within a society.'

From this perspective, the application of the continua framework has raised much broader issues than those addressed by either language acquisition policies or even by linguistic-pluralism ideology . It has forced us – and she hopes the policy makers – to consider who has the power to define such policy and the relation of minority/majority communities. This leads to a theoretical claim that other research of this kind could fruitfully develop: 'By transforming the way of weighting power along the continua of biliteracy, the coercive power relationships will be transformed into collaborative power relationships.' This is expressed more as a hope than a demonstrated process and recalls the problems I raised above about the ways in which power is being analyzed: but from the perspective of the book as a whole it can be taken as indicative of the kind of theoretical and policy issues that arise from applying the continua framework. As Jeon states at the end: 'I conclude that the continua of biliteracy model, incorporated with the notion of language-policy ideology, provides descriptive power to depict the details of the policies, predictive power to anticipate language-acquisition policy outcomes, and explanatory power to elucidate why certain outcomes are anticipated.' These are large claims but they again demonstrate the productivity of the framework for helping researchers and policy makers to think outside of their immediate context.

Again the argument is in favour of addressing the full range of the continua: 'allowing learners to draw on all points of the continua of biliteracy through weighting equal power toward both ends of the continua.' This weighting will, Jeon hopes, help the policy to 'promote secure majorities/minorities and a collaborative power relationship between these groups as well as full development of learners' biliteracy.' This, then, provides the rationale for the program's goals that appeared to be missing when viewed from the narrower perspective of dominant policy and theory perspectives. The model thus has both descriptive and predictive power and offers a theoretical clue to how case studies, of the kind Jeon provides but also that occur throughout the volume, can be used to generate general theory.

Carmen I. Mercado is one of the authors to focus closely on the literacy issue, against a tendency I draw attention to above for the literacy dimension to collapse into language ideology positions. She looks at biliteracy development among Latino youth in New York City communities. Whereas researchers have paid considerable attention to the literacy skills of emergent bilinguals, less interest has been shown in those who have already developed bilingual skills but still fail to write in ways that a native speaker would. She cites McKay who describes such non-native features as 'written discourse accent,' which she defines as a lack of proficiency in grammar, word choice, cohesion, rhetorical organization and topic development. Again, the continua framework is called upon to help deal with the complexity of this situation. She might also have invoked the academic literacies framework (Jones *et al.*, 2001), which considers the discursive and deeper aspects of academic writing that frequently prevent even native speakers from accessing 'written discourse accent.' As with other authors, the continua framework can usefully be harnessed to complementary ones: it is the combination of complementary frameworks, rather than any one in isolation, that provides the productive direction.

Like other authors, Mercado calls upon a strong tradition of home/school studies and interventions, typified by the work of Luis Moll and his colleagues (1992) and considers in the light of these what is the significance of shifts between home and school language and literacy practices, especially when these are respectively Spanish and English. 'Understanding the incipient forms of biliteracy emerging from social uses of literacy in homes and communities moves us toward unraveling the dormant potential that home/community practices have for learning in school and which may be harnessed to promote the development of literacies in and for academic purposes in English and Spanish, and to shape individual and collective destinies.' As in Hull and Schultz's (2002) recent aptly named book *'School's Out,'* she argues for the importance of home literacies in the development of schooled practice, against the dominant trend to value primarily the schooled variety and to see community language and literacy as somehow interfering with this development (see also Street and Street, 1991 for an account of the 'schooling of literacy').

Despite the complex histories of migration of Spanish-speaking peoples across the Americas, 'the bilingual and biliterate potential of Latino youth remains, for the most part, invisible or discredited in settings where students' bilingualism and biliteracy is neither understood nor valued by bilingual and non-bilingual educators.' How to build on these and at the same time facilitate access for Latino students to schooled literacies, writing in particular, was the problem Mercado and her colleagues on a middle school project in NY attempted to address. These literacies 'play vital gatekeeping functions in creating or limiting access to a post-secondary education which is essential to increase the life chances of these students. Latino students are not usually exposed to the forms and functions of literacy (especially writing) likely to increase those chances.' The project's solution was not simply to deliver schooled literacies direct, but rather to enable the students to recognise the literacy dimensions of their own community practices and to build on them. This involved both valorizing of Spanish and recognition of the kinds of social science practices that enable their communities to locate, document and legitimize local knowledge on social issues. Biliteracy, then, was the route to scaffolding for the students the writing skills needed for higher levels of the education system. The author defines this process in terms of the continua framework: 'In terms of the continua, these practices were directed toward the minority, vernacular, and contextualized ends of the continua of biliterate content.' As with other authors, the ideological commitment is, on the one hand, towards the ends of the continua usually marginalized but, more broadly, to a reframing of the dominant discourse so that the full range of the continua become the framing concept for policy and practice, rather than the dominant emphasis on the majority, standard and decontextualized poles. At the same time, again like other authors, complementary perspectives and theory – in this case the 'funds of knowledge' perspective and perhaps implicitly the 'academic literacies' perspective in its US guise at the more radical end of the College Composition tradition – are linked to the continua and new insights and inspirations for practice emerge. From a language policy perspective, there is the recognition that the importance of English is not weakened by drawing upon knowledge of Spanish; and from a literacies perspective, there is the recognition that local literacies can be a fruitful source for the development of the specific registers associated with academic literacy practices. The power of biliteracy is being harnessed by the participants in the project to broaden the communicative repertoires of Latino students and at the same time the power of the model of biliteracy is being harnessed to explicate their experiences and locate them in a broader context.

Felicia Lincoln starts from a similar position to Mercado in recognizing that even where students have adequate dual language facility there is sometimes academic failure in the school system. She provides a case analysis of language minority students in a US public high school in rural Arkansas, using the continua of biliteracy to examine and understand their struggles and to predict ways to enhance their agency. Like other authors, she acknowledges that the issue is not so much language ability as empowerment, voice and discourse, 'how to allow their voices to inform and impact their educational experiences.' The continua can highlight this issue both conceptually and in terms of policy interventions. Language planning and policy (LPP) discourses have been shown to have some impact in urban areas in the US, whatever the limitations exposed by authors in this volume and elsewhere, but in rural areas there has been much less experience and such discourses are not always available to take account of the experience of minority language students.

In classic ethnography of communication terms, the author's aim is 'to incorporate rural "ways of knowing" and understanding educational issues into the canon.' The continua helps her set out this aim in the light of ethnographic-style accounts of students' experience, by indicating the range of features that need to be taken into account. Again the continua are adding to a complementary conceptual framework and the work of the chapter is to make the alliance between these two and language planning and policy (LPP). Her task is to apply these ideas, to assess what are the best practices for language minority student education in the decidedly different rural and isolated regions of 'middle America.' Using interviews and case studies with a small number of students in a local high school, she applies the continua in the way that has become familiar in this volume: 'The continua model predicts that for language minorities to have agency and voice, planners and educators must pay more attention to the typically less powerful ends of the content and media continua, that is, minority ways of knowing, vernacular ways of speaking and writing, and contextualized language use, as well as non-standard or "mixed" language varieties and orthographies.'

Likewise the development and context continua tend towards the written and literate ends: if more attention were paid to the oral ends of both the development and context sets, fewer students might struggle and fail. And at the micro–macro level, again we find administrators and policy makers valuing the macro at the expense of the micro: 'This is an example of power weighting in one set of continua influencing and affecting the power weighting along the other sets in the continua. Administrators affect and influence the microlevel context and policy through the types of curriculum and programming they provide for students.' The complexity of Lincoln's data, however, suggests that this is not simply a matter of ethnographers conflicting with administrators around polarities on the continuum. The position is not as fixed as this and Lincoln's contribution to the debates raised in the book is to bring out the processual dimension: 'Participants' location at any given moment on a particular point on the continua is not static. Where on the continua they are positioned in terms of power weighting often correlates with the presence or lack of student voice.' Another theoretical proposition that is suggestive of future research.

Another rural example comes from *Joel Hardman*'s focus on the differing roles of English language learners, ESL/bilingual teachers, mainstream classroom teachers and other school personnel in the control of content in an ESL/bilingual program. He uses examples from his research in a rural area in the Midwestern United States to explore points of tension at the intersection of continua, in this case those of media and content and between content and context. He brings out the tension between 'content of the school's (or mainstream classroom teachers') choosing' and 'no content at all' (language-only) on the one hand and, on the other, between content which ESL/bilingual teachers perceive to be in the students' best interests aside from mainstream classroom needs, and content they think will support the students' mainstream classroom success. These tensions exemplify the power relations inherent in the control of knowledge and meaning in a social context such as a school. In Hornberger and Skilton-Sylvester's account, one end of the content continuum might be thought of as school-centered content (majority, literary and decontextualized), and the other as learner-centered content (minority, vernacular and contextualized). The question this raises is: whose agendas for biliteracy are being served by the system? Hardman argues that 'The nested nature of Hornberger and Skilton-Sylvester's continua provides a clear framework for exploring how these conflicts relate to the full socio-political environment in which biliteracy develops.'

He provides close account of the classroom struggles over content and media and invokes Rampton's conception of 'ritual' to enable a close focus on the power relations, 'meaning that there is a sense of stepping outside the normal flow of events and modes of interpretation, and reliance on a special set of "formulaic content."' The ritual in this case is Content Based Instruction: 'Seeing CBI as ritualized helps describe the intersection within Hornberger and Skilton-Sylvester's continua framework of content and media.' Again an author is harnessing the continua to other theoretical apparatus and it is the combination that facilitates insights otherwise missed. It is through this ritualization of content and media of curriculum that contestation is resisted and the power relations of apparently innocent classroom practices revealed. Again there is not a fixed application of these concepts, rather the aim is to capture the flow and flexibility of the processes: 'The lines of tension and change vary from teacher to teacher, and are strung out in different directions. The same ritual empowers some teachers, and seems to disempower others.' Hardman, however, concludes on a positive note: 'Despite the complexities of intersecting and nested continua, the framework describes not a kind of web in which teachers and learners are trapped, but rather the possibilities inherent to a language-rich environment, wherein reflective practitioners can take on the power to "christen," along with learners, the knowledge relevant to biliterate development.'

Bertha Pérez, Belinda Flores and Susan Strecker also focus on biliteracy teacher education in the US, in this case in the Southwest. They apply the continua to two groups of bilingual teacher education candidates: US resident 'normalistas' and home-grown 'paraprofessionals.' In San Antonio and other communities in the Southwest, consortiums have formed between schools, universities and community organizations to identify the linguistic and intellectual capital available within the community. Two groups who have the linguistic skills and potential but who have only marginally participated in teacher preparation programs are paraprofessionals in public schools and persons with teacher training or university studies from Mexico. The two groups diverge on certain dimensions of language, discourse, culture, schooling, history, class and power. The authors examine the convergence and divergence of these dimensions along the continua model of biliteracy for participants from each of the two cohort groups. Calling on the ethnography of communication framework as developed by Hymes, they link it to the biliteracy continua. This, they believe, 'provides ways of uncovering both the contextual frames and the items within the frames for specific communicative and literacy events. The notion of context permits examining biliteracy in terms of situated discourse, i.e. language use in context, and recognizes the multiple and alternative social roles and identities available for participants.' For the power dimension of their account they also call upon critical reflection and discourse analysis. Drawing on this complex array of previous theoretical and empirical work, the authors asked two questions, both related to the oral to written, L1 to L2 development continua, and the contexts, media, and content through which they develop. 'First, would the *normalistas,* who had sophisticated Spanish literacy attainment as evident by informal and formal measures, be able to demonstrate English literacy attainment at a level appropriate for university work? And would their literacies assist them to situate themselves when a full range from vernacular to literary language skills in both languages was required in the context of bilingual teacher preparation activities? Second, in the case of the paraprofessionals, would the level of literacy development in Spanish be more on the vernacular end of the continuum and how would that knowledge and the knowledge of more standard and literary forms of English situate them within the context of bilingual teacher preparation activities?'

Using a variety of formal and informal language data they generated case studies to answer these questions that indicated interesting variation amongst the participants: they 'exhibited varying degrees of contextual situatedness and multiple social roles and identities in their texts and discourses, as revealed through both the media and content of their biliterate expression ... all exhibited aspects of situationally emergent language and social identity. That is, through co-membership with their students they created a shared social identity and adapted their communicative style to what was going on during the lesson presentation.' To see this variation the authors had first to see the interrelatedness of the media, content and context continua: this then enables them 'to understand the dynamic of the biliteracy continua in the very diverse language and literacy skills that the *normalistas* and the paraprofessionals had and were developing.' Findings, then, suggest that field experiences allow bilingual teacher candidates to realize the language and power issues within bilingual education and promote the use of the native language as a conduit for the acquisition of equity and power. As with the other accounts, the authors' work highlight's the need to contest the traditional power-weightings of the continua of biliteracy.

Melisa Cahnmann applies the continua to more localized issues in the classroom concerning teachers' efforts to correct errors in biliteracy output. She uses the core aspects of the continua of biliteracy to understand the struggle and contradiction involved in assessment and correction of students' oral and written productions. She presents an expanded definition of biliteracy and uses this definition to explore the development, media, context and content of biliteracy errors and correction. She concludes that the answer to whether a teacher should or should not correct a student's work is better understood as a continuum of complex and multifaceted considerations. Again she brings to attention the use and value of marketplace and vernacular varieties of language within bilingual development. Presaging my suggestion above that some theoretical position on determination might be called for, wherein certain dimensions of the continua could be argued to override others, Cahnmann highlights 'three core continua – monolingual–bilingual (norms), oralcy–literacy, and macro–micro – that I felt best captured the comprehensive meaning of the original twelve.' Her research focus was on a 'grass roots effort to expand bilingual education from the middle school into the high school grades,' focusing on Puerto Rican students in a ninth-grade classroom.

As with other accounts here, she documents how the teacher 'skillfully tapped into the content of students' lives as a way to connect and transfer their background knowledge and interests to more traditional curriculum content with monolingual literacy expectations.' Language switching, mixing and use of norms and content across, in this case, Spanish and English provide fruitful scaffolding opportunities for these pupils' development of the language skills required by schooling. The proposal for policy and for pedagogy builds on the notion of continuity rather than polarity: 'An approach to the correction of bilingual students' literacy errors will be more successful if it eliminates the dichotomy between "yes, one should correct" and "no, one should not correct," and understands the multiple and nested considerations on a continua.' Making decisions as to how to operate in a specific classroom and with a specific student takes the teacher away from the centralized end of the continua and towards a more nuanced recognition of variation in practice. This takes confidence and will be frequently contested. Having a sound conceptual framework on which to base such an approach can play a crucial role in its application. This plus further 'tales from the field' can help validate the work of bilingual teachers and students.

Hornberger's conclusion uses the metaphor of 'ecology of language' invoked in the title of the volume to explore the ideologies underlying multilingual language policies and the continua of biliteracy framework. The continua framework is presented as an ecological heuristic for situating the challenges faced in implementing such policies. Her examples are taken from work in South Africa and Bolivia, both countries which introduced transformative policies in the 1990s. 'As the one language–one nation ideology breaks apart, so too the language planning field increasingly seeks models and metaphors that reflect a multilingual rather than monolingual approach to language planning and policy. One such model is the continua of biliteracy and one such metaphor is the ecology of language; both are premised on a view of multilingualism as a resource.' The notion of ecology of language emphasizes the reciprocity between language and environment, at the level of both psychological and sociological factors. Hornberger focuses on three themes in the metaphor, 'that languages, like living species, evolve, grow, change, live, and die in relation to other languages and also in relation to their environment,' what she terms the *language evolution* and *language environment* themes. A third theme is the notion that 'some languages, like some species and environments, may be endangered and that the ecology movement is about not only studying and describing those potential losses, but also counteracting them'; this she calls the *language endangerment* theme.

How, then, does this metaphor get harnessed to the continua framework? Putting the two together, she suggests, offers a way to situate research, teaching and language planning in multilingual settings. The notion of the biliteracy continua can be seen as ecological in the sense it conveys 'that all points on a particular continuum are interrelated.' The model suggests that 'the more their learning contexts and contexts of use allow learners and users to draw from across the whole of each and every continuum, the greater are the chances for their full biliterate development and expression.' Dominant, especially schooled models of language learning and language policy have tended to focus on one end of the continua and not to invoke the full range.

As the papers in this volume have demonstrated from a variety of contexts, where the range is called upon there is more scope for valuing local knowledge, building on what learners know and developing their new skills in empowering ways. The continua of biliteracy model, like the ecology of language metaphor, is premised on a view of multilingualism as a resource. As Hornberger states: 'The model situates biliteracy development (whether in the individual, classroom, community, or society) in relation to the contexts, media, and content in and through which it develops (i.e. *language environment*); and it provides a heuristic for addressing the unequal balance of power across languages and literacies (i.e. for both studying and counteracting *language endangerment*).' Hornberger uses her own previous experience in Peru and her new learning from colleagues in South Africa (including the work of Bloch and Alexander in this volume) and Bolivia to explore how these theoretical constructs can help us answer difficult policy and political questions. She concludes, like them, on a positive note: 'I share their optimism and their sense of urgency that we linguists and language educators must work hard alongside language planners and language users to fill the ideological and implementational spaces opened up by multilingual language policies; and as researchers to document these new discourses in action so as to keep those ecological policy spaces open into the future.' The continua of biliteracy framework, harnessed in each case to other powerful conceptual tools, has demonstrably made a contribution towards such optimism.

References

Gee, J. (1999) The new literacy studies: From 'socially situated' to the work of the social. In D. Barton, M. Hamilton and R. Ivanic (eds) *Situated Literacies: Reading and Writing in Context.* London: Routledge

Hull, G. and Schultz, K. (2002) *School's Out: Bridging Out-of-school Literacies with Classroom Practice.* New York: Teachers College Press.

Jones, C., Turner, J. and Street, B. (2001) *Student Writing in the University: Cultural and Epistemological Issues.* Amsterdam: John Benjamins.

Kress, G. and van Leeuwen, T. (2001) *Multimodal Discourse: The Modes of Contemporary Communication.* London: Arnold.

Luke, A. (1994) Genres of power? Literacy education and the production of capital. In R. Hasan and G. Williams (eds) *Literacy in Society.* London: Longman.

Martin-Jones, M. and Jones, K. (eds) (2000) *Multilingual Literacies: Comparative Perspectives on Research and Practice.* Amsterdam: John Benjamins.

Moll, L., Amanti, C., Neff, D. and Gonzalez, N. (1992) Funds of knowledge for teaching: Using a qualitative approach to connect homes and classrooms. *Theory into Practice* 31 (2), 131–41.

Street, B. (ed.) (2001) *Literacy and Development: Ethnographic Perspectives* London: Routledge.

Street, B. and Street, J. (1991) The schooling of literacy. In D. Barton and R. Ivanic (eds) *Literacy in the Community* (pp. 143–66). Sage.

Index

Subjects

Authors